Psychological Type, Religion, and Culture

Comprising a selection of contemporary state of the art research that focuses on psychological type, religion, and culture, this book can be divided into two particular areas of research. The first section focuses on the religion and psychological type of Church leaders, while the second section reports on Church members, their religion, and their psychological type.

The book attests to the importance of Jungian Psychological Type theory in understanding individual differences in religiosity within a variety of samples. Authored by a wide range of international scholars, employing a wide range of measures, among diverse samples and in a variety of different cultures, this research provides an important contribution to current and future research. It facilitates future research work in the area outside of the white, Anglo-Saxon, Anglophone, Christian context on which it has traditionally been focused.

The chapters in this book were originally published as a double special issue of the journal *Mental Health, Religion & Culture*.

Christopher Alan Lewis is Professor of Psychology and the Director of the Alister Hardy Religious Experience Research Centre at Glyndŵr University, Wrexham, UK. He is also a Distinguished Visiting Professor at Bashkir State University, Ufa, Russia. He is co-editor of the journal *Mental Health, Religion & Culture*.

Psychological Type, Religion, and Culture

Edited by
Christopher Alan Lewis

LONDON AND NEW YORK

First published 2018
by Routledge
2 Park Square, Milton Park, Abingdon, Oxon, OX14 4RN, UK

and by Routledge
711 Third Avenue, New York, NY 10017, USA

Routledge is an imprint of the Taylor & Francis Group, an informa business

© 2018 Taylor & Francis

All rights reserved. No part of this book may be reprinted or reproduced or utilised in any form or by any electronic, mechanical, or other means, now known or hereafter invented, including photocopying and recording, or in any information storage or retrieval system, without permission in writing from the publishers.

Trademark notice: Product or corporate names may be trademarks or registered trademarks, and are used only for identification and explanation without intent to infringe.

British Library Cataloguing in Publication Data
A catalogue record for this book is available from the British Library

ISBN 13: 978-0-8153-6200-5

Typeset in Times New Roman
by RefineCatch Limited, Bungay, Suffolk

Publisher's Note
The publisher accepts responsibility for any inconsistencies that may have arisen during the conversion of this book from journal articles to book chapters, namely the possible inclusion of journal terminology.

Disclaimer
Every effort has been made to contact copyright holders for their permission to reprint material in this book. The publishers would be grateful to hear from any copyright holder who is not here acknowledged and will undertake to rectify any errors or omissions in future editions of this book.

Contents

Citation Information vii
Notes on Contributors xi

Introduction: psychological type, religion, and culture 1
Christopher Alan Lewis

Part I: Church leaders, religion, and psychological type

1. Confirming the psychological type profile of Anglican churchmen in Wales: a ministry for sensing types 5
   V. John Payne and Christopher Alan Lewis

2. Psychological types and self-assessed leadership skills of clergy in the Church of England 14
   Laura Watt and David Voas

3. Psychological type and the training relationship: an empirical study among curates and training incumbents 26
   Greg Smith

4. Early and late responders to questionnaires: clues from psychological type 36
   Kelvin J. Randall

5. Psychological type profile of Protestant church leaders in Australia: are clergymen and clergywomen different? 46
   Mandy Robbins and Ruth Powell

6. Psychological type profile of clergywomen and clergymen serving in the New York metropolitan area of the Reformed Church in America 56
   Marjorie H. Royle, Jon Norton and Thomas Larkin

7. Work-related psychological health and psychological type: a study among Catholic priests in Italy 63
   Leslie J. Francis and Giuseppe Crea

8. Psychological type functions and biblical scholarship: an empirical enquiry among members of the Society of Biblical Literature 75
   Andrew Village

CONTENTS

Part II: Church members, religion, and psychological type

9. Psychological type differences between churchgoers and church-leavers   92
   Matthew J. Baker

10. The psychological type profile of Christians participating in fellowship groups or in small study groups: insights from the Australian National Church Life Survey   105
    Leslie J. Francis, Mandy Robbins and Ruth Powell

11. Created to be guardians? Psychological type profiles of members of cathedral Friends associations in England   111
    Judith A. Muskett and Andrew Village

12. Unsettling the guardian: quest religiosity and psychological type among Anglican churchgoers   125
    David S. Walker

13. Inside Southwark Cathedral: a study in psychological-type profiling   134
    David W. Lankshear and Leslie J. Francis

14. Spiritual well-being and psychological type: a study among visitors to a medieval cathedral in Wales   145
    Leslie J. Francis, John W. Fisher and Jennie Annis

15. The perceiving process and mystical orientation: a study in psychological type theory among 16- to 18-year-old students   163
    Christopher F.J. Ross and Leslie J. Francis

16. The personality of the Fourth Evangelist   173
    Derek Edwin Noel King

17. Do different psychological types look for different things in sermons? A research note   182
    Leslie J. Francis, Christopher Stone and Mandy Robbins

Index   185

Citation Information

The chapters in this book were originally published in *Mental Health, Religion & Culture*, volume 18, issue 7–8 (September–October 2015). When citing this material, please use the original page numbering for each article, as follows:

Chapter 1
Confirming the psychological type profile of Anglican churchmen in Wales: a ministry for sensing types
V. John Payne and Christopher Alan Lewis
Mental Health, Religion & Culture, volume 18, issue 7–8 (September–October 2015), pp. 535–543

Chapter 2
Psychological types and self-assessed leadership skills of clergy in the Church of England
Laura Watt and David Voas
Mental Health, Religion & Culture, volume 18, issue 7–8 (September–October 2015), pp. 544–555

Chapter 3
Psychological type and the training relationship: an empirical study among curates and training incumbents
Greg Smith
Mental Health, Religion & Culture, volume 18, issue 7–8 (September–October 2015), pp. 556–565

Chapter 4
Early and late responders to questionnaires: clues from psychological type
Kelvin J. Randall
Mental Health, Religion & Culture, volume 18, issue 7–8 (September–October 2015), pp. 566–575

Chapter 5
Psychological type profile of Protestant church leaders in Australia: are clergymen and clergywomen different?
Mandy Robbins and Ruth Powell
Mental Health, Religion & Culture, volume 18, issue 7–8 (September–October 2015), pp. 576–585

CITATION INFORMATION

Chapter 6
Psychological type profile of clergywomen and clergymen serving in the New York metropolitan area of the Reformed Church in America
Marjorie H. Royle, Jon Norton and Thomas Larkin
Mental Health, Religion & Culture, volume 18, issue 7–8 (September–October 2015), pp. 586–592

Chapter 7
Work-related psychological health and psychological type: a study among Catholic priests in Italy
Leslie J. Francis and Giuseppe Crea
Mental Health, Religion & Culture, volume 18, issue 7–8 (September–October 2015), pp. 593–604

Chapter 8
Psychological type functions and biblical scholarship: an empirical enquiry among members of the Society of Biblical Literature
Andrew Village
Mental Health, Religion & Culture, volume 18, issue 7–8 (September–October 2015), pp. 605–621

Chapter 9
Psychological type differences between churchgoers and church-leavers
Matthew J. Baker
Mental Health, Religion & Culture, volume 18, issue 7–8 (September–October 2015), pp. 622–634

Chapter 10
The psychological type profile of Christians participating in fellowship groups or in small study groups: insights from the Australian National Church Life Survey
Leslie J. Francis, Mandy Robbins and Ruth Powell
Mental Health, Religion & Culture, volume 18, issue 7–8 (September–October 2015), pp. 635–640

Chapter 11
Created to be guardians? Psychological type profiles of members of cathedral Friends associations in England
Judith A. Muskett and Andrew Village
Mental Health, Religion & Culture, volume 18, issue 7–8 (September–October 2015), pp. 641–654

Chapter 12
Unsettling the guardian: quest religiosity and psychological type among Anglican churchgoers
David S. Walker
Mental Health, Religion & Culture, volume 18, issue 7–8 (September–October 2015), pp. 655–663

CITATION INFORMATION

Chapter 13
Inside Southwark Cathedral: a study in psychological-type profiling
David W. Lankshear and Leslie J. Francis
Mental Health, Religion & Culture, volume 18, issue 7–8 (September–October 2015),
pp. 664–674

Chapter 14
Spiritual well-being and psychological type: a study among visitors to a medieval cathedral in Wales
Leslie J. Francis, John W. Fisher and Jennie Annis
Mental Health, Religion & Culture, volume 18, issue 7–8 (September–October 2015),
pp. 675–692

Chapter 15
The perceiving process and mystical orientation: a study in psychological type theory among 16- to 18-year-old students
Christopher F.J. Ross and Leslie J. Francis
Mental Health, Religion & Culture, volume 18, issue 7–8 (September–October 2015),
pp. 693–702

Chapter 16
The personality of the Fourth Evangelist
Derek Edwin Noel King
Mental Health, Religion & Culture, volume 18, issue 7–8 (September–October 2015),
pp. 703–711

Chapter 17
Do different psychological types look for different things in sermons? A research note
Leslie J. Francis, Christopher Stone and Mandy Robbins
Mental Health, Religion & Culture, volume 18, issue 7–8 (September–October 2015),
pp. 712–714

For any permission-related enquiries please visit:
http://www.tandfonline.com/page/help/permissions

Notes on Contributors

Jennie Annis is part of the ministry team at St Mary's Centre, Wales, UK.

Matthew J. Baker is based at the Warwick Religions and Education Research Unit, Centre for Education Studies, the University of Warwick, UK.

Giuseppe Crea is based at the Department of Psychology, Salesian Pontifical University, Rome, Italy.

John W. Fisher is Adjunct Associate Professor at the Department of Education, Federation University Australia, Victoria, Australia.

Leslie J. Francis is Professor of Religions and Education within the Warwick Religions and Education Research Unit, UK, and Honorary Distinguished Canon at Manchester Cathedral, UK.

Derek Edwin Noel King is based in the Diocese of St Edmundsbury and Ipswich, Suffolk, UK.

David W. Lankshear is based at the Warwick Religions and Education Research Unit, Centre for Education Studies, the University of Warwick, UK.

Thomas Larkin is based at the Abundant Life Reformed Church, USA.

Christopher Alan Lewis is Professor of Psychology and Director of the Alister Hardy Religious Experience Research Centre at Glyndŵr University, Wrexham, UK. He is also a Distinguished Visiting Professor at Bashkir State University, Ufa, Russia. He is co-editor of the journal *Mental Health, Religion & Culture*.

Judith A. Muskett is Postdoctoral Research Assistant at the Department of Theology and Religious Studies, Faculty of Education and Theology, York St. John University, UK.

Jon Norton is a semi-retired clergyman affiliated with the Regional Synod of New York, Reformed Church in America, USA.

V. John Payne is based at the Department of Psychology, Glyndŵr University, Plas Coch Campus, Wrexham, UK.

Ruth Powell is based at the NCLS Research, Australian Catholic University, Sydney, Australia.

Kelvin J. Randall is based at the Department of Psychology, Institute for Health, Medical Sciences and Society, Glyndŵr University, UK.

Mandy Robbins is a Senior Lecturer at the Department of Psychology, Glyndŵr University, Plas Coch Campus, Wrexham, UK.

NOTES ON CONTRIBUTORS

Christopher F.J. Ross is based at the Department of Religion and Culture, Wilfrid Laurier University, Canada.

Marjorie H. Royle is based at Clay Pots Research, Lincoln Park, USA.

Greg Smith is based at the Warwick Religions and Education Research Unit, Institute of Education, the University of Warwick, UK.

Christopher Stone is based in the Diocese of Rochester, Rochester, UK.

Andrew Village is Professor of Practical and Emprical Theology at the Department of Theology and Religious Studies, Faculty of Education and Theology, York St. John University, UK.

David Voas is based at the Cathie Marsh Institute for Social Research, University of Manchester, UK.

David S. Walker is based at the Department of Psychology, Glyndŵr University, Plas Coch Campus, Wrexham, UK.

Laura Watt is based at the Institute for Social and Economic Research, University of Essex, Wivenhoe Park, UK.

Introduction: psychological type, religion, and culture

Christopher Alan Lewis

Context

In the contemporary empirical psychology of religion, the individual difference tradition remains a dominant perspective (e.g., Hood, Hill, & Spilka, 2009; Wulff, 1997). Within this approach, research has been undertaken that has located religiosity within the various major theoretical models of personality (Piedmont, 2005). From such research, a number of conclusions can be drawn. First, the examination of the Freudian theory (1927/1961) that religion is an obsessional neurosis demonstrates that higher obsessional personality trait scores, rather than obsessional symptoms scores, are associated with greater religiosity (for a review see Lewis, 1998, 2003). Second, the location of religiosity within Eysenck's Three-dimensional Model of Personality (e.g., Eysenck & Eysenck, 1985), demonstrates that lower Psychoticism scores (i.e., tendermindedness), rather than extraversion or neuroticism or Lie Scale scores, are associated with greater religiosity (for a review see Francis, 1992; Lewis & Francis, 2014). Third, the location of religiosity within Costa and McCrae's Five-factor Model of Personality (e.g., McCrae & Costa, 1987, 1999), demonstrates that higher agreeableness scores and conscientiousness, rather than openness, extraversion or neuroticism scores are associated with greater religiosity (for a review see Saroglou, 2002). Fourth, the location of religiosity within Cattell's 16-factor Model of Personality Cattell's (1946, 1957, 1973) has been the subject of limited research. Data from two studies demonstrate that religiosity is significantly associated with five of the 14 personality factors: higher scores on factor G (conformity), factor I (tendermindedness), and factor Q3 (self-discipline), and with lower scores on factor E (submissiveness) and factor F (sobriety). Also religiosity is significantly associated with two of the four second-order factors: lower scores on extraversion (indicating a relationship with introversion), with lower scores on tough-poise (indicating a relationship with emotionality) and with lower scores on independence (indicating a relationship with a lack of independence) (Bourke, Francis, & Robbins, 2007; Francis & Bourke, 2003).

Recently within this research tradition, Jungian psychological type theory (Jung, 1971) has become more visible, as a growing number of studies have demonstrated the explanatory power of type theory to predict individual differences in religiosity (for recent reviews see Francis, 2009; Ross, 2011). Particular contributions to this growing body of knowledge have been made by recent special issues of *Research in the Social Scientific Study of Religion* (Village, 2011) and *Mental Health, Religion & Culture* (Lewis, 2012a, 2012b). Indeed, the success of the previous collection on psychological type (Lewis, 2012a, 2012b) served as the impetus for extending that work further.

The aim of this volume, entitled *Psychological Type, Religion, and Culture* was to bring together a collection of contemporary research articles recently published in the international journal *Mental Health, Religion & Culture* as part of a Special Issue series entitled *Psychological Type, Religion and Culture: Further Empirical Perspectives* (Lewis, 2015a, 2015b). The aim of the Special Issue was to build on the recent research reported by Lewis (2012a, 2012b) and elsewhere (e.g., Francis, 2009; Ross, 2011; Village, 2011), by providing a forum for the review and extension of research on the relationship of psychological type theory to religiosity, with particular reference to culture. Within this collection, psychological type is overwhelmingly measured by the 40-item Francis Psychological Type Scales (FPTS; Francis, 2005). Exceptions are one study (Smith, 2015) that employed the 126-item Form G (Anglicised) of the Myers–Briggs Type Indicator (Myers & McCauley, 1985) and one study (King, 2015) that employed personality-critical analysis (King, 2010).

The present volume comprises 17 empirical articles. These articles are divided thematically and are presented across two sections. Section one comprises of eight articles focused on Church leaders, religion, and psychological type (Payne & Lewis, 2015; Watt & Voas, 2015; Smith, 2015; Randall, 2015; Robbins & Powell, 2015; Royle, Norton, & Larkin, 2015; Francis & Crea, 2015; Village, 2015). Payne and Lewis (2015) report on a sample of 268 Anglican clergymen serving within the Church in Wales using the FPTS. Watt and Voas (2015) report on a sample of 1480 clergy serving within the Church of England using the FPTS. Smith (2015) reports on a sample of 11 curate-training incumbent pairs (and one additional incumbent) during a three-day residential programme organised by an Anglican Diocese in England using the 126-item Form G (Anglicised) of the Myers–Briggs Type Indicator. Randall (2015) reports on a sample of 185 Anglican clergy in England and Wales using the FPTS. Robbins and Powell (2015) report on a sample of 120 clergywomen and 436 clergymen from Protestant denominations who completed the Australian National Church Life Survey using the FPTS. Royle et al. (2015) report on a sample of 26 clergywomen and 89 clergymen serving within the Reformed Church in the US located in two synods in the New York metropolitan using the FPTS. Francis and Crea (2015) report on a sample of 155 Roman Catholic priests in Italy using the FPTS. One article is focused on Biblical scholars, Village (2015) reports on a sample of 338 members of the Society of Biblical Literature using the FPTS.

Section two comprises of nine chapters focussed on Church members, religion, and psychological type (Baker, 2015; Francis, Robbins, & Powell, 2015; Muskett & Village, 2015; Walker, 2015; Lankshear & Francis, 2015; Francis, Fisher, & Annis 2015; Ross & Francis, 2015; King 2015; Francis, Stone, & Robbins, 2015). Baker (2015) reports on three samples taken from the online Personality and Belief in God Survey. All three samples consisted of individuals who grew up attending church as a child. The first sample was made up of 2326 individuals who continue to attend church as adults (1137 females and 1189 males), the second was made up of 10,515 individuals who no longer attend church and are now atheists or agnostics (2677 females and 7838 males), and the third was made up of 1977 individuals who no longer attend church yet still retain some sort of belief in God (1134 females and 843 males) using the FPTS. Francis, Robbins, and Powell (2015) report on a sample of 2355 participants in the 2006 congregation survey of the Australian National Church Life Survey using the FPTS. Muskett and Village (2015) report on a sample of 1356 members of the Friends associations of six English cathedrals (775 women and 581 men) using the FPTS. Walker (2015) reports on a sample of 390 individuals who attended a Christmas carol service in a Church of England cathedral using the FPTS. Lankshear and Francis (2015) report on a sample of 120 men and 161 women attending Sunday services in Southwark Cathedral, England using the FPTS. One article is focused on church visitors. Francis, Fisher, and Annis (2015) report on a sample of 2339 visitors to St David's Cathedral in rural west Wales using the FPTS. One article is focused on young people. Ross and Francis (2015) report on a sample of 149 adolescents (16–18 years of age) using the FPTS. One article is focused on the Bible. King (2015) applies the technique of personality-critical analysis to the Fourth Gospel. One article is focused on Preaching. Francis, Stone, and Robbins (2015) report on a sample of 76 Evangelical Anglican churchgoers using the FPTS

Conclusion

The present aim was to bring together a collection of contemporary research articles recently published in the international journal *Mental Health, Religion & Culture* as part of a Special Issue series entitled *Psychological Type, Religion and Culture: Further Empirical Perspectives*. In doing so, the present volume provides a further forum for the review and extension of research on the relationship of psychological type theory to religiosity, with particular reference to culture. It is hoped that this volume has illustrated further some of the diversity and richness of such research. This collection clearly attests to the ongoing momentum of this specific research tradition, and itself serves as a further spring-board for future research.

This volume would not have been possible without the assistance of a number of people. We wish to acknowledge the authors who provided stimulating articles and efficient revisions, and our reviewers for their judicious and insightful evaluations of the articles submitted. We are particularly grateful to the regular Co-Editors of *Mental Health, Religion & Culture* for their continued enthusiasm and support for this, and indeed previous projects on psychological type.

References

Baker, M. J. (2015). Psychological type differences between churchgoers and church-leavers. *Mental Health, Religion & Culture*, *18*(7), 622–634. doi:10.1080/13674676.2014.961247

Bourke, R., Francis, L. J., & Robbins, M. (2007). Cattell's personality model and attitude toward Christianity. *Mental Health, Religion & Culture*, *10*(4), 353–362. doi:10.1080/13694670600722460

Cattell, R. B. (1946). *The description and measurement of personality*. New York, NY: World Book.

Cattell, R. B. (1957). *Personality and motivation structure and measurement*. New York, NY: World Book.

Cattell, R. B. (1973). *Personality and Mood by Questionnaire*. San Francisco, CA: Jossey-Bass.

Eysenck, H. J., & Eysenck, M. W. (1985). *Personality and individual differences: A natural science approach*. New York, NY: Plenum.

Francis, L. J. (1992). Religion, neuroticism, and psychoticism. In J. F. Schumaker (Ed.), *Religion and mental health* (pp. 149–160). New York, NY: Oxford University Press.

Francis, L. J. (2005). *Faith and psychology: Personality, religion and the individual*. London: Darton, Longman and Todd.

Francis, L. J. (2009). Psychological type theory and religious and spiritual experience. In M. De Souza, L. J. Francis, J. O'Higgins-Norman, & D. G. Scott (Eds.), *International handbook of education for spirituality, care and wellbeing* (pp. 125–146). Dordrecht: Springer.

Francis, L. J., & Bourke, R. (2003). Personality and religion: Applying Cattell's model among secondary school pupils. *Current Psychology*, *22*(2), 125–137. doi:10.1007/s12144-003-1003-9

Francis, L. J., & Crea, G. (2015). Work-related psychological health and psychological type: A study among Catholic priests in Italy. *Mental Health, Religion & Culture*, *18*(7), 593–604. doi:10.1080/13674676.2014.963996

Francis, L. J., Fisher, J. W., & Annis, J. (2015). Spiritual wellbeing and psychological type: A study among visitors to a medieval cathedral in Wales. *Mental Health, Religion & Culture*, *18*(8), 675–692. doi:10.1080/13674676.2014.964002

Francis, L. J., Robbins, M., & Powell, R. (2015). The psychological type profile of Christians participating in fellowship groups or in small study groups: Insights from the Australian National Church Life Survey. *Mental Health, Religion & Culture*, *18*(8), 635–640. doi:10.1080/13674676.2014.964000

Francis, L. J., Stone, C., & Robbins, M. (2015). Do different psychological types look for different things in sermons? A research note. *Mental Health, Religion & Culture*, *18*(8), 712–714. doi:10.1080/13674676.2014.964001

Freud, S. (1927/1961). The future of an illusion. In J. Strachey (Ed. and Trans.). *The standard edition of the complete psychological works of Sigmund Freud* (Vol. 21, pp. 5–58). London: Hogarth Press.

Hood, R. W. Jr., Hill, P. C., & Spilka, B. (2009). *The psychology of religion: An empirical approach* (4th ed.). New York, NY: The Guilford Press.

Jung, C. G. (1971). *Psychological types: The collected works vol 6*. London: Routledge and Kegan Paul.

King, D. E. N. (2010). The author of John's letters – the Evangelist, or another? *Journal of Beliefs and Values*, *31*(1), 81–87. doi:10.1080/13617671003666795

King, D. E. N. (2015). The personality of the fourth Evangelist. *Mental Health, Religion & Culture*, *18*(8), 703–711. doi:10.1080/13674676.2014.961251

Lankshear, D. W., & Francis, L. J. (2015). Inside Southwark Cathedral: A study in psychological type profiling. *Mental Health, Religion & Culture*, *18*(8), 664–674. doi:10.1080/13674676.2014.961705

Lewis, C. A. (1998). Cleanliness is next to godliness: Religiosity and obsessiveness. *Journal of Religion and Health*, *37*(1), 49–61. doi:10.1023/A:1022913117655

Lewis, C. A. (2003). Cleanliness is next to godliness: A further look. *Journal of Beliefs & Values*, *24*(2), 239–244. doi:10.1080/13617670305422

Lewis, C. A. (2012a). Psychological type, religion, and culture: Theoretical and empirical perspectives [Special Issue]. *Mental Health, Religion & Culture*, *15*(10), whole issue.

Lewis, C. A. (2012b). Psychological type, religion, and culture: Theoretical and empirical perspectives. *Mental Health, Religion & Culture*, *15*(9), 817–821. doi:10.1080/13674676.2012.721534

Lewis, C. A., & Francis, L. J. (2014). Personality and religion among female university students in France. *Psychology, Society, & Education*, *6*(2), 68–81. doi:10.25115/psye.v6i2.509

McCrae, R. R., & Costa, P. T., Jr. (1987). Validation of the five-factor model of personality across instruments and observers. *Journal of Personality and Social Psychology*, *52*(1), 81–90. doi:10.1037/0022-3514.52.1.81

McCrae, R. R., & Costa, P. T. Jr. (1999). A five-factor theory of personality. In L. A. Pervin & O. P. John (Eds.), *Handbook of personality: Theory and research* (pp. 139–53). New York, NY: Guilford Press.

Muskett, J. A., & Village, A. (2015). Created to be Guardians? Psychological type profiles of members of cathedral Friends associations in England. *Mental Health, Religion & Culture*, *18*(8), 641–654. doi:10.1080/13674676.2014.961249

Myers, I. B., & McCauley, M. H. (1985). *Manual: A guide to the development and use of the Myers–Briggs Type Indicator*. Palo Alto, CA: Consulting Psychologist Press.

Payne, V. J., & Lewis, C. A. (2015). Confirming the psychological type profile of Anglican clergymen in Wales: A ministry for sensing types. *Mental Health, Religion & Culture*, *18*(7), 535–543. doi:10.1080/13674676.2014.963999

Piedmont, R. L. (2005). The role of personality in understanding religious and spiritual constructs. In R. F. Paloutzian & C. L. Park (Eds.), *Handbook of the psychology of religion and spirituality* (pp. 253–273). New York, NY: Guilford Press.

Randall, K. J. (2015). Early and late responders to questionnaires: Clues from psychological type. *Mental Health, Religion & Culture*, *18*(7), 566–575. doi:10.1080/13674676.2014.961248

Robbins, M., & Powell, R. (2015). Psychological type profile of Protestant church leaders in Australia: Are clergymen and clergywomen different? *Mental Health, Religion & Culture*, *18*(7), 576–585. doi:10.1080/13674676.2014.963997

Ross, C. F. J. (2011). Jungian typology and religion: A perspective from North America. *Research in the Social Scientific Study of Religion*, *22*, 165–191. doi:10.1163/ej.9789004207271.i-360.30

Ross, C. F. J., & Francis, L. J. (2015). The perceiving process and mystical orientation: A study in psychological type theory among 16- to 18-year-old students. *Mental Health, Religion & Culture*, *18*(8), 693–702. doi:10.1080/13674676.2014.961353

Royle, M. H., Norton, J., & Larkin, T. (2015). Psychological type profile of clergywomen and clergymen serving in the New York Metropolitan area of the Reformed Church in America. *Mental Health, Religion & Culture*, *18*(7), 586–592. doi:10.1080/13674676.2014.961264

Saroglou, V. (2002). Religion and the five factors of personality: A meta-analytic review. *Personality and Individual Differences*, *32*(1), 15–25. doi:10.1016/s0191-8869(00)00233-6

Smith, G. (2015). Psychological type and the training relationship: An empirical study among curates and training incumbents. *Mental Health, Religion & Culture*, *18*(7), 556–565. doi:10.1080/13674676.2014.963998

Village, A. (2011). Introduction to special section: Psychological type and Christian ministry. *Research in the Social Scientific Study of Religion*, *22*, 157–164. doi: 10.1163/ej.9789004207271.i-360.28

Village, A. (2015). Psychological type functions and biblical scholarship: An empirical enquiry among members of the Society of Biblical Literature. *Mental Health, Religion & Culture*, *18*(7), 605–621. doi:10.1080/13674676.2014.961246

Walker, D. S. (2015). Unsettling the guardian: Quest religiosity and psychological type among Anglican churchgoers. *Mental Health, Religion & Culture*, *18*(8), 655–663. doi:10.1080/13674676.2014.963291

Watt, L., & Voas, D. (2015). Psychological types and self-assessed leadership skills of clergy in the Church of England. *Mental Health, Religion & Culture*, *18*(7), 544–555. doi:10.1080/13674676.2014.961250

Wulff, D. M. (1997). *Psychology of religion: Classic and contemporary* (2nd ed.). New York, NY: John Wiley & Sons.

Confirming the psychological type profile of Anglican clergymen in Wales: a ministry for sensing types

V. John Payne and Christopher Alan Lewis

Within the psychology of religion, there is growing interest in the theoretical and empirical contributions of psychological type theory. For example, a series of studies has explored the psychological type profile of religious professionals. The present study examined the psychological type profile of Anglican clergymen serving within the Church in Wales. A sample of 268 clergymen completed the Francis Psychological Type Scales. The data demonstrated a group of clergymen who prefer introversion (65%) over extraversion (35%), sensing (57%) over intuition (43%), feeling (68%) over thinking (32%), and judging (78%) over perceiving (27%). The three predominant types among this group of clergymen were ISFJ (22%), ISTJ (13%), and ESFJ (11%). These findings are discussed to illuminate two problems: the significant difference between the psychological type profile of Anglican clergymen in Wales and the UK male population norms, and the contrast between the preference for sensing among Anglican clergymen in Wales and the preference for intuition demonstrated by earlier research among Anglican clergymen in England.

Introduction

Psychological type theory has offered an interesting and fruitful bridge between the empirical psychology of religion and empirical theology (Francis, 2009). Within the psychology of religion, psychological type theory has provided a model of personality useful for exploring and explaining individual differences in religious and spiritual experiences and preferences (Lewis, 2012). Within empirical theology, psychological type theory has provided a vocabulary for connecting observation of human differences with systematic theology and hermeneutical theory (Francis & Village, 2008).

Psychological type theory discusses basic and fundamental psychological differences in terms of typological distinctions: two orientations defined as introversion and extraversion, two perceiving functions defined as sensing and intuition, two judging functions defined as thinking and feeling, and two attitudes towards the outer world defined as judging and perceiving.

The orientations are concerned with identifying the sources of psychological energy. In this area, the two discrete types are defined as extraversion and introversion. For extravert types, the source of energy is located in the outer world of people and things. Extraverts are exhausted by large periods of solitude and silence; and they need to re-energise through the stimulation they receive from people and places. Extraverts are talkative people who feel at home in social contexts. For introvert types, the source of energy is located in the inner world of ideas and reflection. Introverts are exhausted by long periods of social engagements and sounds; and they need to re-energise through the stimulation they receive from their own company and tranquillity.

The perceiving processes are concerned with identifying ways in which individuals take in information. For Jung, the perceiving processes were described as irrational processes because they were not concerned with data evaluation, but simply with data gathering. In this area, the two discrete types are defined as sensing and as intuition. For sensing types, the preferred way of perceiving is through the five senses. Sensers are motivated by facts, details, and information. They build up to the big picture slowly by focusing first on the component parts. They are more comfortable in the present moment rather than in exploring future possibilities. They are realistic and practical people. For intuitive types, the preferred way of perceiving is through their imagination. Intuitives are motivated by theories, ideas, and connections. They begin with the big picture and gradually give attention to the component parts. They are more comfortable planning the future than making do with the present. They are inspirational and visionary people.

The judging processes are concerned with identifying ways in which individuals evaluate information. For Jung, the judging processes were described as the rational processes because they were concerned with data evaluation and with decision-making. In this area, the two discrete types are defined as thinking and as feeling. For thinking types, the preferred way of judging is through objective analysis and dispassionate logic. They are concerned with the good running of systems and organisations and put such strategic issues first. They are logical and fair-minded people who appeal to the God of justice. For feeling types, the preferred way of judging is through subjective evaluation and personal involvement. They are concerned with the good relationships between people and put such inter-personal issues first. They are humane and warm-hearted people who appeal to the God of mercy.

The attitudes (often more fully expressed as the "attitudes toward the outer world") are concerned with identifying which of the two processes (judging or perceiving) individuals prefer to use in the outer world. In this area, the two discrete types are defined by the name of the preferred process, either judging or perceiving. For judging types, their preferred judging function (either thinking or feeling) is employed in their outer world. Because their outer world is where the rational, evaluating, judging, or decision-making process is deployed, judging types appear to others to be well-organised decisive people. For perceiving types, their preferred perceiving function (either sensing or intuition) is employed in their outer world. Because their outer world is where the irrational, data gathering process is deployed, perceiving types appear to others to be laid-back, flexible, even disorganised people.

Since the early 2000s, a connected series of independent but interrelated studies has begun to assemble a composite picture of the psychological type profile of religious professionals working within a variety of church traditions within the UK, including Anglican clergymen serving in the Church of England (Francis, Craig, Whinney, Tilley, & Slater, 2007; Francis, Robbins, Duncan, & Whinney, 2010; Village, 2011; Francis, Robbins, & Whinney, 2011; Francis & Holmes, 2011; Francis, Robbins, & Jones, 2012; Francis & Village, 2012; Village 2013), Anglican clergy serving in the Church in Wales (Francis, Payne, & Jones, 2001; Francis, Littler, & Robbins, 2010), Anglican seminaries (Francis, Craig, & Butler, 2007), Apostolic Network leaders (Kay, Francis, & Robbins, 2011), Bible College students (Francis, Penson, & Jones, 2001; Kay & Francis, 2008; Kay, Francis, & Craig, 2008), Evangelical church leaders (Francis & Robbins, 2002; Craig, Francis, & Robbins, 2004; Francis, Craig, Horsfall, & Ross, 2005), Free Church Ministers (Francis, Whinney, Burton, & Robbins, 2011), missionary personnel (Craig, Horsfall, & Francis, 2005), Methodist circuit ministers (Burton, Francis, & Robbins, 2010), Newfrontiers lead elders (Francis, Gubb, & Robbins, 2009), Roman Catholic priests (Craig, Duncan, & Francis, 2006), and youth ministers (Francis, Nash, Nash, & Craig, 2007).

Two main conclusions emerge from these studies. The first conclusion is that the psychological type profiles of clergymen and clergywomen differ significantly from the population norms generated from men and women in the UK by Kendall (1998). The second conclusion is that there are significant differences between different groups of religious professionals, varying according to denominational affiliation and according to church traditions or styles of believing. One of the most fascinating comparisons to emerge from this set of studies concerns the difference in profile recorded by Anglican clergy serving in the Church of England and Anglican clergy serving in the Church in Wales. Here are two Churches within the same Anglican Communion separated only by the permeable boundary along Offa's Dyke. This observed difference is worth further investigation to ensure that the observed differences are not merely an accident of sampling or an accident of measurement.

To date two studies have reported on the psychological type profile of Anglican clergymen serving in the Church in Wales: Francis, Payne et al. (2001) drew on data from 427 clergymen and Francis, Littler et al. (2010) drew on data from 231 clergymen. Two other studies have reported on the psychological type profile of Anglican clergymen serving in the Church of England: Francis, Craig, Whinney et al. (2007) drew on data from 626 clergymen and Francis, Robbins et al. (2010) drew on data from 622 clergymen. In terms of the orientations, the attitudes and the judging process, clergymen from England and Wales recorded similar profiles, but in terms of the perceiving process the two groups emerge quite differently.

In terms of the orientations, all four studies demonstrate a clear preference for introversion: in Wales 59% according to Francis, Payne et al. (2001) and 69% according to Francis, Littler et al. (2010), and in England 57% according to Francis, Craig, Whinney et al. (2007) and 64% according to Francis, Robbins et al. (2010). Clergy who prefer introversion display distinctive strengths in ministry. They may be energised by private study and by periods of solitary preparation, by one-to-one encounters in counselling and in spiritual direction, by contemplative prayer and reflection, and by focusing deeply on interior spiritual issues. On the other hand, clergy who prefer introversion may be drained by some of the public aspects of ministry, such as attending social events, speaking in public (especially when required to be spontaneous or interactive), talking with strangers as part of evangelism or parish visiting, and assuming a high profile within the parish. Anglican ministry in Wales and England alike is shaped by the quiet reflective spirituality characteristic of a preference for introversion.

In terms of attitude, all four studies demonstrate a clear preference for judging: in Wales 68% according to Francis, Payne et al. (2001) and 78% according to Francis, Littler et al. (2010), and in England 68% according to Francis, Craig, Whinney et al. (2007) and 73% according to Francis, Robbins et al. (2010). Clergy who prefer judging display distinctive strengths in ministry. They may be inspired by taking care of organisational matters, both in their own life and in the life of the parish, by arranging services and events well in advance, by maintaining efficient administrative systems, and by managing local affairs. On the other hand, clergy who prefer judging may be less able to cope with some other aspects of ministry, such as the need for thinking on their feet, responding effectively to unanticipated crises, and adapting to changing situations. Anglican ministry in Wales and England alike is shaped by clear organisation and structure characteristic of a preference for judging.

In terms of the judging process, all four studies demonstrate a clear preference for feeling: in Wales 69% according to Francis, Payne et al. (2001) and 55% according to Francis, Littler et al. (2010), and in England 54% according to Francis, Craig, Whinney et al. (2007) and 56% according to Francis, Robbins et al. (2010). Clergy who prefer feeling display distinctive strengths in ministry. They may be particularly good at spending time caring for others through visiting, counselling or pastoral care, supporting and empathising with those in need, and emphasising the importance of interpersonal values in Christian teaching, such as love, harmony, peace, and compassion. On the other hand, clergy who prefer feeling may be less equipped to deal with some other aspects of ministry, such as having to look at problems objectively and logically, the need to make tough decisions which affect other people's lives, the need to be critical when necessary, and dealing with troublesome people. Anglican ministry in Wales and England alike is shaped by an emphasis on pastoral care and by a love for harmony inspired by allegiance to the God of mercy.

However, a very different picture emerges in terms of the perceiving process. The two studies conducted in Wales demonstrate a clear preference for sensing: 57% according to Francis, Payne et al. (2001) and 64% according to Francis, Littler et al. (2010). The two studies conducted in England demonstrate a clear preference for intuition: 62% according to Francis, Craig, Whinney et al. (2007) and 67% according to Francis, Robbins et al. (2010). Sensing types and intuitive types bring somewhat different strengths to ministry. With ministry leadership shaped by a predominance of intuitive types, the Church of England is a Church that may promote change and development in church structure, church order, liturgy, and teaching. The leadership may encourage an open, enquiring, and more liberal approach to faith. Within ministry leadership shaped by a predominance of sensing types, the Church in Wales is a Church that may be more reluctant to promote change and development in church structures, church order, liturgy, and teaching. The leadership may encourage a stronger commitment to tradition and a more conservative approach to faith and to liturgy. In terms of the perceiving process, the Anglican Churches in England and Wales may present a very different public face for ministry.

One of the key ways in which scientific knowledge is consolidated and tested is through replication. The aim of the present study, therefore, was to replicate the two studies reported earlier by Francis, Payne et al. (2001), and Francis, Littler et al. (2010) among a further sample of Anglican clergymen serving in the Church in Wales. In the analysis of these new data particular attention will be given to the preferences reported on the perceiving process in terms of sensing and intuition.

Method

Sample

Of the 268 clergymen who participated in the project, two were under the age of 30, 15 were in their 30s, 44 were in their 40s, 129 were in their 50s, 72 were in their 60s, five were in their 70s, and one did not disclose his age; 210 were married, 36 were single, 11 were divorced and not remarried, six were divorced and remarried, three were widowed, one was separated, and one did not disclose his marital status; 238 were engaged in stipendiary ministry, and 30 were engaged in non-stipendiary ministry.

Instrument

Psychological type was assessed by the Francis Psychological Type Scales (Francis, 2005). This is a 40-item instrument comprising four sets of 10 forced-choice items related to each of the four components of psychological type: orientation (extraversion or introversion), perceiving process (sensing or intuition), judging process (thinking or feeling), and attitude towards the outer world (judging or perceiving). Recent studies have demonstrated that this instrument functions well in church-related contexts. For example, Francis, Craig, and Hall (2008) reported alpha coefficients of .83 for the EI Scale, .76 for the SN Scale, .73 for the TF Scale, and .79 for the JP Scale. Participants were asked for each pair of characteristics to check the "box next to that characteristic which is closer to the real you, even if you feel both characteristics apply to you. Tick the characteristics that reflect the real you, even if other people see you differently".

Procedure

A questionnaire was posted to all licensed clergy serving in parochial ministry in the Church in Wales. A response rate of 54% produced 268 replies from male clergy, who had completed the relevant measures, which form the basis of the present analysis.

Data analysis

The research literature concerning the empirical investigation of psychological type has developed a highly distinctive method for analysing, handling, and displaying statistical data in the form of "type tables". This convention has been adopted in the following presentation in order to integrate these new data within the established literature and to provide all the detail necessary for secondary analysis and further interpretation within the rich theoretical framework afforded by psychological type. Type tables have been designed to provide information about the 16 discrete psychological types, about the four dichotomous preferences, about the six sets of pairs and temperaments, about the dominant types, and about the introverted and extraverted Jungian types. Commentary on this table will, however, be restricted to those aspects of the data strictly relevant to the research question. In the context of type tables, the statistical significance of the difference between two groups is established by means of the selection ratio index (I), an extension of chi-square (McCaulley, 1985).

Results

Table 1 presents the type distribution for the 268 Anglican clergymen serving in the Church in Wales who participated in the survey. These data confirm that clergymen serving in the Church in Wales prefer introversion (65%) over extraversion (35%), sensing over (57%) over intuition (43%), feeling (68%) over thinking (32%), and judging (78%) over perceiving (22%). The strongest dominant function is sensing (38%), followed by feeling (27%), intuition (25%), and thinking (10%). The three most strongly represented types were ISFJ (22%), ISTJ (13%), and ESFJ (11%).

Table 1 also presents the statistical significance tests comparing the profile of this group of Anglican clergymen with the UK population norms for men presented by Kendall (1998). The data confirm among Anglican clergymen significantly higher proportions of introversion (65% compared with 53%), intuitive types (43% compared with 27%), feeling types (68% compared with 35%), and judging types (78% compared with 55%). In terms of dominant types among Anglican clergymen dominant feeling types are significantly over-represented (27% compared with 15%), dominant intuitive types are significantly over-represented (25% compared with 13%), and dominant thinking types are significantly under-represented (10% compared with 31%). In terms of the 16 complete types, among Anglican clergymen five types are significantly under-represented (ISTJ, ISTP, ESTP, ENTP, and ESTJ) and five types are significantly over-represented (ISFJ, INFJ, INTJ, ESFJ, and ENFJ).

Discussion and conclusion

The current study was established to replicate two earlier studies reported by Francis, Payne et al. 2001), and Francis, Littler et al. (2010) among a sample of Anglican clergymen serving in the Church in Wales. These new data contribute to knowledge in two ways.

Table 1. Type distribution for Anglican clergymen in Wales compared with UK population norms.

The Sixteen Complete Types					Dichotomous Preferences			
ISTJ	ISFJ	INFJ	INTJ	E	$n=$ 95	(35.4%)	$I=0.76***$
$n=35$	$n=58$	$n=26$	$n=23$	I	$n=173$	(64.6%)	$I=1.22***$
(13.1%)	(21.6%)	(9.7%)	(8.6%)				
$I=0.66*$	$I=3.11***$	$I=6.05***$	$I=3.38***$	S	$n=153$	(57.1%)	$I=0.78***$
+++++	+++++	+++++	+++++	N	$n=115$	(42.9%)	$I=1.60***$
+++++	+++++	+++++	++++				
+++	+++++			T	$n=86$	(32.1%)	$I=0.49***$
	+++++			F	$n=182$	(67.9%)	$I=1.93***$
	++						
				J	$n=210$	(78.4%)	$I=1.43***$
				P	$n=58$	(21.6%)	$I=0.48***$
ISTP	ISFP	INFP	INTP		Pairs and Temperaments		
$n=2$	$n=7$	$n=17$	$n=5$				
(0.7%)	(2.6%)	(6.3%)	(1.9%)	IJ	$n=142$	(53.0%)	$I=1.72***$
$I=0.07***$	$I=0.70$	$I=1.76$	$I=0.45$	IP	$n=31$	(11.6%)	$I=0.52***$
+	+++	+++++	++	EP	$n=27$	(10.1%)	$I=0.44***$
		+		EJ	$n=68$	(25.4%)	$I=1.06$
				ST	$n=49$	(18.3%)	$I=0.36***$
				SF	$n=104$	(38.8%)	$I=1.70***$
				NF	$n=78$	(29.1%)	$I=2.37***$
ESTP	ESFP	ENFP	ENTP	NT	$n=37$	(13.8%)	$I=0.95$
$n=1$	$n=9$	$n=17$	$n=0$				
(0.4%)	(3.4%)	(6.3%)	(0.0%)	SJ	$n=134$	(50.0%)	$I=1.13$
$I=0.05***$	$I=0.55$	$I=1.25$	$I=0.00**$	SP	$n=19$	(7.1%)	$I=0.25***$
	+++	+++++		NP	$n=39$	(14.6%)	$I=0.88$
		+		NJ	$n=76$	(28.4%)	$I=2.72***$
				TJ	$n=78$	(29.1%)	$I=0.76**$
				TP	$n=8$	(3.0%)	$I=0.11***$
ESTJ	ESFJ	ENFJ	ENTJ	FP	$n=50$	(18.7%)	$I=1.00$
$n=11$	$n=30$	$n=18$	$n=9$	FJ	$n=132$	(49.3%)	$I=2.97***$
(4.1%)	(11.2%)	(6.7%)	(3.4%)				
$I=0.35***$	$I=1.86***$	$I=3.35***$	$I=0.78$	IN	$n=71$	(26.5%)	$I=2.23***$
++++	+++++	+++++	+++	EN	$n=44$	(16.4%)	$I=1.10$
	+++++	++		IS	$n=102$	(38.1%)	$I=0.92$
	+			ES	$n=51$	(19.0%)	$I=0.60***$
				ET	$n=21$	(7.8%)	$I=0.28***$
				EF	$n=74$	(27.6%)	$I=1.43**$
				IF	$n=108$	(40.3%)	$I=2.53***$
				IT	$n=65$	(24.3%)	$I=0.65***$

Jungian Types (E)				Jungian Types (I)				Dominant Types			
	n	%	Index		n	%	Index		n	%	Index
E-TJ	20	7.5	0.47***	I-TP	7	2.6	0.17***	Dt.T	27	10.1	0.33***
E-FJ	48	17.9	2.23***	I-FP	24	9.0	1.22	Dt.F	72	26.9	1.75***
ES-P	10	3.7	0.26***	IS-J	93	34.7	1.30*	Dt.S	103	38.4	0.94
EN-P	17	6.3	0.73	IN-J	49	18.3	4.41***	Dt.N	66	24.6	1.92***

Note: $N=268$. $+=1\%$ of N.
$*p<.05$.
$**p<.01$.
$***p<.001$.

First, these data confirm the general finding that the psychological type profile of Anglican clergymen differ from the population norms generated for men in the UK in particularly strong and remarkable way. According to the population norms, the majority of women prefer feeling (70%) while the majority of men prefer thinking (65%). Although in the population as a whole only 35% of men prefer feeling, among Anglican clergy, a much higher proportion of men prefer feeling: 69% according to Francis, Payne et al. (2001), 68% according to the present study, 56% according to Francis, Robbins et al. (2010), 55% according to Francis, Littler et al. (2010), and 54% according to Francis, Craig, Whinney et al. (2007). This finding may help to illuminate much of the culture evident in the Anglican Church in both Wales and England. This is a Church in which women predominate in which the male (as well as the female) leadership share the congregations' preference for feeling, a distinctively feminine personality characteristic. This psychological finding may help to explain the Anglican Church's reluctance in England and Wales to tackle tough management issues in a characteristically masculine way, and also the reluctance of men to join the congregations.

Second, these data confirm the specific finding that Anglican clergymen in Wales demonstrate an overall preference for sensing in contrast with their colleagues in England who demonstrate an overall preference for intuition. The differences in leadership style between intuitive types and sensing types may be quite profound, and such differences may lead to quite different experiences for church members. Studies of Anglican congregations, both in Wales and in England show a very strong preference for sensing (Francis & Robbins, 2012; Francis, Robbins, & Craig, 2011; Francis, Robbins, Williams, & Williams, 2007) and for this reason leaders who prefer sensing may find themselves in closer sympathy with the members of other congregations than is the case for leaders who prefer intuition.

With a ministry leadership shaped by a predominance of intuitive types, the Church of England may be more active in promoting change and development at the local level. In such a church the clergy may run ahead of the laity, leave the regular churchgoers frustrated by the pace of change and experimentation, and confuse the large body of occasional churchgoers who turn up at Christmas only to find that the form of service has changed and few of the familiar landmarks remain to nurture them back into the faith with which they once felt both familiar and comfortable. With ministry leadership shaped by a predominance of sensing types, the Church in Wales may be more reluctant to promote change at the local level. In such a church, the clergy may drag behind those regular churchgoers who have had a taste of experimentation in the wider international church, and alienate occasional attenders who seek innovation in marriage services and funeral services connecting with contemporary culture.

The puzzle remains, however, as to why the Church of England and the Church in Wales have taken on such noticeable and important differences in the psychological type profile of their clergymen. Two possible explanations may warrant further investigation. One explanation would look to the selection processes by which the Church of England and the Church in Wales test the vocation of candidates for ordained ministry. Both Churches rely on a specific group of people who serve on the selection boards. The theory that suggests selectors may be inclined to select in their own image is worth empirical scrutiny. A study concerned with assessing the psychological type profile of the selectors may be overdue. Another explanation is that there is an element of self-selection in the two-way traffic across Offa's Dyke of clergy moving from Wales to serve in England and of clergy moving from England to serve in English-speaking parishes in Wales. Clergy in England who prefer sensing may be drawn to ministry in Wales, while clergy in Wales who prefer intuition may be drawn to ministry in England. A study concerned with assessing the psychological type profile of clergy on the transfer list may also be overdue.

A different source of insight could be generated by research in Anglican Churches in other countries to explore how far the preference for sensing and for intuition varies within the Anglican Communion. Differences in the psychological type profile of clergy within the Anglican Communion may help to explain some of the rich diversity in the expression of Anglicanism in different Provinces and some of the internal conflict, struggles, and misunderstandings within this widely spread and diverse Communion. The theory suggested by the data so far available is that some fundamental differences in perspectives on theology and on church order may reflect even more fundamental differences in psychological type preferences.

References

Burton, L., Francis, L. J., & Robbins, M. (2010). Psychological type profile of Methodist circuit minister in Britain: Similarities with and differences from Anglican clergy. *Journal of Empirical Theology, 23,* 64–81. doi:10.1163/157092510X503020

Craig, C. L., Duncan, B., & Francis, L. J. (2006). Psychological type preferences of Roman Catholic priests in the United Kingdom. *Journal of Beliefs and Values, 27,* 157–164. doi:10.1080/13617670600849812

Craig, C. L., Francis, L. J., & Robbins, M. (2004). Psychological type and sex differences among church leaders in the United Kingdom. *Journal of Beliefs and Values, 25,* 3–13. doi:10.1080/1361767042000199004

Craig, C. L. Horsfall, T., & Francis, L. J. (2005). Psychological types of male missionary personnel training in England: A role for thinking type men? *Pastoral Psychology, 53,* 475–482. doi:10.1007/s11089-005-2588-8

Francis, L. J. (2005). *Faith and psychology: Personality, religion and the individual.* London: Darton, Longman and Todd.

Francis, L. J. (2009). Psychological type theory and religious and spiritual experience. In M. De Souza, L.J. Francis, J. O'Higgins-Norman & D. G. Scott (Eds.), *International handbook of education for spirituality, care and wellbeing* (pp. 125–146). Dordrecht: Springer.

Francis, L. J., Craig, C. L., & Butler, A. (2007). Psychological types of male evangelical Anglican seminarians in England. *Journal of Psychological Type, 67,* 11–17.

Francis, L. J., Craig, C. L., & Hall, G. (2008). Psychological type and attitude toward Celtic Christianity among committed churchgoers in the United Kingdom: An empirical study. *Journal of Contemporary Religion, 23,* 181–191. doi:10.1080/13537900802024543

Francis, L. J., Craig, C. L., Horsfall, T., & Ross, C. F. J. (2005). Psychological types of male and female evangelical lay church leaders in England, compared with United Kingdom population norms. *Fieldwork in Religion, 1,* 69–83.

Francis, L. J., Craig, C. L., Whinney, M., Tilley, D., & Slater, P. (2007). Psychological profiling of Anglican clergy in England: Employing Jungian typology to interpret diversity, strengths, and potential weaknesses in ministry. *International Journal of Practical Theology, 11,* 266–284. doi:10.1515/IJPT.2007.17

Francis, L. J., Gubb, S., & Robbins, M. (2009). Psychological type profile of Lead Elders within the Newfrontiers network of churches in the United Kingdom. *Journal of Belief and Values, 30,* 61–69. doi:10.1080/13617670902784568

Francis, L. J., & Holmes, P. (2011). Ordained local ministers: The same Anglican orders, but of different psychological temperaments? *Rural Theology, 9,* 151–160.

Francis, L. J., Littler, K., & Robbins, M. (2010). Psychological type and Offa's Dyke: Exploring differences in the psychological type profile of Anglican clergy serving in England and Wales. *Contemporary Wales, 23,* 240–251.

Francis, L. J., Nash, P., Nash, S., & Craig, C. L. (2007). Psychology and youth ministry: Psychological type preferences of Christian youth workers in the United Kingdom. *Journal of Youth Ministry, 5,* 73–90.

Francis, L. J., Payne, V. J., & Jones, S. H. (2001). Psychological types of male Anglican clergy in Wales. *Journal of Psychological Type, 56,* 19–23.

Francis, L. J., Penson, A. W., & Jones, S. H. (2001). Psychological types of male and female Bible College students in England. *Mental Health, Religion & Culture, 4,* 23–32. doi:10.1080/13674670123953

Francis, L. J., & Robbins, M. (2002). Psychological types of male evangelical church leaders. *Journal of Belief and Values, 23,* 217–220. doi:10.1080/1361767022000010860

Francis, L. J., & Robbins, M. (2012). Not fitting in and getting out: Psychological type and congregational satisfaction among Anglican churchgoers in England. *Mental Health, Religion & Culture, 15*, 1023–1035. doi:10.1080/13674676.2012.676260

Francis, L. J., Robbins, M., & Craig, C. L. (2011). The psychological type profile of Anglican churchgoers in England: Compatible or incompatible with their clergy? *International Journal of Practical Theology, 15*, 243–259. doi:10.1515/IJPT.2011.036

Francis, L. J. Robbins, M., Duncan, B., & Whinney, M. (2010). Confirming the psychological type profile of Anglican clergymen in England: A ministry for intuitives. In B. Ruelas & V. Briseno (Eds.), *Psychology of intuition* (pp. 211–219). New York, NY: Nova Science.

Francis, L. J., Robbins, M., & Jones, S. H. (2012). The psychological type profile of clergywomen in ordained local ministry in the Church of England: Pioneers or custodians? *Mental Health, Religion & Culture, 15*, 919–932. doi:10.1080/13674676.2012.698449

Francis, L. J., Robbins, M., & Whinney, M. (2011). Women priests in the Church of England: Psychological type profile. *Religions, 2*, 389–397. doi:10.3390/rel2030389

Francis, L. J., Robbins, M., Williams, A., & Williams, R. (2007). All types are called, but some are more likely to respond: The psychological profile of rural Anglican churchgoers in Wales. *Rural Theology, 5*, 23–30.

Francis, L. J., & Village, A. (2008). *Preaching with all our souls*. London: Continuum.

Francis, L. J., & Village, A. (2012). The psychological temperament of Anglican clergy in ordained local ministry (OLM): The conserving, serving pastor? *Journal of Empirical Theology, 25*, 57–76. doi:10.1163/157092512X635743

Francis, L. J., Whinney, M., Burton, L., & Robbins, M. (2011). Psychological type preferences of male and female Free Church Ministers in England. *Research in the Social Scientific Study of Religion, 22*, 251–263. doi:10.1163/ej.9789004207271.i-360.55

Kay, W. K., & Francis, L. J. (2008). Psychological type preferences of female Bible College students in England. *Journal of Beliefs and Values, 29*, 101–105. doi:10.1080/13617670801928324

Kay, W. K., Francis, L. J., & Craig, C. L. (2008). Psychological type preferences of male British Assemblies of God Bible College students: Tough minded or tender hearted? *Journal of the European Pentecostal Theological Association, 28*, 6–20.

Kay, W. K., Francis, L. J., & Robbins, M. (2011). A distinctive leadership for a distinctive network of churches? Psychological type theory and the apostolic networks. *Journal of Pentecostal Theology, 20*, 306–322. doi:10.1163/174552511X597170

Kendall, E. (1998). *Myers-Briggs Type Indicator: Step 1 manual supplement*. Palo Alto, CA: Consulting Psychologists Press.

Lewis, C. A. (2012). Psychological type, religion, and culture: Theoretical and empirical perspectives. *Mental Health, Religion & Culture, 15*, 817–821. doi:10.1080/13674676.2012.721534

McCaulley, M. H. (1985). The selection ratio type table: A research strategy for comparing type distributions. *Journal of Psychological Type, 10*, 46–56.

Village, A. (2011). Gifts differing? Psychological type among stipendiary and non-stipendiary clergy. *Research in the Social Scientific Study of Religion, 22*, 230–250. doi:10.1163/ej.9789004207271.i-360.49

Village, A. (2013). Traditions within the Church of England and psychological type: A study among the clergy. *Journal of Empirical Theology, 26*, 22–44. doi:10.1163/15709256-12341252

Psychological types and self-assessed leadership skills of clergy in the Church of England

Laura Watt and David Voas

The study uses data from an online survey of parish churches carried out in 2013 for the Church of England. It obtained a sample of 1480 clergy, mainly stipendiary. As expected from previous studies, there were relatively high frequencies of psychological types marked by introversion, intuition, feeling, and judging. Gender differences were small. Clergy also provided self-assessments of their abilities in a number of areas related to parish ministry. Personality has substantial effects on these leadership strengths, although the types that have positive associations are often not those most commonly found among Anglican clergy. A single scale can be created for most of the qualities (including managing, motivating, innovating, etc.), but empathising and connecting do not belong on the same dimension. If clergy are to be deployed effectively, it may be desirable to distinguish between positions calling for good general leaders and those where the emphasis is on pastoral work.

Introduction

The relationship between personality and leadership has been discussed by psychologists, sociologists, economists, and others. These discussions address various questions such as: Are people of some personality types more likely to emerge as leaders than others? Can we predict the *kind* of leader a person will become from his or her personality? Do certain traits make for better leaders?

Studies that have addressed the last of these questions in particular have tended to focus on corporate leadership and to measure personality via the "Big Five" dimensions: extraversion, agreeableness, emotional stability (versus neuroticism), conscientiousness, and openness to experience (Digman, 1990). Many of these studies show that this five-factor model of personality can be used to predict leadership effectiveness. There are, however, inconsistencies between them in terms of which personality traits appear to have an effect and the size of those effects. For example, McCrae, Costa, and Yik (1996) found extraversion, agreeableness, emotional stability, and conscientiousness to be most related to leadership effectiveness, with openness to experience much less so. Meanwhile, in their meta-analysis of existing empirical work, Judge, Bono, Ilies, and Gerhardt (2002) found that agreeableness had no effect on leadership effectiveness. Different again are the results of Silverthorne (2001) who, in his cross-national study of leadership and personality, found that all of the big five personality traits had a positive effect upon leadership (at least in the USA).

The most consistent finding in studies of leadership and personality seems to be the association between extraversion and leadership effectiveness: extraverts tend to make better leaders than introverts (Colbert, Judge, Choi, & Wang, 2012; Ployhart, Lim, & Chan, 2001). Colbert et al. (2012) claim that many studies of personality and leadership actually underestimate the association between these two constructs because of the ways in which they are measured. They argue that while most of these studies rely upon self-reported measures of personality, in order to see the real effect personality has upon leadership, observer-reported measures should be used instead. Oh, Wang, and Mount (2011) agree with this view, reporting stronger associations between leadership and extraversion when the latter is rated by an observer rather than the subject.

While there is some evidence that such individual differences can be used to predict leadership effectiveness, authors such as Andersen (2006) strongly criticise this emphasis on personality. They argue instead for the instrumental approach, which is more concerned with what leaders do than who they are as a means of distinguishing between the successful and unsuccessful. Andersen (2006) claims that while a leader's personality might be associated with his or her success, it will only be so to the extent that personality affects his or her behaviour. In his view, it is the action of the leader that makes the difference. This action might be the result of personality but it might also result from situational factors. Farkas and Wetlaufer (1996) found, for example, that the corporate environment was a key influence on the behaviour of company leaders, regardless of their personality. Andersen (2006), therefore, questions the relationship between personality and leadership, suggesting that traits alone are not enough to explain leadership effectiveness and are at best preconditions that might encourage certain behaviours.

This debate raises interesting questions regarding leadership and the age-old question of nature versus nurture: are leaders born, or are they made? We enter this debate by investigating the association between personality and leadership among clergy in the Church of England. In particular, we are interested in whether people of certain psychological types appear to be better suited than others to ordained leadership. The ways in which personality is associated with leadership in a corporate setting may not apply to the religious sphere. In their study of personality and job performance, Barrick and Mount (1991) found that different personality traits can have different effects in different occupational settings.

Scholarly interest has been growing in the distribution of clergy by psychological type and the implications of that distribution (see, for example, Francis, Craig, Whinney, Tilley, & Slater, 2007; Francis & Village, 2012). In 2013, measures of personality were included as part of the Church of England's survey for the Church Growth Research Programme, which was designed to explore potential causes of church growth and decline. Results from the study suggest that church growth is significantly associated with the personality of the ordained minister, and specifically with extraversion, intuition, and emotional stability (Voas & Watt, 2014).

Growth of a congregation could be used as a measure of leadership effectiveness for clergy, though of course it would be a limited one. Increasing the size of the flock is just one aspect of church leadership; clergy are also expected to tend to the existing flock by providing religious instruction, pastoral care, and administering the sacrament as well as managing lay leaders, organising finances, and liaising with members of the wider community – to mention just a few of their functions. Each of these varied roles could be associated with personality in different ways. In the present study, we look at how psychological type might influence leadership strengths more broadly among the clergy. Alongside the issue of personality, we also explore how age and sex affect this relationship.

Method

Sample

The data used in this study come from a large online survey administered between April and July 2013 as part of the Church of England's Church Growth Research Programme. The survey was designed to identify factors related to numerical change in church attendance. Invitations were sent by e-mail to ordained ministers – most with incumbent status – in a large sample of parishes. More detail regarding the sample and overall study can be found in Voas and Watt (2014).

The survey consisted of two main parts. The first was principally concerned with profiling the church in terms of size, worship style, activities, and so on. Responses were received from 1703 churches. The second part was to be completed by the ordained minister most closely associated with the church. Here the questions included age, date of ordination, type of post, theological orientation, and other characteristics. This section also featured the batteries on personality and leadership that are used in the work described below.

The clergy portion of the questionnaire was completed for the large majority of churches in the achieved sample, with the result that we have full data on nearly 1500 Anglican clergymen and women. All respondents are in parish ministry; 95% are stipendiary and 90% full time. Incumbents are over-represented in the sample and curates, self-supporting ministers and ordained local ministers are under-represented.

Measures

Psychological type

The survey included the battery of items used for the Francis Personality Type Scales (FPTS; Francis, 2005). Like the familiar Myers-Briggs system, these scales represent an attempt to operationalise psychological type theory rooted in the pioneering work of Jung (1971). The strength of the FPTS is that it was designed for use in large-scale surveys rather than in individual consultation or clinical contexts. There are four dimensions, identified by the letter in upper case: Extraversion – Introversion, Sensing – iNtuition, Thinking – Feeling, Judging – Perceiving. An additional dimension in the FPTS was called neuroticism and is also in the Big-Three (Eysenck & Eysenck, 1985) and the Five-Factor model of personality (Costa & McCrae, 1985), though it might more helpfully be referred to as emotional stability.

E and I distinguish between two orientations: towards the outside world in the case of Extraversion or the inner world in the case of Introversion. Extraverts thrive off company, feeling energised through contact with others, preferring to socialise than to be alone. Introverts, on the other hand, tend to feel drained by social events and too much contact with other people; they gain their energy from being alone, working out problems in solitude rather than talking them through.

S and N distinguish between two ways of perceiving or processing information, either through one's senses or intuition. Sensing types look to, and prioritise, the specific and concrete details of a situation, concerned with the finer practical points of how something might be accomplished. Intuitive types are less concerned with such detail, preferring to look at the general picture of what they observe and what they would like to accomplish rather than focusing on the practicalities of how it might happen. Francis and Village (2012) note that people of this type can appear to be "up in the air" and "idealistic dreamers".

T and F distinguish between ways of making judgements. Thinking types make judgements, or decisions, based on knowledge, facts about the situation, and values they hold and adhere to. As such, they tend to remain objective even when tough decisions need to be made. Conversely, feeling types are more subjective in their decision-making, prioritising the desire to make people happy or keeping the peace above adherence to external criteria and rules.

J and P concern a person's attitude towards the outside world. Judging types have an organised and structured approach to doing things. They enjoy routine and schedules, finding it difficult to be spontaneous or to deal with unexpected situations or change in general. Perceiving types have a much less fixed approach to life, enjoy being spontaneous, and welcome change. They tend to be more impulsive than judging types and so are less likely to stick to previously made plans and decisions.

A fifth dimension in Francis' (2005) instrument distinguishes between emotional stability and instability. Those inclined towards the latter tend to be more susceptible to worry and stress than the emotionally stable, who are more likely to remain calm and rational in any situation and are better able to cope with problems that arise.

Each of these five dimensions of personality is measured on an 11-point scale. These measures can be dichotomised, as has been done for some analyses reported here. In general, however, we treat the dimensions as continuous variables. We label each dimension using one or the other pole (e.g., extraversion rather than introversion) as a matter of convenience. Choosing the other pole would give the same results with the opposite sign.

On the basis of the four main dimensions (excluding emotional stability), every respondent can be assigned one of 16 possible psychological types, combining a dominant orientation (extraversion or introversion), a dominant perceiving process (sensing or intuition), a dominant judging process (thinking or feeling), and a dominant attitude towards the outside word (judging or perceiving). The result is described by a four-letter combination such as ENTJ or ISFP. This categorical typology is also used in this study.

Leadership measure

The principal aim of the survey was to help identify factors associated with church growth or decline, which might include characteristics of the ordained minister. A great deal of work in this area has been done by National Church Life Survey (NCLS) Research in Australia, and we took particular inspiration from their analysis of leadership strengths. Their investigations follow the psychometric tradition: respondents complete a large battery of questions and are scored on the basis of their answers. Time and space constraints meant that it was not possible to adopt the same approach in our survey, and so we asked clergy to assess their own strengths in eight areas. The question was as follows:

What do you see as your strengths? Some of your qualities will be more or less developed, either in relation to each other or relative to the characteristics of others. How would you rate yourself on each of the following attributes? [The questionnaire presented a 7-point Likert scale with the endpoints marked "no special talent" (1) and "better than most people" (7).]

- Empathising: sensing what other people are feeling; listening and counselling.
- Speaking: being confident when giving a sermon or addressing a formal meeting.
- Innovating: regularly coming up with new ways of doing things.
- Connecting: spending time with people in the community and listening to their views.
- Managing: creating good systems and providing clear expectations to lay leaders.
- Envisioning: having a clear vision for the future and being focused on achieving it.
- Persisting: finishing what you start, despite obstacles in the way.
- Motivating: generating enthusiasm and inspiring people to action.

While we believe that these eight qualities encompass important aspects of clerical leadership, we recognise that there may be relevant strengths that are not measured here. A larger concern is that the self-perceptions underlying these assessments may be inaccurate. Inflated scores would not be too serious if the bias is either universal or randomly occurring, but it seems possible that the degree of over-estimation may be influenced by personality. For example, one might expect that extraverts rate themselves more highly than similarly talented introverts, or that neuroticism leads to lower self-confidence.

In fact, our results do show positive associations between both extraversion and emotional stability and the various leadership strengths. While it is highly plausible that people of these psychological types are indeed more able leaders, they might also be more prone to high self-regard. Identifying the extent of causality in each direction is far from straightforward.

Results

Psychological type: descriptive statistics

The findings on psychological type from the current study are broadly consistent with previous research on Anglican clergy, both male and female (Francis et al., 2007; Francis, Robbins, Duncan, & Whinney, 2010; Francis, Robbins, & Whinney, 2011). As shown in Table 1, introversion, intuition, feeling, and judging are the dominant types. The gender differences are relatively small. Francis et al. (2007) report that male and female Anglican clergy are similarly likely to belong to types I, N, and J, but that a considerably higher proportion of ordained women should be classed as Feeling (as is the case for women generally). The same contrast can be observed in comparing the findings of Francis et al. (2010) and Francis et al. (2011) for male and female Anglican clergy, respectively. We found a much smaller gap that is not statistically significant.

Francis and colleagues report that upwards of 60% of Church of England clergy have intuition rather than sensing as their perceiving function, and we find slightly smaller majorities of this type for both men and women. On the other dimensions our figures for men are close to those in either Francis et al. (2007) or Francis et al. (2010). The current study shows a lower prevalence of Feeling and also a higher prevalence of Judging among female Anglican clergy than reported in earlier work.

The differences between clergy and the general population in psychological type are much as have already been described in the literature. Anglican clergymen are considerably more likely than other men to be classed as N, F, and J, although their level of introversion is not distinctive. For women, N and J are also high for Anglican clergy, but otherwise the contrast comes in higher

Table 1. Psychological type of male and female Anglican clergy (%).

Type	UK	Francis et al. (2007)	Francis et al. (2010)/ Francis et al. (2011)	Church growth research
Men				
I	53	57	64	55
N	27	62	67	55
F	35	54	56	59
J	55	68	73	75
Sample size	*748*	*626*	*622*	*1172*
Women				
I	43	54	63	59
N	21	65	60	56
F	70	74	76	63
J	62	65	55	76
Sample size	*865*	*247*	*83*	*308*

Source: UK population norms are provided by Kendall (1998). Figures in the penultimate column are taken from Francis et al. (2010) for men and Francis et al. (2011) for women.

levels of Introversion, with F being similar to the population norm. To put the matter another way, a majority of Anglican clergymen have what might seem to be feminine levels of feeling and judging, while ordained women are somewhat more introverted than the gender norm. The preference for intuition is relatively high among both male and female clergy in the Church of England.

Despite the preponderance of intuition, we found ISFJ to be the most prevalent psychological type among both male and female Anglican clergy (12.8% and 18.9%, respectively). INFJ, which combines the types that taken individually are observed most frequently, characterises 10.9% of men and 10.4% of women in our sample. Other common types are INTJ (10.4% and 10.7% for men and women, respectively) and ISTJ (10.4% of ordained men). The last three columns of Table 5 show the full list for all clergy (men and women combined), as compared to the general UK population.

Leadership strengths: descriptive statistics

Table 2 lists the mean scores for each leadership quality. Anglican clergy appear to have a relatively high degree of confidence in their own abilities: the means range from 4.27 to 5.77 on a 7-point scale, and for all factors with the exception of "managing" the median score is at least 5.

Respondents were most likely to be positive about their "speaking" ability, that is, feeling confident when giving a sermon or addressing a formal meeting. Speaking, empathising, and motivating are all near the top of the list with mean ratings over 5. Respondents were least confident about "managing", defined as creating good systems and providing clear expectations to lay leaders.

Bivariate associations with leadership strengths

Age is not strongly correlated with any of the self-reported leadership strengths, but in three instances there are statistically significant associations. Younger ordained ministers are more likely to say that they are good at innovating and envisioning, while older clergy score highly in persisting ("finishing what you start, despite obstacles in the way").

These results are consistent with stereotypes about the young and old. Youth is associated with a desire to change; innovating is about creating new ways of doing things, while envisioning involves having a vision for the future. Younger leaders may be relatively forward thinking. In contrast, older leaders may be more reliable and effective at following through on a plan, though persistence may also translate into inflexibility (Voas & Watt, 2014).

Table 2. Self-reported leadership scores among Church of England clergy.

	Mean	Std. dev.	Men	Women
Speaking	5.77	1.08	5.85	5.49
Empathising	5.26	1.30	5.15	5.69
Motivating	5.14	1.21	5.06	5.43
Persisting	4.86	1.43	4.86	4.86
Envisioning	4.85	1.35	4.86	4.82
Innovating	4.73	1.45	4.73	4.76
Connecting	4.49	1.35	4.43	4.72
Managing	4.27	1.43	4.25	4.36
Sample size	*1480*		*1172*	*308*

Note: Scale from 1 ("no special talent") to 7 ("better than most people").

Table 3. Correlations between leadership strengths and psychological types.

	Empathising	Speaking	Innovating	Connecting	Managing	Envisioning	Persisting	Motivating
Extraversion	0.05	0.16**	0.26**	0.30**	0.11**	0.18**	0.00	0.36**
Intuition	0.11**	0.18**	0.45**	0.09**	−0.05*	0.29**	−0.13**	0.22**
Feeling	0.27**	−0.14**	−0.13**	0.15**	−0.20**	−0.19**	−0.17**	0.04
Judging	−0.09**	−0.06*	−0.20**	−0.13**	0.35**	0.05*	0.29**	−0.09**
Emotional stability	−0.09**	0.10**	0.07**	0.08**	0.19**	0.14**	0.11**	0.17**

*$p < 0.05$.
**$p < 0.01$.

There are some significant differences between the mean scores of male and female clergy. Ordained women appear to be stronger at empathising (5.69 compared to 5.15 for men), connecting (4.72 versus 4.43), and motivating (5.43 versus 5.06). Male clergy give themselves relatively high marks for speaking (5.85 compared to 5.49 for women). It is no surprise that women have the edge with empathy and connecting (defined as "spending time with people in the community and listening to their views"), or that men feel especially confident in public performance. The result for motivating is more intriguing, not least because this strength is one that emerges as particularly important for church growth, although there is no association between clergy gender and growth (Voas & Watt, 2014).

Table 3 shows the correlations between the five personality traits (extraversion, intuition, thinking, judging, and emotional stability) and the eight leadership qualities. The main associations with each strength are consistent with expectations: empathising goes hand in hand with high scores on feeling; connecting and motivating are linked to extraversion; innovating and envisioning are promoted by intuition; and both managing and persisting relate to judging.

Note that the psychological types that are found most frequently among Anglican clergy are not always those most closely correlated to leadership strengths. In particular, extraversion has a significantly positive association with most of the qualities, but the majority of ordained ministers are introverts. Similarly, clergy tend to be strong on feeling, which is negatively correlated with managing, envisioning, persisting, speaking, and innovating. The position with judging is somewhat better, though this type does not rate highly on innovating. The most promising observation is that a majority of these ordained ministers are of the intuitive type, which is positively correlated with most of the strengths. While "there is a danger that the wider population [three quarters of whom prefer sensing to intuition] may view clergy as having little to say to 'the real world'" (Francis et al., 2007, p. 281), it is at least possible that these individuals are more effective leaders than others.

Multivariate versus bivariate analyses

To go beyond the bivariate correlations described above, we used linear regression to investigate the relative effect of age, sex, and each personality trait on the self-assessed leadership ratings. Table 4 shows the results, where each of the eight leadership strengths was taken in turn as the dependent variable. The rows list the independent variables (age, sex, and the five psychological types), and the values in the table are the standardised coefficients for each. We are thus able to assess the relative effects of each variable on the different measures of leadership.

The results of the multivariate analysis are largely in line with those reviewed above from the bivariate analyses, suggesting that for the most part the factors have independent effects. The differences that are observed are related to intuition and judging, which are inversely related: in this data set the correlation between these two types is −0.425. Considering both variables simultaneously using regression techniques is particularly helpful in distinguishing their effects.

Table 4. Standardised coefficients from linear regression models showing effects of age, sex, and personality on leadership strengths.

	Empathising	Speaking	Innovating	Connecting	Managing	Envisioning	Persisting	Motivating	Scale
Age	0.04	−0.00	−0.02	0.04	0.03	−0.01	0.15**	0.03	0.05*
Female	0.15**	−0.13**	0.02	0.10**	0.05*	−0.00	0.01	0.14**	0.03
Extraversion	0.03	0.15**	0.21**	0.28**	0.19**	0.18**	0.07**	0.33**	0.28**
Intuition	0.10**	0.16**	0.42**	0.05	0.11**	0.36**	−0.01	0.21**	0.32**
Feeling	0.27**	−0.15**	−0.15**	0.12**	−0.12**	−0.16**	−0.11**	0.02	−0.17**
Judging	0.02	0.01	−0.01	−0.01	0.41**	0.22**	0.29**	0.08**	0.26**
Emotional stability	−0.05*	0.09**	0.07**	0.06*	0.19**	0.15**	0.11**	0.18**	0.20**
Adjusted R^2	0.11	0.10	0.27	0.12	0.22	0.20	0.14	0.20	0.25

Note: As described in the text, the scale is the mean value for speaking, innovating, managing, envisioning, persisting, and motivating, that is, all qualities except empathising and connecting.
*$p < 0.05$.
**$p < 0.01$.

Table 5. Scale measure of leadership strengths by psychological type.

Psychological type	Mean	Std. error of mean	N	%	SSR
ENTJ	5.46	0.08	91	6.3	2.14
ENFJ	5.37	0.07	128	8.8	3.21
ESTJ	5.30	0.07	89	6.2	0.59
ENTP	5.25	0.12	46	3.2	1.15
INTJ	5.20	0.07	149	10.3	7.32
INTP	5.00	0.13	34	2.3	0.96
ESFJ	4.96	0.08	134	9.3	0.73
ENFP	4.94	0.07	112	7.7	1.23
ESFP	4.85	0.15	31	2.1	0.25
ISTJ	4.84	0.06	144	10.0	0.73
INFJ	4.75	0.07	156	10.8	6.29
INFP	4.72	0.11	72	5.0	1.56
ESTP	4.67	0.22	14	1.0	0.17
ISFJ	4.52	0.06	205	14.2	1.11
ISFP	4.12	0.14	32	2.2	0.36
ISTP	4.08	0.31	10	0.7	0.11

Note: The self-selection ratio (SSR) is the ratio of the relative frequency of the type in this dataset to that in the general UK population (OPP, 2011).

Innovating, for example, shows a substantial negative correlation with judging. Intuition is even more strongly associated with innovating, however, and judging ceases to have any effect when controlling for that characteristic. In other words, the correlation arises only because of the connection between intuition and perceiving; the first type is strongly related to innovating but the second is not. The same phenomenon can be seen in reverse with persisting, where the strong association with judging produces a "spurious" negative correlation with intuition.

There are also shifts in the strength and even the direction of the associations with respect to managing, envisioning, and motivating. Judging has a strong influence on managing, which shows a small negative correlation with intuition. In a multivariate analysis, however, it turns out that the influence of intuition is actually positive. The story with envisioning and motivating is essentially the same in reverse: the positive effect of judging is suppressed in the bivariate correlation because intuition is so important.

Finally, connecting is unusual in that the small but significant bivariate associations with intuition and judging do not survive in multivariate analysis, where sex has a more important role.

Findings from the multivariate analysis

As one might expect, empathising is most strongly associated with feeling. While thinking types try to remain objective in judging situations, making decisions based on external values, feeling types tend to place greater importance on ensuring the peace and happiness of those with whom they interact. Such people would seem more naturally empathetic. Interestingly, empathising is the only leadership quality that is negatively associated with emotional stability. The effect is small yet significant and points to the fact that sensitivity can be a positive attribute.

Speaking is not strongly associated with any personality trait though it is moderately, and positively, linked to extraversion, intuition, thinking, and emotional stability. These traits seem plausibly related to having confidence when speaking to groups of people.

The strongest relationship in the entire table is between intuition and innovating. People who lean towards the intuition (rather than sensing) end of the perceiving dimension are inclined to look at the bigger picture rather than concrete details when processing information. They are more interested in an overall vision of what might be accomplished than in the practicalities of how that vision will come to pass. The intuitive way of perceiving the world, therefore, seems to lend itself to innovation or coming up with new ways of doing things. A tendency to overlook the details of how something might work seems potentially valuable, at least in the first instance, when creating new systems. For similar reasons, envisioning is also strongly linked to intuition.

Connecting is most strongly associated with extraversion. The fact that extraverts thrive off interacting with other people would suggest that they are more comfortable (and therefore better at) connecting, defined here as spending time with people in the community and listening to their views. Motivating is also strongly associated with extraversion. Again, an outgoing personality seems suited to this leadership quality; someone who gains energy from being with others is arguably better at motivating others to action than someone more reserved.

Finally, both managing and persisting are strongly linked to judging. Judgers, unlike perceivers, like to be organised and structured rather than impulsive and spontaneous, qualities that help to support these strengths.

Overall, the results suggest that extraversion and intuition are most consistently associated with the leadership qualities being considered here. The effects of emotional stability are somewhat more modest, but with a single exception (empathising) it is positively and significantly associated with the various leadership strengths. As noted earlier, we need to be cautious about interpreting some of these findings. Extraverts and introverts, and the emotionally stable and unstable, might have different perceptions of their own abilities.

A scale measure of leadership

Both factor analysis and classical reliability analysis indicate that a good scale can be formed by combining six out of the eight leadership strengths (all except empathising and connecting). The value of Cronbach's alpha is 0.73. The multi-item scale is created by calculating the mean of the six original leadership measures.

By creating a single measure of leadership that combines most of these qualities, we can produce a model to measure the relative effect of each independent variable on leadership more generally. The last column in Table 4 shows the results of a linear regression treating this multi-item leadership scale as the dependent variable. Gender has no significant effect on overall leadership ratings. Being female is positively associated with empathising and connecting, both of which have been excluded from the scale. The only other significant effects are counterbalancing: men rate themselves as better at speaking while women give themselves higher marks for motivating. The effect of age is small, but older clergy do tend to have higher leadership scores. Each of the personality traits is found to have a significant effect on this combined measure of leadership; starting from the most important, the positive influences come from intuition, extraversion, judging, emotional stability, and finally thinking (as opposed to feeling).

Psychological types and leadership ratings

The results in Table 4 for the scale measure imply that ENTJs are likely to score most highly in self-assessed leadership strengths, which is indeed the case. Table 5 shows the full set of 16 psychological types in descending order of leadership scale scores.

There are striking differences between the EN (extroversion + intuition) and IS (introversion + sensing) psychological types. Three of the top four positions in the table are occupied by the former; the bottom three places are taken by the latter. These results go some way to explaining the finding that IS clergy are three times as likely to preside over decline as substantial growth, whereas EN clergy are twice as likely to report substantial growth as decline (Voas & Watt, 2014). Personality matters to church growth in part because some key abilities come more or less naturally to different types of people, not least motivating (generating enthusiasm and inspiring people to action) and envisioning (having a clear vision for the future and being focused on achieving it).

Of course, Table 5 shows mean values, and it should be remembered that there will be considerable dispersion of scores for people of any given type. Moreover, some introvert types rank higher than some extravert types (e.g., INTJ versus ESTP), just as some sensing types score better than some intuitive types (e.g., ESTJ versus ENFP). There will be considerable overlap in the strengths of people belonging to different types, whether we are considering one, two, or all four dimensions combined.

In addition, one should bear in mind that the qualities of empathising and connecting are not included in this leadership scale. Those strengths are associated with different psychological types. The highest rating for empathising goes to INFP, which only barely escapes the lowest quartile in Table 5. The Church of England would not be well served by a unidimensional approach to the selection of ordinands.

Encouragingly for the Church, the psychological types with higher mean scores on the leadership scale tend to be over-represented among clergy, relative to the general population. Whether they should be much more so is another question. It is clear from comparing the top and bottom halves of the last column in Table 5 that ordained ministers are already selected – or self-selected – to have some of the qualities needed for the role. The best candidate for the psychological type that might be the parochial all-rounder – both a good leader and a good listener – is ENFJ: it takes second place in the mean scores on both the leadership scale and the empathising dimension. There are more than three times as many Anglican clergy of this type as one would find in the UK population. Whether by accident or design, at least some people seem to be finding their vocation.

Conclusion

As previous studies have shown, Church of England clergy have a distinctive psychological type profile. They are more likely than other people in the UK to be characterised by introversion, intuition, feeling, and judging. We do not find large differences between the ordained men and women in our sample in personality.

Anglican clergy tend to see themselves as having better than average abilities in a number of areas related to the parish ministry. They have most confidence in speaking and empathising, and least in managing and connecting. Although the gender differences in self-assessed leadership strengths are not great, they do emerge with particular qualities. Consistent with stereotypes, men generate the highest marks for public speaking, while women are strong in one-to-one empathising. Perhaps less expectedly, women also score more highly on both motivating and managing.

Personality has substantial effects on these leadership strengths. Unfortunately the types that have positive associations are often not those most commonly found among Anglican clergy. In particular, there is arguably a shortage of ordained ministers characterised by extraversion and thinking (rather than introversion and feeling). That said, the considerable bias towards intuition and judging (as opposed to sensing and perceiving) may benefit the Church of England.

Most of the qualities considered here – managing, motivating, innovating, and so on – can be regarded as manifestations of an underlying aptitude. Only empathising is clearly a separate dimension; the primary scale is slightly improved by leaving out connecting, but the difference is marginal. The implications for recruitment and deployment of clergy are interesting. On the one hand, many of the required strengths do go together, and it should be possible to identify which individuals seem well or less well suited to the demands of ordained ministry. On the other hand, a focus on that single dimension would neglect empathising, which must be a key attribute for some roles. It may be necessary to distinguish the good general leaders – strong on extraversion, thinking, judging, and emotional stability – from the good pastoral workers, whose effectiveness is promoted by feeling and is not inconsistent with a degree of emotional instability. Whether certain types of people are genuinely strong in both areas is a topic for further study.

While personality matters considerably to leadership – we have accounted for a quarter of the variance on our scale measure – it is just as clearly not the whole story. Some people may be born to lead, but others achieve leadership, and many clergy have leadership thrust upon them. Parish ministry makes broad demands. The environment may make the minister, and some qualities might be nurtured beyond nature's initial endowment. Nevertheless, the well-being of both clergy and the churches they serve would be promoted by fitting the right pegs in the right holes.

References

Andersen, J. A. (2006). Leadership, personality and effectiveness. *The Journal of Socio-Economics, 35*, 1078–1091. doi: 10.1016/j.socec.2005.11.066

Barrick, M. R., & Mount, M. K. (1991). The big five personality dimensions and job performance: A meta-analysis. *Personnel Psychology, 44*(1), 1–26. doi: 10.1111/j.1744-6570.1991.tb00688.x

Colbert, A. E., Judge, T. A., Choi, D., & Wang, G. (2012). Assessing the trait theory of leadership using self and observer ratings of personality: The mediating role of contributions to group success. *The Leadership Quarterly, 23*, 670–685. doi: 10.1016/j.leaqua.2012.03.004

Costa, P. T. Jr., & McCrae, R. R. (1985). *The NEO Personality Inventory manual.* Odessa, FL: Psychological Assessment Resources.

Digman, J. (1990). Personality structure: Emergence of the five-factor model. *Annual Review of Psychology, 41*, 417–440. doi: 10.1146/annurev.ps.41.020190.002221

Eysenck, H. J., & Eysenck, M. W. (1985). *Personality and individual differences: A natural science approach.* New York, NY: Plenum Press.

Farkas, C. M., & Wetlaufer, S. (1996). The ways chief executive officers lead. *Harvard Business Review, 74*(3), 110–122.

Francis, L. J. (2005). *Faith and psychology: Personality, religion and the individual.* London: Darton, Longman and Todd.

Francis, L. J., Craig, C. L., Whinney, M., Tilley, D., & Slater, P. (2007). Psychological typology of Anglican clergy in England: Diversity, strengths, and weaknesses in ministry. *International Journal of Practical Theology, 11*, 266–284. doi: 10.1515/IJPT.2007.17

Francis, L. J., Robbins, M., Duncan, B., & Whinney, M. (2010). Confirming the psychological type profile of Anglican clergymen in England: A ministry for intuitives. In B. Ruelas & V. Brisero (Eds.), *Psychology of intuition* (pp. 211–219). New York, NY: Nova Science.

Francis, L. J., Robbins, M., & Whinney, M. (2011). Women priests in the Church of England: Psychological type profile. *Religions, 2*, 389–397. doi: 10.3390/rel2030389

Francis, L. J., & Village, A. (2012). The psychological temperament of Anglican clergy in Ordained Local Ministry (OLM): The conserving, serving pastor? *Journal of Empirical Theology, 25*, 57–76. doi: 10.1163/157092512X635743

Judge, T. A., Bono, J. E., Ilies, R., & Gerhardt, M. (2002). Personality and leadership: A qualitative and quantitative review. *Journal of Applied Psychology, 87*, 765–780.

Jung, C. G. (1971). *Psychological types: The collected works, volume 6*. London: Routledge and Kegan Paul.

Kendall, E. (1998). *Myers-Briggs Type Indicator: Step 1 manual supplement*. Palo Alto, CA: Consulting Psychologists Press.

McCrae, R. R., Costa, P. T. Jr., & Yik, M. S. M. (1996). Universal aspects of Chinese personality structure. In M. H. Bond (Ed.), *The handbook of Chinese psychology* (pp. 189–207). Hong Kong: Oxford University Press.

Oh, I. S., Wang, G., & Mount, M. K. (2011). Validity of observer ratings of the five-factor model of personality: A meta-analysis. *Journal of Applied Psychology, 96*, 762–773.

OPP. (2011). *MBTI step 1 instrument: European data supplement*. Oxford: Author.

Ployhart, R. E., Lim, B. C., & Chan, K. Y. (2001). Exploring relations between typical and maximum performance ratings and the five factor model of personality. *Personal Psychology, 54*(4), 809–843.

Silverthorne, C. (2001). Leadership effectiveness and personality: A cross cultural evaluation. *Personality and Individual Differences, 30*, 303–309.

Voas, D., & Watt, L. (2014). *Numerical change in church attendance: National, local and individual factors*. Report commissioned by the Church of England. Retrieved from http://www.churchgrowthresearch.org.uk/progress_findings_reports

Psychological type and the training relationship: an empirical study among curates and training incumbents

Greg Smith

This study draws on Jungian psychological type theory to illuminate the relationship between curates and training incumbents. During a three-day residential programme organised by an Anglican Diocese in England, 11 curate–incumbent pairs (and one additional incumbent) completed the Myers–Briggs Type Indicator and participated in four workshops organised, respectively, according to their scores recorded on the orientations (extraversion and introversion), on the perceiving process (sensing and intuition), on the judging process (thinking or feeling), and on the attitudes (judging and perceiving). The data generated from these four workshops illustrated the importance of individual differences in psychological type for shaping emphases in approaches to pastoral practice. The implications of these findings are discussed for the relationship between curates and their training incumbents.

Introduction

Psychological type theory has been brought into conversation with practical theology both at the level of theory and at the level of empirical science. For example, theoretical discussions have considered the relevance of psychological type theory for areas concerned with: congregational dynamics (Baab, 1998), prayer styles (Duncan, 1993), and preaching (Francis & Village, 2008). Empirical research employing psychological type measures has illuminated areas like: ministry styles (Francis & Payne, 2002), work-related psychological health (Francis, Robbins, Kaldor, & Castle, 2009), charismatic phenomena (Jones, Francis, & Craig, 2005), mystical experience (Francis, Village, Robbins, & Ineson, 2007), and interpretation of scripture (Village, 2010).

Psychological type theory

Psychological type theory has its roots in the work of Jung (1971) and has been subsequently developed, extended, and operationalised through a series of type indicators, temperament sorters and type scales, including the Myers–Brigg Type Indicator (Myers & McCaulley, 1985), the Keirsey Temperament Sorter (Keirsey & Bates, 1978), and the Francis Psychological Type Scales (Francis, 2005). At its core psychological type theory suggests that individuals differ in terms of four bi-polar preferences: the two orientations of extraversion (E) and introversion (I); the two perceiving functions of sensing (S) and intuition (N); the two judging functions of thinking (T) and feeling (F); and the two attitudes towards the outer world of judging (J) and perceiving (P).

Extraversion and introversion are dichotomous *orientations*, that is two different ways in which people focus their psychological energy. Extraverts focus their energy on and gain energy from the outside world of people and things. They enjoy communicating and thrive in stimulating and exciting environments. They prefer to act in a situation rather than to reflect on it and they may vocalise a problem or an idea rather than think it through privately. They may be bored and frustrated by silence and solitude. More often they focus their attention on what is happening outside them and may be influenced by others' opinions. They are usually open people, easy to get to know, and they enjoy having many friends. In contrast, introverts focus their energy on and gain energy from their inner world of ideas and reflections. They may feel drained by events and people around them and they prefer to reflect on a situation rather than to act on it. They enjoy solitude, silence, and contemplation, as they tend to focus their attention on what is happening in their inner life. They may appear reserved and detached as they are difficult to get to know and they may prefer to have a small circle of intimate friends rather than many acquaintances.

Sensing and intuition are dichotomous *perceiving functions*, that is two different ways in which people take in information. Sensing types gather information by focusing on the facts of a situation using the five senses. They tend to focus on specific details, rather than the overall picture. They are concerned with the actual, the real, and the practical and tend to be down to earth and matter of fact. They may feel that particular details are more significant than general patterns and they are frequently fond of the traditional and conventional. They may be conservative and tend to prefer what is known and well established. In contrast, intuitive types gather information by focusing on wider meanings and relationships using their imagination. They may feel that perception by the senses is not as valuable as information gained from the unconscious mind; indirect associations and concepts impact their perceptions. They focus on the overall picture, rather than specific facts and data. They follow their inspirations enthusiastically, but not always realistically and they may be seen as idealistic dreamers. They often aspire to bring innovative change to established conventions.

Thinking and feeling are dichotomous *judging functions*, that is two different ways in which people make decisions and judgements. Thinking types make decisions by using objective, analytical logic. They value integrity and justice and are often known for their truthfulness and desire for fairness. They consider conforming to principles to be of more importance than cultivating harmony. They are often good at making difficult decisions as they are able to analyse problems to reach an unbiased and reasonable solution. When working with others, they may consider it to be more important to be honest and correct than to be tactful. In contrast, feeling types make decisions by using subjective, personal values. They value compassion and mercy and are often known for their tactfulness and desire for peace. They are more concerned to promote harmony, than to adhere to abstract principles and they may be thought of as "people-persons", as they are able to take into account other people's feelings and values in decision-making and problem solving, ensuring that they reach a solution that satisfies everyone. They may find it difficult to criticise others, even when it is necessary. They find it easy to empathise with other people, and they tend to be trusting and encouraging of others.

Judging and perceiving are dichotomous *attitudes towards the outside world*, that is, two different ways in which people approach the world around them. Judging types present a systematic, ordered attitude towards the outside world. They enjoy routine and established patterns. They prefer to follow schedules in order to reach an established goal and may make use of lists, timetables, or diaries. They tend to be punctual, organised, and tidy and they may find it difficult to deal with unexpected disruptions of their plans. Likewise, they are inclined to be resistant to changes to established methods. They prefer to make decisions quickly and to stick to their conclusions once made. In contrast, perceiving types present a spontaneous, explorative attitude towards the outside world. They enjoy change and spontaneity and they prefer to leave projects open in order to adapt and improve them. They may find plans and schedules restrictive and tend to be easygoing about issues such as punctuality, deadlines, and tidiness. Indeed, they may consider last minute pressure to be a necessary motivation in order to complete projects. They are often good at dealing with the unexpected and they may welcome change and variety as routine bores them. Their behaviour may often seem impulsive and unplanned.

Psychological type theory and clergy training

A significant contribution to the application of psychological type theory for understanding the dynamics of clergy was made by Oswald and Kroeger (1988) in their book, *Personality type and religious leadership*. More recently, in an empirical study among Anglican clergy serving within the Church in Wales, Francis and Payne (2002) have confirmed the power of psychological type theory to predict individual differences in the ways in which clergy express their vocation to ordained ministry. Different priorities are given in the day-to-day exercise of ministry by extraverts and introverts, by sensing types and intuitive types, by thinking types and feeling types, and by judging types and perceiving types.

Francis and Payne's (2002) study may have interesting implications for the way in which Anglican clergy are currently trained within the Church of England. The model of continuing training after ordination to the diaconate, serving as assistant curate under the supervision of a training incumbent, is a long-established practice in the Church of England. The most recent document governing the training of clergy in the Church of England, *Formation for ministry within a learning church: Shaping the future* (Church of England, 2003), suggests that the training incumbent should be self-aware and allow colleagues to develop in ways different from their own (p. 115).

Drawing on Francis and Payne's (2002) study, Tilley, Francis, Robbins, and Jones (2011) hypothesised that psychological type theory may be an important consideration in understanding the working relationship between curates and their training incumbents. Drawing on data provided by 98 curates, Tilley et al. (2011) found that the ministry expectations placed on curates reflected more strongly the psychological type profile of training incumbents than of the curates themselves. These data suggest that training incumbents may be more prone to shaping curates in their own image than to enabling curates to develop their own preferred ministry styles.

Putting the insights of this genre of research into practice, the Diocese of Winchester has since 2009 employed psychological type theory in its developmental programme for curates and training incumbents, operating a three-day residential workshop during the January following ordination to the diaconate and a two-day residential workshop 22 months later towards the end of the curacy. These workshops are designed to explore the ways in which psychological type theory may illuminate areas of strength and areas of potential disagreement or conflict in the training relationships. The present study reflects on the learning opportunities provided by these residential workshops.

Research question

Against this background, the aim of the present study was to engage in a form of action research with a group of training incumbents and their curates from the Diocese of Winchester during their first residential workshop. Taking each of the four components of psychological type theory in turn, workshops were constructed in ways designed to bring each of the psychological type components into focus. The research team monitored and documented the feedback from the workshops.

Method

Participants

Twelve sets of training incumbents and their curates accepted the invitation to participate in the residential programme. Illness prevented one curate from attending, resulting in participation from 11 curates and 12 incumbents (8 women and 15 men). The dichotomous type preferences identified by the Myers–Briggs Type Indicator described a group characterised by preference for introversion (13) over extraversion (10), preference for intuition (14) over sensing (9), preference for feeling (13) over thinking (10), and preference for judging (13) over perceiving (10).

Measure

The 126-item Form G (Anglicised) of the Myers–Briggs Type Indicator (Myers & McCaulley, 1985) was used. This instrument was a forced-choice questionnaire to indicate preferences between the two orientations (introversion and extraversion), the two perceiving functions (sensing and intuition), the two judging functions (thinking and feeling), and the two attitudes (judging and perceiving).

Procedure

In the context of a residential programme conducted during January 2011, the participants were invited to complete the 126-item Form G (Anglicised) of the Myers–Briggs Type Indicator (Myers & McCaulley, 1985). The participants were then invited to experience working in groups structured on the basis of psychological type theory, examining in turn the orientations, the perceiving functions, the judging functions, and the attitudes.

Results

Orientations

Procedure

The participants were divided into three groups: seven high-scoring extraverts, seven high-scoring introverts, and a mixture of low-scoring introverts and low-scoring extraverts. Each group was invited to discuss the aspects of ministry that they found draining and the aspects of ministry that they found energising.

Findings

The group of high-scoring *introverts* settled to the task quickly, quietly, and seriously. The first thing they did was to appoint someone to take notes and to report back. They arrived back at the plenary session in good time and well prepared. When reporting back they began by identifying the aspects of ministry that they found draining. Their main points emerged in this order: the telephone and the need to make immediate responses to the requests and questions raised by phone; the immediacy of the mobile phone; having to think of things to say to miscellaneous groups, like the Mothers' Union; having to say things to lot of people; being at social occasions when it is necessary to move from person to person; family communion when there is a full and noisy church. Aspects of ministry that were found energising included: dealing with emails; driving alone between appointments; being part of stimulating discussions that they did not have to lead; going on retreat; periods of silence; and watching food events on television.

The group of high-scoring *extraverts* showed high energy in engaging with the task. Twenty minutes into the conversation one of them remarked how none of them had so far actually finished their sentence before someone else had interrupted, and they had not yet sorted out note-taking and feedback. They arrived back at the plenary session late and all chipped in with reporting. They began by identifying the aspects of ministry that they found energising. Their main points emerged in this order: being with people; being in the middle of activity and "holy pandemonium"; leading worship, with the emphasis on the event and on preaching; leading groups with lots of buzz and interest; working with children, enjoying the spontaneity and mess; preparing sermons in the coffee shop or with the television on in the background. Aspects of ministry that were found draining included: routine and monotony; being in meetings where the same conversations kept coming back over and over again; indecision; and being left to get on with things alone and without conversation and support.

Perceiving process

Procedure

The participants were invited to read the following scenario and then to go away to write a letter to the bishop responding to the three questions posed at the end of the scenario. In reaching their conclusions, the participants were invited to take a careful look at the large country house where the programme was being held (Park Place).

> The Bishop has invited training incumbent and curate to go together to look at a new parish. There are development opportunities there, says the Bishop, that need the skills of an experienced incumbent and have enormous training potential. When you arrive the churchwarden explains that a large country house has just been bequeathed to the parish (like the original Park Place), but there is a restricted covenant that says the property must be maintained and managed as part of the ministry of the parish, otherwise it will pass to the British Humanist Association. What do you see and what do you perceive? What opportunities and challenges do you envisage? And are you likely to accept the Bishop's invitation?

Findings

From the 23 individual letters that emerged from this exercise a good contrast is provided by giving close attention to the four responses generated by the two highest scoring sensing types and by the two highest scoring intuitive types. The responses from the sensing types emphasised the practical issues. The highest scoring sensing type began his letter by showing that he had noticed the appeal notice in the foyer of Park Place. Currently £200 k was urgently needed for essential maintenance; but already £100 k had been raised and there should be ways of raising the rest. Currently, the diocese possesses one residential centre, offering only 16 beds. There is a need for an alternative and larger facility. Moreover, a centre of this size could serve a range of needs, locally, regionally, and even nationally. This individual was interested in setting up a fully costed feasibility study into the project so that a good decision could be made.

The second highest scoring sensing type took a similar line. He described the environment as a large historic house with large grounds. Such an environment will incur significant maintenance costs and significant running costs. On the other hand, such an environment offers considerable opportunities for development and for promoting the ministry and mission of the local church. This individual would accept the offer, subject to a viable business plan. Both sensing types wanted to ensure that the project was going to be practicable before jumping in.

The responses from the intuitive types emphasised the possibilities and proposed imaginative (if not necessarily realistic strategies) for overcoming obstacles in the way of realising their vision. The highest scoring intuitive type began his letter by saying that his instinct was to begin with the opportunities. He saw a large country house and envisaged a Centre for Performing Arts and Creative Ministries (drawing on his previous professional experience). He envisioned dance studios, drama studios, Creative Studies, Artists in Residence and educational courses that would be revenue generating, but supported by grants intended for educational purposes and for community development. He saw a large country house and envisaged a Centre for Ministries, combining a Retreat Centre and a Young People's Adventure Centre. He saw the large grounds and envisaged opportunities for parish and for community use.

The second highest scoring intuitive type took a similar starting point. He began his letter by saying that the opportunities would be legion, if the people of the parish were open to them. Here was a space for hospitality, for meetings for training events, for informal worship. Here was an opportunity for residential use. The vicarage and curate's house could be sold (to release capital for renovation) and the vicar and curate could move in to live there. Others could be invited to join them to form a religious community. Perhaps links could be made with an established religious community. The Centre could become a resource for the wider Deanery, Diocese, and Church. The house and the grounds could by widely used by the local community, including exercise groups, a drop-in centre, an advice centre, archery in the grounds. It would provide a wonderful opportunity for an experiment in a new form of parish ministry and community life. Both intuitive types wanted to accept the bishop's invitation and jump in before exploring detailed costings.

Judging process

Procedure

On this occasion training incumbents and curates were invited to work together, irrespective of their psychological type preferences. They were asked to consider the following scenario.

> Donna is responsible for baptism ministry in your church. She is a divorcee, who has been single for four years, but has recently started dating. Donna has always got on very well with the vicar, but has carefully avoided any conversation about her new relationship. Her relationship with the curate is cordial but not especially warm. Both vicar and curate hear independently, but at third hand, that the man Donna is seeing is married, with children, but has defended her action on the grounds that he is going to leave his wife very soon. Curate and vicar meet in supervision to discuss the situation. Donna has said she would like to surrender responsibility for the baptism ministry after nearly three years, but she and her 18 year old daughter both intend to continue as youth leaders. What do you decide to do (if anything)? Record your decision, but also record the other options you discussed and the process you went through.

Findings

From the 11 responses to this exercise a good contrast is provided by giving close attention to an occasion where both curate and training incumbent recorded preferences for thinking and to an occasion where both curate and training incumbent recorded preferences for feeling.

The curate and training incumbent who preferred thinking began by identifying the facts of the situation and noted where further testing and substantiation was needed. They set out to weigh the evidence and to formulate a strategy. Since Donna had always got on well with the vicar, the vicar was commissioned to get into discussion with Donna and to ascertain the facts of the matter. Depending on the outcome of the discussion, Donna would be asked to give up her role as youth leader. In many ways, the solution seemed to follow on naturally and clearly from the evidence.

The curate and training incumbent who preferred feeling began by trying to work out the implications of the situation for Donna herself, for her daughter, and for other members of the church. They decided that they wanted to find a pretext for getting into conversation with Donna so that they could broach the subject of her new relationship in a casual and non-confrontational way. They agreed that it was very important to ensure that Donna knew how much her previous ministry and work for the church had been appreciated. They wanted Donna to have the opportunity to reflect on the implications of her current relationship for the church and to make the decision herself that it would be best for her to step down from the role of youth leader.

Attitude

Procedure

The participants were divided into three groups: seven high-scoring judging types, seven high-scoring perceiving types, and a mixture of low-scoring judging types and low-scoring perceiving types. Each group was asked to respond to the following scenario. They had recently been appointed as rector and curate of St Andrew's Church, Tuna Juxta Mare, and they needed to consider the "Sea Sunday Celebration". The five questions were: When? Where? What? Who? and Why?

Finding

The group of high-scoring judging types decided to use the question as a framework for addressing the issue. In response to the first question, "who?", they listed: sea cadets, RNLI, coastguards, harbour master, seafarers, band, choir, the Mission to Seafarers (for whom a collection could be taken). In response to the second question, "where?", one answer was offered and quickly agreed. The celebration could take place at the harbour, and it was agreed that arrangements would be made well in advance to ensure that the harbour would be available. In response to the third question, "what?", the theme was quickly agreed. The celebration would focus on the safety of those at sea. The theme would be reflected in blessing the boats and singing appropriate hymns. Further consideration of the hymns identified: "Will your anchor hold"; "Eternal father strong to save"; and "Lead us heavenly father lead us". The response to the fourth question, "when?", was easy. Sea Sunday is always held on the second Sunday in June. Only the question "why" was overlooked. Further signs of detailed planning involved arranging the fish and chip lunch, and ensuring that a full risk assessment had taken place and that full and proper safeguarding procedures were implemented. A wet weather alternative plan was also discussed. The group concluded by saying that, if everything were not fully ready at least three weeks before Sea Sunday, they would feel the need to cancel the celebration.

The group of high-scoring perceiving types began by realising that none of them had listened carefully to the task and tried to recreate it. Then they launched into wide-ranging brainstorming with ideas emerging in no particular order. Perhaps the celebration could be held on the beach with a barbeque, or perhaps in a local leisure centre and swimming pool complex, or perhaps out at sea on a boat, on a flotilla of boats, or on the ferry from Lymington to the Isle of Wight. Perhaps the point of the celebration could be thanksgiving for the provisions of the oceans, and perhaps prayer for those who work at sea, or for submariners (perhaps a nuclear submarine could be booked for the day and good use made of the psalm "Out of the depths, O Lord, have I cried unto thee"). Perhaps the theme could be stewardship of the seas, with a fishermen's market (like a farmers' market), with local restaurants setting up stalls on the harbour. There would be opportunities to bless the boats and (via the Orthodox tradition) link the blessing of the boats with the Baptism of Jesus and hold a baptism service. There would be opportunities to set well-known hymns to the tunes of sea shanties. A quiz could be held about all the goods found in our shops that are transported to our island by sea. The Sea Sunday Celebration could involve the whole community, introducing craft stalls offering driftwood sculptures, shell boxes, sea-weed weaving, sand sculptures, and fish costumes. Innovative liturgy was suggested with rewriting the creed, "I believe in Cod", and with passing "the Peace of Cod that passes all understanding" as people greet each other. The group concluded by recognising that they had not yet fixed a date for the celebration, but then considered that it might be wise to leave the date flexible, depending on the weather.

Conclusion

Building on theoretical insights advanced by Oswald and Kroeger (1988) and on quantitative research findings offered by Francis and Payne (2002) and by Tilley et al. (2011), the present study employed qualitative research methods to explore whether psychological type theory may illuminate the ways in which curates and training incumbents approach day-to-day issues raised within parish ministry. The data suggest that each of the four main components of psychological type theory, considered separately, indicate important differences in approaches to ministry. Each of these four differences will be discussed in turn.

First, the two orientations (introversion and extraversion) distinguish between different sources of energy. Introverts are energised by their inner world and drained by too much activity in the outer world. Extraverts are energised by the outer world and drained by too much solitude. The evidence of the first workshop not only confirmed that introverted and extraverted clergy provided very different accounts of what energises and of what drains them in ministry, but also demonstrated that introverts and extraverts set about the task of engaging with the topic in very different ways. When an extravert and an introvert have been paired together as curate and training incumbent they may need to learn and to respect each other's preferred way of working. One may wish to talk about things, while the other may wish to reflect alone. When tired or under pressure these different styles may become frustrating and annoying.

Second, the two perceiving functions (sensing and intuition) distinguish between different ways of looking at the world. Sensing types are looking for the evidence and are practical people. Intuitive types are looking for the possibilities and are visionary people. The evidence of the second workshop not only confirmed that sensing type clergy and intuitive type clergy looked at a common situation through very different eyes, but also demonstrated that their ways of setting about the task were very different. When a sensing type and an intuitive type have been paired together as curate and training incumbent they may need to learn how to view situations through each other's preferred lenses. One may wish to focus on the present reality, while the other may wish to speculate about the future potential. When tired or under pressure these different styles may become frustrating and annoying.

Third, the two judging functions (thinking and feeling) distinguish between different ways of evaluating situations. Thinking types are concerned to identify the principles and issues at stake and to apply logical analysis. Feeling types are concerned to identify the human values and interpersonal relationship involved and to apply pastoral concern. The evidence of the third workshop confirmed that two feelings types working together produced a very different strategy from two thinking types working together. When a thinking type and a feeling type have been paired together as curate and training incumbent they may need to learn how to assess situations through each other's preferred lenses. One may wish to prioritise obedience to the God of justice (the thinking preference), while the other may wish to prioritise allegiance to the God of mercy (the feeling preference). When tired or under pressure these different styles may become frustrating and annoying.

Fourth, the two attitudes towards the outside world distinguish between different ways of living life in the public domain. Judging types are concerned to have the outside world organised and structured. Perceiving types are concerned to keep things flexible and open. Judging types work best when there is time to plan well in advance, while perceiving types work best under the pressure of the last minute. The evidence of the fourth workshop not only confirmed that judging type clergy and perceiving type clergy provided very different visions for a future event, but also demonstrated that they approached the task in very different ways. When a judging type and a perceiving type have been paired together as curate and training incumbent they may need to learn how to appreciate each other's perspective. One may wish to plan the last details of the Sunday service well in advance, while the other may not be ready to make his or her best contribution until Sunday has arrived. When tired or under pressure these different styles may find working together frustrating and annoying.

Overall, the evidence generated by this approach to action research among a group of training incumbents and their curates supports the wisdom of the Diocese of Winchester in employing psychological type theory as a tool to enable trainee and trainer to reflect on their working relationship. At the same time, however, the evidence also raises a more fundamental question regarding the purpose of the curacy and the way in which curates are matched with training incumbents. For example, if the Church of England were to recognise that the ministry style of extraverts and introverts are equally acceptable in the eyes of God and continues to select and train both introverts and extraverts for ordained ministry, the point of placing an introvert curate with an extravert incumbent or an extravert curate with an introvert incumbent may benefit from further strategic investigation. One strategic approach might be to allow an introvert curate to learn from the experience of an introvert incumbent and to allow an extravert curate to learn from the experience of an extravert incumbent. The same point would apply also to the other components of psychological type theory: to sensing and intuition, to thinking and feeling, and to judging and perceiving.

An alternative strategic approach, in the light of the Church of England's express requirement that training incumbents should have a record of allowing colleagues to develop in ways different from their own (Church of England, 2003, p. 115) might argue that dioceses would benefit from a concerted use of psychological type theory. This tool might be utilised to assure that it is entirely explicit in the training relationship that an extravert training incumbent does not expect an introvert curate to undertake ministry and be refreshed in ministry in the same way as the training incumbent. The key learning outcome is that curates understand that there is more than one way of exercising ministry and that they should be encouraged to explore what suits them best, while appreciating that other means may suit other people better.

References

Baab, L. M. (1998). *Personality type in congregations: How to work with others more effectively.* Washington, DC: Alban Institute.

Church of England. (2003). *Formation for ministry within a learning church.* London: Church House Publishing.

Duncan, B. (1993). *Pray your way: Your personality and God.* London: Darton, Longman and Todd.

Francis, L. J. (2005). *Faith and psychology: Personality, religion and the individual*. London: Darton, Longman and Todd.

Francis, L. J., & Payne, V. J. (2002). The Payne Index of Ministry Styles (PIMS): Ministry styles and psychological type among male Anglican clergy in Wales. *Research in the Social Scientific Study of Religion, 13*, 125–141.

Francis, L. J., Robbins, M., Kaldor, K., & Castle, K. (2009). Psychological type and work-related psychological health among clergy in Australia, England and New Zealand. *Journal of Psychology and Christianity, 28*, 200–212.

Francis, L. J., & Village, A. (2008). *Preaching with all our souls*. London: Continuum.

Francis, L. J., Village, A., Robbins, M., & Ineson, K. (2007). Mystical orientation and psychological type: An empirical study among guests staying at a Benedictine Abbey. *Studies in Spirituality, 17*, 207–223. doi: 10.2143/SIS.17.0.2024649

Jones, S. H., Francis, L. J., & Craig, C. L. (2005). Charismatic experience and psychological type: An empirical enquiry. *Journal of the European Pentecostal Theological Association, 25*, 39–53.

Jung, C. G. (1971). *Psychological types: The collected works* (Vol. 6). London: Routledge and Kegan Paul.

Keirsey, D., & Bates, M. (1978). *Please understand me*. Del Mar, CA: Prometheus Nemesis.

Myers, I. B., & McCaulley, M. H. (1985). *Manual: A guide to the development and use of the Myers-Briggs Type Indicator*. Palo Alto, CA: Consulting Psychologists Press.

Oswald, R. M., & Kroeger, O. (1988). *Personality type and religious leadership*. Washington, DC: The Alban Institute.

Tilley, D., Francis, L. J., Robbins, M., & Jones, S. H. (2011). Apprentice clergy? The relationship between expectations in ministry and the psychological type profile of training incumbents and curates in the Church of England. *Research in the Social Scientific Study of Religion, 22*, 286–305. doi: 10.1163/ej.9789004207271.i-360.65

Village, A. (2010). Psychological type and biblical interpretation among Anglican clergy in the UK. *Journal of Empirical Theology, 23*, 179–200. doi: 10.1163/157092510X527349

Early and late responders to questionnaires: clues from psychological type

Kelvin J. Randall

As part of a longitudinal study of Anglican clergy in England and Wales, a measure of Jungian psychological type, the Francis Psychological Type Scales, was used. When early responders to the survey were compared to late responders, the main difference between the two groups was located in the judging process. There was a significantly higher proportion of feeling types among the late responders (72% compared with 56%). Among late responders, 43% were dominant feeling types compared with 28% among the early responders.

Introduction

For the empirical quantitative researcher, postal questionnaires have a number of advantages. They are relatively low in cost. They are geographically flexible and can reach a widely dispersed population almost simultaneously. Their relative or promised anonymity can encourage respondents to divulge freely quite private information. In addition they permit leisurely or thoughtful replies (Kanuk & Berenson, 1975).

Researchers tend to feel that the response rate to a questionnaire is an indicator of survey quality (Aday, 1996; Babbie, 1990; Backstrom & Hirsh, 1963; Rea & Parker, 1997), and so there is a large amount of research into methods which will increase response rates to postal questionnaire studies. The systematic review of such methods by Edwards et al. (2002) found that the likelihood of a response more than doubled when a monetary incentive was used. Response was more likely when short questionnaires were used. Personalised questionnaires and letters increased response, as did the use of coloured ink. The likelihood of response more than doubled when the questionnaires were sent by recorded delivery, and increased when stamped return envelopes were used and questionnaires were sent by first-class post. Contacting participants before sending questionnaires increased response. So did follow-up contact and providing non-respondents with a second copy of the questionnaire. Questionnaires originating from universities were more likely to be returned than questionnaires from other sources, such as commercial organisations.

Though researchers tend to feel that a higher response rate indicates a higher quality survey, there have been few studies rigorously designed to provide empirical evidence to document the consequences of lower response rates. Visser, Krosnick, Marquette, and Curtin (1996) showed that surveys with lower response rates (near 20%) yielded more accurate measurements than did surveys with higher response rates (near 60% or 70%). In another study, Keeter, Kennedy, Dimock, Best, and Craighill (2006) compared the results of a 5-day survey employing the Pew Research Centre's usual methodology (with a 25% response rate) with the results from a more rigorous survey conducted over a much longer period and achieving a higher response rate of 50%. In 77 out of 84 comparisons, the two surveys yielded results that were statistically indistinguishable. Among the items that manifested significant differences across the two surveys, the differences in proportions of people giving a particular answer ranged from 4 to 8 percentage points.

A study by Curtin, Presser, and Singer (2000) tested the effect of lower response rates on estimates of the Index of Consumer Sentiment (ICS). They assessed the impact of excluding respondents who initially refused to cooperate (which reduces the response rate by between 5 and 10 percentage points), respondents who required more than five calls to complete the interview (reducing the response rate by about 25 percentage points), and those who required more than two calls (a reduction of about 50 percentage points). They found no effect of excluding these respondent groups on estimates of the ICS using monthly samples of hundreds of respondents. For yearly estimates, based on thousands of respondents, the exclusion of people who required more calls had a very small effect.

Holbrook, Krosnick, and Pfent (2007) assessed whether lower response rates were associated with a less demographically representative sample. By examining the results of 81 national surveys with response rates varying from 5% to 54%, they found that surveys with much lower response rates were only minimally less accurate.

There do seem to be differences, though, between early and late responders to questionnaires. Paganini-Hill, Hsu, Chao, and Ross (1993) mailed a health survey to the 18,408 residents of a California retirement community and compared the 11,550 respondents on a number of characteristics by time of response. Early respondents were more likely to be the "worried well", that is, healthy individuals who see their doctor regularly, receive disease detection screening, and follow healthy lifestyle practices. Late respondents tended to answer questions regarding their mental function and emotional status more negatively.

It seemed, therefore, that the field of personality theory might provide a useful lens through which to view and interpret these differences in response times. Accordingly Chen, Wei, and Syme (2003), in a study of Scottish dockyard painters, used the Neuroticism (N) Scale and Lie (L) Scale from the short-form of the Revised Eysenck Personality Questionnaire (EPQR-S: Eysenck, Eysenck, & Barrett, 1985) in a study on work environment and health. They found that "there were no significant differences in scores of N or L scales among early, intermediate and late respondents" (Chen et al., 2003, p. 200). In addition, Vink and Boomsma (2008) used the Amsterdam Biographical Questionnaire (Wilde, 1970) which includes an Extraversion Scale and a Neuroticism Scale in an ongoing study of families with twins. They found no significant correlation between either of these scales and early or late responding.

A different model of personality from the models proposed by Eysenck (Eysenck et al., 1985) or Wilde (1970) is the model of psychological type. Instead of discussing personality factors, this model proposes 16 discrete psychological types. The underlying theory for this model has already been quite widely applied within the area of practical theology (Baab, 1998; Duncan, 1993; Fowke, 1997; Francis, 2005; Keating, 1987; Martínez, 2001; Michael & Norrisey, 1984; Osborn & Osborn, 1991).

The Jungian model of psychological type has been operationalised and developed through a set of psychometric instruments, including the Myers–Briggs Type Indicator (Myers & McCaulley, 1985), the Keirsey Temperament Sorter (Keirsey & Bates, 1978), and the Francis Psychological Type Scales (Francis, 2005). At its core, psychological type theory suggests that individuals differ in terms of four bipolar preferences: two orientations, two perceiving preferences, two judging preferences, and two attitudes towards the outer world. Taken together, these four bipolar preferences generate 16 discrete psychological types.

The two orientations are defined as introversion (I) and extraversion (E). Introverts draw their energy from the inner world of ideas and reflection, while extraverts draw their energy from the outer world of people and things. Extraverts are energised by people and drained by large periods of solitude and silence, while introverts are energised by solitude and drained by too many people.

The two perceiving functions are defined as sensing (S) and intuition (N). Sensing types perceive their environment through the five senses and focus on the details of the here and now, on facts, details, and information, while intuitive types perceive their environment by making use of the imagination and inspiration: they are motivated by theories, ideas, and connections. Sensing types are distrustful of jumping to conclusions and of envisioning the future, while intuitive types are overloaded by too many details and long to try out new approaches.

The two judging functions are defined as thinking (T) and feeling (F). Thinking types reach their judgements by relying on objective analysis and dispassionate logic, while feeling types reach their judgements by relying on subjective appreciation of the personal and interpersonal factors involved. Thinking types strive for truth, fairness, and justice, while feeling types strive for harmony, peace, and reconciliation.

The two attitudes towards the outer world are defined as judging (J) and perceiving (P). Judging types use their preferred judging function (either thinking or feeling) to deal with the outside world. Their outside world is organised, scheduled, and planned. Perceiving types use their preferred perceiving functions (either sensing or intuition) to deal with the outside world. Their outside world is flexible, spontaneous, and unplanned.

A significant and useful body of research has been undertaken to document the psychological type profile of clergy. The foundations for this research tradition were established during the 1980s in the USA through studies summarised by Macdaid, McCaulley, and Kainz (1986) in their *Atlas of Type Tables* and by Myers and McCaulley (1985) in their *Manual* for the Myers–Briggs Type Indicator. This research tradition has more recently been extended to the UK with studies reported among Anglican clergy (Francis, Craig, Whinney, Tilley, & Slater, 2007; Francis & Robbins, 2008), Anglican women priests (Francis, Robbins, & Whinney, 2011), Welsh Anglican male clergy (Francis, Payne, & Jones, 2001), Anglican clergy in Ordained Local Ministry (Francis & Village, 2012), Roman Catholic priests (Craig, Duncan, & Francis, 2006), Free Church ministers (Francis, Whinney, Burton, & Robbins, 2011), Bible College students (Francis, Penson, & Jones, 2001; Kay, Francis, & Craig, 2008), Evangelical church leaders (Francis & Robbins, 2002), interdenominational church leaders (Craig, Francis, & Robbins, 2004), lead elders in the Newfrontiers network (Francis, Gubb, & Robbins, 2012), missionary personnel (Craig, Horsfall, & Francis, 2005), youth ministers (Francis, Nash, Nash, & Craig, 2007), and Evangelical seminarians (Francis, Craig, & Butler, 2007).

Through the pages of the *Journal of Psychological Type* in particular, there has been continuing research on the uses of psychological type theory in a number of different settings, for example, work motivation (Barbuto, Fritz, Lim, & Xu, 2008); academic performance (DiRienzo, Kitts, Das, McGrath, & Synn, 2010); and person–job fit (Jarlstrom & Valkealahti, 2010). Since studies using the EPQR-S (Eysenck et al., 1985) and the Amsterdam Biographical Questionnaire (Wilde, 1970) had found no correlation between personality and early or late responding, this study was undertaken in order to see whether psychological type theory could provide insights into early or late responding.

Method

Participants

As part of a longitudinal study the same cohort of clergy, all those ordained to stipendiary ministry in 1994 in the Church of England and the Church in Wales, answered postal questionnaires in their 1st, 2nd, 3rd, 7th, and 14th years of ministry. The data for this study are taken from the seventh year questionnaire. In 1994, 340 had been ordained to parish ministry: of these 77% were male and 23% female.

Accompanying the first questionnaire was a letter explaining the purpose of the survey and its longitudinal nature and requesting their cooperation. In order to increase the response rate, a stamped addressed envelope was included with the questionnaire. To assure anonymity regarding the content of the replies, a separate database for responses was established with only a numerical code to differentiate each respondent. With the first and subsequent questionnaires, a reminder letter was sent after six weeks by post enclosing a copy of the original questionnaire.

A total of 275 replies were received for the first year questionnaire: 80.8% of the total. A response rate of 72.6% was achieved in the second year. In the third year the response rate was 82%. In the seventh year, the year of this study, because of changes among the clergy, only 313 questionnaires were sent out. From the questionnaires distributed a total of 234 completed questionnaires were returned, making a response rate of 74.7% of this group or 69% of the original population. The present analyses were conducted on the 185 respondents who provided a full set of data. Early responders ($N = 120$) are categorised as those who responded before the reminder letter was sent, six weeks after the initial mailing. Late responders ($N = 65$) responded after the reminder letter.

Measure

Psychological type was assessed by the Francis Psychological Type Scales (Francis, 2005). This instrument proposes 40 forced choice items to distinguish between the two orientations (E or I), the two perceiving functions (S or N), the two judging functions (T or F), and the two attitudes towards the outside world (J or P). Extraversion and introversion are distinguished by 10 questions such as "Are you energised by others (E) or drained by too many people (I)?" Sensing and intuition are distinguished by 10 questions such as "Do you tend to be more concerned for meaning (N) or concerned about detail (S)?" Thinking and feeling are distinguished by 10 questions such as "Are you warm-hearted (F) or fair-minded (T)?" Judging and perceiving are distinguished by 10 questions such as "Do you tend to be more happy with routine (J) or unhappy with routine (P)?"

Analysis

The psychological type literature has developed a highly distinctive method for displaying type data in the format of type tables. The present data are presented in this way in Tables 1 and 2 in order to facilitate clear comparison with other studies in the field. The data will be discussed in two steps.

Results

The Francis Psychological Type Scales generated the following alpha coefficients: extraversion and introversion, .83; sensing and intuition, .81; feeling and thinking, .74; perceiving and judging, .83. All of these alphas are in excess of DeVellis' (2003) recommended threshold of .65.

Table 1. Type distribution for early responders.

The Sixteen Complete Types

ISTJ	ISFJ	INFJ	INTJ
n = 9	n = 13	n = 12	n = 17
6.0%	10.8%	10.0%	14.2%
+++++	+++++	+++++	+++++
+	+++++	+++++	+++++
	+		++++

ISTP	ISFP	INFP	INTP
n = 3	n = 3	n = 7	n = 1
2.5%	2.5%	5.8%	0.8%
+++	+++	+++++	+
		+	

ESTP	ESFP	ENFP	ENTP
n = 1	n = 2	n = 6	n = 4
0.8%	1.7%	5.0%	3.3%
+	++	+++++	+++

ESTJ	ESFJ	ENFJ	ENTJ
n = 12	n = 13	n = 11	n = 6
10.0%	10.8%	9.2%	5.0%
+++++	+++++	+++++	+++++
+++	+++++	++++	
	+		

Dichotomous Preferences

E	n = 55	45.8%
I	n = 65	54.2%
S	n = 56	46.7%
N	n = 64	53.3%
T	n = 53	44.2%
F	n = 67	55.8%
J	n = 93	77.5%
P	n = 27	22.5%

Pairs and Temperaments

IJ	n = 51	42.5%
IP	n = 14	11.7%
EP	n = 13	10.8%
EJ	n = 42	35.0%
ST	n = 25	20.8%
SF	n = 31	25.8%
NF	n = 36	30.0%
NT	n = 28	23.3%
SJ	n = 47	39.2%
SP	n = 9	7.5%
NP	n = 18	15.0%
NJ	n = 46	38.3%
TJ	n = 44	36.7%
TP	n = 9	7.5%
FP	n = 18	15.0%
FJ	n = 49	40.8%
IN	n = 37	30.8%
EN	n = 27	22.5%
IS	n = 28	23.3%
ES	n = 28	23.3%
ET	n = 23	19.2%
EF	n = 32	26.7%
IF	n = 35	29.2%
IT	n = 30	25.0%

Jungian Types (E)	n	%	Jungian Types (I)	n	%	Dominant Types	n	%
E-TJ	18	15.0	I-TP	4	3.3	Dt.T	22	18.3
E-FJ	24	20.0	I-FP	10	8.3	Dt.F	34	28.3
ES-P	3	2.5	IS-J	22	18.3	Dt.S	25	20.8
EN-P	10	8.3	IN-J	29	24.2	Dt.N	39	32.5

Notes: N = 120; "+" indicates 1% of N.

Table 2. Type distribution for late responders compared with early responders.

The Sixteen Complete Types					Dichotomous Preferences			
ISTJ	ISFJ	INFJ	INTJ	E	$n = 32$	58.5%	$I = 1.28$
$n = 4$	$n = 6$	$n = 8$	$n = 2$	I	$n = 27$	41.5%	$I = 0.77$
6.2%	9.2%	12.3%	3.1%				
$I = 82$	$I = 0.85$	$I = 1.23$	$I = 0.22*$	S	$n = 36$	55.4%	$I = 1.19$
+++++	+++++	+++++	+++	N	$n = 29$	44.6%	$I = 0.84$
+	+++	+++++					
		++		T	$n = 18$	27.7%	$I = 0.63*$
				F	$n = 47$	72.3%	$I = 1.30*$
				J	$n = 53$	81.5%	$I = 1.05$
				P	$n = 12$	18.5%	$I = 0.82$
ISTP	ISFP	INFP	INTP				
$n = 0$	$n = 1$	$n = 4$	$n = 2$		Pairs and Temperaments		
0%	1.5%	6.2%	3.1%	IJ	$n = 20$	30.8%	$I = 0.72$
$I = 0.0$	$I = 0.62$	$I = 1.05$	$I = 0.27$	IP	$n = 7$	10.8%	$I = 0.92$
	++	+++++	+++	EP	$n = 5$	7.7%	$I = 0.71$
		+		EJ	$n = 33$	50.8%	$I = 1.45*$
				ST	$n = 10$	15.4%	$I = 0.74$
				SF	$n = 26$	40.0%	$I = 1.55*$
				NF	$n = 21$	32.3%	$I = 1.08$
ESTP	ESFP	ENFP	ENTP	NT	$n = 8$	12.3%	$I = 0.53$
$n = 0$	$n = 1$	$n = 4$	$n = 0$				
0%	1.5%	6.2%	0%	SJ	$n = 34$	52.3%	$I = 1.34$
$I = 0.0$	$I = 0.92$	$I = 1.23$	$I = 0.0$	SP	$n = 2$	3.1%	$I = 0.41$
	++	+++++		NP	$n = 10$	15.4%	$I = 1.03$
		+		NJ	$n = 19$	29.2%	$I = 0.76$
				TJ	$n = 16$	24.6%	$I = 0.67$
				TP	$n = 2$	3.1%	$I = 0.41$
				FP	$n = 10$	15.4%	$I = 1.03$
				FJ	$n = 37$	56.9%	$I = 1.39*$
ESTJ	ESFJ	ENFJ	ENTJ	IN	$n = 16$	24.6%	$I = 0.80$
$n = 6$	$n = 18$	$n = 5$	$n = 4$	EN	$n = 13$	20.0%	$I = 0.89$
9.2%	17.7%	7.7%	6.2%	IS	$n = 11$	16.9%	$I = 0.73$
$I = 0.92$	$I = 2.56**$	$I = 0.84$	$I = 1.23$	ES	$n = 25$	35.5%	$I = 1.65*$
+++++	+++++	+++++	+++++				
++++	+++++	+++	+	ET	$n = 10$	15.4%	$I = 0.80$
	+++++			EF	$n = 28$	43.1%	$I = 1.62*$
	+++			IF	$n = 19$	29.2%	$I = 1.00$
				IT	$n = 8$	12.3%	$I = 0.49*$

Jungian Types (E)				Jungian Types (I)				Dominant Types			
	n	%	Index		n	%	Index		n	%	Index
E-TJ	10	15.4	1.03	I-TP	2	3.1	0.92	Dt.T	12	18.5	1.01
E-FJ	23	35.4	1.77*	I-FP	5	7.7	0.92	Dt.F	28	43.1	1.52*
ES-P	1	1.5	0.62	IS-J	10	15.4	0.84	Dt.S	11	16.9	0.81
EN-P	4	6.2	0.74	IN-J	10	15.4	0.64	Dt.N	14	21.5	0.66

Note: $N = 65$; "+" indicates 1% of N.
*$p < .05$.
**$p < .01$.

The first step discusses the psychological type profile of the early responders and the late responders. According to the data in Table 1, early responders show clear preferences for introversion (54%) over extraversion (46%), for intuition (53%) over sensing (47%), for feeling (56%) over thinking (44%), and for judging (78%) over perceiving (23%). In terms of dominant type, 33% of the early responders projected the imaginative profile of intuition, 28% the humane profile of feeling, 21% the practical profile of sensing, and 18% the logical profile of thinking. The three most strongly represented types were INTJ, ISFJ, and ESFJ which accounted for 14%, 11%, and 11% of the early responders, respectively.

According to the data in Table 2, late responders show clear preferences for extraversion (59%) over introversion (42%), for sensing (55%) over intuition (45%), for feeling (72%) over thinking (28%), and for judging (82%) over perceiving (19%). In terms of dominant type, 43% of late responders projected the humane profile of feeling, 22% the imaginative profile of intuition, 19% the logical profile of thinking, and 17% the practical profile of sensing. The two most strongly represented types were ESFJ and INFJ, which accounted for 18% and 12% of the late responders, respectively.

The second step compares the psychological profiles of the early responders with those of the late responders. The statistical significances of differences between the two groups are tested by means of the Selection Ratio Index (I), an extension of the classic chi-square test (Myers & McCaulley, 1985), and these results are shown in Table 2. In terms of the dichotomous preferences there were no significant differences between the two groups on the orientations, the perceiving process, or the attitudes. There were, however, significant differences between the groups on the judging process: while 72% of the late responders preferred feeling, the proportion fell to 56% among the early responders.

In terms of dominant type preferences, there was a significant difference between the two groups in the proportions of dominant feeling types (43% among the late responders and 28% among the early responders).

In terms of the 16 complete types, among the early responders there was a significantly higher proportion of INTJs (14% compared with 3%). There was also a significantly lower proportion of ESFJs (11% compared to 18%).

Discussion

Myers (2000) describes the INTJ, the largest group among the early responders.

> People with INTJ preferences have a clear vision of future possibilities coupled with the drive and organisation to implement their ideas. They love complex challenges and readily synthesize complicated theoretical and abstract matters. Once they have created their general structure, they devise strategies to achieve their goals ... INTJs value knowledge and expect competence of themselves and others. They especially abhor confusion, mess and inefficiency. (Myers, 2000, p. 18)

These insights point to early responders as disliking inefficiency, valuing competence, and having the drive and organisation to implement their ideas. Speedy response, sometimes as soon as they receive the posted questionnaire, indicates an urge to efficient handling of post that crosses the clergy desk.

Myers (2000) describes the ESFJ, the largest group among the late responders.

> People with ESFJ preferences like to organise people and situations and then work with others to complete tasks accurately and on time. They are conscientious and loyal, following through even in small matters, and they want others to be the same. They value security and stability ... They

are encouraged by approval and hurt by indifference or unkindness. Conflict-filled or tense situations make them uncomfortable, and they work to ensure these don't occur. (Myers, 2000, p. 28)

These insights indicate that the follow-up letter has been a reminder that someone, a real person, is waiting to receive their completed questionnaire. Their delay has created a problem for someone else so they are encouraged to work to complete the task accurately and on time. "They greatly like to have things settled, or at least to *feel* that things are settled" (Myers & Myers, 1995, p. 93).

Conclusion

In this study psychological type theory using the Francis Psychological Type Scales (Francis, 2005) has been able to provide an indicator to the personality preferences of those who respond early or late to postal questionnaire surveys. Early responders with their preference for the dominant function of intuition show that an awareness of the big picture, moving quickly to conclusions, drives them to complete and return a questionnaire quickly. Late responders with their preference for the dominant function of feeling show that the striving for harmony and positive interactions with others drives them to respond to the follow-up letter by completing and returning their questionnaire somewhat later than others. Further research with longitudinal studies may be able to indicate any differences in personality preferences between responders and non-responders.

References

Aday, L. A. (1996). *Designing and conducting health surveys: A comprehensive guide*. San Francisco, CA: Jossey-Bass.

Baab, L. M. (1998). *Personality type in congregations: How to work with others more effectively*. Washington, DC: Alban Institute.

Babbie, E. R. (1990). *Survey research methods*. Belmont, CA: Wadsworth.

Backstrom, C. H., & Hirsh, G. D. (1963). *Survey research*. Evanston, IL: Northwestern University Press.

Barbuto, J. E., Fritz, S. M., Lim, J. C. S., & Xu, Y. (2008). Using the MBTI instrument and the Motivation Sources Inventory to test the relationship between Jung's psychological types and sources of work motivation. *Journal of Psychological Type, 68*, 139–147.

Chen, R., Wei, L., & Syme, P. D. (2003). Comparison of early and delayed respondents to a postal health survey: A questionnaire study of personality traits and neuropsychological symptoms. *European Journal of Epidemiology, 18*, 195–202.

Craig, C. L., Duncan, B., & Francis, L. J. (2006). Psychological type preferences of Roman Catholic priests in the United Kingdom. *Journal of Beliefs and Values, 27*, 157–164. doi:10.1080/13617670600849812

Craig, C. L. Francis, L. J., & Robbins, M. (2004). Psychological type and sex differences among church leaders in the United Kingdom. *Journal of Beliefs and Values, 25*, 3–13. doi:10.1080/13617670420000199004

Craig, C. L. Horsfall, T., & Francis, L. J. (2005). Psychological types of male missionary personnel training in England: A role for thinking type men? *Pastoral Psychology, 53*, 475–482. doi: 10.1007/s11089-005-2588-8

Curtin, R., Presser, S., & Singer, E. (2000). The effects of response rate changes on the Index of Consumer Sentiment. *Public Opinion Quarterly, 64*, 413–428.

DeVellis, R. F. (2003). *Scale development: Theory and applications*. London: Sage.

DiRienzo, C., Kitts, J., Das, J., McGrath, K., & Synn, W. (2010). The relationship between MBTI and academic performance: A study across academic disciplines. *Journal of Psychological Type, 70*, 53–67.

Duncan, B. (1993). *Pray your way: Your personality and God*. London: Darton, Longman and Todd.

Edwards, P., Roberts, I., Clarke, M., DiGuiseppi, C., Pratap, S., Wentz, R., & Kwan, I. (2002). Increasing response rates to postal questionnaires: Systematic review. *British Medical Journal, 324*, 1183–1185. doi:10.1002/14651858.MR000008.pub4

Eysenck, S. B. G., Eysenck, H. J., & Barrett, P. (1985). A revised version of the Psychoticism Scale. *Personality and Individual Differences, 6*, 21–29. doi:10.1016/0191-8869(85)90026-1

Fowke, R. (1997). *Personality and prayer: Finding and extending the prayer style that suits your personality.* Guildford: Eagle.

Francis, L. J. (2005). *Faith and psychology: Personality, religion and the individual.* London: Darton, Longman and Todd.

Francis, L. J., Craig, C. L., & Butler, A. (2007). Psychological types of male evangelical Anglican seminarians in England. *Journal of Psychological Type, 67*, 11–17.

Francis, L. J., Craig, C. L., Whinney, M., Tilley, D., & Slater, P. (2007). Psychological profiling of Anglican clergy in England: Employing Jungian typology to interpret diversity, strengths, and potential weaknesses in ministry. *International Journal of Practical Theology, 11*, 266–284.

Francis, L. J., Gubb, S., & Robbins, M. (2012). Work-related psychological health and psychological type among lead elders within the Newfrontiers network of churches in the United Kingdom. *Journal of Prevention and Intervention in the Community, 40*, 233–245. doi:10.1080/10852352.2012.680422

Francis, L. J., Nash, P., Nash, S., & Craig, C. L. (2007). Psychology and youth ministry: Psychological type preferences of Christian youth workers in the United Kingdom. *Journal of Youth Ministry, 5*, 73–90.

Francis, L. J., Payne, V. J., & Jones, S. H. (2001). Psychological types of male Anglican clergy in Wales. *Journal of Psychological Type, 56*, 19–23. doi:10.1080/13674670123953

Francis, L. J., Penson, A. W., & Jones, S. H. (2001). Psychological types of male and female Bible College students in England. *Mental Health, Religion & Culture, 4*, 23–32.

Francis, L. J., & Robbins, M. (2002). Psychological types of male evangelical church leaders. *Journal of Belief and Values, 23*, 217–220. doi:10.1080/1361767022000010860

Francis, L. J., & Robbins, M. (2008). Psychological type and prayer preferences: A study among Anglican clergy in the United Kingdom. *Mental Health, Religion & Culture, 11*, 67–84. doi:10.1080/13674670701619445

Francis, L. J., Robbins, M., & Whinney, M. (2011). Women priests in the Church of England: Psychological type profile. *Religions, 2*, 389–397. doi: 10.3390/rel2030389

Francis, L. J., & Village, A. (2012). The psychological temperament of Anglican clergy in Ordained Local Ministry (OLM): The conserving, serving pastor? *Journal of Empirical Theology, 25*, 57–76. doi:10.1163/157092512X635743

Francis, L. J., Whinney, M., Burton, L., & Robbins, M. (2011). Psychological type preferences of male and female Free Church ministers in England. *Research in the Social Scientific Study of Religion, 22*, 251–263.

Holbrook, A., Krosnick, J., & Pfent, A. (2007). The causes and consequences of response rates in surveys by the news media and government contractor survey research firms. In J. M. Lepkowski, N. C. Tucker, J. M. Brick, E. D. De Leeuw, L. Japec, P. J. Lavrakas, M. W. Link, R. L. Sangster (Eds.), *Advances in telephone survey methodology* (pp. 499–678). New York, NY: Wiley. doi:10.1002/9780470173404.ch23

Jarlstrom, M., & Valkealahti, K. (2010). Person-job fit related to psychological type of Finnish business students and managers: Implications for change in the management environment. *Journal of Psychological Type, 70*, 41–52.

Kanuk, L., & Berenson, C. (1975). Mail surveys and response rates: A literature review. *Journal of Marketing Research, 12*, 440–453.

Kay, W. K., Francis, L. J., & Craig, C. L. (2008). Psychological type preferences of male British Assemblies of God Bible College students: Tough minded or tender hearted? *Journal of the European Pentecostal Theological Association, 28*, 6–20.

Keating, C. J. (1987). *Who we are is how we pray: Matching personality and spirituality.* Mystic, CT: Twenty-Third.

Keeter, S., Kennedy, C., Dimock, M., Best, J., & Craighill, P. (2006). Gauging the impact of growing nonresponse on estimates from a National RDD telephone survey. *Public Opinion Quarterly, 70*, 759–779. doi:10.1093/poq/nfl035

Keirsey, D., & Bates, M. (1978). *Please understand me.* Del Mar, CA: Prometheus Nemesis.

Macdaid, G. P., McCaulley, M. H., & Kainz, R. I. (1986). *Myers-Briggs Type Indicator: Atlas of type tables.* Gainesville, FL: Centre for Application of Psychological Type.

Martinez, P. (2001). *Prayer life: How your personality affects the way you pray.* Carlisle: Paternoster.

Michael, C. P., & Norrisey, M. C. (1984). *Prayer and temperament: Different prayer forms for different personality types.* Charlottesville, VA: The Open Door.

Myers, I. B. (2000). *Introduction to type: A guide to understanding your results on the Myers-Briggs Type Indicator.* Oxford: OPP.

Myers, I. B., & McCaulley, M. H. (1985). *Manual: A guide to the development and use of the Myers-Briggs Type Indicator*. Palo Alto, CA: Consulting Psychologists Press.

Myers, I. B., & Myers, P. B. (1995). *Gifts differing: Understanding personality type*. Mountain View, CA: CPP.

Osborn, L., & Osborn, D. (1991). *God's diverse people*. London: Daybreak.

Paganini-Hill, A., Hsu, G., Chao, A., & Ross, R. K. (1993). Comparison of early and late respondents to a postal health survey questionnaire. *Epidemiology, 4*, 375–379.

Rea, L. M., & Parker, R. A. (1997). *Designing and conducting survey research: A comprehensive guide*. San Francisco, CA: Jossey-Bass.

Vink, J. M., & Boomsma, D. I. (2008). A comparison of early and late respondents in a twin-family survey study. *Twin Research and Human Genetics: The Official Journal of the International Society for Twin Studies, 11*, 165–173. doi:10.1375/twin.11.2.165

Visser, P. S., Krosnick, J. A., Marquette, J., & Curtin, M. (1996). Mail surveys for election forecasting? An evaluation of the Colombia Dispatch Poll. *Public Opinion Quarterly, 60*, 181–227. doi:10.1086/297748

Wilde, G. J. S. (1970). *Neurotische labiliteit gemeten volgens de vragenlijst methode* [The questionnaire method as a means of measuring neurotic instability]. Amsterdam: van Rossen.

Psychological type profile of Protestant church leaders in Australia: are clergymen and clergywomen different?

Mandy Robbins and Ruth Powell

A sample of 120 clergywomen and 436 clergymen from Protestant denominations in Australia participated in the 2011 National Church Life Survey completing form LS2 that included the Francis Psychological Type Scales, an operationalisation of psychological type theory. The type profiles of the clergymen and clergywomen are compared, and demonstrate only one difference, clergywomen are significantly more likely to report a feeling preference than clergymen but the difference is not strong. The type profiles of the clergy are compared to the Australian population norms and, in the case of both men and women, found to be different. The personality profiles of clergymen and clergywomen have more in common based on being clergy, rather than being either male or female. The implications of these findings for the ministry and mission of Protestant denominations in Australia are discussed.

Introduction

The number of Protestant denominations who ordain women has grown significantly since the late 1980s. This has been documented by a number of studies within different contexts (Blohm, 2004; Chaves, 1997; Jones, 2004; Robbins, 2008). One reason that is cited for this move, whether implicitly or explicitly, is that the ordination of women brings "balance" to ministry by providing a "complementary" approach to ministry when compared with clergymen (Webster, 1994). This has particularly been the case among groups that have been set up to campaign for the necessary changes within church structures to enable the ordination of women, for example, the Movement for the Ordination of Women in the UK and the Movement for the Ordination of Women in Australia. Those who argue against the ordination of women take a different perspective and suggest that women bring a complementary approach to ministry that does not require ordination.

Against this changing background of ministry in Protestant denominations, a research strand has been developing that seeks to chart the psychological type profile of leaders and congregations across church communities. This paper explores the psychological type profile of clergymen and clergywomen in Protestant denominations in Australia. This group are also compared with the Australian male and female population norms, respectively. From an individual differences perspective, psychological type theory is able to explore whether having both clergymen and clergywomen in ministry does indeed bring a greater balance to ministry.

Psychological type theory was first proposed by Jung (1971) and has been operationalised by a number of different instruments including the Myers–Briggs Type Indicator (MBTI; Myers, McCaulley, Quenk, & Hammer, 2003); the Keirsey Temperament Sorter (Keirsey & Bates, 1978); and the Francis Psychological Type Scales (FPTS: Francis, 2005). Psychological type theory is based on four preferences: two orientations, two perceiving functions, two judging functions, and two attitudes towards the outer world. The two orientations are Extraversion (E) and Introversion (I). The orientations indicate whether individuals have a preference for gaining their energy from the outside world (E) or from their inside world (I). The two perceiving functions are Sensing (S) and Intuition (N). The perceiving functions indicate whether individuals prefer to take in information through their five senses (S) or through inspiration and imagination (N). The two judging functions are Thinking (T) and Feeling (F). The judging functions indicate whether individuals prefer to make decisions based on objective logic (T) or subjective understanding (F). The two attitudes towards the outer world are Judging (J) and Perceiving (P). The attitudes indicate whether individuals prefer to organise their outer work in an orderly way (J) or in a spontaneous way (P). These four preferences work together to produce 16 discrete types, for example, ENFP or ISTJ.

A number of studies have charted the psychological type profile of male church leaders in the UK, USA, and Australia. Within the UK, psychological type profiles are published for Anglicans in the Church in Wales (Francis & Payne, 2002; Francis, Payne, & Jones, 2001). Francis and Payne (2002) found a preference for introversion (61%), sensing (61%), feeling (64%), and judging (73%) among 191 Church in Wales clergymen. Francis et al. (2001) found preferences for introversion (59%), sensing (57%), feeling (69%), and judging (68%) among a sample of 427 Church in Wales clergymen.

Francis, Gubb, and Robbins (2009) found among a sample of 134 male Newfrontiers lead elders a preference for extraversion (52%), sensing (52%), thinking (54%), and judging (78%). The same preferences for extraversion over introversion, for sensing over intuition, for thinking over feeling, and for judging over perceiving were found in a study of 92 male evangelical missionary personnel using the Form G(Anglicised) of the MBTI (Craig, Horsfall, & Francis, 2005).

Among Roman Catholic priests in the USA preferences for introversion (61%), sensing (61%), and judging (73%) have been found. Priests were more likely to have the predominant type of ISTJ (27%), compared with 16% of men in the USA population (Burns, Francis, Village, & Robbins, 2013). Roman Catholic priests in the UK have also shown preferences for introversion, and judging, with near equal preferences for sensing and intuition (Craig, Duncan, & Francis, 2006). A similar Australian study of Roman Catholic priests found preferences for introversion (58%), sensing (77%), feeling (67%), and judging (84%) (Francis, Powell, & Robbins, 2012).

Across the UK, USA, and Australia and across denominations, a picture is beginning to emerge of a Sensing and Judging leadership among male clergy. Type theory describes the SJ temperament as the "guardian" and summarise this in the following way:

> Guardians need to know they are doing the responsible thing. They value stability, security, and a sense of community. They trust hierarchy and authority and may be surprised when others go against these. Guardians prefer cooperative actions with a focus on standards and norms. Their orientation is to their past experiences, and they like things sequenced and structured. (Myers et al., 2003, pp. 59–60)

One example of a study of female clergy and psychological type is of 212 Australian clergywomen across 14 denominations in the 2006 National Church Life Survey. These clergywomen had clear preferences for introversion (55%) over extraversion (45%); for sensing (60%) over intuition (40%); for feeling (61%) over thinking (39%); and for judging (84%) over perceiving (17%). The two most strongly represented types were ISFJ (21%) and ISTJ (14%) (Robbins, Francis, & Powell, 2012). Relatively few studies have made comparisons of the personality profiles of clergymen and clergywomen in the same sample. In the Church of England women were first ordained to the priesthood in 1994. Just prior to this time, data were collected from 373 male and 560 female Anglican clergy in parishes using Eysenck's three-dimensional model of personality. Robbins, Francis, and Rutledge (1997) found that the personality profiles of clergymen and clergywomen were indistinguishable. In a comparable study in 2004 among 182 clergywomen and 540 clergymen in similar posts, Brewster, Francis, and Robbins (2011) found that little change had taken place.

Using psychological type measures among Anglicans in the UK, Francis, Craig, Whinney, Tilley, and Slater (2007) compared 626 clergymen and 237 clergywomen. The clergymen and clergywomen present significantly different profiles compared with the population norms and are more like each other.

Among a sample of 135 women and 164 men from different denominations who were attending an evangelical event (Spring Harvest), Craig, Francis, and Robbins (2004) found a preference for ESFJ among the women and ISTJ among the men. This sample may not provide a representative sample of men and women in ministry as they have self-selected in attending an event such as Spring Harvest. Nonetheless it does demonstrate again that while there are some significant differences between the psychological profile of male and female church leaders, the SJ temperament is consistent across the male and female leaders.

In terms of differences between countries, the 2001 International Church Life Survey provided the opportunity to explore the psychological type profile of 2972 male and 720 female clergy from three countries: Australia, England, and New Zealand. This study found preferences for introversion (62%), sensing (61%), feeling (59%), and judging (77%). However, this study did not compare the personality profiles of clergymen and clergywomen (Francis, Robbins, Kaldor, & Castle, 2009).

In summary these findings have shown that, in terms of psychological type, the dominant temperament among both male and female clergy is SJ. These preferences for sensing over intuition and for judging over perceiving was found in the UK, USA, and Australia and across denominations. Across nearly all of these studies, preferences for introversion and for feeling were also evident. While the pattern for women to express a preference for feeling has been well-established in general population samples, this emphasis on feeling in male clergy has led some researchers to draw conclusions about the feminine personality profile of clergy in general (Francis et al., 2007).

Further, these findings show that clergymen and clergywomen are more like each other than they are like the population norms. This suggests that clergywomen may not necessarily bring "balance" to ministry in terms of their psychological type profile. The evidence presented in this review has also demonstrated that the most frequent whole type among clergy is ISFJ. The ISFJ can be summarised as:

> Quiet, friendly, responsible, and conscientious. Work devotedly to meet their obligations. Lend stability to any project or group. Thorough, painstaking, accurate. Their interests are usually not technical. Can be patient with necessary details. Loyal, considerate, perceptive, concerned with how other people feel. (Myers et al., 2003, p. 64)

There are three aims for the present study. The first aim is to explore the psychological type profile of Protestant clergy who took part in the 2011 National Church Life Survey in Australia to test the reliability of the FPTS among this population. The second aim is to compare the psychological type profile of clergymen and clergywomen to consider if they bring different personalities to their ministry. The third aim is to compare the psychological type profile of clergymen and clergywomen to the population norms for Australia. Previous research suggests that clergymen and clergywomen will present profiles that are more like each other than the population norms. The 2011 National Church Life Surveys provides the opportunity to test this finding across more than 20 Protestant denominations within an Australian context.

Method

Procedure

In 2011 a total of 556 Protestant clergy completed the National Church Life Survey Leaders Form LS2 which contained the 40-item FPTS (Francis, 2005) and background questions on age, sex, and denomination.

Participants

Of the 556 clergy, 22% were clergywomen and 78% were clergymen. Of the female respondents, 10% were under the age of 30, 13% were in their 30s, 15% were in their 40s, 36% were in their 50s, 20% were in their 60s, and 6% were aged 60 or over.

Of the male respondents, 6% were under the age of 30, 22% were in their 30s, 23% were in their 40s, 29% were in their 50s, 16% were in their 60s, and 4% were aged 60 or over. Ten Protestant denominations were represented, 46% Anglican, 18% Baptist, and 13% Uniting Church. The remaining 23% were divided between Churches of Christ, Independent, Lutheran, Presbyterian, Salvation Army, Seventh-day Adventist, and Vineyard.

Measure

Psychological type was assessed by the FPTS (Francis, 2005). This 40-item instrument comprises four sets of 10 forced-choice items related to each of the components of psychological type. Participants are asked to tick the characteristic that is closest to their preference for each pair. The four components are orientation (extraversion or introversion), the perceiving process (sensing or intuition), the judging process (thinking or feeling), and attitude towards the outer world (judging or perceiving). This instrument has been designed to operationalise Jungian psychological type theory within the research context (Francis, 2005). Recent studies have demonstrated that this instrument functions well in terms of reliability in the Australian context. For example, Robbins et al. (2012) reported reliabilities of .84 for extraversion and introversion, .79 for sensing and intuition, .71 for feeling and thinking, and .81 for judging and perceiving among a sample of Australian clergywomen from the 2006 National Church Life Survey.

Age, sex, and denomination were measured by three closed questions.

Data analysis

Type tables are the recognised way of reporting psychological type within the research literature and this convention has been applied in this paper. Type tables provide information on the 16 complete types, the four dichotomous preferences, the six sets of pairs and temperaments, the four dominant types, and the introverted and extraverted Jungian types. Australian population norms have yet to be published by CPP Asia Pacific so the comparison data used in the analysis are supplied by the Australian Archive of the Psychological Type Research Unit at Deakin University (Ball, 2008). These data have been used in other studies employing psychological type theory as a comparative group (Francis et al., 2012).

Table 1. Type distribution for Protestant clergywomen in Australia, compared with the female population norms.

The Sixteen Complete Types				Dichotomous Preferences			
ISTJ	ISFJ	INFJ	INTJ	E	$n=53$	(44.2%)	0.96
$n=18$	$n=24$	$n=9$	$n=6$	I	$n=67$	(55.8%)	1.04
(15.0%)	(20.0%)	(7.5%)	(5.0%)				
1.55*	1.57*	1.25	0.95	S	$n=74$	(61.7%)	1.18**
+++++	+++++	+++++	+++++	N	$n=46$	(38.3%)	0.80**
+++++	+++++	+++++	+++				
+++++	+++++			T	$n=44$	(36.7%)	0.87
	+++++			F	$n=76$	(63.3%)	1.09
				J	$n=98$	(81.7%)	1.38***
				P	$n=22$	(18.3%)	0.45***

				Pairs and Temperaments			
ISTP	ISFP	INFP	INTP	IJ	$n=57$	(47.5%)	1.41**
$n=1$	$n=3$	$n=6$	$n=0$	IP	$n=10$	(8.3%)	0.41***
(0.8%)	(2.5%)	(5.0%)	(0%)	EP	$n=12$	(10.0%)	0.48**
0.31	0.52	0.59	0.00*	EJ	$n=41$	(34.2%)	1.35*
+	+++	+++++		ST	$n=26$	(21.7%)	0.96
				SF	$n=48$	(40.0%)	1.35*
				NF	$n=28$	(23.3%)	0.82
				NT	$n=18$	(15.0%)	0.77
ESTP	ESFP	ENFP	ENTP	SJ	$n=67$	(55.8%)	1.46***
$n=0$	$n=3$	$n=3$	$n=6$	SP	$n=7$	(5.8%)	0.42**
(0.0%)	(2.5%)	(2.5%)	(5.0%)	NP	$n=15$	(12.5%)	0.46***
0.00	0.65	0.28*	0.92	NJ	$n=31$	(25.8%)	1.24
	+++	+++	+++++	TJ	$n=37$	(30.8%)	1.13
				TP	$n=7$	(5.8%)	0.39**
				FP	$n=15$	(12.5%)	0.48***
ESTJ	ESFJ	ENFJ	ENTJ	FJ	$n=61$	(50.8%)	1.60***
$n=7$	$n=18$	$n=10$	$n=6$	IN	$n=21$	(17.5%)	0.74
(5.8%)	(15.0%)	(8.3%)	(5.0%)	EN	$n=25$	(20.8%)	0.87
0.76	1.83**	1.73	1.08	IS	$n=46$	(38.3%)	1.28*
+++++	+++++	+++++	+++++	ES	$n=28$	(23.3%)	1.05
+	+++++	+++		ET	$n=19$	(15.8%)	0.78
	+++++			EF	$n=34$	(28.3%)	1.09
				IF	$n=42$	(35.0%)	1.09
				IT	$n=25$	(28.8%)	0.96

Jungian Types (E)				Jungian Types (I)				Dominant Types			
	n	%	Index		n	%	Index		n	%	Index
E-TJ	13	10.8	0.88	I-TP	1	0.8	0.12**	Dt.T	14	11.7	0.61*
E-FJ	28	23.3	1.79***	I-FP	9	7.5	0.56	Dt.F	37	30.8	1.17
ES-P	3	2.5	0.39	IS-J	42	35.0	1.56***	Dt.S	45	37.5	1.30*
EN-P	9	7.5	0.52*	IN-J	15	12.5	1.11	Dt.N	24	20.0	0.78

Note: $N=120$ (NB + = 1% of N).
*$p<.05$.
**$p<.01$.
***$p<.001$.

Table 2. Type distribution for Protestant clergymen in Australia, compared with the male population norms.

The Sixteen Complete Types				Dichotomous Preferences			
ISTJ	ISFJ	INFJ	INTJ	E	$n = 193$	(44.3%)	0.95
$n = 74$	$n = 60$	$n = 27$	$n = 35$	I	$n = 243$	(55.7%)	1.04
(17.0%)	(13.8%)	(6.2%)	(8.0)				
0.80*	3.49***	2.39***	0.92	S	$n = 246$	(56.4%)	0.98
+++++	+++++	+++++	+++++	N	$n = 190$	(43.6%)	1.03
+++++	+++++	+	+++				
+++++	++++			T	$n = 214$	(49.1%)	0.63***
++				F	$n = 222$	(50.9%)	2.28***
				J	$n = 340$	(78.0%)	1.18***
				P	$n = 96$	(22.0%)	0.64***

Pairs and Temperaments

ISTP	ISFP	INFP	INTP	IJ	$n = 196$	(45.0%)	1.23***
$n = 4$	$n = 7$	$n = 26$	$n = 10$	IP	$n = 47$	(10.8%)	0.63***
(0.9%)	(1.6%)	(6.0%)	(2.3%)	EP	$n = 49$	(11.2%)	0.66***
0.16***	0.83	1.87***	0.36***	EJ	$n = 144$	(33.0%)	1.13
+++++	++	+++++	++				
+++++		+		ST	$n = 127$	(29.1%)	0.62***
				SF	$n = 119$	(27.3%)	2.62***
				NF	$n = 103$	(23.6%)	1.99***
				NT	$n = 87$	(20.0%)	0.66***
ESTP	ESFP	ENFP	ENTP	SJ	$n = 218$	(50.0%)	1.13*
$n = 9$	$n = 8$	$n = 19$	$n = 13$	SP	$n = 28$	(6.4%)	0.47***
(2.1%)	(1.8%)	(4.4%)	(3.0%)	NP	$n = 68$	(15.6%)	0.76*
0.44**	1.28	1.08	0.44**	NJ	$n = 122$	(28.0%)	1.29**
++	++	++++	+++++				
			+++++	TJ	$n = 178$	(40.8%)	0.75***
			+++	TP	$n = 36$	(8.3%)	0.35***
				FP	$n = 60$	(13.8%)	1.30*
ESTJ	ESFJ	ENFJ	ENTJ	FJ	$n = 162$	(37.2%)	3.18***
$n = 40$	$n = 44$	$n = 31$	$n = 29$	IN	$n = 98$	(22.5%)	1.07
(9.2%)	(10.1%)	(7.1%)	(6.7%)	EN	$n = 92$	(21.1%)	0.99
0.58***	3.24***	3.47***	0.79	IS	$n = 145$	(33.3%)	1.02
+++++	+++++	+++++	+++++	ES	$n = 101$	(23.2%)	0.92
++++	+++++	++	++				
				ET	$n = 91$	(20.9%)	0.58***
				EF	$n = 102$	(23.4%)	2.20***
				IF	$n = 120$	(27.5%)	2.36***
				IT	$n = 123$	(28.2%)	0.67***

Jungian Types (E)				Jungian Types (I)				Dominant Types			
	n	%	Index		n	%	Index		n	%	Index
E-TJ	69	15.8	0.66***	I-TP	14	3.2	0.27***	Dt.T	83	19.0	0.53***
E-FJ	75	17.2	3.33***	I-FP	33	7.6	1.48*	Dt.F	108	24.8	2.41***
ES-P	17	3.9	0.63	IS-J	134	30.7	1.22**	Dt.S	151	34.6	1.10
EN-P	32	7.3	0.67*	IN-J	62	14.2	1.26	Dt.N	94	21.6	0.97

Note: $N = 436$ (NB + = 1% of N).
*$p < .05$.
**$p < .01$.
***$p < .001$.

Table 3. Type distribution for Protestant church leaders in Australia, clergymen compared with clergywomen

The Sixteen Complete Types

ISTJ	ISFJ	INFJ	INTJ
n = 74	n = 60	n = 27	n = 35
(17.0%)	(13.8%)	(6.2%)	(8.0%)
1.13	0.69	0.83	1.61
+++++	+++++	+++++	+++++
+++++	+++++	+	+++
+++++	++++		
++			

ISTP	ISFP	INFP	INTP
n = 4	n = 7	n = 26	n = 10
(0.9%)	(1.6%)	(6.0%)	(2.3%)
1.10	0.64	1.19	
+	++	+++++	++
		+	

ESTP	ESFP	ENFP	ENTP
n = 9	n = 8	n = 19	n = 13
(2.1%)	(1.8%)	(4.4%)	(3.0%)
	0.73	1.74	0.60
++	++	++++	+++

ESTJ	ESFJ	ENFJ	ENTJ
n = 40	n = 44	n = 31	n = 29
(9.2%)	(10.1%)	(7.1%)	(6.7%)
1.57	0.67	0.85	1.33
+++++	+++++	+++++	+++++
++++	+++++	++	++

Dichotomous Preferences

E	n = 193	(44.3%)	1.00
I	n = 243	(55.7%)	1.00
S	n = 246	(56.4%)	0.91
N	n = 190	(43.6%)	1.14
T	n = 214	(49.1%)	1.34*
F	n = 222	(50.95)	0.80*
J	n = 340	(78.0%)	0.95
P	n = 96	(22.0%)	1.20

Pairs and Temperaments

IJ	n = 196	(45.0%)	0.95
IP	n = 47	(10.8%)	1.29
EP	n = 49	(11.2%)	1.12
EJ	n = 144	(33.0%)	0.97
ST	n = 127	(29.1%)	1.34
SF	n = 119	(27.3%)	0.68
NF	n = 103	(23.6%)	1.01
NT	n = 87	(20.0%)	1.33
SJ	n = 218	(50.0%)	0.90
SP	n = 28	(6.4%)	1.10
NP	n = 68	(15.6%)	1.25
NJ	n = 122	(28.0%)	1.08
TJ	n = 178	(40.8%)	1.32
TP	n = 36	(8.3%)	1.42
FP	n = 60	(13.8%)	1.10
FJ	n = 162	(37.2%)	0.73
IN	n = 98	(22.5%)	1.28
EN	n = 92	(21.1%)	1.01
IS	n = 145	(33.3%)	0.87
ES	n = 101	(23.2%)	0.99
ET	n = 91	(20.9%)	1.32
EF	n = 102	(23.4%)	0.83
IF	n = 120	(27.5%)	0.79
IT	n = 123	(28.2%)	1.35

Jungian Types (E)

	n	%	Index
E-TJ	69	15.8	1.46
E-FJ	75	17.2	0.74
ES-P	17	3.9	1.55
EN-P	32	7.3	0.98

Jungian Types (I)

	n	%	Index
I-TP	14	3.2	3.85
I-FP	33	7.6	1.01
IS-J	134	30.7	0.88
IN-J	62	14.2	1.14

Dominant Types

	n	%	Index
Dt.T	83	19.0	1.63
Dt.F	108	24.8	0.80
Dt.S	151	34.6	0.92
Dt.N	94	21.6	1.08

Note: N = 436 (NB + = 1% of N).
*p < .05.
**p < .01.
***p < .001.

Results

The FPTS produced the following alpha coefficients: extraversion and introversion .84; sensing and intuition .76; thinking and feeling .72; and judging and perceiving .79. The alpha coefficients for all the four scales exceed the threshold recommended by DeVellis (2003) of .65. This confirms the findings of previous studies within church populations in Australia that demonstrate that the FPTS perform well in this context.

Table 1 tests the statistical significance between the clergywomen and the Australian female population norms provided by Ball (2008). The data demonstrate that the clergywomen are significantly more likely to be judging (82%) than the female population (59%; $p < .001$). The clergywomen are also significantly more likely to be feeling (63%) than the female population (58%), although this difference is not as pronounced ($p < .05$). The SJ "guardian" profile is represented by 56% of the clergywomen but by only 38% of the female population norms ($p < .001$).

Table 2 tests the statistical significance between the clergymen and the Australian male population norms provided by Ball (2008). The data demonstrate that the clergymen are significantly more likely to be judging (78%) than the male population (66%; $p < .001$). The clergymen are also significantly more likely to be feeling (51%) than the male population (22%; $p < .001$). The SJ "guardian" profile is reported by half of the clergymen (50%) and 44% of the male population ($p < .05$).

Table 3 tests the statistical significant differences between the clergymen and clergywomen employing an extension of the chi-square test (McCaulley, 1985). The type table demonstrates that the clergymen prefer introversion (56%) over extraversion (44%); sensing (56%) over intuition (44%); feeling (51%) over thinking (49%); and judging (78%) over perceiving (22%). The predominant types are ISTJ (17%) and ISFJ (14%). The type tables demonstrate that both the clergywomen and the clergymen have a preference for introversion, sensing, feeling, and judging. The dominant types for both clergywomen and clergymen are sensing (38% and 35%, respectively) and feeling (31% and 25%, respectively). The SJ temperament accounts for over half of the clergywomen (56%) and half of the clergymen (50%). The table demonstrates that there is only one small significant difference ($p < .05$) between the clergymen and clergywomen with respect to feeling and thinking. Clergywomen score higher on feeling (63%) than clergymen (51%). With respect to the other dichotomous pairs there are no significant differences. There are also no significant differences with respect to the 16 complete psychological types, any of the pairs and temperaments or the dominant types.

Conclusion

This paper set out to explore the psychological type profile of Protestant clergymen and clergywomen who took part in the 2011 National Church Life Survey in Australia. Four main findings emerge from this study.

First, the FPTS provide alpha coefficients that give confidence to employing this scale to measure psychological type among clergy in Australia.

Second, the argument that women will bring a greater balance to ordained ministry in terms of individual differences is not supported in terms of psychological type theory. Neither is any argument against the ordination of women that relies on psychological reasoning about the female temperament. Australian clergywomen do not present a different psychological type profile to their male counterparts. The only small difference is that clergywomen are significantly more likely to report a feeling preference than the clergymen. Overall, clergymen and clergywomen are more alike than different when it comes to their psychological type profile.

Third, both clergymen and clergywomen report an ISFJ profile with no significant differences reported on the "guardian" SJ profile. This psychological type profile may find change difficult both to instigate and to manage. If the churches are looking to maintain their status quo then they have clergymen and clergywomen who are both likely to support this. Those clergy who do not share these preferences and are in the minority may well find that their colleagues do not understand them and may even find their approach to ministry difficult to understand and work with. In addition, the emphasis on feeling types among both male and female church leaders is once again confirmed, supporting the overall conclusion of a feminine personality profile among clergy.

Fourth, the clergymen and clergywomen are more like each other than they are like their respective population norms. That is, being a clergyperson is associated with certain personality types, more than being male or female. In a sense, there is an occupational psychological type profile for clergy. This not only highlights the strengths that these clergy bring to ministry, but also highlights the types of activities that may be more difficult, stressful or de-energising.

Future studies would benefit from exploring denominational differences to identify the faith traditions where these patterns are maintained and where they diverge. Other potential avenues for research to increase understanding may include age differences and ethnic differences.

Acknowledgement

The authors wish to thank the Australian Catholic University for the award of Distinguished Visiting Research Fellow for the first author which enabled this collaboration.

References

Ball, I. L. (2008). Australian data on the distribution of psychological types. *Bulletin of Psychological Type, 31*, 53–55.

Blohm, U. (2004). *Religious traditions and personal stories: Women working as priests, ministers and rabbis*. Frankfurt am Main: Peter Lang.

Brewster, C., Francis, L. J., & Robbins, M. (2011). Maintaining a public ministry in rural England: Work-related psychological health and psychological type among Anglican clergy serving in multi-church benefices. In L. J. Francis & H-G. Ziebertz (Eds.), *The public significance of religion* (pp. 241–266). Leiden: Brill.

Burns, J., Francis, L. J., Village, A., & Robbins, M. (2013). Psychological type profile of Roman Catholic priests: An empirical enquiry in the United States. *Pastoral Psychology, 62*, 239–246. doi 10.1007/s11089-012-0483-7.

Chaves, M. (1997). *Ordaining women: Culture and conflict in religious organizations*. Cambridge, MA: Harvard University Press.

Craig, C. L., Duncan, B., & Francis, L. J. (2006). Psychological type preferences of Roman Catholic priests in the United Kingdom. *Journal of Beliefs and Values, 27*, 157–164. doi: 10.1080/13617670600849812.

Craig, C. L., Francis, L. J., & Robbins, M. (2004). Psychological type and sex differences among church leaders in the United Kingdom. *Journal of Beliefs and Values, 25*, 3–13. doi:10.1080/1361767042000199004.

Craig, C. L. Horsfall, T., & Francis, L. J. (2005). Psychological types of male missionary personnel training in England: A role for thinking type men? *Pastoral Psychology, 53*, 475–482. doi: 10.1007/s11089-005-2588-8.

DeVellis, R. F. (2003). *Scale development: Theory and applications*. London: Sage.

Francis, L. J. (2005). *Faith and psychology: Personality, religion and the individual*. London: Darton, Longman and Todd.

Francis, L. J., Craig, C. L., Whinney, M., Tilley, D., & Slater, P. (2007). Psychological profiling of Anglican clergy in England: Employing Jungian typology to interpret diversity, strengths, and potential weaknesses in ministry. *International Journal of Practical Theology, 11*, 266–284. doi: 10.1515/IJPT.2007.17.

Francis, L. J., Gubb, S., & Robbins, M. (2009). Psychological type profile of Lead Elders within the Newfrontiers network of churches in the United Kingdom. *Journal of Beliefs and Values, 30*, 61–69.

Francis, L. J., & Payne, V. J. (2002). The Payne Index of Ministry Styles (PIMS): Ministry styles and psychological type among male Anglican clergy in Wales. *Research in the Social Scientific Study of Religion, 13*, 125–141.

Francis, L. J., Payne, V. J., & Jones, S. H. (2001). Psychological types of male Anglican clergy in Wales. *Journal of Psychological Type, 56*, 19–23.

Francis, L. J., Powell, R., & Robbins, M. (2012). Profiling Catholic priests in Australia. In A. W. Ata (Ed.), *Catholics and Catholicism in contemporary Australia* (pp. 282–298). Melbourne: David Lovell Publishing.

Francis, L. J., Robbins, M., Kaldor, P., & Castle, K. (2009). Psychological type and work-related psychological health among clergy in Australia, England and New Zealand. *Journal of Psychology and Christianity, 28*(3), 200–212. doi: 10.1080/13617670902784568.

Jones, I. (2004). *Women and priesthood in the Church of England ten years on*. London: Church House Publishing.

Jung, C. G. (1971). *Psychological types: The collected works, volume 6*. London: Routledge and Kegan Paul.

Keirsey, D., & Bates, M. (1978). *Please understand me*. Del Mar, CA: Prometheus Nemesis.

McCaulley, M. H. (1985). The selection ratio type table: A research strategy for comparing type distributions. *Journal of Psychological Type, 10*, 46–56.

Myers, I. B., McCaulley, M. H., Quenk, N. L., & Hammer, A. L. (2003). *MBTI manual: A guide to the development and use of the Myers-Briggs type indicator*. Mountain View, CA: CPP.

Robbins, M. (2008). *Clergywomen in the Church of England: A psychological study*. New York, NY: Edwin Mellen Press.

Robbins, M., Francis, L., & Powell, R. (2012). Work-related psychological health among clergywomen in Australia. *Mental Health, Religion & Culture, 15*, 933–944. doi 10.1080/13674676.2012.698044.

Robbins, M., Francis, L. J., & Rutledge, C. (1997). The personality characteristics of Anglican stipendiary parochial clergy in England: Gender differences revisited. *Personality and Individual Differences, 23*, 199–204. doi: 10.1016/S0191-8869(97)00042-1.

Webster, M. (1994). *A new strength, a new song: Journey to a whole priesthood*. London: Mowbray.

Psychological type profile of clergywomen and clergymen serving in the New York metropolitan area of the Reformed Church in America

Marjorie H. Royle, Jon Norton and Thomas Larkin

This study of the psychological types of clergymen and clergywomen in the Reformed Church in America (RCA) extends the body of research to an additional mainline American denomination. It uses a sample of 89 RCA clergymen and 26 RCA clergywomen from two synods in the New York metropolitan area who completed the Francis Psychological Type Scales as part of a study of clergy stress. The 16 psychological types were calculated separately for men and women. The type distributions were compared with US population norms by gender and with those of Presbyterian (PC(USA)) clergymen and clergywomen. Like the PC(USA) clergy, RCA clergy had psychological types differing significantly from those of the population at large. Similar to other clergy, the majority preferred intuition, feeling, and judging. However, clergymen in the RCA were about equally divided in preferring extraversion to introversion, and clergywomen were more likely to prefer introversion and about equally likely to prefer thinking and feeling in their judging process. These findings generally are similar to those found among Presbyterian clergy.

Introduction

One approach to studying individual differences is psychological type theory, based on the work of Jung (1971) and developed in the USA by Myers and Briggs (Myers & Myers, 1980) and in Great Britain by Francis and colleagues (Village, 2011). The concept has been used widely with clergy in a variety of denominations both in the USA and the UK, as well as in other English-speaking countries, both in empirical research and in application in religious and other organisations to address interpersonal differences and conflicts (Keirsey & Bates, 1984). Francis, Robbins, and Wulff (2011) describe much of the research, citing three major empirical findings. First, type profiles of clergy differ significantly from those in the general population. Second, profiles are similar between clergymen and clergywomen. Third, profiles differ significantly among clergy from different denominations.

The largest empirical study using a US sample included 561 clergy from a representative panel study in the Presbyterian Church (USA) (PC(USA)) (Francis et al., 2011). The sample included 413 clergymen and 148 clergywomen. Results from this sample were in general agreement with previous work in the UK and elsewhere, with profiles for clergy differing significantly from those of the population at large, profiles for clergymen and clergywomen being similar, and profiles for PC(USA) clergy being similar to those for clergy in the Church of England, both relatively liberal denominations.

The Reformed Church in America (RCA) shares the Reformed tradition with the Presbyterian Church. Its beginnings were in the Netherlands in the seventeenth century, under the influence of the German and Swiss reformers. It was brought to North America by immigrants in the seventeenth and eighteenth centuries. Currently, about 1000 RCA congregations with 170,000 confessing members are located throughout the USA and Canada, clustered in the New York/New Jersey metropolitan area and in New York State, Michigan, Iowa, and California. Theologically, the RCA is located within mainline (or oldline) Protestantism, but with somewhat more pietistic practices. Today, the RCA includes clergy and laity of diverse races and ethnicities and many cultures.

Given this similarity in tradition, the distribution of psychological types of the RCA clergymen and clergywomen would be predicted to be similar to that of PC(USA) clergymen and clergywomen. RCA clergymen and women would be predicted to be similar to each other in psychological type, as were the PC(USA) clergy. Finally, the distribution of psychological types of the RCA clergymen and clergywomen would be predicted to differ from that of the psychological types of the US population at large in ways that are similar to the differences seen between (PC(USA) clergymen and clergywomen and the population at large. A study of psychological type and stress conducted in 2013 among RCA parish clergy (Royle, Norton, & Larkin, 2014) provided an opportunity to extend the study of psychological type among clergy to a new, but related group of clergy and test these predictions.

Method

Participants

In 2013, 115 parish clergy in the RCA from the metropolitan New York/New Jersey area completed a measure of psychological type as part of a study of psychological type and stress (Royle et al., 2014). Recruitment was by mail, email, and personal invitation, and participants represented 42% of all those who were invited. Of the group, 89 were male and 26 were female. Most (83%) were married, and the sample included a representative mix of ages and time in the ministry. Of the group, 86% were white, 8% were African-American, and 4% were Latino.

Measures

Psychological type was assessed by the Francis Psychological Type Scales (FPTS; Francis, 2005). This is a 40-item instrument comprising four sets of 10 forced-choice items related to each of the four components of psychological type: orientations (extraversion or introversion), perceiving functions (sensing or intuition), judging functions (thinking or feeling), and attitude towards the outer world (judging or perceiving).

Data analysis

Responses on the FPTS were scored to provide a four-letter psychological type score for each participant. Tables of the distributions of the 16 type scores for both men and women were created using the type table format generally used in the research literature of the empirical investigation of psychological type. These tables include information about the 16 discrete psychological types, the four dichotomous preferences, the six sets of pairs and temperaments, the dominant types, and the introverted and extraverted Jungian types.

The types for RCA clergymen and clergywomen were compared with those for clergymen and women in the PC (USA) (Francis et al., 2011). Types for RCA clergymen were compared with those for RCA clergywomen, and types for RCA clergymen and clergywomen were compared with those for men and women in the US population. Comparisons were tested for statistical significance using the *I* statistic or Selection Ratio Index, an extension of the Chi-square test.

Results

The most common psychological type for RCA clergymen in this sample was INFJ with 15% of the sample in this type (Table 1), with ESFJ and ENFJ nearly as common with 12% each. No one had an ISTP, INTP, or ESTP psychological type. RCA clergymen were almost evenly divided in their preferences for extraversion and introversion, with 51% preferring extraversion. For the perceiving process, those preferring intuition were more common with 60% preferring it, compared to 40% preferring sensing. For the judging process, differences were larger, with two-thirds (67%) preferring feeling and a third (33%) preferring thinking. Finally, for attitudes towards the outer world, over three quarters (76%) preferred judging, while only a quarter (24%) preferred perceiving.

For clergywomen, three psychological types, ISTJ, INFJ, and INTJ, were equally common with 15% of the sample having each type (Table 2). ENFJ was next most common with 12%. No one had an ISFP, INTP, ESTP, or ESFP. Nearly two-thirds (65%) had a preference for introversion over extraversion. For the perceiving process, those preferring intuition were more common, with 62% preferring it. For the judging process, clergywomen were about equally divided, with 46% preferring thinking and 54% preferring feeling. Finally, for attitudes towards the outer world, the great majority (81%) preferred judging, while only 19% preferred perceiving. These percentages are imprecise due to the small sample size.

The psychological type preferences for RCA clergymen and clergywomen among the 16 types were quite similar, as can be seen by comparing Tables 1 and 2. None of the comparisons was statistically significant, using the *I* statistic. INFJ was the most common type for men and one of the most common for women. Although the percentages varied somewhat, the patterns were similar. Clergymen and clergywomen differed more in dichotomous preferences, although differences were not statistically significant, due in part to the small sample sizes. For example, although clergymen were about evenly divided between extraversion and introversion, clergywomen preferred introversion. Clergymen were more likely to prefer feeling, while clergywomen were about equally divided. Preferences for intuition over sensing and judging over perceiving were similar for men and women.

Type preferences of RCA clergymen did not differ significantly from those of PC(USA) clergymen. No differences between the two groups were statistically significant (Table 1). Differences between RCA clergywomen and PC(USA) clergywomen were larger, although most differences also were not statistically significant (Table 2). RCA clergywomen were significantly more likely than PC(USA) women to prefer thinking, and less likely to prefer feeling, with differences significant at $p < .01$. Among the pairs and temperaments, RCA clergywomen were more likely to be in the ST (23%), TJ (38%), and IT (35%) type groups than PC(USA) clergywomen (with 7%, 16%, and 12%, respectively).

RCA clergymen differed significantly in their type preferences from the male US population at large. In complete types, 14% of RCA clergymen were INFJ, as compared to 1% in the US male population, and 11% were ENFJ, as compared to 2% in the population. None were ISTP or INTP, while 8% of men in the US population are ISTP and 5% are INTP. Statistically significant differences were also found in INTJ, with 8% of RCA clergymen having this type but only 3% of US men, and ESTJ, with only 4% of RCA clergy but 11% of US men having this type.

Table 1. Type distribution for clergymen serving in the Synods of New York and Mid-Atlantics of the RCA compared with PC(USA) clergymen.

The Sixteen Complete Types				Dichotomous Preferences			
ISTJ $n = 9$ (10.1%) $I = 1.02$ +++++ +++++	ISFJ $n = 8$ (9.0%) $I = 0.80$ +++++ ++++	INFJ $n = 13$ (14.6%) $I = 1.21$ +++++ +++++	INTJ $n = 7$ (7.9%) $I = 0.96$ +++++ +++	E I S N T F J P	$n = 45$ $n = 44$ $n = 36$ $n = 53$ $n = 29$ $n = 60$ $n = 68$ $n = 21$	(50.6%) (49.4%) (40.4%) (59.6%) (32.6%) (67.4%) (76.4%) (23.6%)	$I = 1.08$ $I = 0.93$ $I = 0.91$ $I = 1.07$ $I = 0.95$ $I = 1.02$ $I = 1.03$ $I = 0.91$
ISTP $n = 0$ (0.0%) $I = 0.00$	ISFP $n = 2$ (2.2%) $I = 0.80$ ++	INFP $n = 5$ (5.6%) $I = 0.83$ +++++ +	INTP $n = 0$ (0.0%) $I = 0.00$		Pairs and Temperaments		
				IJ IP EP EJ ST SF NF NT SJ SP NP NJ TJ TP FP FJ	$n = 37$ $n = 7$ $n = 14$ $n = 31$ $n = 13$ $n = 23$ $n = 37$ $n = 16$ $n = 32$ $n = 4$ $n = 17$ $n = 36$ $n = 25$ $n = 4$ $n = 17$ $n = 43$	(41.6%) (7.9%) (15.7%) (34.8%) (14.6%) (25.8%) (41.6%) (18.0%) (36.0%) (4.5%) (19.1%) (40.4%) (28.1%) (4.5%) (19.1%) (48.3%)	$I = 1.02$ $I = 0.65$ $I = 1.14$ $I = 1.05$ $I = 0.91$ $I = 0.90$ $I = 1.11$ $I = 0.99$ $I = 0.93$ $I = 0.74$ $I = 0.96$ $I = 1.14$ $I = 0.98$ $I = 0.81$ $I = 0.94$ $I = 1.06$
ESTP $n = 0$ (0.0%) $I = 0.00$	ESFP $n = 2$ (2.2%) $I = 0.90$ ++	ENFP $n = 8$ (9.0%) $I = 1.06$ +++++ +++	ENTP $n = 4$ (4.5%) $I = 1.86$ ++++				
ESTJ $n = 4$ (4.5%) $I = 0.88$ ++++	ESFJ $n = 11$ (12.4%) $I = 1.00$ +++++ +++++ ++	ENFJ $n = 11$ (12.4%) $I = 1.24$ +++++ +++++ ++	ENTJ $n = 5$ (5.6%) $I = 1.05$ +++++ +	IN EN IS ES ET EF IF IT	$n = 25$ $n = 28$ $n = 19$ $n = 17$ $n = 13$ $n = 32$ $n = 28$ $n = 16$	(28.1%) (31.5%) (21.3%) (19.1%) (14.6%) (36.0%) (31.5%) (18.0%)	$I = 0.96$ $I = 1.20$ $I = 0.90$ $I = 0.92$ $I = 1.10$ $I = 1.07$ $I = 0.98$ $I = 0.86$

Jungian Types (E)				Jungian Types (I)				Dominant Types			
	n	%	Index		n	%	Index		n	%	Index
E-TJ	9	(10.1)	0.97	I-TP	0	(0.0)	0.00	Dt.T	9	(10.1)	0.77
E-FJ	22	(24.7)	1.09	I-FP	7	(7.8)	0.83	Dt.F	29	(32.6)	1.01
ES-P	2	(2.2)	0.77	IS-J	17	(19.1)	0.93	Dt.S	19	(21.3)	0.91
EN-P	12	(13.5)	1.24	IN-J	20	(22.5)	1.10	Dt.N	32	(36.0)	1.15

Note: $N = 89$ (NB: + = 1% of N).

Table 2. Type distribution for clergywomen serving in the Synods of New York and Mid-Atlantics of the RCA compared with PC(USA) clergywomen.

The Sixteen Complete Types				Dichotomous Preferences			
ISTJ $n = 4$ (15.4%) $I = 3.79$* +++++ +++++ +++++	ISFJ $n = 2$ (7.7%) $I = 0.50$ +++++ +++	INFJ $n = 4$ (15.4%) $I = 0.91$ +++++ +++++ +++++	INTJ $n = 4$ (15,4%) $I = 2.53$ +++++ +++++ +++++	E I S N T F J P	$n = 9$ $n = 17$ $n = 10$ $n = 16$ $n = 12$ $n = 14$ $n = 21$ $n = 5$	(34.6%) (65.4%) (38.5%) (61.5%) (46.2%) (53.8%) (80.8%) (19.2%)	$I = 0.80$ $I = 1.15$ $I = 1.07$ $I = 0.96$ $I = 2.36$** $I = 0.67$** $I = 1.18$ $I = 0.61$
ISTP $n = 1$ (3.8%) $I = 2.85$ ++++	ISFP $n = 0$ (0.0%) $I = 0.00$	INFP $n = 2$ (7.7%) $I = 0.71$ +++++ +++	INTP $n = 0$ (0.0%) $I = 0.00$	\multicolumn{3}{l}{Pairs and Temperaments}	
				IJ IP EP EJ ST SF NF NT SJ SP NP NJ TJ TP FP FJ IN EN IS ES ET EF IF IT	$n = 14$ $n = 3$ $n = 2$ $n = 7$ $n = 6$ $n = 4$ $n = 10$ $n = 6$ $n = 9$ $n = 1$ $n = 4$ $n = 12$ $n = 10$ $n = 2$ $n = 3$ $n = 11$ $n = 10$ $n = 6$ $n = 7$ $n = 3$ $n = 3$ $n = 6$ $n = 8$ $n = 9$	(53.8%) (11.5%) (7.7%) (26.9%) (23.1%) (15.4%) (38.5%) (23.1%) (34.6%) (3.8%) (15.4%) (46.2%) (38.5%) (7.7%) (11.5%) (42.3%) (38.5%) (23.1%) (26.9%) (11.5%) (11.5%) (23.1%) (30.8%) (34.6%)	$I = 1.26$ $I = 0.81$ $I = 0.44$ $I = 1.05$ $I = 3.10$* $I = 0.54$ $I = 0.74$ $I = 1.90$ $I = 1.14$ $I = 0.71$ $I = 0.58$ $I = 1.22$ $I = 2.37$** $I = 2.28$ $I = 0.41$ $I = 0.81$ $I = 1.12$ $I = 0.78$ $I = 1.21$ $I = 0.85$ $I = 1.55$ $I = 0.64$ $I = 0.69$ $I = 2.85$**
ESTP $n = 0$ (0.0%) $I = 0.00$	ESFP $n = 0$ (0.0%) $I = 0.00$	ENFP $n = 1$ (3.8%) $I = 0.28$ ++++	ENTP $n = 1$ (3.8%) $I = 2.85$ ++++				
ESTJ $n = 1$ (3.8%) $I = 1.90$ ++++	ESFJ $n = 2$ (7.7%) $I = 0.90$ +++++ +++	ENFJ $n = 3$ (11.5%) $I = 1.07$ +++++ +++++ ++	ENTJ $n = 1$ (3.8%) $I = 0.95$ ++++				

Jungian Types (E)				Jungian Types (I)				Dominant Types			
	n	%	Index		n	%	Index		n	%	Index
E-TJ	2	(7.7)	1.26	I-TP	1	(3.8)	1.90	Dt.T	3	(11.5)	1.42
E-FJ	5	(19.2)	0.98	I-FP	2	(7.7)	0.63	Dt.F	7	(26.9)	0.85
ES-P	0	(0.0)	0.00	IS-J	6	(23.1)	1.18	Dt.S	6	(23.1)	1.03
EN-P	2	(7.7)	0.52	IN-J	8	(30.8)	1.34	Dt.N	10	(38.5)	1.02

Note: $N = 26$ (NB: + = 1% of N).
*$p < 0.05$.
**$p < 0.01$.

Table 3. Comparing psychological type preferences of clergy in the RCA with clergy in the Presbyterian Church (USA) and US norms.

	Men					Women				
Sample size	RCA 89	PC(USA) 413		US norm 1473		RCA 26	PC(USA) 138		US norm 1531	
	%	%	I	%	I	%	%	I	%	I
Orientation										
Extraversion	50.6	47.0	1.08	45.9	1.10	34.6	43.2	0.80	52.6	0.66
Introversion	49.4	53.0	0.93	54.1	0.91	65.4	56.6	1.15	47.4	1.38
Perceiving process										
Sensing	40.4	44.6	0.91	71.8	0.56***	38.5	35.8	1.07	74.9	0.51***
Intuition	59.6	55.4	1.07	28.2	2.11***	61.5	64.2	0.96	25.1	2.45***
Judging process										
Thinking	32.6	34.1	0.95	56.5	0.58***	46.2	19.6	2.36**	24.5	1.88*
Feeling	67.4	65.9	1.02	43.5	1.55***	53.8	80.4	0.67**	75.5	0.71*
Attitude towards the outer world										
Judging	76.4	74.1	1.03	52.1	1.47***	80.8	68.2	1.18	56.1	1.44*
Perceiving	23.6	25.9	0.91	47.9	0.49***	19.2	31.8	0.61	43.9	0.44*

*$p < 0.05$.
**$p < 0.01$.
***$p < 0.001$.

Table 3, comparing dichotomous preferences among RCA with that of PC(USA) and US normative groups, shows these differences clearly. The percentages of RCA and PC(USA) clergymen preferring intuition over sensing, feeling over thinking, and judging over perceiving were quite similar, while both differed significantly from the population at large. Differences in extraversion/introversion were not statistically significant.

RCA clergywomen, like RCA clergymen, differed significantly from the US female population, preferring intuition over sensing and judging over perceiving. In addition, they were significantly less likely than women in the US population to prefer feeling over thinking. This lack of preference for feeling also set them apart from PC(USA) clergywomen, whose preference for feeling was similar to women in the US population. Differences in intuition were significant at $p < .001$, differences in thinking and judging were significant at $p < .05$, while differences in extraversion/introversion were not statistically significant.

Among the 16 complete types, RCA clergywomen were significantly more likely to be INFJ, INTJ, and ENFJ (15% each) than women in the US population (2%, 1%, and 3%, respectively). In general, RCA clergywomen were more like RCA clergymen than they were like US women with regard to the norms. They were also more like RCA clergymen than they were like PC(USA) clergywomen.

Discussion

Although this study extends the body of research on psychological types among clergy by describing the psychological type profiles from another US denomination, it has two significant limitations. First, the sample size is small, particularly for clergywomen, which limits the reliability of the profiles, and decreases the power for finding differences from other groups of clergywomen. Second, the sample is limited to one geographic area within the denomination, and one that may not be typical of the entire denomination, in general being more theologically liberal than those in other regions. RCA clergy in other parts of the USA and Canada may have somewhat different profiles. Further research with RCA clergy would address these limitations.

Results from the study generally were in agreement with the existing body of research on psychological types of religious professionals. Type profiles were very similar to those of PC (USA) clergymen and clergywomen in the Francis et al. (2011) study, although the clergywomen were significantly more likely to have a preference for feeling in the judging process. The type profiles of both RCA clergymen and women differed from US population norms in ways that were similar to those found in the PC(USA) study. This lack of difference is not surprising across denominations that are more similar in many ways than they are different.

RCA clergywomen were about equally likely to prefer thinking and feeling in how they evaluate information and make decisions. In this they were similar to male (but not female) US norms. In all other comparison groups in the study, RCA and PC(USA) clergymen and PC(USA) clergywomen, as well as the female US norms, the majority were much more likely to prefer feeling. The higher preference for thinking rather than feeling in the judging process among RCA clergywomen may be due simply to a small and unrepresentative sample. However, clergywomen's acceptance in the RCA has been a relatively recent development. Having a preference for introversion, judging in their attitude to the outer world, and thinking rather than feeling in the judging process could have helped ease the way for these pioneer women in the denomination. Further research with larger samples or in denominations in which clergywomen are more established may help understand this anomaly.

Conclusion

This study of the psychological types of clergymen and clergywomen in the RCA extends the body of research to an additional mainline American denomination. RCA and PC(USA) clergymen had very similar psychological types, with the majority in both groups preferring intuition, feeling, and judging. Differences between RCA and PC(USA) clergywomen were significant only in that more RCA women preferred thinking to feeling. Psychological types were similar for RCA clergywomen and clergymen, again similar to the PC(USA) findings. Clergy in both denominations differed in types from the US population at large in similar ways.

References

Francis, L. J. (2005). *Faith and psychology: Personality, religion and the individual.* London: Darton, Longman and Todd.

Francis, L. J., Robbins, M., & Wulff, K. (2011). Psychological type profile of clergywomen and clergymen serving in the Presbyterian Church (USA): Implications for strengths and weaknesses in ministry. *Research in the Social Scientific Study of Religion, 22*, 192–211.

Jung, C. G. (1971). *Psychological types: The collected works, Vol. 6.* London: Routledge and Kegan Paul.

Kiersey, D., & Bates, M. (1984). *Please understand me: Character and temperament types.* Del Mar, CA: Prometheus Nemesis Book Co.

Myers, I. B., & Myers, P. B. (1980). *Gifts differing.* Palo Alto, CA: Consulting Psychologist Press.

Royle, M. H., Norton, J., & Larkin, T. (2014). Stress and psychological type among clergy in the Reformed Church in America. *Review of Religious Research, 56*, 337–338. doi:10.1007/s13644-014-0152-7

Village, A. (2011). Introduction to special section: Psychological type and Christian ministry. *Research in the Social Scientific Study of Religion, 22*, 157–164.

Work-related psychological health and psychological type: a study among Catholic priests in Italy

Leslie J. Francis and Giuseppe Crea

This paper explores the connection between psychological type and burnout among a sample of 155 Catholic priests serving in Italy. Burnout was assessed by the Francis Burnout Inventory that draws on Bradburn's classic model of balanced affect to conceptualise poor work-related psychological health (burnout) in terms of high levels of emotional exhaustion in ministry in the absence of good levels of satisfaction in ministry. Psychological type was assessed by the Francis Psychological Type Scales that draw on the development of Jung's classic model that distinguishes between two orientations (extraversion and introversion), two perceiving functions (sensing and intuition), two judging functions (thinking and feeling), and two attitudes (judging and perceiving). The data demonstrated that higher levels of burnout were experienced by introverts than by extraverts. These findings are consistent with the view that the clerical profession has been shaped by inter-personal expectations that are more readily met by extraverts.

Introduction

The scientific study of work-related psychological health among the clergy has been gaining interest in recent years (see Francis, Gubb, & Robbins, 2012; Lewis, Turton, & Francis, 2007). Two main research questions are of particular concern in this developing research literature. The first research question concerns the conceptualisation and measurement of work-related psychological health among the clergy. The second research question concerns identifying the personality correlates and predictors of individual differences in work-related psychological health among the clergy. The present study addresses both of these questions among a sample of 155 Catholic priests serving in Italy.

Conceptualisation and measurement of work-related psychological health

One of the best established conceptualisations and operationalisations of work-related psychological health is provided by the Maslach Burnout Inventory as proposed by Maslach and Jackson (1986). The Maslach Burnout Inventory assesses work-related psychological health across three domains according to which professional burnout is characterised by high scores of emotional exhaustion, high scores of depersonalisation, and low scores of personal accomplishment.

In the original form of the Maslach Burnout Inventory, emotional exhaustion is assessed by a nine-item subscale. The items describe feelings of being emotionally overextended and exhausted by engagement in professional care. The item with the highest factor loading on this dimension is one referring directly to burnout, "I feel burned out from my work". Depersonalisation is assessed by a five-item subscale. The items describe an unfeeling and impersonal response towards the recipients of professional care. An example item on this dimension is "I feel I treat some recipients as if they were impersonal objects". Personal accomplishment is assessed by an eight-item subscale. The items describe feelings of competence and successful achievement in work with people. An example item on this dimension is "I feel I'm positively influencing other people's lives through my work".

The model of burnout proposed by Maslach and Jackson (1986) and operationalised through the *Maslach Burnout Inventory* has been used (in its original form) in a series of studies among clergy, including those reported by Warner and Carter (1984), Strümpfer and Bands (1996), Rodgerson and Piedmont (1998), Stanton-Rich and Iso-Ahola (1998), Virginia (1998), Evers and Tomic (2003), Golden, Piedmont, Ciarrocchi, and Rodgerson (2004), Raj and Dean (2005), Miner (2007a, 2007b), Doolittle (2007), Buys and Rothmann (2010), Joseph, Corveleyn, Luyten, and de Witte (2010), Parker and Martin (2011), Joseph, Luyten, Corveleyn, and de Witte (2011), and Küçüksüleymanoğlu (2013). The Maslach Burnout Inventory has also been specifically modified for use among clergy and employed in a series of studies, including those reported by Francis and Rutledge (2000), Francis, Louden, and Rutledge (2004), Francis and Turton (2004a, 2004b), Randall (2004, 2007, 2013), Rutledge and Francis (2004), Rutledge (2006), Francis, Turton, and Louden (2007), and Turton and Francis (2007).

One of the key theoretical problems with the Maslach model of burnout concerns giving an account of the relationship between the three components (emotional exhaustion, depersonalisation, and lack of personal accomplishment). One account of this relationship is in terms of a sequential progression, according to which emotional exhaustion leads to depersonalisation and depersonalisation leads to loss of personal accomplishment.

Challenging the adequacy of the empirical foundations for this sequential model and recognising the apparent independence of personal accomplishment from the other two components (emotional exhaustion and depersonalisation), Francis, Kaldor, Robbins, and Castle (2005) revisited the insights of Bradburn's (1969) classic notion of "balanced affect" in order to give a coherent account of the observed phenomena of poor work-related psychological health. Drawing on Bradburn's notion of balanced affect, they proposed a model of work-related psychological health according to which positive affect and negative affect are not opposite ends of a single continuum, but two separate continua. According to this model, it is reasonable for individuals to experience at one and the same time high levels of positive affect and high levels of negative affect. According to this model of balanced affect, warning signs of poor work-related psychological health occur when *high* levels of negative affect coincide with *low* levels of positive affect.

Francis (2005) tested this balanced affect approach to work-related psychological health in an international study conducted among clergy in Australia, New Zealand, and the UK. For research among clergy, they translated the notion of negative affect into emotional exhaustion (measured by the Scale of Emotional Exhaustion in Ministry; SEEM) and the notion of positive affect into ministry satisfaction (measured by the Satisfaction in Ministry Scale; SIMS). Put together, these two 11-item scales form the Francis Burnout Inventory (FBI).

The SEEM drew together items expressing lack of enthusiasm for ministry, frustration, impatience, negativity, cynicism, inflexibility, profound sadness, the sense of being drained and exhausted by the job, and withdrawal from personal engagement with the people among whom ministry is exercised. The SIMS drew together items expressing personal accomplishment, personal satisfaction, the sense of dealing effectively with people, really understanding and influencing people positively, being appreciated by others, deriving purpose and meaning from ministry, and being glad that they entered ministry.

The internal consistency reliability and construct validity of the two component scales of the FBI have been recently tested and supported in a study by Francis, Village, Robbins, and Wulff (2011). More importantly, this study has tested and supported the balanced affect model of work-related psychological health by demonstrating how high levels of positive affect serve to offset high levels of negative affect in order to maintain a form of psychological equilibrium. Although a relatively new measure, the FBI has already been included in a number of studies concerning clergy work-related psychological health, including Francis, Wulff, and Robbins (2008), Francis, Robbins, Kaldor, and Castle (2009), Robbins and Francis (2010), Brewster, Francis, and Robbins (2011), Francis et al. (2012), Robbins, Francis, and Powell (2012), Barnard and Curry (2012), Randall (2013), and Francis, Payne, and Robbins (2013).

Against this background, the first aim of the present study is to explore the psychometric properties of the FBI among a different group of clergy, namely Catholic priests serving in Italy, and to assess the levels of work-related psychological health reported by this group.

Conceptualisation and measurement of psychological type

Among the range of personality theories currently employed in studies conducted among clergy, psychological type theory has played an increasingly central part in recent years within the UK. Psychological type theory has its roots in the pioneering work of Jung (1971) and has been developed and made more widely known through a series of type indicators, including the Myers–Briggs Type Indicator (Myers & McCaulley, 1985), the Keirsey Temperament Sorter (Keirsey & Bates, 1978), and the Francis Psychological Type Scales (FPTS; Francis, 2005). At its core, psychological type theory identifies four key psychological characteristics and distinguishes between two expressions of each of these characteristics. The first characteristic is concerned with the source of psychological energy, and distinguishes between the two orientations of introversion and extraversion. The second characteristic is concerned with the way in which information is gathered, and distinguishes between the two perceiving functions of sensing and intuition. The third characteristic is concerned with the way in which information is evaluated, and the way in which decisions are made, and distinguishes between the two judging functions of thinking and feeling. The fourth characteristic is concerned with the way in which the outside world is approached, and distinguishes between the two attitudes of judging and perceiving.

The orientations are concerned with identifying the sources of psychological energy. In this area, the two discrete types are defined as extraversion and introversion. For extravert types, the source of energy is located in the outer world of people and things. Extraverts are exhausted by large periods of solitude and silence; and they need to re-energize through the stimulation they receive from people and places. Extraverts are talkative people who feel at home in social contexts. For introvert types, the source of energy is located in the inner world of ideas and reflection. Introverts are exhausted by long periods of social engagements and sounds; and they need to re-energise through the stimulation they receive from their own company and tranquillity.

The perceiving processes are concerned with identifying ways in which individuals take in information. For Jung, the perceiving processes were described as irrational processes because they were not concerned with data evaluation, but simply with data gathering. In this area, the two discrete types are defined as sensing and as intuition. For sensing types, the preferred way of perceiving is through the five senses. Sensers are motivated by facts, details, and information. They build up to the big picture slowly by focusing first on the component parts. They are more comfortable in the present moment rather than in exploring future possibilities. They are realistic and practical people. For intuitive types, the preferred way of perceiving is through their imagination. Intuitives are motivated by theories, ideas, and connections. They begin with the big picture and gradually give attention to the component parts. They are more comfortable planning the future than making do with the present. They are inspirational and visionary people.

The judging processes are concerned with identifying ways in which individuals evaluate information. For Jung, the judging processes were described as the rational processes because they were concerned with data evaluation and with decision-making. In this area, the two discrete types are defined as thinking and as feeling. For thinking types, the preferred way of judging is through objective analysis and dispassionate logic. They are concerned with the good running of systems and organisations and put such strategic issues first. They are logical and fair-minded people who appeal to the God of justice. For feeling types, the preferred way of judging is through subjective evaluation and personal involvement. They are concerned with the good relationships between people and put such inter-personal issues first. They are humane and warm-hearted people who appeal to the God of mercy.

The attitudes (often more fully expressed as the "attitudes towards the outer world") are concerned with identifying which of the two processes (judging or perceiving) individuals prefer to use in the outer world. In this area, the two discrete types are defined by the name of the preferred process, either judging or perceiving. For judging types, their preferred judging function (either thinking or feeling) is employed in their outer world. Because their outer world is where the rational, evaluating, judging, or decision-making process is deployed, judging types appear to others to be well-organised decisive people. For perceiving types, their preferred perceiving function (either sensing or intuition) is employed in their outer world. Because their outer world is where the irrational, data gathering process is deployed, perceiving types appear to others to be laid-back, flexible, even disorganised people.

Working within the context of practical theology, pastoral theology, and empirical theology, a series of studies published over the past 20 years has profiled the psychological type characteristics of men and women working in pastoral ministry within various churches in the UK, as illustrated by studies conducted among: clergy within the Church of Wales (Francis, Littler, & Robbins, 2010; Francis, Payne, & Jones, 2001), clergy within the Church of England (Francis, Craig, Whinney, Tilley, & Slater, 2007; Francis & Holmes 2011; Francis, Robins, Duncan, & Whinney, 2010; Francis, Robbins, & Jones, 2012; Francis, Robbins, & Whinney, 2011; Francis & Village, 2012; Village, 2011, 2013), ministers within the Methodist Church (Burton, Francis, & Robbins, 2010), ministers within the Free Churches (Francis, Whinney, Burton, & Robbins, 2011), priests within the Roman Catholic Church (Craig, Duncan, & Francis, 2006), lead elders within the Newfrontiers network of churches (Francis, Gubb, & Robbins, 2009), and leaders within the Apostolic Networks (Kay, Francis, & Robbins, 2011).

Work-related psychological health and psychological type

Early research exploring the connection between work-related psychological health and psychological type was reviewed by Reid (1999), who drew together four unpublished doctoral dissertations and one published study which had assessed the relationship between psychological type and scores recorded on the Maslach Burnout Inventory. The consistent finding across four of these five studies was that individuals with a preference for introversion appeared to be more prone to burnout than individuals with a preference for extraversion. Later findings reported by Myers, McCaulley, Quenk, and Hammer (1998, p. 238) confirmed that introverts recorded significantly higher scores than extraverts on the Emotional Exhaustion Scale and on the Depersonalisation Scale.

Building on this earlier research, a series of seven recent studies have examined the connection between psychological type and work-related psychological health among different groups of clergy. All seven studies have assessed work-related psychological health by means of the two measures of emotional exhaustion and satisfaction in ministry proposed by the FBI (Francis et al., 2005). All seven studies have assessed psychological type by means of the FPTS (Francis, 2005). These seven studies have been conducted among 748 clergy serving in the Presbyterian Church (USA) by Francis et al. (2008), among 3715 clergy from Australia, England, and New Zealand by Francis et al. (2009), among 521 clergy serving in rural ministry in the Church of England by Brewster et al. (2011), among 874 clergywomen serving in the Church of England by Robbins and Francis (2010), among 134 lead elders within the Newfrontiers network of churches serving in the UK by Francis et al. (2012), among 212 Australian clergywomen drawn from 14 denominations or streams of churches by Robbins et al. (2012), and among 266 clergymen serving in the Church in Wales by Francis et al. (2013).

In terms of emotional exhaustion, all seven studies reported significantly higher scores recorded by introverts than by extraverts. Four of the seven studies also reported significantly higher scores recorded by thinking types than by feeling types. One of the seven studies reported significantly higher scores recorded by perceiving types than by judging types. In terms of satisfaction in ministry, six of the seven studies reported significantly higher scores recorded by extraverts than by introverts. Four of the seven studies also reported significantly higher scores recorded by feeling types than by thinking types. Three of the seven studies reported significantly higher scores recorded by intuitive types than by sensing types. The clearest message from these findings is that extraverted feeling types fare better than thinking types.

Research question

The research so far reported on the connection between work-related psychological health and psychological type has been conducted in Australia, the UK, and the USA, and among Protestant, Reformed, and Anglican clergy. The aim of the present study is to extend this research tradition to Roman Catholic priests serving in Italy. Specifically, there are three research questions addressed by this study. The first research question concerns testing the psychometric properties of the scales proposed by the FBI among Roman Catholic priests serving in Italy. The second research question concerns profiling the psychological health of Roman Catholic priests serving in Italy in terms of the levels of positive affect (satisfaction in ministry) and negative affect (emotional exhaustion in ministry) reported by these priests. The third research question concerns testing the association between psychological type and work-related psychological health among Roman Catholic priests serving in Italy.

Method

Procedure

In the context of programmes operated in Rome for Catholic priests on the topic of personality and spirituality, participants were invited to complete a questionnaire covering issues relevant to the programme. Participation in the programme was voluntary and responses to the questionnaire were confidential and anonymous. Full data were provided by 155 priests.

Participants

Three-fifths of the participants were Italians (63%) and the remaining 37% were from a number of other countries; 56% were diocesan priests, and 44% were religious priests. Participants' age ranged from 24 to 76 years with an average age of 46 years (SD = 12.16); 8% of the participants were in their 20s, 29% in their 30s, 30% in their 40s, 21% in their 50s, 6% in their 60s, and 7% in their 70s.

Measures

Psychological type was assessed by the FPTS (Francis, 2005). This is a 40-item instrument comprising four sets of 10 forced-choice items related to each of the four components of psychological type: orientation (extraversion or introversion), perceiving process (sensing or intuition), judging process (thinking or feeling), and attitude towards the outer world (judging or perceiving). Recent studies have demonstrated that this instrument functions well in church-related contexts. For example, Francis, Craig, and Hall (2008) reported alpha coefficients of .83 for the EI Scale, .76 for the SN Scale, .73 for the TF Scale, and .79 for the JP Scale. Participants were asked for each pair of characteristics to check the "box next to that characteristic which is closer to the real you, even if you feel both characteristics apply to you. Tick the characteristics that reflect the real you, even if other people see you differently".

Work-related psychological health was assessed by the two scales reported by the FBI (Francis, 2005). This 22-item instrument comprises the SEEM and the SIMS. Each item is assessed on a five-point scale: ranging from "agree strongly" (5) to "disagree strongly" (1).

Data analysis

These data were analysed by means of the SPSS statistical package using the reliability and *t*-test routines.

Results

Table 1 presents the scale properties of the two indices proposed by the FBI, in terms of the item rest-of-test correlations, together with the item endorsement as the sum of the agree strongly and agree responses. Both scales function with a high level of internal consistency reliability: SIMS, α = .79; SEEM, α = .81. The item endorsement suggests that overall the priests display a high level of satisfaction in ministry, coupled with significant indicators of emotional exhaustion in ministry.

In terms of satisfaction in ministry, over three-quarters of the priests are really glad that they entered the ministry (90%), feel that their ministry gives real meaning and purpose to their life (83%), feel that they have accomplished many worthwhile things in their current ministry (77%), feel that this pastoral ministry has a positive influence on people's lives (77%), and feel that their teaching ministry has a positive influence on people's faith (76%). Over two-thirds of the priests say that they can easily understand how those among whom they minister feel about things (75%), feel that their ministry is really appreciated by people (74%), feel that they deal very effectively with the problems of people in their current ministry (73%), gain a lot of personal satisfaction from fulfilling their ministry roles (71%), gain a lot of personal satisfaction from working with people in their current ministry (70%), and feel very positive about their current ministry (68%).

In terms of emotional exhaustion in ministry, at least one in every five priests say that fatigue and irritation are part of their daily experience (28%), have been discouraged by the lack of personal support for them in their ministry (23%), and recognise that their humour has a cynical and biting tone (20%). At least one in every 10 priests feel themselves spending less and less time with those among whom they minister (16%), are less patient with those among whom they minister than they used to be (15%), feel drained by fulfilling their ministry roles (14%), find themselves

Table 1. FBI: scale properties.

	r	%
Scale of Emotional Exhaustion in Ministry		
I feel drained by fulfilling my ministry roles	.57	14
Fatigue and irritation are part of my daily experience	.48	28
I am invaded by sadness I cannot explain	.49	13
I am feeling negative or cynical about the people with whom I work	.47	12
I always have enthusiasm for my work[a]	.10	57
My humour has a cynical and biting tone	.51	20
I find myself spending less and less time with those among whom I minister	.46	16
I have been discouraged by the lack of personal support for me here	.50	23
I find myself frustrated in my attempts to accomplish tasks important to me	.57	14
I am less patient with those among whom I minister than I used to be	.52	15
I am becoming less flexible in my dealings with those among whom I minister	.53	13
Satisfaction in Ministry Scale		
I have accomplished many worthwhile things in my current ministry	.36	77
I gain a lot of personal satisfaction from working with people in my current ministry	.42	70
I deal very effectively with the problems of the people in my current ministry	.31	73
I can easily understand how those among whom I minister feel about things	.25	75
I feel very positive about my current ministry	.61	68
I feel that my pastoral ministry has a positive influence on people's lives	.47	77
I feel that my teaching ministry has a positive influence on people's faith	.24	76
I feel that my ministry is really appreciated by people	.58	74
I am really glad that I entered the ministry	.51	90
The ministry here gives real purpose and meaning to my life	.55	83
I gain a lot of personal satisfaction from fulfilling my ministry roles	.63	71

[a]This item has been reverse coded to compute the correlations, but not the percentage endorsement.

frustrated in their attempts to accomplish tasks important to them (14%), are invaded by sadness they cannot explain (13%), are becoming less flexible in their dealing with those among whom they minister (13%), and are feeling negative or cynical about the people with whom they work (12%).

Table 2 sets the mean scale scores recorded by the Roman Catholic priests on the two indices of emotional exhaustion in ministry and satisfaction in ministry alongside the scores of the clergy recorded within the previous seven studies in this series. These data suggest that in terms of satisfaction in ministry, the Roman Catholic priests record the highest mean score among the eight groups; and in terms of emotional exhaustion in ministry, the Roman Catholic priests are close to the lowest scores recorded by the eight groups.

Table 3 presents basic information about the type profile of the Roman Catholic priests. These data demonstrate that among these priests there are preferences for introversion (59%) over extraversion (41%), for sensing (81%) over intuition (19%), for feeling (60%) over thinking (40%), and for judging (92%) over perceiving (8%). Table 3 also examines the relationship between the dichotomous-type preferences and scores recorded on the two indices of emotional exhaustion in ministry and satisfaction in ministry. These data confirm that the statistically significant link between psychological type and work-related psychological health is in respect of the orientations. Compared with extraverts, introverts recorded significantly higher scores on the index of emotional exhaustion and significantly lower scores on the index of satisfaction in ministry. These data did not find significant differences in terms of the perceiving process (sensing and intuition), the judging process (thinking and feeling), and the attitudes (judging and perceiving).

Table 2. Mean scores of SEEM and SIMS across seven studies.

	N	SEEM Mean	SEEM SD	SIMS Mean	SIMS SD
1. USA[a]	748	27.8	7.9	44.5	5.7
2. Australia, England and New Zealand[b]	3715	26.0	6.5	43.2	4.9
3. Church of England clergymen[c]	874	27.6	6.6	43.7	4.5
4. Church of England clergy[d]	521	29.6	7.4	39.5	4.9
5. Australian clergywomen[e]	212	24.3	5.9	44.2	4.5
6. Newfrontiers lead elders[f]	134	25.3	6.9	45.2	4.6
7. Church in Wales clergymen[g]	266	28.2	7.4	42.1	5.1
8. Catholic priests in Italy[h]	155	25.5	6.9	42.6	5.1

[a]From Francis et al. (2008).
[b]From Francis et al. (2009).
[c]From Robbins and Francis (2010).
[d]From Brewster, Francis, and Robbins (2011).
[e]From Robbins et al. (2012).
[f]From Francis et al. (2012).
[g]From Francis et al. (2013).
[h]The present study.

Table 3. Mean scores of emotional exhaustion and satisfaction in ministry by dichotomous-type preferences.

	N	Mean	SD	t	p<
Satisfaction in Ministry					
extraversion	64	43.9	3.2		
introversion	91	41.6	5.9	3.0	.01
sensing	125	42.6	4.7		
intuition	30	42.7	6.6	0.1	NS
thinking	62	42.9	3.9		
feeling	93	42.3	5.8	0.8	NS
judging	142	42.8	4.9		
perceiving	13	40.4	6.7	1.6	NS
Scale of Emotional Exhaustion in Ministry					
extraversion	64	23.9	6.4		
introversion	91	26.6	7.0	2.5	.01
sensing	125	25.4	7.0		
intuition	30	25.8	6.4	0.3	NS
thinking	62	25.7	6.8		
feeling	93	25.4	6.9	0.3	NS
judging	142	25.4	6.9		
perceiving	13	26.4	6.7	0.5	NS

Conclusion

Building on an established research tradition among Protestant, Reformed, and Anglican clergy in Australia, the UK, and the USA, the present study was designed to address three research questions among Roman Catholic priests serving in Italy. The first research question concerned testing the psychometric properties of the two scales proposed by the FBI (the SEEM and the SIMS) among Roman Catholic priests in Italy. Both scales reported satisfactory alpha coefficients of internal consistency reliability, suggesting that the instruments transferred satisfactorily to this different population.

The second research question concerned profiling the psychological health of Roman Catholic priests in Italy in terms of the levels of positive affect (satisfaction in ministry) and negative affect (emotional exhaustion in ministry) as identified by the FBI. Closer inspection of the individual items of the two scales suggested a high level of satisfaction in ministry, coupled with significant indicators of emotional exhaustion in ministry. When the mean scale scores recorded by these Roman Catholic priests on the SEEM and the SIMS were set alongside the mean scale scores recorded by clergy in other studies, this group of priests fared somewhat better than the other groups with which they were compared.

The third research question concerned testing the association between psychological type and work-related psychological health among Roman Catholic priests in Italy. Here, the new data confirmed the main conclusion emerging from previous studies among other groups of clergy. This conclusion is that introverted priests experience a poorer level of work-related psychological health in comparison with extraverted priests both in terms of recording higher levels of emotional exhaustion in ministry and in terms of recording lower levels of satisfaction in ministry. The finding that introverts fare less well in ministry than extraverts is particularly interesting in light of the fact that ministry attracts a higher proportion of introverts than extraverts: in the present sample, 59% of the priests are introverts.

The reported observation that extraverts record better levels of work-related psychological health in ministry than introverts is explicable in light of the nature of the roles and functions that priests are called upon to fulfil. The clerical profession requires considerable periods of extraverted activity. Priests can often be seen as the public face of the Church, and as such they are expected and required to engage with a wide range of people across a wide range of contexts. It is such activities that introverts may experience as particularly draining. Those exercising a duty of care for the psychological well-being of priests may need to reflect on ways in which an introverted priesthood can be better resourced and better equipped to respond to the extraverted demands of ministry.

This is the first study to have explored the connection between work-related psychological health and psychological type among Roman Catholic priests serving in Italy. The study has been limited by the sample size ($N = 155$) which has restricted the depth at which the connection between work-related psychological health and psychological type can be explored. Further studies are now needed to build on and to extend this initial enquiry.

References

Barnard, L. K., & Curry, J. F. (2012). The relationship of clergy burnout to self-compassion and other personality dimensions. *Pastoral Psychology*, 61, 149–163. doi: 10.1007/s11089-011-0377-0

Bradburn, N. M. (1969). *The structure of psychological well-being*. Chicago, IL: Aldine.

Brewster, C. E., Francis, L. J., & Robbins, M. (2011). Maintaining a public ministry in rural England: Work-related psychological health and psychological type among Anglican clergy serving in multi-church benefices. In H-G. Ziebertz & L. J. Francis (Eds.), *The public significance of religion* (pp. 241–265). Leiden: Brill. doi: 10.1163/ej.9789004207066.i-495.90

Burton, L., Francis, L. J., & Robbins, M. (2010). Psychological type profile of Methodist circuit minister in Britain: Similarities with and differences from Anglican clergy. *Journal of Empirical Theology, 23,* 64–81. doi: 10.1163/157092510X503020

Buys, C., & Rothman, S. (2010). Burnout and engagement of reformed church ministers. *SA Journal of Industrial Psychology, 36*(1), Art # 825, 11 pages. doi: 10.4102/sajip.v36i1.825

Craig, C. L., Duncan, B., & Francis, L. J. (2006). Safeguarding tradition: Psychological type preferences of male vergers in the Church of England. *Pastoral Psychology, 54,* 457–463. doi: 10.1007/s11089-005-0010-1

Doolittle, B. R. (2007). Burnout and coping among parish-based clergy. *Mental Health, Religion & Culture, 10,* 31–38. doi: 10.1080/13674670600857591

Evers, W., & Tomic, W. (2003). Burnout among Dutch reformed pastors. *Journal of Psychology and Theology, 31,* 329–338.

Francis, L. J. (2005). *Faith and psychology: Personality, religion and the individual.* London: Darton, Longman and Todd.

Francis, L. J., Craig, C. L., & Hall, G. (2008). Psychological type and attitude toward Celtic Christianity among committed churchgoers in the United Kingdom: An empirical study. *Journal of Contemporary Religion, 23,* 181–191. doi: 10.1080/13537900802024543

Francis, L. J., Craig, C. L., Whinney, M., Tilley, D., & Slater, P. (2007). Psychological profiling of Anglican clergy in England: Employing Jungian typology to interpret diversity, strengths, and potential weaknesses in ministry. *International Journal of Practical Theology, 11,* 266–284. doi: 10.1515/IJPT.2007.17

Francis, L. J., Gubb, S., & Robbins, M. (2009). Psychological type profile of lead elders within the newfrontiers network of churches in the United Kingdom. *Journal of Belief and Values, 30,* 61–69. doi: 10.1080/13617670902784568

Francis, L. J., Gubb, S., & Robbins, M. (2012). Work-related psychological health and psychological type among lead elders within the newfrontiers network of churches in the United Kingdom. *Journal of Prevention and Intervention in the Community, 40,* 233–245. doi: 10.1080/10852352.2012.680422

Francis, L. J., & Holmes, P. (2011). Ordained local ministers: The same Anglican orders, but of different psychological temperaments? *Rural Theology, 9,* 151–160.

Francis, L. J., Kaldor, P., Robbins, M., & Castle, K. (2005). Happy but exhausted? Work-related psychological health among clergy. *Pastoral Sciences, 24,* 101–120.

Francis, L. J., Littler, K., & Robbins, M. (2010). Psychological type and Offa's Dyke: Exploring differences in the psychological type profile of Anglican clergy serving in England and Wales. *Contemporary Wales, 23,* 240–251.

Francis, L. J., Louden, S. H., & Rutledge, C. J. F. (2004). Burnout among Roman Catholic parochial clergy in England and Wales: Myth or reality? *Review of Religious Research, 46,* 5–19. doi: 10.2307/3512249

Francis, L. J., Payne, V. J., & Jones, S. H. (2001). Psychological types of male Anglican clergy in Wales. *Journal of Psychological Type, 56,* 19–23.

Francis, L. J., Payne, V. J., & Robbins, M. (2013). Psychological type and susceptibility to burnout: A study among Anglican clergymen in Wales. In B. R. Doolittle (Ed.), *Psychology of burnout: New research* (pp. 179–192). New York, NY: Nova Science.

Francis, L. J. Robbins, M., Duncan, B., & Whinney, M. (2010). Confirming the psychological type profile of Anglican clergymen in England: A ministry for intuitives. In B. Ruelas & V. Briseno (Eds.), *Psychology of intuition* (pp. 211–219). New York, NY: Nova Science.

Francis, L. J., Robbins, M., & Jones, S. H. (2012). The psychological type profile of clergywomen in ordained local ministry in the Church of England: Pioneers or custodians? *Mental Health, Religion & Culture, 15,* 945–953. doi: 10.1080/13674676.2012.676257

Francis, L. J., Robbins, M., Kaldor, K., & Castle, K. (2009). Psychological type and work-related psychological health among clergy in Australia, England and New Zealand. *Journal of Psychology and Christianity, 28,* 200–212.

Francis, L. J., Robbins, M., & Whinney, M. (2011). Women priests in the Church of England: Psychological type profile. *Religions, 2,* 389–397. doi: 10.3390/rel2030389

Francis, L. J., & Rutledge, C. J. F. (2000). Are rural clergy in the Church of England under greater stress? A study in empirical theology. *Research in the Social Scientific Study of Religion, 11,* 173–191.

Francis, L. J. & Turton, D. W. (2004a). Recognising and understanding burnout among the clergy: A perspective from empirical theology. In D. Herl & M. L. Berman (Eds.), *Building bridges over troubled waters: Enhancing pastoral care and guidance* (pp. 307–331). Lima, OH: Wyndham Hall Press.

Francis, L. J. & Turton, D. W. (2004b). Reflective ministry and empirical theology: Antidote to clergy stress? In C. A. M. Hermans & M. E. Moore (Eds.), *Hermeneutics and empirical research in practical theology: The contribution of empirical theology by Johannes A van der Ven* (pp. 245–265). Leiden: Brill.

Francis, L. J., Turton, D. W., & Louden, S. H. (2007). Dogs, cats and Catholic parochial clergy in England and Wales: Exploring the relationship between companion animals and work-related psychological health. *Mental Health, Religion & Culture, 10*, 47–60. doi: 10.1080/13674670601012329

Francis, L. J., & Village, A. (2012). The psychological temperament of Anglican clergy in ordained local ministry (OLM): The conserving, serving pastor? *Journal of Empirical Theology, 25*, 57–76. doi: 10.1163/157092512X635743

Francis, L. J., Village, A., Robbins, M., & Wulff, K. (2011). Work-related psychological health among clergy serving in the Presbyterian Church (USA): Testing the idea of balanced affect. *Review of Religious Research, 53*, 9–22. doi: 10.1007/s13644-011-0003-8

Francis, L. J., Whinney, M., Burton, L., & Robbins, M. (2011). Psychological type preferences of male and female free Church Ministers in England. *Research in the Social Scientific Study of Religion, 22*, 251–263. doi: 10.1163/ej.9789004207271.i-360.55

Francis, L. J., Wulff, K., & Robbins, M. (2008). The relationship between work-related psychological health and psychological type among clergy serving in the Presbyterian Church (USA). *Journal of Empirical Theology, 21*, 166–182. doi: 10.1163/157092508X349854

Golden, J., Piedmont, R. L., Ciarrocchi, J. W., & Rodgerson, T. (2004). Spirituality and burnout: An incremental validity study. *Journal of Psychology and Theology, 32*, 115–125.

Joseph, E., Corveleyn, J., Luyten, P., & de Witte, H. (2010). Does commitment to celibacy lead to burnout or enhanced engagement. *European Journal of Mental Health, 5*, 187–204. doi: 10.1556/EJMH.5.2010.2.2

Joseph, N. J., Luyten, P., Corveleyn, J., & de Witte, H. (2011). The relationship between personality, burnout, and engagement among the Indian clergy. *International Journal for the Psychology of Religion, 21*, 276–288. doi: 10.1080/10508619.2011.607412

Jung, C. G. (1971). *Psychological types: The collected works* (Vol. 6). London: Routledge and Kegan Paul.

Kay, W. K., Francis, L. J., & Robbins, M. (2011). A distinctive leadership for a distinctive network of churches? Psychological type theory and the Apostolic Networks. *Journal of Pentecostal Theology, 20*, 306–322. doi: 10.1163/174552511X597170

Keirsey, D., & Bates, M. (1978). *Please understand me*. Del Mar, CA: Prometheus Nemesis.

Küçüksüleymanoğlu, R. (2013). Occupational burnout levels of Turkish imams. *Review of Religious Research, 55*, 27–42. doi: 10.1007/s13644-012-0057-2

Lewis, C. A., Turton, D. W., & Francis, L. J. (2007). Clergy work-related psychological health, stress, and burnout: An introduction to this special issue of Mental Health, Religion & Culture. *Mental Health, Religion & Culture, 10*, 1–8. doi: 10.1080/13674670601070541

Maslach, C., & Jackson, S. (1986). *The Maslach Burnout Inventory* (2nd ed.). Palo Alto, CA: Consulting Psychologists Press.

Miner, M. H. (2007a). Changes in burnout over the first 12 months in ministry: Links with stress and orientation to ministry. *Mental Health, Religion & Culture, 10*, 9–16. doi: 10.1080/13674670600841819

Miner, M. H. (2007b). Burnout in the first year of ministry: Personality and belief style as important predictors. *Mental Health, Religion & Culture, 10*, 17–29. doi: 10.1080/13694670500378017

Myers, I. B., & McCaulley, M. H. (1985). *Manual: A guide to the development and use of the Myers–Briggs Type Indicator*. Palo Alto, CA: Consulting Psychologists Press.

Myers, I. B., McCaulley, M. H., Quenk, N. L., & Hammer, A. L. (1998). *MBTI manual: A guide to the development and use of the Myers–Briggs Type Indicator*. Palo Alto, CA: Consulting Psychologists Press.

Parker, P. D., & Martin, A. J. (2011). Clergy motivation and occupational well-being: Exploring a quadripolar model and its role in predicting burnout and engagement. *Journal of Religion and Health, 50*, 656–674. doi: 10.1007/s10943-009-9303-5

Raj, A., & Dean, K. E. (2005). Burnout and depression among Catholic priests in India. *Pastoral Psychology, 54*, 157–171. doi: 10.1007/s11089-005-6200-z

Randall, K. (2004). Burnout as a predictor of leaving Anglican parish ministry. *Review of Religious Research, 46*, 20–26. doi: 10.2307/3512250

Randall, K. (2007). Examining the relationship between burnout and age among Anglican clergy in England and Wales. *Mental Health, Religion & Culture, 10*, 39–46. doi: 10.1080/13674670601012303

Randall, K. (2013). Clergy burnout: Two different measures. *Pastoral Psychology, 62*, 333–341. doi: 10.1007/s11089-012-0506-4

Reid, J. (1999). The relationships among personality type, coping strategies, and burnout in elementary teachers. *Journal of Psychological Type, 51*, 22–33.

Robbins, M., & Francis, L. J. (2010). Work-related psychological health among Church of England clergywomen: Individual differences and psychological type. *Review of Religious Research, 52*, 57–71.

Robbins, M., Francis, L. J., & Powell, R. (2012). Work-related psychological health among clergywomen in Australia. *Mental Health, Religion & Culture, 15*, 933–944. doi: 10.1080/13674676.2012.698044

Rodgerson, T. E., & Piedmont, R. L. (1998). Assessing the incremental validity of the Religious Problem-Solving Scale in the prediction of clergy burnout. *Journal for the Scientific Study of Religion, 37*, 517–527. doi: 10.2307/1388058

Rutledge, C. J. F. (2006). Burnout and the practice of ministry among rural clergy: Looking for the hidden signs. *Rural Theology, 4*, 57–65.

Rutledge, C. J. F., & Francis, L. J. (2004). Burnout among male Anglican parochial clergy in England: Testing a modified form of the Maslach Burnout Inventory. *Research in the Social Scientific Study of Religion, 15*, 71–93.

Stanton-Rich, H. M., & Iso-Ahola, S. E. (1998). Burnout and leisure. *Journal of Applied Social Psychology, 28*, 1931–1950. doi: 10.1111/j.1559-1816.1998.tb01354.x

Strümpfer, D. J. W., & Bands, J. (1996). Stress among clergy: An exploratory study on South African Anglican priests. *South African Journal of Psychology, 26*(2), 67–75. doi: 10.1177/008124639602600201

Turton, D. W., & Francis, L. J. (2007). The relationship between attitude toward prayer and professional burnout among Anglican parochial clergy in England: Are praying clergy healthier clergy? *Mental Health, Religion & Culture, 10*, 61–74. doi: 10.1080/13674670601012246

Village, A. (2011). Gifts differing? Psychological type among stipendiary and non-stipendiary clergy. *Research in the Social Scientific Study of Religion, 22*, 230–250. doi: 10.1163/ej.9789004207271.i-360.49

Village, A. (2013). Traditions within the Church of England and psychological type: A study among the clergy. *Journal of Empirical Theology, 26*, 22–44. doi: 10.1163/15709256-12341252

Virginia, S. G. (1998). Burnout and depression among Roman Catholic secular, religious, and monastic clergy. *Pastoral Psychology, 47*, 49–67. doi: 10.1023/A:1022944830045

Warner, J., & Carter, J. D. (1984). Loneliness, marital adjustment and burnout in pastoral and lay persons. *Journal of Psychology and Theology, 12*, 125–131.

Psychological type functions and biblical scholarship: an empirical enquiry among members of the Society of Biblical Literature

Andrew Village

Psychological type theory would suggest that the two perceiving functions (sensing and intuition) and the two judging functions (thinking and feeling) shape the way that readers engage with biblical texts. Previous studies of churchgoers have demonstrated associations between psychological function preferences and preferences for interpretation. Building on this work, the current study examines whether biblical scholars engage with texts in ways that are predicted by their psychological function preferences. A sample of 338 members of the Society of Biblical Literature completed an online survey that measured their subject disciplines and methods of study, four psychological functions and four corresponding text-handling styles. Scholars who used "postmodern" methods such as reader response, ideological criticism or cultural studies were more likely to prefer intuition to sensing and feeling to thinking. There were significant correlations between text-handling styles and psychological type preferences, suggesting that psychological function has some influence on how biblical scholars perceive and evaluate texts.

Introduction

The Society of Biblical Literature (SBL) is the foremost organisation of biblical scholars, boasting over 8000 members and hosting well-attended conferences in the USA and elsewhere. The number and diversity of the 200 or so programme units at the SBL annual conference (Society of Biblical Literature, 2012) are evidence of the multiplicity of approaches within this scholarly discourse. The well-documented shift in biblical studies from the use of mainly historical criticism to a greater variety of methodological approaches (Anderson & Moore, 2008; Barton, 1998; Meyer, 1991; Tate, 2008; Thiselton, 1992) has been accompanied by an interest in "real" readers and what is sometimes referred to as "ordinary hermeneutics" or "cultural studies" (Barton, 2002; Briggs, 1995; Cranmer & Eck, 1994; Fowler, 1985; Freund, 1987; Kitzberger, 1999; Lategan, 1996; Mesters, 1991; Segovia, 1995a, 1995b; Svensson, 1990; Village, 2007; West & Dube, 1996). Biblical scholars are increasingly realising that interpretation is not simply a matter of what lies within a text, but also that it depends on what individual readers bring to the text. The emphasis in biblical scholarship has been on the way that socially derived locations such as gender, nationality, ethnicity and economic status influence the way that biblical texts are understood and interpreted (Segovia, 1995a, 1995b; Segovia & Tolbert, 1995a, 1995b).

Biblical scholars operating within the discourses of cultural studies, ideological criticism or reader-centred criticism are becoming familiar with having to include a self-aware description of their background as a preamble to, or integral part of, their analysis of biblical texts. In some cases, this description may be highly personalised and autobiographical (Kitzberger, 1999). Although every interpreter is a unique individual, it is not unusual for scholars to assume that common social factors may shape the handling of biblical texts in particular ways, hence the notion of discourses such as "feminist", "post-colonial" or "queer" biblical studies. These may be very diverse disciplines, but they share a common understanding that some attention must be given to who is doing the interpretation. Given these kinds of interests, it is perhaps surprising that there has been relatively little attention given to the role of psychology in shaping Bible reading.

Psychological approaches to the Bible draw on insights from the field of psychology to examine texts and their interpretations (Cranmer & Eck, 1994; Kille, 2001). The emphases to date have been on analysing the psychology of Bible characters, the psychological power of biblical images and symbols, the psychological dynamics operating within texts and the interaction of biblical texts on reading communities (Rollins & Kille, 2007). To judge by what is probably the definitive work to date (Ellens & Rollins, 2004), relatively little attention has been given to ways in which the psychology of "real" Bible readers (as opposed to the implied readers of literary-critical studies) may shape interpretation. There are, however, a growing number of empirical studies that examine how people in churches interpret the Bible. Some of these stem from liberation hermeneutics in places such as South America (Mesters, 1980, 1991; Segovia & Tolbert, 1995a, 1995b) and South Africa (Sibeko & Haddad, 1997; West, 1991, 1994; West & Dube, 1996), which have a strong focus on the contexts of Bible readers. More recent empirical and ethnographic studies of readers in Europe and North America (Bielo, 2009; Malley, 2004; Todd, 2005; Village, 2005a, 2005b, 2006, 2007) have shown how people in churches interpret the Bible in relation to their particular social contexts, beliefs, attitudes or tradition.

One strand of these studies has used psychological type to understand how personality influences the way that churchgoers respond to biblically based sermons or Bible reading (Francis & Atkins, 2000, 2001, 2002; Francis & Village, 2008). A number of studies based on self-reported quantitative or qualitative data have now shown that psychological type predicts several different aspects of biblical interpretation among lay people (Village, 2009; Village & Francis, 2005), lay preachers (Francis, Robbins, & Village, 2009) and clergy (Village, 2010, 2012a). The evidence that both lay people and clergy show similar effects of psychological type function preferences on biblical interpretation led Village (2010) to suggest that psychology may also affect how biblical scholars interpret the Bible. He made predictions about the way in which different styles of handling texts might be linked to different psychological type function preferences. This paper reports on a survey among members of the SBL designed to test these ideas.

Psychological type and biblical interpretation

The core of the psychological type model of personality lies in the two processes of perceiving and judging, thought to represent the mechanisms by which individuals acquire and evaluate information (Jung, 1923; Myers & McCaulley, 1985; Myers & Myers, 1980). Jung and those who later developed the model postulated that each of these two processes operates with two functions, and that individuals tend to have a preference for one or other function in each process. For perceiving, the functions are sensing (S) and intuition (N); for judging, the two functions are feeling (F) and thinking (T).

The two perceiving functions are concerned with the ways in which people gather and process information. The sensing function processes the realities of a situation as perceived by the senses, drawing attention to specific details rather than to the wider picture. The interests of those who prefer to use their sensing function lie mainly with practical issues and they are typically down-to-earth and matter-of-fact. The intuitive function, on the other hand, processes the possibilities of a situation as perceived by the imagination, attending to wider patterns and relationships rather than to specific details. The interests of those who prefer to use their intuitive function lie mainly with abstract theories and they are typically imaginative and innovative.

The two judging functions are concerned with the ways in which people make decisions and judgements. The thinking function processes decisions objectively, attending to logic and principles rather than to relationships and personal values. Those who prefer to use their thinking function value integrity and justice, and they are typically truthful and fair, even at the expense of harmony. The feeling function, on the other hand, processes information subjectively, attending to personal values and relationships rather than to abstract principles. Those who prefer to use their feeling function value compassion and mercy, and they are typically tactful and empathetic, even at the expense of fairness and consistency.

The theory linking psychological type and interpretation is based on the idea that preferred ways of psychological functioning might shape the way that readers attend to different aspects of texts (Francis, 1997, 2003; Francis & Village, 2008). Sensers, it is argued, will value interpretations that highlight the details in the text, especially those that draw on sensory information. They will be drawn to factual details and may take a fairly literal approach. Interpretations that begin with a repeat of the text and draw attention to minor details will appeal to sensing types, which will be reluctant to speculate too widely on "what else" the text might mean. For the senser, interpreting a text may be largely about attending to what is actually there.

Intuitives, it is argued, will value interpretations that fire the imagination and raise new possibilities and challenges. They will be drawn to brain-storming links, which may not always be obvious but which draw parallels with analogous ideas and concepts. Interpretations that raise wider questions and that look for overarching or underlying concepts will appeal to intuitive types, who may find the plain or literal sense rather uninteresting. For the intuitive, interpreting a text may be largely about using the text as a springboard to imaginative ideas.

Thinkers, it is argued, will value interpretations that highlight ideas, concepts and abstract principles. They will be drawn to analysing the ideas in a text and the particular truth claims that it makes. Interpretations that apply rationality and logic to highlight theological claims in a text will appeal to thinking types, who may be less interested in trying to understand the characters described by the text. For the thinking type, interpreting a text may largely be about seeing what the text means in terms of evidence, moral principles or theology.

Feelers, it is argued, will value interpretations that stress values and relationships. They will be drawn to empathising with the characters in a narrative and will want to understand their thoughts, motives and emotions. Interpretations that try to understand what it was like to be there will appeal to feeling types, who may be less interested in the abstract theological ideas that might be drawn from the text. For the feeling type, interpreting a text may largely be about applying the human dimensions to present-day issues of compassion, harmony and trust.

These ideas have previously been examined in a study of 404 lay Anglicans from the Church of England (Village, 2007; Village & Francis, 2005) and 718 recently ordained clergy from the same denomination (Village, 2010). Short interpretative statements that were related to a particular healing story in Mark 9:14–29 were developed using psychological type theory and following interviews with around 30 people from a range of Anglican congregations. A pool of items designed to appeal to particular psychological functions were then tested by asking psychological type practitioners to assign them "type-unseen" to one of the four functions in the perceiving and judging processes. Those that were most often assigned to the intended function were used in questionnaires given to lay and ordained Anglicans. Interpretative items were presented in pairs to respondents who, having read the test passage in Mark, were then asked to choose between sensing and intuition interpretations and between feeling and thinking interpretations. The results showed that there were significant associations between preferences for different types of interpretative items and corresponding psychological type preferences in both the perceiving and judging processes. People with high sensing scores (and therefore low intuition scores) were more likely to prefer sensing interpretations to intuitive ones, and vice versa. People with high feeling scores (and therefore low thinking scores) were more likely to prefer feeling interpretations to thinking ones, and vice versa.

The fact that clergy (who have some training in biblical studies) showed similar responses to lay people suggested that biblical scholars might also interpret texts in ways that are related to their psychological type preferences. Village (2010) speculated on ways that different psychological functions might influence how scholars read the Bible:

The sensing function will help scholarly readers to negotiate the complexity of texts, noticing small details that are easily missed. The tendency to "stay with the text" is important to those who examine passages for clues about their historical origin or literary structure. The ability to attend to the sensory information in texts may foster interpretations that highlight the rich meanings associated with words and the ways in which they work together to produce complex patterns of meaning.

The intuitive function may enable scholarly readers to draw on apparently unconnected material from a range of sources to create new insights. The ability to handle Scripture by analogy, allegory and metaphor may foster access to some valuable interpretative traditions that have stressed the "fuller" meaning of Scripture. The ability to see the same underlying ideas expressed in very different ways might foster canonical readings that allow Hebrew Scriptures and the New Testament to witness to continuing truths.

The thinking function would seem to be connected to the traditional skills required for scholarly engagement with Scripture. The ability to analyse logically, discern theological principles and apply objective reason has long been the hallmark of biblical and theological study, suggesting that many biblical scholars will prefer their thinking function when they evaluate ideas. Thinking types should favour rational and logical interpretations but resist subjectivity in their interpretative strategies. In a postmodern environment, with its stress on personal contexts and individuality, the thinking function may help scholars avoid overly subjective or absurd interpretations.

The feeling function may help scholarly readers to identify more closely with the authors of texts, the characters within them or the emotional content of texts. This sort of reading might sometimes produce unwarranted harmonisation of original and current contexts, but its strength is the ability to recognise the commonality of values expressed in Scripture and owned by contemporary reading communities. Scholars who prefer the feeling function may use it to evaluate texts in terms of the relationships, values and ethics of interpreting communities.

This application of psychological type theory to biblical scholarship focuses on the ways in which scholars handle texts, rather than the particular disciplines in which they work. Although there may be a link between disciplines and styles of handling texts, the theory posits a more direct relationship between psychological type and style than between psychological type and discipline. What area a scholar works in may be related to a wide range of factors, but the way they operate within it should be more closely shaped by their general psychological functioning.

This study tests these ideas in two stages: first, by creating new scales that relate to the ways in which the four psychological type functions are predicted to influence how scholars handle texts and second by presenting these scales alongside psychological type scales to a sample of biblical scholars through an online survey.

Method

Developing the text-handling style instrument

Using type theory, four sets of items were produced to reflect how the sensing, intuitive, thinking and feeling functions might influence the way that biblical scholars handle texts. Each set consisted of around 10 statements that were designed to appeal to one of the four functions in the perceiving and judging psychological processes. Items were randomised and tested for validity on a group of 20 psychological type practitioners who were familiar with type theory, but not necessarily its application to the handling of texts. The purpose of the study was explained, and for each item the practitioners were asked to decide which style it represented. Items that were correctly linked to their psychological function by at least 75% of the experts were used to produce the final instrument, which consisted of seven items in each function group.

The chosen items were used as Likert-type items (Likert, 1932) with a five-point response scale ranging from "strongly agree" (= 5) to "strongly disagree" (= 1). The two styles related to the perceiving process (sensing and intuitive) were introduced by the heading:

> How do you study texts in general? Below are a number of statements that describe different ways in which you might operate, or different priorities you might have, when you study texts. Please indicate how strongly you agree or disagree with each statement.

The items were then preceded by "When I study texts I tend to ... ", followed by 14 items (seven related to sensing style and seven to intuitive style) in random order. The two styles in the judging process (thinking and feeling) were introduced by the heading:

> How do you decide about texts? Below are a number of statements that describe different ways in which you might operate, or different priorities you might have, when you come to interpret or evaluate texts. This might be evaluating texts themselves, or other people's ideas about texts. Please indicate how strongly you agree or disagree with each statement

and preceded by "When I decide about texts I tend to ... ".

For each style, the sum of item scores was used as an indication of strength of preference for that style.

The survey

The survey was delivered through Bristol Online Surveys (BOS, 2011) and consisted of 70 questions in three main sections. The first section enquired about disciplines of study, methods employed and styles of handling texts. The second section consisted of a widely used measure of psychological type, the Francis Psychological Type Scales (FPTS; Francis, 2005). The third section included questions related to country of residence, age, sex, educational qualifications and religion. Most answers required participants to click boxes or select from a list and were coded automatically by the software.

Sample

The SBL online newsletters for February and March 2011 were used to invite participation in the survey. The newsletter is circulated to those members who have email addresses in the society membership database, and 338 replies were received by the time the survey closed in June 2011. The respondents came from 24 different countries, though 74% were from the USA. The majority were male (69%) and 50% were aged 50 or older. When asked about their main role, 42% chose teaching/supervision, 25% student, 11% research, 7% minister of religion and 7% retired. When asked to indicate their religious affiliation, 5% indicated none, 7% Jewish, 86% Christian and 2% other. In terms of qualifications, 70% had some sort of doctoral-level qualifications and 60% had doctoral qualifications in biblical studies. It was difficult to tell if this was a representative sample of SBL members, or biblical scholars generally, but the profile suggests a sample of largely religiously affiliated people, qualified in biblical studies and mostly engaged as students, teachers or researchers in the discipline.

Dependent variables

The first set of dependent variables related to the disciplines of study and methods used by participants. The complexity and diversity of biblical studies make it difficult to collect data on subject specialism without being either too restrictive or soliciting open answers that are then difficult to categorise. As a compromise, questions were grouped by broad discipline or methodological approaches, and each of these had options specifying sub-disciplines or particular methods within the general area (see Appendix). Participants could click on any answer in any section, so there was a wide choice of how they could describe their work. For analysis, responses within the main sections were coded as 1 or 0 depending on whether any of the options in the section were chosen. This allowed individuals to be classified according to whether or not they engaged in specified disciplines of biblical studies or used specified methodological approaches. The items related to text-handling styles were scored and used to create four summated rating scales, which were tested for internal consistency reliability using Cronbach's alpha coefficient (Cronbach, 1951).

Predictor variables

The main predictor variables were psychological preferences within each of the four dimensions as measured by the FPTS (Francis, 2005) which are similar to other measures of type such as the Keirsey Temperament Sorter (Keirsey, 1998; Keirsey & Bates, 1978) and the Myers–Briggs Type Inventory (Myers, 2006). The FPTS have been used to study psychological type in a wide range of Christian denominations and other religions in different parts of the world, and seem to function well in these contexts (see, e.g., Burns, Francis, Village, & Robbins, 2013; Francis & Datoo, 2012; Francis, Robbins, & Wulff, 2011; Lewis, 2012; Lewis, Varvatsoulias, & Williams, 2012; Powell, Robbins, & Francis, 2012; Robbins & Francis, 2011; Village, 2011). The instrument consists of 40 forced-choice items with 10 related to each of the four dimensions (E/I, S/N, F/T and J/P) of the psychological type model.[1] Items were presented in pairs and respondents were asked to select the one in each pair that was closest to their preference. Choices were summed to give a score for each function, and preferences assigned according to which of the pair scored highest. Alpha reliabilities for the type scales in this study were E/I = .79, S/N = .74, F/T = .71 and J/P = .76, which is similar to those reported elsewhere from other samples (Francis, Craig, & Hall, 2008; Francis, Robbins, & Wulff, 2008; Village, 2011).

Controls: sex and religiosity

Sex was used as a control variable because of the widely reported difference between men and women in the judging process, where women in most populations are more likely to prefer feeling over thinking compared with men (Kendall, 1998; Myers, 2006). Psychological type has also been shown to be related to a range of religious variables, some of which might in turn be related to interpretative choices (Village, 2010). The questionnaire included a widely used question related to religiosity, "How religious are you" measured on a scale from 0 (not at all) to 10 (very). This was strongly correlated with another item in the questionnaire measuring attendance at religious services ($r = .53, p < .001$).

Research questions and analyses

The analysis of data was designed to answer two main research questions. The first research question was: Did a scholar's psychological type preferences in the perceiving or judging processes predict either their disciplines of study or the methods of study? The usual practice for handling psychological type is to dichotomise the scores to indicate preferences, and this enables the type classification to be produced. This procedure was suitable for comparing the relationships between psychological type and scholarly discipline/method because the latter were measured as binary scores, suitable for contingency table analyses. Counts were used to test associations using chi-squared analysis, though results are presented as percentages for ease of comparison.

The second research question was: Did psychological type scores predict text-handing styles in accordance with theory? Dichotomising psychological type scores results in some unnecessary information loss (DeCoster, Iselin, & Gallucci, 2009), so analyses for style preferences used the scores in each psychological type process as predictor variables. Due to the way that the FPTS operate, scores for sensing and intuition are complementary, as are those for thinking and feeling, so it was necessary to use only one score per process in a multiple regression analysis. The psychological type score used depended on which one was predicted to be positively correlated with a given text-handing style. So, for example, sensing psychological type score was used with sensing style, and intuition psychological type score was used with intuitive style, and so on. Sex and religiosity were included as controls in multiple regression analyses.

Results

Psychological type

Psychological type preferences for this sample are reported in detail elsewhere (Village, 2012b). There was an overall preference for introversion over extraversion, thinking over feeling, and judging over perceiving, but no preference between sensing and intuition. These preferences are similar to those reported in a sample of Anglican clergy (Village, 2011), except for the judging process, where the scholars showed a much higher preference for thinking than the clergy. This was true for both sexes, which is unusual because women in most populations show a preference for feeling over thinking (Kendall, 1998; Myers, 2006). The main types were ISTJ (27%), INTJ (22%) and INFJ (10%), which is as might be expected from this particular population of people who belong to a guild of scholars.

Text-handling style scales

All four scales showed acceptable internal reliability, with alpha values between .70 and .75 (Tables 1 and 2). The high endorsement of some items suggested they may be common features among scholars irrespective of psychological function preferences, whereas most items showed some variation in endorsement. Mean (SD) scores for each were sensing, 24.1 (4.3); intuitive, 25.9 (4.4); thinking, 26.9 (3.6); and feeling, 21.0 (4.5). As expected, there was a negative correlation between sensing style and intuitive style, and between thinking style and feeling style

Table 1. Scales related to perceiving styles for handling texts.

When I study texts I tend to:

Sensing style (alpha = 0.73)	%D	%?	%A	IRC
Use well-tried and familiar methods	11	15	74	0.29
Follow a routine step-by-step procedure	47	20	33	0.36
Establish the facts rather than speculate on possibilities	25	25	49	0.61
Build carefully on what is already known	13	19	68	0.42
Be meticulous in gathering data	6	13	81	0.40
Avoid speculation	47	23	30	0.49
Build knowledge carefully without leaving gaps	19	28	53	0.56

Intuitive style (alpha = 0.77)	%D	%?	%A	IRC
Find unlikely links between texts	19	26	55	0.44
Use my imagination	10	15	75	0.54
Speculate on what might be so	16	22	61	0.43
Try something new	8	20	72	0.63
Draw on ideas from lots of different places	7	11	82	0.42
Look for the ground-breaking idea	23	22	54	0.48
Explore unusual or fringe ideas	23	25	52	0.52

Note: $N = 338$; %D = disagreeing; %? = not certain; %A = agreeing and IRC = item-rest-of-scale correlation coefficient.

Table 2. Scales related to judging styles for handling texts.

When I decide about texts I tend to:

Thinking style (alpha = 0.70)	%D	%?	%A	IRC
Identify weaknesses in hypotheses	3	5	92	0.35
Critique illogical or unfounded ideas	4	7	89	0.39
Not be swayed by what others think of my work	17	29	54	0.38
Expose truth, even if it is uncomfortable for some	1	10	89	0.53
Challenge or confront in the service of truth	7	19	74	0.42
Prevent my values or beliefs clouding my objectivity	22	23	55	0.40
Apply objective criteria impartially	17	28	55	0.47

Feeling style (alpha = 0.75)	%D	%?	%A	IRC
Interpret according to my values	34	19	47	0.55
Decide on the basis of what feels best to me	61	22	17	0.31
Avoid harmful interpretations, even if they are true	77	13	10	0.41
Be aware of how my work might affect other people	18	14	68	0.54
Interpret texts in ways that are helpful to others	15	21	64	0.51
Allow my heart to guide my thinking	53	30	17	0.55
Be sensitive to the emotional content of texts	11	20	69	0.40

Note: For explanation, see Table 1.

Table 3. Correlation matrix for text-handling styles.

Style for handling texts	Thinking	Feeling	Intuitive
Sensing	0.34***	−0.08	−0.35***
Intuitive	0.01	0.24***	
Feeling	−0.21**		

Note: $N = 338$.
**$p < .01$.
***$p < .001$.

(Table 3), indicating these scales may indicate opposite text-handling preferences. Style scores showed some positive correlations across the perceiving and judging processes, that is, between sensing and thinking, and intuition and feeling. It seemed that a sensing style of studying texts was partially linked to a thinking style of evaluating them, and an intuitive style of studying was linked to a feeling style of evaluation.

Associations between discipline or method and psychological functions

Engagement in biblical texts was (as expected) virtually universal, as was work in the areas of hermeneutics and interpretation. Less frequent disciplines were theological or historical/archaeological, while philosophical/ethical disciplines were the least reported. There was little difference between an individual's reported frequencies of using various disciplines and psychological

Table 4. Frequency of discipline or methodological approach by psychological function preferences.

	Perceiving process		Judging process	
	S	N	T	F
(a) Discipline	160	178	253	85
Biblical	97%	96%	98%	93%*
Hermeneutical	88%	84%	85%	88%
Theological	58%	62%	60%	59%
Philosophical	34%	42%	36%	43%
Historical	69%	66%	66%	70%
Social	73%	78%	74%	80%
(b) Method	S	N	T	F
Historical	84%	87%	85%	86%
Literary	78%	90%**	82%	90%*
Reader	48%	70%***	54%	71%**
Ideological	41%	61%***	47%	62%**
Theological	59%	65%	63%	61%
Philosophical	24%	43%***	33%	36%

Note: Table shows the percentage those with a preferred function in the perceiving or judging psychological type process that indicated they worked in a particular discipline or used a particular method. Differences between S/N and T/F preferences tested on counts using chi-squared with 1 df.
*$p < .05$.
**$p < .01$.
***$p < .001$.

Table 5. Linear multiple regression of text handing styles.

	Text-handling styles			
	Perceiving		Judging	
Predictor	Sensing β	Intuitive β	Thinking β	Feeling β
Sex	0.08	−0.10*	0.05	0.01
Religiosity	0.16**	−0.10*	0.06	0.35***
Type scores:				
Sensing	0.39***	–	0.04	–
Intuition	–	0.43***	–	0.13*
Thinking	0.09	–	0.27***	–
Feeling	–	0.06	–	0.24***
R^2	0.19	0.21	0.08	0.22

Note: β = standardised regression coefficient.
*$p < .05$.
**$p < .01$.
***$p < .001$.

function preferences in either the perceiving or judging processes (Table 4(a)). Thinking types showed slightly more frequent engagement with biblical disciplines than feeling types, but in both cases engagement was over 90% and the difference was barely statistically significant. There were more differences when it came to methods (Table 4(b)), with intuitive types being more likely to use literary, reader-centred, ideological or philosophical methods than sensing types. These methods may require imaginative ability, or the ability to work across different disciplines, which would suit intuitives. In the judging process, feeling types were more likely to use literary, reader-centred or ideological criticisms than were thinking types. Evaluation in these disciplines may require more subjective attention to values, and less attention to the objective analysis of data, than with historical-critical, theological or philosophical analyses.

Associations between handling texts and psychological functions

The two perceiving text-handling styles were each positively correlated with the relevant psychological function scores (Table 5, Columns 2 and 3). Those who scored high for sensing psychological function also scored high in the sensing text-handling style, and those who score high for intuitive psychological function also scored high in the intuition text-handling style. There were also significant correlations with religiosity (positive for sensing and negative for intuition), suggesting that text handling that draws on the sensing rather than the intuitive function is more likely to be adopted by religious than non-religious scholars, irrespective of their psychological function preferences.

A similar pattern emerged for the judging text-handling styles (Table 5, Columns 4 and 5), with positive correlations between feeling psychological function and feeling text-handling style, and between thinking psychological function and thinking text-handling style. For feeling text-handling, there was also a positive correlation with religiosity, suggesting that this style of evaluating texts is favoured by more religious scholars, irrespective of their psychological type preferences. There was also a small but statistically significant correlation between feeling text-handling style and intuitive psychological function score which indicated that intuitive types may have been slightly more likely to favour feeling text-handling styles than were sensing types.

Discussion

Subject area, method and psychological functions

There was little or no relationship between a scholar's discipline specialism within biblical studies and their psychological preferences. Perhaps the areas that scholars work in depend on particular interests that arise for a host of reasons, or even by chance. When it came to the methods employed, however, there was some evidence that psychology may be more important in shaping choices. The most obvious trends were between a preference for intuitive perception and those approaches that might broadly be described as "postmodern", in particular reader-centred and ideological criticisms. Within these, examination of associations with particular methods suggested that intuitives were particularly likely to work with cultural studies, autobiographical, post-colonial and postmodern criticisms. It seems that the intuitive function is suited to methods that draw on multidisciplinary discourses that cross methodological boundaries. There was also a link between preference for feeling-type judging and the broad areas of reader-centred and ideological criticism. This may be because these areas are developing more values-based ethics of interpretation which require application of the feeling rather than the thinking function.

Biblical text-handling and psychological functions

The results support the idea that psychological functions may shape the way that biblical scholars handle texts, as suggested by Village (2010). Each of the four different text-handling scales was positively correlated with the corresponding score on the psychological function scales. These different styles of handling texts thus seem to represent the application of different psychological functions applied to the perception and judging of biblical information.

Sensing engagement tends towards establishing fact, rather than speculating on possibilities. It encourages the meticulous gathering of data, building carefully on what is known in a step-by-step process that avoids leaving gaps. Intuitive engagement, by contrast, tends to give more weight to imaginative or speculative possibilities and is more likely to look for unusual or ground-breaking ideas. To some extent, these approaches may be diametrically opposed, but there are some ways of engaging texts that seem common to most scholars, notably the detailed examination of the text (perhaps a more sensing type of approach) and linking to wider trends in Scripture (perhaps a more intuitive-type approach).

When it comes to evaluating texts or interpretations of texts, feeling engagement draws on the interpreter's values, with a strong awareness of the ethical implications of different interpretations. Thinking engagement is more concerned with issues of truth, and the careful application of objective criteria. Again, there are some evaluative practices that seem common to many scholars, such as the need to understand the values that underpin texts (perhaps a more feeling-type approach) and the need to identify weaknesses in hypotheses (perhaps a more thinking-type approach).

The two psychological processes of perceiving and judging are generally held to be related to the ways that information is collected and evaluated (Francis & Village, 2008). Preferences in each process are theoretically independent, but in any given population there may be links between the preferred perceiving function and the preferred judging function. In this sample, the majority of respondents were either STs (36%) or NTs (35%), and this may partly explain the correlations between the different styles of handling texts (Table 3). However, this was not the only explanation and the strongest positive correlations between text-handling styles were between (a) perceiving with a sensing style and judging with a thinking style, and (b) between perceiving with an intuitive style and judging with a feeling style. This may be no accident:

the kind of evidence gathered by using the sensing function may lend itself to the kind of objective, evidence-based decision-making that is the hallmark of the thinking function. For example, the evidence to support textual variants, based on methodical and detailed data collection, may be best evaluated by logical and objective analysis based on wider principles. In contrast, the sort of imaginative evidence gathered using the intuitive function may lend itself to the kind of subjective, value-based decision-making that is the hallmark of the feeling function. For example, the evidence that a biblical narrative can be used to shape present-day ethical decisions, based on the ability to move between different textual "worlds", may best be evaluated by the subjective values of interpreters that are sensitive to the impact of such interpretations on reading communities. In psychological type terms, there may be a general division among biblical scholars between the "ST type" of approach and the "NF type" of approach which seems to be reflected in the distinctions between those methods that arose from "modernist" approaches (such as historical, literary-critical and traditional theological study) and those that arose from "postmodernist" approaches (such as reader-centred and ideological study).

Despite the ubiquity of some ways of handling texts, there are profound differences among interpreters, and this study has shown that some of these can be explained by differences in more general psychological dispositions. This is in line with studies among clergy and lay people that have shown that interpretative styles are related to the core psychological type functions (Francis et al., 2009; Village, 2009, 2010, 2012a; Village & Francis, 2005). The difference with this study is that it has used new scales that relate to the general way that texts are handled by scholars, rather than the specific interpretations of particular passages. Clearly the two are related, especially for scholars where the final interpretations of a text are likely to be the product of explicit methodological awareness and the application of techniques shared by a guild of interpreters operating in a shared discourse.

Biblical studies have seen a flowering of discourses and stormy debates about what constitutes "correct" method. In particular, the postmodern turn has forced scholars to both recognise and accept the "situated-ness" of all interpretations. Although this is often seen as being about social location (Segovia & Tolbert, 1995a, 1995b) or individual history (Kitzberger, 1999), it is also about the "psychological location" of interpreters. The way that interpreters go about their task will affect how they perceive and judge texts, and this will dispose them to favour some methods over others. Scholarly "interpretive communities" (Fish, 1980, 1989) may not form by chance, but may attract people with particular dispositions and interpretive skills that are related to their psychological profile. The members of the SBL form themselves into "like-minded" groups that are termed "programme units" in the annual conference. These units may not be held together solely by a common interest in subject matter or a common methodological approach: they may also reflect the coming together of scholars who share similar ways of psychological functioning that dispose them to handle texts in particular ways, making some forms of discourse seem more "natural" than others. Being able to overtly identify and understand these psychological differences may help scholars with very different approaches to better relate to one another and recognise that biblical scholarship, no less than any other form of engagement with the Bible, is the product of the interaction of readers and texts.

Limitations and future work

This study was based on a relatively small sample of scholars who were mostly from the USA, and it would be good to investigate the relationship of psychological type to scholarly style among a wider range of scholars from different countries and cultures. The self-report instruments used to measure type and interpretative style seemed to have reasonable internal consistency reliabilities for these sorts of psychometric measures, but further refinements would help. Although validity was assessed in the initial construction of the scales, more work is needed to confirm that the scales do indeed tap into the function preferences they are designed to assess. This might be done by more "blind" matching by type experts, or by more detailed qualitative studies on a smaller sample of biblical scholars.

Acknowledgements

I thank the board of the Society of Biblical Literature for permission to advertise the survey in the society's newsletter, and all those colleagues who took time to complete the survey.

Note

1. Those dimensions measured by the type scales but not used in this analysis were orientation (extraversion, E, versus introversion, I) and attitude towards the outer world (judging, J, versus perceiving, P).

References

Anderson, J. C., & Moore, S. D. (Eds.). (2008). *Mark and method. New approaches in biblical studies* (2nd ed.). Minneapolis, MN: Augsburg Fortress Press.
Barton, J. (Ed.). (1998). *The Cambridge companion to biblical interpretation*. Cambridge: Cambridge University Press.
Barton, J. (2002). Thinking about reader-response criticism. *The Expository Times, 113*(5), 147–151. doi:10.1177/0014524602113005 02
Bielo, J. S. (2009). *Words upon the word: An ethnography of evangelical group bible study*. New York, NY: New York University Press.
BOS. (2011). Bristol Online Surveys. Retrieved June 1, 2011, from http://survey.bris.ac.uk/
Briggs, R. (1995). "Let the reader understand". The role of the reader in biblical interpretation. *Evangel, 13*(3), 72–77.
Burns, J., Francis, L., Village, A., & Robbins, M. (2013). Psychological type profile of Roman Catholic priests: An empirical enquiry in the United States. *Pastoral Psychology, 62*, 239–246. doi:10.1007/s11089-012-0483-7
Cranmer, D. J., & Eck, B. E. (1994). God said it: Psychology and biblical interpretation, how text and reader interact through the glass darkly. *Journal of Psychology and Theology, 22*(3), 207–214.
Cronbach, L. J. (1951). Coefficient alpha and the internal structure of tests. *Psychometrika, 16*(3), 297–334. doi:10.1007/BF02310555
DeCoster, J., Iselin, A.-M. R., & Gallucci, M. (2009). A conceptual and empirical examination of justifications for dichotomization. *Psychological Methods, 14*(4), 349–366. doi:10.1037/a0016956
Ellens, J. H., & Rollins, W. G. (Eds.). (2004). *Psychology and the bible: A new way to read the scriptures* (Vol. 1–4). Westport, CT: Praeger.
Fish, S. (1980). *Is there a text in this class?* Cambridge, MA: Harvard University Press.
Fish, S. (1989). *Doing what comes naturally: Change, rhetoric and the practice of theory in literary and legal studies*. Oxford: Clarendon Press.
Fowler, R. M. (1985). Who is "The Reader" in reader response criticism? *Semeia, 31*(1), 5–23.
Francis, L. J. (1997). *Personality type and scripture: Exploring St Mark's Gospel*. London: Mowbray.
Francis, L. J. (2003). Psychological type and biblical hermeneutics: SIFT method of preaching. *Rural Theology, 1*(1), 13–23.
Francis, L. J. (2005). *Faith and psychology: Personality, religion and the individual*. London: Darton, Longman & Todd.
Francis, L. J., & Atkins, P. (2000). *Exploring Luke's Gospel: A guide to the Gospel readings in the Revised Common Lectionary*. London: Continuum.
Francis, L. J., & Atkins, P. (2001). *Exploring Matthew's Gospel: A guide to the Gospel readings in the Revised Common Lectionary*. London: Continuum.
Francis, L. J., & Atkins, P. (2002). *Exploring Mark's Gospel: An aid for readers and preachers using Year B of the Revised Common Lectionary*. London: Continuum.

Francis, L. J., Craig, C. L., & Hall, G. (2008). Psychological type and attitude towards Celtic Christianity among committed churchgoers in the United Kingdom: An empirical study. *Journal of Contemporary Religion, 23*(2), 181–191. doi:10.1080/13537900802024543

Francis, L. J., & Datoo, F. A. (2012). Inside the mosque: A study in psychological-type profiling. *Mental Health, Religion & Culture, 15*(10), 1037–1046. doi:10.1080/13674676.2012.709723

Francis, L. J., Robbins, M., & Village, A. (2009). Psychological type and the pulpit: An empirical enquiry concerning preachers and the SIFT method of biblical hermeneutics. *HTS Teologiese Studies/ Theological Studies, 65*(1), *Art. #161, 7 pages*. doi:10.4102/hts.v65i1.161

Francis, L. J., Robbins, M., & Wulff, K. (2008). The relationship between work-related psychological health and psychological type among clergy serving in the Presbyterian Church (USA). *Journal of Empirical Theology, 21*(2), 166–182. doi:10.1163/157092508X349854

Francis, L. J., Robbins, M., & Wulff, K. (2011). Psychological type profile of clergywomen and clergymen serving in the Presbyterian Church (USA): Implications for strengths and weaknesses in ministry. *Research in the Social Scientific Study of Religion, 22*, 192–211. http://dx.doi.org/10.1163/ej.9789004207271.i-360.38

Francis, L. J., & Village, A. (2008). *Preaching with all our souls*. London: Continuum.

Freund, E. (1987). *The return of the reader: Reader-response criticism*. London, NY: Methuen.

Jung, C. G. (1923). *Psychological types*. London: Routledge.

Keirsey, D. (1998). *Please understand me II: Temperament, character and intelligence*. Del Mar, CA: Prometheus Nemesis.

Keirsey, D., & Bates, M. (1978). *Please understand me* (3rd ed.). Del Mar, CA: Prometheus Nemesis.

Kendall, E. (1998). *Myers-Briggs Type Indicator: Step 1 manual supplement*. Palo Alto, CA: Consulting Psychologists Press.

Kille, D. A. (2001). *Psychological biblical criticism*. Minneapolis, MN: Fortress Press.

Kitzberger, I. R. (Ed.). (1999). *The personal voice in biblical interpretation*. London, NY: Routledge.

Lategan, B. C. (1996). Scholar and ordinary reader- more than a simple interface. *Semeia, 73*(1), 243–255.

Lewis, C. A. (2012). Psychological type, religion, and culture: Theoretical and empirical perspectives. *Mental Health, Religion & Culture, 15*(9), 817–821. doi:10.1080/13674676.2012.721534

Lewis, C. A., Varvatsoulias, G., & Williams, E. (2012). The psychological type profile of practising Greek Orthodox churchgoers in London. *Mental Health, Religion & Culture, 15*(10), 979–986. doi:10.1080/13674676.2012.720753

Likert, R. (1932). A technique for the measurement of attitudes. *Archives of Psychology, 140*(1), 1–55.

Malley, B. (2004). *How the Bible works: An anthropological study of evangelical Biblicism*. Walnut Creek, CA: AltaMira Press.

Mesters, C. (1980). How the Bible is interpreted in some basic communities in Brazil. *Concilium, 138*(1), 41–46.

Mesters, C. (1991). "Listening to what the Spirit is saying to the churches." Popular interpretation of the Bible in Brazil. In W. Beuken, S. Freyne, & A. Weiler (Eds.), *The Bible and its readers* (pp. 100–111). London: SCM.

Meyer, B. F. (1991). The challenges of text and reader to the historical-critical method. *Concilium, 49*(1), 3–12.

Myers, I. B. (2006). *MBTI manual: A guide to the development and use of the Myers-Briggs Type Indicator*. Palo Alto, CA: Consulting Psychologists Press.

Myers, I. B., & McCaulley, M. H. (1985). *Manual: A guide to the development and use of the Myers-Briggs Type Indicator*. Palo Alto, CA: Consulting Psychologists Press.

Myers, I. B., & Myers, P. B. (1980). *Gifts differing*. Palo Alto, CA: Consulting Psychologists Press.

Powell, R., Robbins, M., & Francis, L. J. (2012). The psychological-type profile of lay church leaders in Australia. *Mental Health, Religion & Culture, 15*(9), 905–918. doi: 10.1080/13674676.2012.686478

Robbins, M., & Francis, L. J. (2011). All are called, but some psychological types are more likely to respond: Profiling churchgoers in Australia. *Research in the Social Scientific Study of Religion, 22*, 212–229. http://dx.doi.org/10.1163/ej.9789004207271.i-360.44

Rollins, W. G., & Kille, D. A. (2007). *Psychological insight into the bible: Texts and readings*. Grand Rapids, MI: Eerdmans.

Segovia, F. F. (1995a). "And they speak in other tongues": Competing modes of discourse in contemporary biblical studies. In F. F. Segovia & M. A. Tolbert (Eds.), *Reading from this place: Social location and biblical interpretation in the United States* (Vol. 1, pp. 1–34). Minneapolis, MN: Fortress Press.

Segovia, F. F. (1995b). Cultural studies and contemporary biblical criticism: Ideological criticism as a mode of discourse. In F. F. Segovia & M. A. Tolbert (Eds.), *Reading from this place: Social location and biblical interpretation in global perspective* (Vol. 2, pp. 1–17). Minneapolis, MN: Fortress Press.

Segovia, F. F., & Tolbert, M. A. (Eds.). (1995a). *Reading from this place, volume 1: Social location and biblical interpretation in the United States.* Minneapolis, MN: Fortress Press.

Segovia, F. F., & Tolbert, M. A. (Eds.). (1995b). *Reading from this place, volume 2: Social location and biblical interpretation in global perspective.* Minneapolis, MN: Fortress Press.

Sibeko, M., & Haddad, B. (1997). Reading the Bible "with" women in poor and marginalized communities in South Africa. *Semeia, 78*(1), 83–92.

Society of Biblical Literature. (2012). SBL Annual Meeting. Retrieved August 27, 2012, from http://www.sbl-site.org/meetings/annualmeeting.aspx

Svensson, C. (1990). The Bible and the real reader: World view and interpretive strategies. In G. Hansson (Ed.), *Bible reading in Sweden: Studies related to the translation of the New Testament* (pp. 117–148). Stockholm: Almqvist & Wiksell International.

Tate, W. R. (2008). *Biblical interpretation* (3rd ed.). Peabody, MA: Hendrickson.

Thiselton, A. C. (1992). *New horizons in hermeneutics.* London: HarperCollins.

Todd, A. (2005). Repertoires or Nodes? Constructing meanings in Bible-study groups. *Journal of Applied Linguistics, 2*(2), 219–238.

Village, A. (2005a). Assessing belief about the Bible: A study among Anglican laity. *Review of Religious Research, 46*(3), 243–254. doi: 10.2307/3512554

Village, A. (2005b). Factors shaping biblical literalism: A study among Anglican laity. *Journal of Beliefs and Values, 26*(1), 29–38. doi: 10.1080/13617670500047566

Village, A. (2006). Biblical interpretative horizons and ordinary readers: An empirical study. *Research in the Social Scientific Study of Religion, 17*(1), 157–176.

Village, A. (2007). *The Bible and lay people: An empirical approach to ordinary hermeneutics.* Aldershot: Ashgate.

Village, A. (2009). The influence of psychological type preferences on readers trying to imagine themselves in a New Testament healing story. *HTS Teologiese Studies/Theological Studies, 65*(1), Art. #162, 6 pages. doi:10.4102/hts.v65i1.162, http://www.hts.org.za

Village, A. (2010). Psychological type and biblical interpretation among Anglican clergy in the UK. *Journal of Empirical Theology, 23*(2), 179–200. doi:10.1163/157092510X527349

Village, A. (2011). Gifts differing? Psychological type among stipendiary and non-stipendiary Anglican clergy. *Research in the Social Scientific Study of Religion, 22,* 230–250. http://dx.doi.org/10.1163/ej.9789004207271.i-360.49

Village, A. (2012a). The Charismatic imagination: Clergy reading Mark 9: 14–29. *Pentecostudies, 11*(2), 212–237.

Village, A. (2012b). Psychological-type profiles of biblical scholars: An empirical enquiry among members of the Society of Biblical Literature. *Mental Health, Religion & Culture, 15*(10), 1047–1053. doi:10.1080/13674676.2012.681484

Village, A., & Francis, L. J. (2005). The relationship of psychological type preferences to biblical interpretation. *Journal of Empirical Theology, 18*(1), 74–89. doi:10.1163/1570925054048929

West, G. O. (1991). The relationship between different modes of reading (the Bible) and the ordinary reader. *Scriptura, 39*(1), 87–110.

West, G. O. (1994). Difference and dialogue: Reading the Joseph story with poor and marginalized communities in South Africa. *Biblical Interpretation, 2*(2), 152–170. doi:10.1163/156851594X00196

West, G. O., & Dube, M. W. (Eds.). (1996). *"Reading with": An exploration of the interface between critical and ordinary readings of the Bible. African overtures* (Vol. 73). Atlanta, GA: Scholars Press.

Appendix

Categories for biblical disciplines and methods used in the questionnaire.

Disciplines	
1. Biblical or textual studies	96.4%
Biblical/textual general	46.4%
Hebrew Scriptures	54.7%
New Testament	50.9%
Non-canonical texts	24.0%
Non-biblical Ancient Near East literature	16.0%
Linguistics/translations	18.3%
Other	5.6%
2. Hermeneutics or interpretation	85.5%
Hermeneutics/interpretation general	50.6%
Theological interpretation	27.5%
Exegetical study	59.5%
Interpretation in faith communities	32.8%
Preaching/homiletics	17.8%
Other	4.4%
3. Theological studies	60.1%
Theological general	16.9%
Biblical theology	47.3%
Systematic theology	6.5%
Practical/applied theology	11.2%
Historical theology	15.7%
Other	3.3%
4. Philosophical or ethical studies	38.2%
Philosophical/ethical general	12.4%
Historical philosophy	8.9%
Contemporary philosophy	5.0%
Ethical and moral philosophy	11.2%
Ethics of interpretation	14.5%
Other	3.8%
5. Historical or archaeological studies	67.5%
Historical/archaeological general	20.7%
History of biblical world	43.2%
History: Ancient Near East	24.6%
History: Greco-Roman	31.4%
Archaeology: Ancient Near East	16.3%
Archaeology: Greco-Roman	10.1%
Other	4.7%
6. Social or cultural studies	75.4%
Social/cultural general	19.5%
Bible and ancient culture	51.8%
Bible and modern culture	27.2%
Bible in faith communities	20.7%
Social world of ancient communities	37.9%
Contemporary faith communities	10.1%
Other	2.4%
7. Other	24.0%

Methods

1. Textual criticism	83.7%
Textual criticism general	47.0%
Exegetical study	63.9%
Linguistics	26.9%
Semiotics	8.0%
Other	3.0%
2. Historical criticism	85.5%
Historical criticism general	62.1%
Source criticism	21.0%
Form criticism	21.9%
Redaction criticism	30.8%
Social scientific criticism	35.8%
Other	6.8%
3. Literary criticism	84.0%
Literary criticism general	57.4%
Narrative criticism	46.4%
Structural criticism	13.6%
Rhetorical criticism	35.8%
Psychological criticism	6.5%
Other	4.1%
4. Reader-centred criticism	59.2%
Reader-centred criticism general	23.1%
Reception history	28.1%
Reader response	18.9%
Ordinary readers	10.7%
Autobiographical	2.7%
Psychological	5.9%
Other	1.5%
5. Ideological criticism	51.5%
Ideological criticism general	22.2%
Cultural studies	27.2%
Liberation	10.1%
Feminist/womanist	21.0%
Ethnic	4.7%
Post-colonial	11.5%
Lesbian Gay Bisexual/queer studies	6.2%
Other	3.6%
6. Theological criticism	62.1%
Theological general	21.9%
Theological interpretation	29.9%
Biblical theology	44.7%
Canonical criticism	24.3%
Practical theology	10.1%
Other	1.5%
7. Philosophical criticism	34.3%
Philosophical general	13.0%
Existential	5.3%
Postmodern	17.2%
Deconstruction	7.4%
Post-structuralist	5.3%
Other	4.1%
8. Other	11.2%

Note: Scholars often work in multiple disciplines and use a variety of textual methods. Each respondent could tick any of the (unnumbered) sub-categories. For main (numbered) headings, the table shows the percentage ($n = 338$) who selected at least one sub-category in that group.

Psychological type differences between churchgoers and church-leavers

Matthew J. Baker

Differences in psychological type were examined among three samples taken from the online Personality and Belief in God Survey. All three samples consisted of individuals who grew up attending church as a child. The first sample was made up of 2326 individuals who continue to attend church as adults (1137 females and 1189 males), the second was made up of 10,515 individuals who no longer attend church and are now atheists or agnostics (2677 females and 7838 males), and the third was made up of 1977 individuals who no longer attend church yet still retain some sort of belief in God (1134 females and 843 males). Of the three groups, the atheist/agnostic church-leavers differed the most from current churchgoers in terms of psychological type. Compared to the female churchgoers, the types most significantly over-represented among the female atheist/agnostic church-leavers were ISTP ($I = 3.79$), INTP ($I = 2.29$), and ISTJ (introversion, sensing, thinking, and judging) ($I = 1.91$). Compared to the male churchgoers, the types most significantly over-represented among the male atheist/agnostic church-leavers were ISTP ($I = 3.20$), ESTP ($I = 2.19$), and INTP ($I = 1.81$). These findings support the hypothesis that psychological type plays a role in church-leaving, particularly among those who become atheists or agnostics.

Introduction

One of the key findings of the 2008 American Religious Identification Survey is that Christianity, although still the dominant religion in America, is on the decline and that that decline is not due to the growth of non-Christian religions, but, rather, is due to individuals leaving organised forms of Christianity and becoming non-religious (Kosmin & Keysar, 2009). This trend is by no means a new one and, as such, researchers have been trying to understand the reasons behind church-leaving and apostasy for many decades now. To date, explanations have included rebellion against parents and traditional values by young people (Caplovitz & Sherrow, 1977), intellectualism and a low emphasis on religion in the home during childhood (Hunsberger & Brown, 1984), and simple demographic conditions such as being a young, single, male, city-dweller with a higher education (Hadaway & Roof, 1988).

More recently however, it has been suggested that innate personality differences might also play a role and that psychological type theory in particular might prove to be a useful model when it comes to understanding why some people end up leaving church while others do not (Francis & Robbins, 2012). Psychological type theory, originally proposed by Jung (1971) and developed by others, holds that personality differences can be best explained in terms of four dichotomies: extraversion (E) vs introversion (I), sensing (S) vs intuition (N), thinking (T) vs feeling (F), judging (J) vs perceiving (P). The first dichotomy, extraversion (E) vs introversion (I), is concerned with how individuals obtain their energy with extroverts preferring to draw energy from the outer world of people and things and introverts preferring to draw energy from the inner world of ideas. The second dichotomy, sensing (S) vs intuition (N), is concerned with how individuals perceive the world, with sensors preferring to focus on the details and on present realities and intuitives preferring to focus on the "big picture" and on future possibilities. The third dichotomy, thinking (T) vs feeling (F), is concerned with how individuals reach their judgements with thinkers preferring to rely on objective logic and feelers preferring to rely on their subjective appreciation of the personal and interpersonal factors involved. The fourth and final dichotomy, judging (J) vs perceiving (P), is concerned with how individuals approach day-to-day life with judgers preferring an organised and planned approach and perceivers preferring a more flexible and spontaneous approach. Taken together, an individual's preference on each of the four dichotomies generates one of 16 discrete psychological types (e.g., ESTJ).

Over the last decade, psychological type theory has been increasingly used to explore various issues related to the psychology of religion. Areas of empirical research have included examining psychological type's role in attitude towards Christianity (e.g., Francis, Jones & Craig, 2004), profiling members of the Christian clergy (e.g., Francis, Craig, Whinney, Tilley, & Slater, 2007), and comparing Christian churchgoers to the general population (e.g., Robbins & Francis, 2011). The growing consensus view from these studies is that Christian churches tend towards preferences for introversion, sensing, feeling, and judging (ISFJ). More recently, several studies have focused on non-Christian religious groups as well, including the psychological type profiling of Buddhists (Silver, Ross, & Francis, 2012), Muslims (Francis & Datoo, 2012), and Neopagans (Williams, Francis, Billington, & Robbins, 2012). However, more data are needed before any major conclusions can be made about these non-Christian religious groups.

Only one study to date has focused on psychological type and the non-religious. Baker and Robbins (2012) compared the psychological type of 10,627 American atheists to the 3009 members that comprise the US national representative sample and found a tendency among atheists towards preferences for introversion, thinking, and judging (I_TJ). However, this study had a major weakness, in that the two samples used were not ideal for making a comparison due to major differences in data collection and measurement. The data for the atheists were collected online in 2011 and 2012 using the Francis Psychological Types Scales (FPTS), whereas the data for the national representative samples were collected offline in 1996 using the Myers–Briggs Type Indicator®. In addition to this, it is important to note that Baker and Robbins (2012) focused on atheists in general, and thus the sample included both individuals who had never attended church as well as those who had. Therefore, the results are not directly applicable to the present topic of church-leavers.

The first study to use psychological type theory to examine directly issues related to church-leaving was Francis and Robbins (2012). This study, based on 1867 churchgoers, measured both psychological type and overall satisfaction with one's congregation. The data confirmed a general leaning towards ISFJ among churchgoers. It also demonstrated for the first time that those who hold the opposite preferences, in particular intuition, thinking, and perceiving (_NTP), feel less satisfied within their congregations. This feeling of "not fitting in" would certainly give such individuals a strong reason for leaving altogether. One might therefore predict that preferences for intuition, thinking, and perceiving (_NTP) would be common among those who do actually end up leaving church.

Further evidence that church-leavers might have a tendency towards preferences for thinking and perceiving (__TP), if not intuition (N), can be found in research based on the five-factor model, a personality model with certain similarities to the psychological type model. In a large ($N = 21,715$) meta-analysis of the literature on personality and religion, Saroglou (2010) found that two basic personality traits, agreeableness and conscientiousness, are positively correlated with high levels of religiousness on a consistent basis across gender, age, and culture. These two traits correlate with feeling (F) and judging (J) in the psychological type model (Myers, McCaulley, Quenk, & Hammer, 2003, p. 178) and thus one would expect to find greater preferences for feeling and judging (__FJ) among those who are religious and greater preferences for thinking and perceiving (__TP) among those who are not. It could also be argued that a tendency towards thinking and perceiving (__TP) would be especially strong among atheist church-leavers. Atheists are known to rely heavily on logic and rational reasoning and also to be less conformist than religious individuals (Caldwell-Harris, 2012, pp. 10–11), traits that match the descriptions of thinking (T) and perceiving (P), respectively.

The aim of the present study is to build on the work of Francis and Robbins (2012) by testing to see whether or not church-leavers do indeed tend towards preferences for intuition, thinking, and perceiving (_NTP) by comparing church-leavers directly with current churchgoers. By separating atheist and agnostic church-leavers from those church-leavers who still retain some sort of belief in God, the present study also aims to build on the work of Baker and Robbins (2012) in trying to determine which psychological types are most common among atheists and agnostics in particular.

Method

Procedure

During 2011 and 2012, the Personality and Belief in God Survey was made available online and individuals over the age of 18 were invited to participate via social media websites using a snowball sampling technique. From the data collected, three samples were extracted for the present study, all of which consisted of individuals who indicated that they regularly attended a Christian place of worship for at least one full year prior to the age of 19. The churchgoing sample was based on those who indicated that they currently attend a Christian place of worship at least six times per year. The atheist/agnostic sample was based on those who agreed with the statement "I do not believe in any sort of God, gods, or Higher Power" and/or selected "atheist" or "agnostic" as the word that best described their current stance on God. The third sample was based on those who indicated that they still believe in some sort of God or Higher Power but no longer attend church regularly. This final, "believing but not belonging" group included stay-at-home Christians, deists, and neopagans, as well as those who consider themselves "spiritual but not religious". However, it did not include those who converted to another major world religion such as Islam, Judaism, Hinduism, or Buddhism.

Participants

The churchgoing sample consisted of 2326 individuals (1137 females and 1189 males), the atheist/agnostic sample consisted of 10,515 individuals (2677 females and 7838 males), and the "believing but not belonging" sample consisted of 1977 individuals (1134 females and 843 males). Analysis of the visitor statistics for the survey website indicated that the majority of the participants accessed the study via Facebook, Reddit (a social news website), or Pharyngula (a popular atheist blog written by biologist PZ Myers).

The three samples were all very similar in terms of age with the churchgoing and "believing but not belonging" samples having a mean age of 35 (with standard deviations of 13 and 12, respectively) and the atheist/agnostic sample having a mean age of 34 (SD = 12). The samples were also quite similar with regard to nationality and ethnicity, although the atheist/agnostic sample stood out as being slightly more Caucasian (90% as opposed to 87% for the churchgoers and 86% for the "believing but not belonging" group) and the churchgoer sample stood out as being slightly more American (77% as opposed to 72% for the atheists/agnostics and 73% for the "believing but not belonging" group).

The most important difference between the three samples was sex, with the atheist/agnostic sample having a much larger percentage of males than the other two samples. Because of this imbalance and because sex is known to be a factor in psychological type differences (Myers et al., 2003, p. 122), each sample was divided into male and female subsamples for the data analysis.

Measure

Psychological type was assessed by the FPTS (Francis, 2005) which were included as part of the Personality and Belief in God Survey. This 40-item instrument comprises four sets of 10 forced-choice items related to each of the four components of psychological type: extraversion vs introversion, sensing vs intuition, thinking vs feeling, and judging vs perceiving. Recent studies have demonstrated that this instrument functions well in terms of reliability. For example, Francis, Craig, and Hall (2008) reported alpha coefficients of .83 for the E–I Scale, .76 for the S–N Scale, .73 for the T–F Scale, and .79 for the J–P Scale.

Data analysis

Because the 16 psychological types are not distributed equally within the general population (Myers et al., 2003, p. 122), the type distribution of any given sample is expected to be uneven with some types appearing in greater number than other types. Therefore, the percentages of each psychological type within a given sample are of less importance than how those percentages compare to a control sample. Thus, for the present study, the churchgoing sample was considered the control group and the other two samples were compared to it with a focus on which types were the most over-represented and under-represented. The research literature on psychological type has developed the distinctive method of displaying the results of such type comparisons in the form of "type tables". Type tables are designed to test the statistical significance of over-representations and under-representations between groups by means of the selection ratio (I), an extension of the chi-square, and this convention was used in the present study.

Results

The four scales of the FPTS achieved satisfactory alpha coefficients according to DeVellis (2003): extraversion vs introversion .80; sensing vs intuition .65; thinking vs feeling .70; judging vs perceiving .74.

Table 1 presents the type distribution for the 1137 female churchgoers. These data demonstrated that the female churchgoers displayed overall preferences for introversion (63%) over extraversion (37%), sensing (60%) over intuition (40%), feeling (54%) over thinking (46%), and judging (82%) over perceiving (18%). In terms of the 16 discreet types, the two most common types among the female churchgoers were introversion, sensing, thinking, and judging (ISTJ) (20%) and ISFJ (16%), and the two least common types were ISTP (1%) and ESTP (1%).

Table 1. Type distribution for female churchgoers.

The Sixteen Complete Types

ISTJ	ISFJ	INFJ	INTJ
n = 224	n = 182	n = 101	n = 95
(19.7%)	(16.0%)	(8.9%)	(8.4%)
+++++	+++++	+++++	+++++
+++++	+++++	++++	+++
+++++	+++++		
+++++	+		

ISTP	ISFP	INFP	INTP
n = 13	n = 17	n = 61	n = 26
(1.1%)	(1.5%)	(5.4%)	(2.3%)
+	++	+++++	++

ESTP	ESFP	ENFP	ENTP
n = 16	n = 19	n = 40	n = 17
(1.4%)	(1.7%)	(3.5%)	(1.5%)
+	++	++++	++

ESTJ	ESFJ	ENFJ	ENTJ
n = 96	n = 120	n = 75	n = 35
(8.4%)	(10.6%)	(6.6%)	(3.1%)
+++++	+++++	+++++	+++
+++	+++++	++	
	+		

Dichotomous Preferences

E	n = 418	(36.8%)
I	n = 719	(63.2%)
S	n = 687	(60.4%)
N	n = 450	(39.6%)
T	n = 522	(45.9%)
F	n = 615	(54.1%)
J	n = 928	(81.6%)
P	n = 209	(18.4%)

Pairs and Temperaments

IJ	n = 602	(52.9%)
IP	n = 117	(10.3%)
EP	n = 92	(8.1%)
EJ	n = 326	(28.7%)
ST	n = 349	(30.7%)
SF	n = 338	(29.7%)
NF	n = 277	(24.4%)
NT	n = 173	(15.2%)
SJ	n = 622	(54.7%)
SP	n = 65	(5.7%)
NP	n = 144	(12.7%)
NJ	n = 306	(26.9%)
TJ	n = 450	(39.6%)
TP	n = 72	(6.3%)
FP	n = 137	(12.0%)
FJ	n = 478	(42.0%)
IN	n = 283	(24.9%)
EN	n = 167	(14.7%)
IS	n = 436	(38.3%)
ES	n = 251	(22.1%)
ET	n = 164	(14.4%)
EF	n = 254	(22.3%)
IF	n = 361	(31.8%)
IT	n = 358	(31.5%)

Jungian Types (E)

	n	%
E-TJ	131	11.5
E-FJ	195	17.2
ES-P	35	3.1
EN-P	57	5.0

Jungian Types (I)

	n	%
I-TP	39	3.4
I-FP	78	6.9
IS-J	406	35.7
IN-J	196	17.2

Dominant Types

	n	%
Dt.T	170	15.0
Dt.F	273	24.0
Dt.S	441	38.8
Dt.N	253	22.3

Note: N = 1137 (NB: + = 1% of N).

Table 2. Type distribution for female atheist/agnostic church-leavers.

The Sixteen Complete Types

ISTJ	ISFJ	INFJ	INTJ
n = 1009	n = 203	n = 135	n = 328
(37.7%)	(7.6%)	(5.0%)	(12.3%)
I = 1.91***	I = 0.47***	I = 0.57***	I = 1.47***
+++++++	+++++	+++++	+++++
+++++++	+++		+++++
++++++			++
++++++			
++++++			
++++++			

ISTP	ISFP	INFP	INTP
n = 116	n = 43	n = 83	n = 140
(4.3%)	(1.6%)	(3.1%)	(5.2%)
I = 3.79***	I = 1.07	I = 0.58***	I = 2.29***
++++	++	+++	+++++

ESTP	ESFP	ENFP	ENTP
n = 50	n = 22	n = 38	n = 56
(1.9%)	(0.8%)	(1.4%)	(2.1%)
I = 1.33	I = 0.49*	I = 0.40***	I = 1.40
++	+	+	++

ESTJ	ESFJ	ENFJ	ENTJ
n = 248	n = 82	n = 41	n = 83
(9.3%)	(3.1%)	(1.5%)	(3.1%)
I = 1.10	I = 0.29***	I = 0.23	I = 1.01
+++++	+++	++	+++
++++			

Dichotomous Preferences

	n	%	I
E	260	(23.2%)	I = 0.63***
I	2057	(76.8%)	I = 1.22***
S	1773	(66.2%)	I = 1.10***
N	904	(33.8%)	I = 0.85***
T	2030	(75.8%)	I = 1.65***
F	647	(24.2%)	I = 0.45***
J	2129	(79.5%)	I = 0.97
P	548	(20.5%)	I = 1.11

Pairs and Temperaments

	n	%	I
IJ	1675	(62.6%)	I = 1.18***
IP	382	(14.3%)	I = 1.39***
EP	166	(6.2%)	I = 0.77*
EJ	454	(17.0%)	I = 0.59***
ST	1423	(53.2%)	I = 1.73***
SF	350	(13.1%)	I = 0.44***
NF	297	(11.1%)	I = 0.46***
NT	607	(22.7%)	I = 1.49***
SJ	1542	(57.6%)	I = 1.05
SP	231	(8.6%)	I = 1.51**
NP	317	(11.8%)	I = 0.93
NJ	587	(21.9%)	I = 0.81***
TJ	1668	(62.3%)	I = 1.57***
TP	362	(13.5%)	I = 2.14***
FP	86	(6.9%)	I = 0.58***
FJ	461	(17.2%)	I = 0.41***
IN	686	(25.6%)	I = 1.03
EN	218	(8.1%)	I = 0.55***
IS	1371	(51.2%)	I = 1.34***
ES	402	(15.0%)	I = 0.68***
ET	437	(16.3%)	I = 1.13
EF	183	(6.8%)	I = 0.31***
IF	464	(17.3%)	I = 0.55***
IT	1593	(59.5%)	I = 1.89***

Jungian Types (E)

	n	%	Index
E-TJ	331	12.4	1.07
E-FJ	123	4.6	0.27***
ES-P	72	2.7	0.87
EN-P	94	3.5	0.70*

Jungian Types (I)

	n	%	Index
I-TP	256	9.6	2.79***
I-FP	126	4.7	0.69**
IS-J	1212	45.3	1.27***
IN-J	463	17.3	1.00

Dominant Types

	n	%	Index
Dt.T	587	21.9	1.47***
Dt.F	249	9.3	0.39***
Dt.S	1284	48.0	1.24***
Dt.N	557	20.8	0.94

Note: N = 2677 (NB: + = 1% of N).
*p < 0.05.
**p < 0.01.
***p < 0.001.

Table 3. Type distribution for female "believing but not belonging" church-leavers.

The Sixteen Complete Types					Dichotomous Preferences		
ISTJ $n=240$ (21.2%) $I=1.07$ +++++ +++++ +++++ +++++ +	ISFJ $n=158$ (13.9%) $I=0.87$ +++++ +++++ ++++	INFJ $n=118$ (10.4%) $I=1.17$ +++++ +++++	INTJ $n=134$ (11.8%) $I=1.41**$ +++++ +++++ ++	E I S N T F J P	$n=333$ $n=801$ $n=574$ $n=560$ $n=578$ $n=556$ $n=870$ $n=264$	(29.4%) (70.6%) (50.6%) (49.4%) (51.0%) (49.0%) (76.7%) (23.3%)	$I=0.80***$ $I=1.12***$ $I=0.84***$ $I=1.25***$ $I=1.11*$ $I=0.91*$ $I=0.94**$ $I=1.27**$
ISTP $n=16$ (1.4%) $I=1.23$ +	ISFP $n=15$ (1.3%) $I=0.88$ +	INFP $n=67$ (5.9%) $I=1.10$ +++++ +	INTP $n=53$ (4.7%) $I=2.04***$ +++++	\multicolumn{3}{c}{Pairs and Temperaments}		
				IJ IP EP EJ	$n=650$ $n=151$ $n=113$ $n=220$	(57.3%) (13.3%) (10.0%) (19.4%)	$I=1.08*$ $I=1.29*$ $I=1.23$ $I=0.68***$
				ST SF NF NT	$n=325$ $n=249$ $n=307$ $n=253$	(28.7%) (22.0%) (27.1%) (22.3%)	$I=0.93$ $I=0.74***$ $I=1.11$ $I=1.47***$
ESTP $n=11$ (1.0%) $I=0.69$ +	ESFP $n=17$ (1.5%) $I=0.90$ ++	ENFP $n=60$ (5.3%) $I=1.50*$ +++++	ENTP $n=25$ (2.2%) $I=1.47$ ++	SJ SP NP NJ	$n=515$ $n=59$ $n=205$ $n=355$	(45.4%) (5.2%) (18.1%) (31.3%)	$I=0.83***$ $I=0.91$ $I=1.43***$ $I=1.16*$
				TJ TP FP FJ	$n=473$ $n=105$ $n=159$ $n=397$	(41.7%) (9.3%) (14.0%) (35.0%)	$I=1.05$ $I=1.46**$ $I=1.16$ $I=0.83***$
ESTJ $n=58$ (5.1%) $I=0.61***$ +++++	ESFJ $n=59$ (5.2%) $I=0.49***$ +++++	ENFJ $n=62$ (5.5%) $I=0.83$ +++++ +	ENTJ $n=41$ (3.6%) $I=1.17$ ++++	IN EN IS ES	$n=372$ $n=188$ $n=429$ $n=145$	(32.8%) (16.6%) (37.8%) (12.8%)	$I=1.32***$ $I=1.13$ $I=0.99$ $I=0.58***$
				ET EF IF IT	$n=135$ $n=198$ $n=358$ $n=443$	(11.9%) (17.5%) (31.6%) (39.1%)	$I=0.83$ $I=0.78**$ $I=0.99$ $I=1.24***$

Jungian Types (E)				Jungian Types (I)				Dominant Types			
	n	%	Index		n	%	Index		n	%	Index
E-TJ	99	8.7	0.76*	I-TP	69	6.1	1.77**	Dt.T	168	14.8	0.99
E-FJ	121	10.7	0.62***	I-FP	82	7.2	1.05	Dt.F	203	17.9	0.75***
ES-P	28	2.5	0.80	IS-J	398	35.1	0.98	Dt.S	426	37.6	0.97
EN-P	85	7.5	1.50*	IN-J	252	22.2	1.29**	Dt.N	337	29.7	1.34***

Note: $N=1134$ (NB: $+ = 1\%$ of N).
*$p < 0.05$.
**$p < 0.01$.
***$p < 0.001$.

Table 4. Type distribution for male churchgoers.

The Sixteen Complete Types					Dichotomous Preferences		
ISTJ	ISFJ	INFJ	INTJ	E	$n = 358$	(30.1%)
$n = 308$	$n = 83$	$n = 72$	$n = 194$	I	$n = 831$	(69.9%)
(25.9%)	(7.0%)	(6.1%)	(16.3%)			
+++++	+++++	+++++	+++++	S	$n = 611$	(51.4%)
+++++	++	+	+++++	N	$n = 578$	(48.6%)
+++++			+++++			
+++++			+	T	$n = 812$	(68.3%)
+++++				F	$n = 377$	(31.7%)
+						
				J	$n = 906$	(76.2%)
				P	$n = 283$	(23.8%)
ISTP	ISFP	INFP	INTP		Pairs and Temperaments	
$n = 30$	$n = 19$	$n = 70$	$n = 55$			
(2.5%)	(1.6%)	(5.9%)	(4.6%)	IJ	$n = 657$	(55.3%)
+++	++	+++++	+++++	IP	$n = 174$	(14.6%)
		+		EP	$n = 109$	(9.2%)
				EJ	$n = 249$	(20.9%)
				ST	$n = 448$	(37.7%)
				SF	$n = 163$	(13.7%)
				NF	$n = 214$	(18.0%)
ESTP	ESFP	ENFP	ENTP	NT	$n = 364$	(30.6%)
$n = 13$	$n = 17$	$n = 40$	$n = 39$			
(1.1%)	(1.4%)	(3.4%)	(3.3%)	SJ	$n = 532$	(44.7%)
+	+	+++	+++	SP	$n = 79$	(6.6%)
				NP	$n = 204$	(17.2%)
				NJ	$n = 374$	(31.5%)
				TJ	$n = 675$	(56.8%)
				TP	$n = 137$	(11.5%)
				FP	$n = 146$	(12.3%)
				FJ	$n = 231$	(19.4%)
ESTJ	ESFJ	ENFJ	ENTJ	IN	$n = 391$	(32.9%)
$n = 97$	$n = 44$	$n = 32$	$n = 76$	EN	$n = 187$	(15.7%)
(8.2%)	(3.7%)	(2.7%)	(6.4%)	IS	$n = 440$	(37.0%)
+++++	++++	+++	+++++	ES	$n = 171$	(14.4%)
+++			+			
				ET	$n = 225$	(18.9%)
				EF	$n = 133$	(11.2%)
				IF	$n = 144$	(20.5%)
				IT	$n = 587$	(49.4%)

Jungian Types (E)			Jungian Types (I)			Dominant Types		
	n	%		n	%		n	%
E-TJ	173	14.6	I-TP	85	7.1	Dt.T	258	21.7
E-FJ	76	6.4	I-FP	89	7.5	Dt.F	165	13.9
ES-P	30	2.5	IS-J	391	32.9	Dt.S	421	35.4
EN-P	79	6.6	IN-J	266	22.4	Dt.N	345	29.0

Note: $N = 1189$ (NB: + = 1% of N).

Table 5. Type distribution for male atheist/agnostic church-leavers.

The Sixteen Complete Types				Dichotomous Preferences			
ISTJ	ISFJ	INFJ	INTJ	E	$n=1639$	(20.9%)	$I=0.69$***
$n=3158$	$n=229$	$n=136$	$n=1169$	I	$n=6199$	(79.1%)	$I=1.13$***
(40.3%)	(2.9%)	(1.7%)	(14.9%)				
$I=1.56$***	$I=0.42$***	$I=0.29$***	$I=0.91$	S	$n=5094$	(65.0%)	$I=1.26$***
+++++++	+++	++	+++++	N	$n=2744$	(35.0%)	$I=0.72$***
+++++++			+++++				
+++++++			+++++	T	$n=7016$	(89.5%)	$I=1.31$***
+++++++			+++++	F	$n=822$	(10.5%)	$I=0.33$***
++++++							
++++++				J	$n=5784$	(73.8%)	$I=0.97$
				P	$n=2054$	(26.2%)	$I=1.10$
ISTP	ISFP	INFP	INTP		Pairs and Temperaments		
$n=632$	$n=73$	$n=144$	$n=658$				
(8.1%)	(0.9%)	(1.8%)	(8.4%)	IJ	$n=4692$	(59.9%)	$I=1.08$**
$I=3.20$***	$I=0.58$*	$I=0.31$***	$I=1.81$***	IP	$n=1507$	(19.2%)	$I=1.31$***
+++++	+	++	+++++	EP	$n=547$	(7.0%)	$I=0.76$**
+++			+++	EJ	$n=1092$	(13.9%)	$I=0.67$***
				ST	$n=4682$	(59.7%)	$I=1.59$***
				SF	$n=412$	(5.3%)	$I=0.38$***
				NF	$n=410$	(5.2%)	$I=0.29$***
ESTP	ESFP	ENFP	ENTP	NT	$n=2334$	(29.8%)	$I=0.97$
$n=188$	$n=47$	$n=84$	$n=228$				
(2.4%)	(0.6%)	(1.1%)	(2.9%)	SJ	$n=4154$	(53.0%)	$I=1.18$***
$I=2.19$**	$I=0.42$***	$I=0.32$***	$I=0.89$	SP	$n=940$	(12.0%)	$I=1.81$***
++	+	+	+++	NP	$n=1114$	(14.2%)	$I=0.83$**
				NJ	$n=1630$	(20.8%)	$I=0.66$***
				TJ	$n=5310$	(67.7%)	$I=1.19$***
				TP	$n=1706$	(21.8%)	$I=1.89$***
				FP	$n=348$	(4.4%)	$I=0.36$***
				FJ	$n=474$	(6.0%)	$I=0.31$***
ESTJ	ESFJ	ENFJ	ENTJ				
$n=704$	$n=63$	$n=46$	$n=279$	IN	$n=2107$	(26.9%)	$I=0.82$***
(9.0%)	(0.8%)	(0.6%)	(3.6%)	EN	$n=637$	(8.1%)	$I=0.52$***
$I=1.10$	$I=0.22$***	$I=0.22$***	$I=0.56$***	IS	$n=4092$	(52.2%)	$I=1.41$***
+++++	+	+	++++	ES	$n=1002$	(12.8%)	$I=0.89$
++++							
				ET	$n=1399$	(17.8%)	$I=0.94$
				EF	$n=240$	(3.1%)	$I=0.27$***
				IF	$n=582$	(7.4%)	$I=0.36$***
				IT	$n=5617$	(71.7%)	$I=1.45$***

Jungian Types (E)				Jungian Types (I)				Dominant Types			
	n	%	Index		n	%	Index		n	%	Index
E-TJ	983	12.5	0.86	I-TP	1290	16.5	2.30***	Dt.T	2273	29.0	1.34***
E-FJ	109	1.4	0.22***	I-FP	217	2.8	0.37***	Dt.F	326	4.2	0.30***
ES-P	235	3.0	1.19	IS-J	3387	43.2	1.31***	Dt.S	3622	46.2	1.31***
EN-P	312	4.0	0.60***	IN-J	1305	16.6	0.74***	Dt.N	1617	20.6	0.71***

Note: $N=7838$ (NB: $+=1\%$ of N).
*$p < 0.05$.
**$p < 0.01$.
***$p < 0.001$.

Table 6. Type distribution for male "believing but not belonging" church-leavers.

The Sixteen Complete Types				Dichotomous Preferences			
ISTJ $n=251$ (29.8%) $I=1.15$ +++++ +++++ +++++ +++++ +++++ +++++	ISFJ $n=43$ (5.1%) $I=0.73$ +++++	INFJ $n=53$ (6.3%) $I=1.04$ +++++ +	INTJ $n=141$ (16.7%) $I=1.03$ +++++ +++++ +++++ ++	E I S N T F J P	$n=196$ $n=647$ $n=424$ $n=419$ $n=622$ $n=221$ $n=610$ $n=233$	(23.3%) (76.7%) (53.0%) (49.7%) (73.8%) (26.2%) (72.4%) (27.6%)	$I=0.77$*** $I=1.10$*** $I=0.98$ $I=1.02$ $I=1.08$** $I=0.83$** $I=0.95$* $I=1.16$*
ISTP $n=35$ (4.2%) $I=1.65$* ++++	ISFP $n=10$ (1.2%) $I=0.74$ +	INFP $n=39$ (4.6%) $I=0.79$ +++++	INTP $n=75$ (8.9%) $I=1.92$*** +++++ ++++	\multicolumn{4}{l}{**Pairs and Temperaments**}
				IJ IP EP EJ ST SF NF NT SJ SP NP NJ TJ TP FP FJ	$n=488$ $n=159$ $n=74$ $n=122$ $n=350$ $n=74$ $n=147$ $n=272$ $n=356$ $n=68$ $n=165$ $n=254$ $n=476$ $n=146$ $n=87$ $n=134$	(57.9%) (18.9%) (8.8%) (14.5%) (41.5%) (8.8%) (17.4%) (32.3%) (42.2%) (8.1%) (19.6%) (30.1%) (56.5%) (17.3%) (10.3%) (15.9%)	$I=1.05$ $I=1.29$** $I=0.96$ $I=0.69$*** $I=1.10$ $I=0.64$*** $I=0.97$ $I=1.05$ $I=0.94$ $I=1.21$ $I=1.14$ $I=0.96$ $I=0.99$ $I=1.50$*** $I=0.84$ $I=0.82$*
ESTP $n=16$ (1.9%) $I=1.74$ ++	ESFP $n=7$ (0.8%) $I=0.58$ +	ENFP $n=31$ (3.7%) $I=1.09$ ++++	ENTP $n=20$ (2.4%) $I=0.72$ ++				
ESTJ $n=48$ (5.7%) $I=0.70$* +++++ +	ESFJ $n=14$ (1.7%) $I=0.45$** ++	ENFJ $n=24$ (2.8%) $I=1.06$ +++	ENTJ $n=36$ (4.3%) $I=0.67$* ++++	IN EN IS ES ET EF IF IT	$n=308$ $n=111$ $n=339$ $n=85$ $n=120$ $n=76$ $n=145$ $n=502$	(36.5%) (13.2%) (40.2%) (10.1%) (14.2%) (9.0%) (17.2%) (59.5%)	$I=1.11$ $I=0.84$ $I=1.09$ $I=0.70$** $I=0.75$** $I=0.81$ $I=0.84$ $I=1.21$***

Jungian Types (E)				Jungian Types (I)				Dominant Types			
	n	%	Index		n	%	Index		n	%	Index
E-TJ	84	10.0	0.68**	I-TP	110	13.0	1.83***	Dt.T	194	23.0	1.06
E-FJ	38	4.5	0.71	I-FP	49	5.8	0.78	Dt.F	87	10.3	0.74*
ES-P	23	2.7	1.08	IS-J	294	34.9	1.06	Dt.S	317	37.6	1.06
EN-P	51	6.0	0.91	IN-J	194	23.0	1.03	Dt.N	245	29.1	1.00

Note: $N=843$ (NB: += 1% of N).
*$p < 0.05$.
**$p < 0.01$.
***$p < 0.001$.

Table 2 compares the type distribution for the 2677 female atheist/agnostic church-leavers with the type distribution for the 1137 churchgoing females. These data demonstrated that the female atheist/agnostic church-leavers displayed a significant over-representation of introversion over extraversion, sensing over intuition, and thinking over feeling. There was no significant difference between judging and perceiving. In terms of the 16 discrete types, the female atheist/agnostic church-leavers had significant over-representations of ISTP, INTP, ISTJ, and INTJ, and significant under-representations of ENFJ, ESFJ, ENFP, ISFJ, ESFP, INFJ, and INFP. There were no significant differences in the percentages of ISFP, ESTP, ENTP, ESTJ, or ENTJ.

Table 3 compares the type distribution for the 1134 female "believing but not belonging" church-leavers with the type distribution for the 1137 churchgoing females. These data demonstrated that the female "believing but not belonging" church-leavers displayed a significant over-representation of introversion over extraversion, intuition over sensing, thinking over feeling, and perceiving over judging. In terms of the 16 discrete types, only two types were significantly over-represented among the female "believing but not belonging" church-leavers (INTP and INTJ) and only two were significantly under-represented (ESFJ and ESTJ). There were no significant differences in the percentages of the other 12 types.

Table 4 presents the type distribution for the 1189 male churchgoers. These data demonstrated that the male churchgoers displayed overall preferences for introversion (70%) over extraversion (30%), sensing (51%) over intuition (49%), thinking (68%) over feeling (32%), and judging (76%) over perceiving (24%). In terms of the 16 discreet types, the two most common types among the male churchgoers were ISTJ (26%) and INTJ (16%), and the two least common types were ESTP (1%) and ESFP (1%).

Table 5 compares the type distribution for the 7838 male atheist/agnostic church-leavers with the type distribution for the 1189 male churchgoers. These data demonstrated that the male atheist/agnostic church-leavers displayed a significant over-representation of introversion over extraversion, sensing over intuition, and thinking over feeling. There was no significant difference between judging and perceiving. In terms of the 16 discrete types, the male atheist/agnostic church-leavers had significant over-representations of ISTP, ESTP, INTP, and ISTJ, and significant under-representations of ENFJ, ESFJ, INFJ, INFP, ENFP, ISFJ, ESFP, ENTJ, and ISFP. There were no significant differences in the percentages of INTJ, ENTP, or ESTJ.

Table 6 compares the type distribution for the 843 male "believing but not belonging" church-leavers with the type distribution for the 1189 male churchgoers. These data demonstrated that the male "believing but not belonging" church-leavers displayed a significant over-representation for introversion over extraversion, thinking over feeling, and perceiving over judging. There was no significant difference between sensing and intuition. In terms of the 16 discrete types, only two types were significantly over-represented among male "believing but not belonging" church-leavers: INTP and ISTP, and only three were significantly under-represented: ESFJ, ENTJ, and ESTJ. There were no significant differences in the percentages of the other 11 types.

Conclusion

The present study set out to compare the psychological type profile of current churchgoers with those who left and became atheists or agnostics as well as those who left and retained some sort of belief in God. From the results, three main conclusions can be drawn. First, when it comes to the growing consensus view that Christian churches tend towards preferences for ISFJ, the data mostly confirmed this notion. Female churchgoers were found to have an overall preference for ISFJ, whereas male churchgoers were found to have an overall preference for ISTJ.

Second, the data demonstrated that the atheist/agnostic population differs more from the churchgoing population than the "believing but not belonging" population does in terms of psychological type. Among the "believing but not belonging" group, there were significant differences in the percentages of only four out of the 16 types (females) and five out of the 16 types (males) when compared to the churchgoing group. However, among the atheist/agnostic group, there were significant differences in 11 out of 16 (females) and 13 out of 16 (males). In addition to this, the over-representations in the atheist/agnostic group were, in most cases, greater than the over-representations in the "believing but not belonging" group. For example, ISTPs were significantly over-represented among males in both groups. However, among the atheist/agnostic group, there were over three times as many ISTPs as compared to the churchgoers, but among the "believing but not belonging" group, there were only one and a half times as many. This finding seems to indicate that psychological type plays a greater role in why atheists and agnostics end up leaving church than those who leave yet retain some sort of belief. Further research is needed in order to test this hypothesis further.

Third, the data demonstrated consistency in terms of which psychological types were the most over-represented and under-represented among the atheist/agnostic church-leavers. ISTP was by far the most over-represented type for both male and female atheist/agnostic church-leavers, with INTP coming in second among females and third among males. In addition to this, the two diametrically opposite types, ENFJ and ESFJ, were the first and second most under-represented types for both male and female atheist/agnostic church-leavers.

These findings support the prediction, based on Francis and Robbins (2012), Saroglou (2010) and Caldwell-Harris (2012), that church-leavers would tend towards preferences for thinking and perceiving (__TP) as opposed to feeling and judging (__FJ). However, they do not support the prediction from Francis and Robbins (2012) that church-leavers would also tend towards a preference for intuition (N) over sensing (S), with the exception of the female church-leavers in the "believing but not belonging" group. The findings also agreed with the data from Baker and Robbins (2012), in that they confirmed that atheists tend towards preferences for introversion and thinking (I_T_). However, the findings from the present study disagreed significantly from the findings from Baker and Robbins (2012) when it came to the J-P dimension. Baker and Robbins (2012) found a tendency towards judging (J) among atheists, whereas the present study found a tendency towards perceiving (P).

Although a general picture is starting to emerge on the psychological type profile of atheists as well as on the role psychological type plays in church-leaving, additional research is needed in order to clarify that picture further. Such discoveries will hopefully lead to improved communication and understanding between the religious and the non-religious, both in the public sphere and in the private.

References

Baker, M. J., & Robbins, M. (2012). American on-line atheists and psychological type. *Mental Health, Religion & Culture, 15*, 1077–1084. doi:10.1080/13674676.2012.707433

Caldwell-Harris, C. L. (2012). Understanding atheism/non-belief as an expected individual-differences variable. *Religion, Brain and Behaviour, 2*, 4–23. doi:10.1080/2153599X.2012.668395

Caplovitz, D., & Sherrow, F. (1977). *The religious drop-outs: Apostasy among college students*. Beverly Hills, CA: Sage Press.

DeVellis, R. F. (2003). *Scale development: Theory and applications*. London: Sage.

Francis, L. J., Jones, S. H., & Craig, C. L. (2004). Personality and religion: The relationship between psychological type and attitude toward Christianity. *Archive for the Psychology of Religion, 26*, 15–34. doi:10.1163/0084672053597987

Francis, L. J. (2005). *Faith and psychology: Personality, religion and the individual*. London: Darton, Longman and Todd.

Francis, L. J., Craig, C. L., Whinney, M., Tilley, D., & Slater, P. (2007). Psychological profiling of Anglican clergy in England: Employing Jungian typology to interpret diversity, strengths, and potential weaknesses in ministry. *International Journal of Practical Theology, 11*, 266–284. doi:10.1515/IJPT.2007.17

Francis, L. J., Craig, C. L., & Hall, G. (2008). Psychological type and attitude toward Celtic Christianity among committed churchgoers in the United Kingdom: An empirical study. *Journal of Contemporary Religion, 23*, 181–191. doi:10.1080/13537900802024543

Francis, L. J., & Datoo, F. A. (2012). Inside the mosque: A study in psychological-type profiling. *Mental Health, Religion & Culture, 15*, 1037–1046. doi:10.1080/13674676.2012.709723

Francis, L. J., & Robbins, M. (2012). Not fitting in and getting out: Psychological type and congregational satisfaction among Anglican churchgoers in England. *Mental Health, Religion & Culture, 15*, 1023–1035. doi:10.1080/13674676.2012.676260

Hadaway, C. K., & Roof, W. C. (1988). Apostasy in American churches: Evidence from national survey data. In D. G. Bromley (Ed.), *Falling from faith* (pp. 29–46). Newbury Park, CA: Sage.

Hunsberger, B., & Brown, L. B. (1984). Religious socialization, apostasy, and the impact of family background. *Journal for the Scientific Study of Religion, 23*, 239–251.

Jung, C. G. (1971). *Psychological types: The collected works* (Vol. 6). London: Routledge and Kegan Paul.

Kosmin, B. A., & Keysar, A. (2009). *American Religious Identification Survey (ARIS 2008) summary report*. Hartford, CT: Institute for the Study of Secularism in Society & Culture. Retrieved April 10, 2013, from http://commons.trincoll.edu/aris/publications/aris-2008-summary-report/

Myers, I. B., McCaulley, M. H., Quenk, N. L., & Hammer, A. L. (2003). *MBTI manual: A guide to the development and use of the Myers-Briggs Type Indicator*. Mountain View, CA: CPP.

Robbins, M. J., & Francis, L. J. (2011). All are called, but some psychological types are more likely to respond: Profiling churchgoers in Australia. *Research in the Social Scientific Study of Religion, 22*, 212–229. doi:10.1163/ej.9789004207271.i-360.44

Saraglou, V. (2010). Religiousness as a cultural adaptation of basic traits: A five-factor model perspective. *Personality and Social Psychology Review, 14*, 108–125. doi:10.1177/1088868309352322

Silver, C., Ross, F. J., & Francis, L. J. (2012). New Kadampa Buddhists and Jungian psychological type. *Mental Health, Religion & Culture, 15*, 1055–1064. doi:10.1080/13674676.2012.678578

Williams, E., Francis, L. J., Billington, U., & Robbins, M. (2012). The psychological-type profile of practicing British druids compared to Anglican churchgoers. *Mental Health, Religion & Culture, 15*, 1065–1075. doi:10.1080/13674676.2012.681483

The psychological type profile of Christians participating in fellowship groups or in small study groups: insights from the Australian National Church Life Survey

Leslie J. Francis, Mandy Robbins and Ruth Powell

The Australian National Church Life Survey draws on psychological type theory to facilitate insights into the connection between individual psychological profiles and preferences for different religious expressions. Drawing on data provided by 2355 participants in the 2006 congregation survey, this analysis profiles those members of church congregations who are drawn to participation in small prayer, discussion or Bible study groups, or to participation in fellowship and social groups. The key findings are that extraverts and feeling types are over-represented in the fellowship and social groups and that intuitive types are over-represented in small prayer, discussion or Bible study groups.

Introduction

Psychological type theory

Psychological type theory has its origins in the pioneering work of Jung (1971) and has been developed and has been operationalised in a series of type indicators, temperament sorters or type scales, including the Myers–Briggs Type Indicator (Myers & McCaulley, 1985), the Keirsey Temperament Sorter (Keirsey & Bates, 1978) and the Francis Psychological Type Scales (FPTS; Francis, 2005).

At its heart psychological type theory distinguishes between two core psychological processes. The perceiving process is concerned with how data are gathered; in Jung's terms this is the irrational process. The judging process is concerned with how data are evaluated; in Jung's terms this is the rational process. Within the perceiving process the two perceiving functions are defined as sensing (S) and intuition (N). Sensing types are concerned with facts and with details. They are the practical people who prefer to rely on past experience rather than to look for future possibilities. Intuitive types are concerned with meanings and with associations. They are the imaginative people who prefer to trust their inspirations about future possibilities rather than to rely on past experience. Within the judging process, the two judging functions are defined as thinking (T) and feeling (F). Thinking types are concerned with objectivity and truth. They are the logical people who test the coherence of systems and institutional structures. Feeling types are concerned with interpersonal relationships and human values. They are the humane people who care about the people operating the system and the people whose lives are affected by institutional structures.

Alongside the two processes (perceiving and judging), psychological type theory also distinguishes between the orientations and the attitudes towards the outer world. The orientations are concerned with the sources of psychological energy. The distinction is between introversion (I) and extraversion (E). Introverts are energised by the inner world and by their inner life. Introverts need quiet for reflection and space for themselves. Extraverts are energised by the outer world of people and theory. Extraverts need people and social company. They reflect best with others.

The attitudes are concerned with how people function in the outer world. The distinction is between judging (J) and perceiving (P). Judging types turn their preferred judging function (thinking or feeling) to the outer world. There they are seen to be organised, planned and structured people. Perceiving types turn their preferred perceiving function (sensing or intuition) to the outer world. There they are seen to be flexible, spontaneous and open people.

Congregational studies

Psychological type theory has made a useful contribution to congregational studies in a variety of ways: by identifying the distinctive psychological profile of churchgoers compared with the general population; by documenting differences in the psychological profile of those attracted to different church traditions; and by charting the connections between psychological profile and spirituality. Psychological type theory has been introduced to congregational studies in North America by Gerhardt (1983), Delis-Bulhoes (1990), Ross (1993, 1995) and Rehak (1998), in the UK by Craig, Francis, Bailey, and Robbins (2003), Francis, Duncan, Craig, and Luffman (2004), and Francis, Robbins, and Craig (2011), and in Australia by Robbins and Francis (2011). An overview of developments in this field has been provided by Francis (2009).

An initial comparison of the psychological type profile of male and female churchgoers with the wider population is illustrated, for example, by Francis, Robbins, Williams, and Williams (2007), drawing on a sample of Anglican churchgoers in England and the population norms published by Kendall (1998). The main finding from this comparison concerned the undue weighting towards sensing, feeling and judging in church congregations. Among women ISFJ accounted for 32% of churchgoers, compared with 18% of the general population, and ESFJ accounted for 28% of churchgoers compared with 19% of the general population. Among men ISFJ accounted for 19% of churchgoers, compared with 7% of the general population, and ESFJ accounted for 27% of churchgoers, compared with 6% of the general population. Over-representation of ISFJ and ESFJ among churchgoers led to under-representation of other types.

A more extensive profile of Anglican churchgoers in England was reported by Francis et al. (2011) in a study including 2135 women and 1169 men. This study analysed the profiles of men and women separately alongside the population norms published by Kendall (1998). Exploring the dichotomous preferences, the data demonstrated that female churchgoers are more introverted than women in the general population (49% compared with 43%) and more inclined to prefer judging (85% compared with 62%). On the other hand, there are no significant differences in levels of preferences for sensing by female churchgoers (81%) and women in the general population (79%), or in levels of preference for feeling by female churchgoers (70%) and women in the general population. The data also demonstrated that male churchgoers are more introverted than men in the general population (62% compared with 53%), more inclined to prefer sensing

(78% compared with 73%), more inclined to prefer feeling (42% compared with 35%), and more inclined to prefer judging (86% compared with 55%).

The comparison of the psychological type profile of people who attend different styles of services or forms of worship, even within the same denomination is illustrated, for example, by Village, Francis, and Craig (2009) who found significant differences in type profiles between individuals attending evangelical Anglican churches and individuals attending Anglo-Catholic churches in England. These data demonstrated a significantly higher proportion of intuitives in the Anglo-Catholic congregations.

The connection between psychological type profile and preferred experiences of spirituality is illustrated, for example, by Francis, Village, Robbins, and Ineson (2007) who examined the associations between psychological type and mystical orientation. Their data demonstrate a significant relationship between mystical orientation and the perceiving processing (sensing or intuition), but no relationship between mystical orientation and psychological orientation (introversion and extraversion), the judging process (feeling or thinking) and attitudes towards the outer world (judging or perceiving). Intuitive types were more open than sensing types to mystical orientation.

Research question

The Australian National Church Life Survey (NCLS) Research team has conducted regular survey work among church congregations over two decades (Bellamy & Castle, 2004; Bellamy et al., 2006; Kaldor, Bellamy, Correy, & Powell, 1992; Kaldor et al., 1995; Kaldor, Bellamy, Powell, Castle, & Hughes, 1999; Kaldor, Bellamy, Powell, Hughes, & Castle, 1997; Kaldor, Dixon, Powell, et al., 1999; Kaldor & McLean, 2009; Kaldor, McLean, Brady, Jacka, & Powell, 2009). The more recent surveys conducted by this team have routinely included a measure of psychological type in order to explore ways in which psychological type theory may promote further insights into congregational life. In particular, data from the 2006 NCLS congregational survey explored levels of participation in various types of congregational group activities. Drawing on these data the research aim of the present study is to examine the extent to which different types of congregational group activities attract participation reflecting individual psychological type preferences.

Method

Participants

The present analysis was conducted on the data provided by 2355 participants in the 2006 wave of the Australian NCLS who completed Form D of the congregational questionnaire, responding to all the items of the FPTS and to the item concerning group activities. This group of participants comprised 923 Catholics, 487 Anglicans, 719 Protestants and 226 Pentecostals; 993 men, 1345 women and 17 individuals who did not disclose their sex; 386 individuals under the age of 30, 672 in their 30s and 40s, 873 in their 50s or 60s, 370 aged 70 or over, and 54 who did not disclose their age.

Measures

Psychological type was assessed by the FPTS (Francis, 2005). This is a 40-item instrument comprising four sets of 10 forced-choice items relating to each of the four components of psychological type: the two orientations (extraversion and introversion), the two perceiving functions (sensing and intuition), the two judging functions (thinking and feeling), and the two attitudes towards the outer world (judging and perceiving). Participants were asked for each pair of

Table 1. Participation by dichotomous type preferences.

	Participation Yes %	Participation No %	I	$p <$
Fellowship groups				
Extraverts	49	41	0.83	.001
Intuitive types	21	17	0.84	NS
Feeling types	57	52	0.91	.05
Judging types	87	88	1.01	NS
N (2192)	763	1429		
Small prayer or study groups				
Extraverts	46	42	0.93	NS
Intuitive types	23	16	0.71	.001
Feeling types	55	53	0.96	NS
Judging types	86	89	1.04	NS
N (2194)	789	1405		

characteristics to check "the box next to that characteristic which is closer to the real you, even if you feel both characteristics apply to you. Tick the characteristic that reflects the real you, even if other people see you differently".

Involvement with group activities was assessed by the question, "Are you regularly involved in any group activities here? (Mark ALL that apply)". The two categories applied in the present analysis are: "Yes, in small prayer, discussion or Bible study group" and "Yes in fellowship clubs, social and other groups".

Analysis

The scientific literature on psychological type employs the self-selection ratio (I) developed by McCaulley (1985), as an extension of Chi square, to test simultaneously the component parts of type theory. Full type tables were constructed and compared for those who participated in the two categories of group activities with those who did not participate in each activity. Only the relevant information from these type tables will be displayed.

Results

Table 1 compares first the proportions of extraverts, intuitive types, feeling types, and judging types who participate in fellowship groups with those who do not participate in fellowship groups. Then Table 1 compares the proportions of extraverts, intuitive types, feeling types, and judging types who participate in small prayer or study groups with those who do not participate in small prayer or study groups. These data show that extraverts and feeling types are over-represented in fellowship groups, with the consequence that introverts and thinking types are under-represented in fellowship groups. These data also show that intuitive types are over-represented in small prayer or study groups, with the consequence that sensing types are under-represented in small prayer or study groups.

Conclusion

This study set out to explore whether psychological type theory could help to illuminate ways in which various types of congregational group activities might appeal to different types of participants. Data provided by 2355 churchgoers in the 2006 Australian NCLS have demonstrated a small but statistically significant connection between personal psychological type preferences and participation in two different and distinctive forms of congregational group activities, namely fellowship groups and small prayer or study groups. The difference reported by the data is highly consistent with the underlying theory.

The fellowship groups attracted an over-representation of extraverts. This finding is consistent with the underlying theory that extraverts are energised by the outer world of people and things. Extraverts enjoy meeting people, conversation and activities. Fellowship groups clearly resource these aspects of the extraverted personality. Churches should not be unduly surprised that introverted churchgoers may prefer to allow the fellowship groups to pass them by. Introverted churchgoers are resourced in other ways.

The fellowship groups also attracted an over-representation of feeling types. This finding is consistent with the underlying theory that feeling types are more concerned with the relational side of church life than with the more abstract and cerebral aspects of the faith. Feeling types enjoy getting alongside other people; feeling types enjoy sharing other people's stories, experiences and concerns; and feeling types enjoy supporting other people. Fellowship groups clearly resource these aspects of the feeling side of personality. Churches should not be unduly surprised that thinking types in the church congregation may prefer to allow the fellowship groups to pass them by. Thinking types in the church congregation are resourced in other ways.

The small prayer or study groups attract an over-representation of intuitive types. This is consistent with the underlying theory that intuitive types are more concerned with the exploratory side of religious faith than with getting on with the practical expression of faith. Intuitive types are keen to explore new ideas, discover new things and test new theories. Small prayer or study groups clearly resource these aspects of the intuitive side of personality. Churches should not be unduly surprised that sensing types in the church congregation may prefer to allow the prayer and study groups to pass them by. Sensing types in the church congregation are resourced in other ways.

The present study has worked with a relatively small number of churchgoers (2355) to test the connection between psychological type preferences and participation in just two different types of congregational group activity. In the light of the sample size analysis has been restricted to just one aspect of psychological type theory, the dichotomous preferences have not looked at men and women separately. The results, however, support the overall usefulness of the theory to help to account for the distinctive appeal of these two different types of congregational group activity. Future research in this tradition would benefit from including a wider range of more specifically defined congregational group activities and gathering data from a larger sample of participants in order to allow further analysis of the 16-complete types among men and women separately.

References

Bellamy, J., & Castle, K. (2004). *2001 church attendance estimates* (Occasional Paper No. 3). Sydney: NCLS Research.

Bellamy, J., Cussen, B., Sterland, S., Castle, K., Powell, R., & Kaldor, P. (2006). *Enriching church life: A practical guide for local churches*. Adelaide: Openbook.

Craig, C. L., Francis, L. J., Bailey, J., & Robbins, M. (2003). Psychological types in Church in Wales congregations. *The Psychologist in Wales, 15*, 18–21.

Delis-Bulhoes, V. (1990). Jungian psychological types and Christian belief in active church members. *Journal of Psychological Type, 20*, 25–33.

Francis, L. J. (2005). *Faith and psychology: Personality, religion and the individual.* London: Darton, Longman and Todd.

Francis, L. J. (2009). Psychological type theory and religious and spiritual experience. In M. De Souza, L. J. Francis, J. O'Higgins-Norman, & D. G. Scott (Eds.), *International handbook of education for spirituality, care and wellbeing* (pp. 125–146). Dordrecht: Springer. doi:10.1007/978-1-4020-9018-9_8

Francis, L. J., Duncan, B., Craig, C. L., & Luffman, G. (2004). Type patterns among Anglican congregations in England. *Journal of Adult Theological Education, 1*, 65–77. doi:10.1558/jate.1.1.65.36058

Francis, L. J., Robbins, M., & Craig, C. L. (2011). The psychological type profile of Anglican churchgoers in England: Compatible or incompatible with their clergy? *International Journal of Practical Theology, 15*, 243–259. doi:10.1515/IJPT.2011.036

Francis, L. J., Robbins, M., Williams, A., & Williams, R. (2007). All types are called, but some are more likely to respond: The psychological profile of rural Anglican churchgoers in Wales. *Rural Theology, 5*, 23–30.

Francis, L. J., Village, A., Robbins, M., & Ineson, K. (2007). Mystical orientation and psychological type: An empirical study among guests staying at a Benedictine Abbey. *Studies in Spirituality, 17*, 207–223. doi:10.2143/SIS.17.0.2024649

Gerhardt, R. (1983). Liberal religion and personality type. *Research in Psychological Type, 6*, 47–53.

Jung, C. G. (1971). *Psychological types: The collected works* (Vol. 6). London: Routledge and Kegan Paul.

Kaldor, P., Bellamy, J., Correy, M., & Powell, R. (1992). *First look in the mirror: Initial findings of the 1991 National Church Life Survey.* Homebush West: Lancer.

Kaldor, P., Bellamy, J., Moore, S., Powell, R., Castle, K., & Correy, M. (1995). *Mission under the microscope: Keys to effective and sustainable mission.* Adelaide: Openbook.

Kaldor, P., Bellamy, J., Powell, R., Castle, K., & Hughes, B. (1999). *Build my church: Trends and possibilities for Australian churches.* Adelaide: Openbook.

Kaldor, P., Bellamy, J., Powell, R., Hughes, B., & Castle, K. (1997). *Shaping a future: Characteristics of vital congregations.* Adelaide: Openbook.

Kaldor, P., Dixon, R., Powell, R., Bellamy, J., Hughes, B., Moore, S., & Dalziel, J. (1999). *Taking stock: A profile of Australian church attenders.* Adelaide: Openbook.

Kaldor, P., & McLean, J. (2009). *Lead with your strengths: Making a difference wherever you are.* Sydney South: NCLS Research.

Kaldor, P., McLean, J., Brady, M., Jacka, K., & Powell, R. (2009). *Introduction to lead with your strengths booklet.* Sydney South: NCLS Research.

Keirsey, D., & Bates, M. (1978). *Please understand me.* Del Mar, CA: Prometheus Nemesis.

Kendall, E. (1998). *Myers-Briggs Type Indicator: Step 1 manual supplement.* Palo Alto, CA: Consulting Psychologists Press.

McCaulley, M. H. (1985). The selection ratio type table: A research strategy for comparing type distributions. *Journal of Psychological Type, 10*, 46–56.

Myers, I. B., & McCaulley, M. H. (1985). *Manual: A guide to the development and use of the Myers-Briggs Type Indicator.* Palo Alto, CA: Consulting Psychologists Press.

Rehak, M. C. (1998). Identifying the congregation's corporate personality. *Journal of Psychological Type, 44*, 39–44.

Robbins, M., & Francis, L. J. (2011). All are called, but some psychological types are more likely to respond: Profiling churchgoers in Australia. *Research in the Social Scientific Study of Religion, 22*, 213–229. doi:10.1163/ej.9789004207271.i-360.44

Ross, C. F. J. (1993). Type patterns among active members of the Anglican Church: Comparisons with Catholics, evangelicals and clergy. *Journal of Psychological Type, 26*, 28–35.

Ross, C. F. J. (1995). Type patterns among Catholics: Four Anglophone congregations compared with Protestants, Francophone Catholics and priests. *Journal of Psychological Type, 33*, 33–41.

Village, A., Francis, L. J., & Craig, C. L. (2009). Church tradition and psychological type preferences among Anglicans in England. *Journal of Anglican Studies, 7*, 93–109. doi:10.1017/S1740355309000187

Created to be guardians? Psychological type profiles of members of cathedral Friends associations in England

Judith A. Muskett and Andrew Village

A sample of 1356 members of the Friends associations of six English cathedrals (775 women and 581 men) completed the Francis Psychological Type Scales. Compared with psychological type profiles published for the Church of England laity, both male and female Friends showed greater preferences for introversion over extraversion, for sensing over intuition, and for judging over perceiving. Female Friends showed less preference for feeling over thinking than other female Anglican churchgoers or women in the general population. Overall, the most frequent psychological profile was the Epimethean (SJ) temperament, which was significantly more frequent than among Anglicans generally in the Church of England. This is a profile expected from people who have a strong desire to maintain tradition and heritage and who have been called "guardians" of the church.

Introduction

The relationship between personality and religion has been demonstrated in a wide range of domains and in many different contexts (Hood, Hill, & Spilka, 2009; Pargament, 2013). Psychological type has proved to be a particularly fruitful model with which to investigate these connections, offering insight into why particular types of people may belong to certain religious traditions and why those within traditions often prefer particular sorts of religious expression (Francis, 2005; Francis, Robbins, & Craig, 2011; Robbins & Francis, 2011; Village, 2011; Village, Baker, & Howat, 2012). As the field develops, these connections are being tested among a wider range of traditions and in relation to a wider range of religious expression. Describing type profiles of different groups adds to the overall picture that is emerging. Where those groups are unusual or comprise fringe members of a religious tradition, the comparison with typical group profiles can be particularly useful in helping to understand the underlying psychological processes.

Friends associations are a common means of raising money to maintain ancient buildings and heritage sites in the UK and elsewhere (Hayes & Slater, 2003; Slater, 2003, 2004, 2005a; Slater & Armstrong, 2010). By joining, members support the upkeep of the fabric by their subscription fee, additional donations, or supporting fund-raising activities. Religious organisations often have

Friends associations, especially those that must support iconic places of worship of particular architectural or cultural significance. English cathedrals fall into this category, and all have Friends associations (Muskett, 2012).

The decline in churchgoing in England over recent decades is well documented (Davie, 1994; Gill, 1999). In a changing religious context (Woodhead & Catto, 2012), when less than one million now attend services in the Church of England on an average Sunday (Archbishops' Council Research & Statistics, 2013a), new ways of belonging have been recognised (Day, 2011; Walker, 2011); and affiliation to the Friends groups of historic religious buildings is a way that individuals with an interest in heritage and architecture, who do not necessarily wish to belong to the worshipping community, may contribute nonetheless to the life and upkeep of such churches (Cameron, 2003). Such people may have very different goals for the building compared with the worshipping community. This sometimes surfaces when congregations are looking for money to develop and change a building to make it more useable (for example, improving heating, seating, or installing modern facilities), especially if this might require change to the ancient fabric. A question of both theoretical and practical interest is whether the differences in goals that emerge in these situations are simply a matter of what people believe a religious building is for, or whether the differences reflect in part some more fundamental, underlying psychological dispositions related to how any change or deviation from tradition is perceived.

Some models of personality predict that certain profiles will be more generally inclined than others to foster tradition and resist change. In particular, the development of psychological type (Jung, 1923) by Keirsey and Bates (Keirsey, 1998; Keirsey & Bates, 1978) posited combinations of psychological preference that describe four different temperaments. Among these, the Epimethean temperament is said to reflect the tendency to be dutiful members of social groups and to protect the status quo. Are people with this sort of temperament the ones most likely to join Friends associations? The aim of the present paper is to assess the psychological temperament of Friends of Anglican cathedrals and compare it with that of Anglican churchgoers in general, to determine whether Friends have a distinctive psychological profile.

Cathedrals and their Friends

Anglican cathedrals are of particular interest because, notwithstanding the general decline in church attendance, there has been a steady growth in the cathedral sector in recent years. Thus, the Anglican cathedrals are regarded as a success story (Davie, 2012; Inge, 2006), on account of the way they attract increasing numbers of worshippers (especially to services held during the week), volunteers, and visitors (Archbishops' Council Research & Statistics, 2013b; Francis & Muskett, in press). In addition, the cathedrals are renowned for having a significant role in contemporary society (Platten & Lewis, 1998, 2006; Theos & The Grubb Institute, 2012); and they also have the capacity to play a distinctive part in the mission of the church (Muskett, in press; Rowe, 2010). All 42 cathedrals in England have Friends groups, the overall membership of which has been said to total about 55,000 (Beeson, 2004, p. 2).

The Friends organisations of places of worship were audited by Slater (2003, 2005a), and subsequently studied at the initiative of the National Conference of Friends of Cathedrals, Abbeys, and Greater Churches (Slater, 2005b). Until very recently, little attention had been given to understanding the distinctive motivations and characteristics underlying the national cathedral Friends movement. The first of two new analyses (Muskett, 2012) set the formation of the earliest associations in the context of cathedral outreach in the 1920s and 1930s; and the second (Muskett, 2011) demonstrated that conspicuous sponsorship and patronage from members of the royal family added weight to the new societies. A third study demonstrated that cathedrals provide distinctive settings, not only where people can befriend a place of worship, but also where they can form and conduct personal friendships (through social events, learning opportunities, and volunteering activities) (Muskett, in press). An ontological analysis of cathedral friendship has revealed that the relationship between Friend/cathedral is worthy of the name: behaviours and norms are comparable to those observed in relationships where both sides of the dyad are mortal (Muskett, 2013).

Psychological type

Psychological type is a model of human personality suggested by Jung (1923) and developed by others (Myers, 2006; Myers & Myers, 1980). It is based on the idea that personality is partly derived from preferences for different modes of psychological processing. The most widely used current model includes two orientations, two perceiving functions, two judging functions, and two attitudes towards the outer world. Type models assume that although all the various aspects of psychological processing are available to everyone, most people have preferences for where and how they perform these processes.

The two orientations describe where people function psychologically. This may be in the outer world through interaction with others. Extraverts (E) prefer this mode of functioning and they tend to be open, sociable people with many friends. People can also function psychologically in the inner world, through solitude, silence, and contemplation. Introverts (I) prefer this mode of functioning and they tend to be more reserved and private people, with a small circle of intimate friends.

The two perceiving functions describe how people collect and process information. This may be through the senses, noticing specific details in the here and now. Sensing types (S) prefer to function in this way and they tend to focus on practical issues in a down-to-earth and matter-of-fact manner. Information can also be processed using the imagination, attending to wider relationships or future possibilities. Intuitive types (N) prefer to function in this way and they tend to focus on abstract theories, innovative ideas, and future possibilities.

The two judging functions describe how people make decisions and judgments. This can be done objectively using logic and principles. Thinking types (T) prefer to make decisions in this way, placing high value on integrity and justice and being truthful and fair, even if this might upset others. Decisions can also be made subjectively using personal values and attending to our relationships with others. Feeling types (F) prefer to make decisions in this way, placing high value on compassion and mercy and being tactful and empathetic, even if this means sometimes being unfair or inconsistent.

The two attitudes indicate how people orientate to the world around them, and are thought to indicate which of the two sets of functions (that is, perceiving S/N or judging T/F) are projected externally. The thinking or feeling functions can be employed to actively evaluate the external world. Judging types (J) prefer to do this and are most comfortable with routine and established patterns, preferring to reach goals using schedules, lists, timetables, or diaries. The sensing or intuitive functions can be employed to passively observe the external world. Perceiving types (P) prefer to do this and have a flexible, open-ended approach to life that is most comfortable with change and spontaneity, preferring to attend to the moment rather than to plan too far ahead.

These four sets of binary preferences imply 16 possible psychological types (ESTJ, ISTJ, ENTJ, etc.) that are the basis for a variety of human personalities. The interactions of preferences across the dimensions are thought to explain some of the key characteristics of each type. Although the details of these interactions, termed "type-dynamics", are controversial and not universally accepted (Bayne, 1997), there is growing evidence that type preferences within dimensions correspond to some of the traits in other personality models (Bayne, 1994; Crump,

Furnham, & Moutafi, 2003; Francis & Jones, 2000; Furnham, 1996; Garden, 1991; Lloyd, 2012; MacDonald, Anderson, Tsagarakis, & Holland, 1995; McCrae & Costa, 1989; Tobacyk, Livingston, & Robbins, 2008; Tucker & Gillespie, 1993), suggesting they are assessing fundamental aspects of human personality.

Temperament theory (Keirsey & Bates, 1978) uses the dimensions of psychological type but rejects Jung's emphasis on psychological functioning. Instead it draws on a range of other psychological models to suggest that individuals have innate temperaments that determine behaviour by creating distinctive needs that different behaviours are designed to meet. Keirsey and Bates argued for two important links between Jungian dimension preferences that give rise to temperament. The first is between the perceiving process and attitude towards the outer world, and leads to two temperaments among those who prefer sensing to intuition. The Epimethean (SJ) temperament describes those who have a longing for duty and to be useful to the societies or social groups to which they belong. Epimetheans have a desire to belong, but assume that belonging is something that is earned by fulfilling obligations to service and caring. The Dionysian (SP) temperament, by contrast, describes those who prize freedom and their ability to experience and enjoy the present moment. Dionysians value the unfettered chance to enjoy action and can become bored with the status quo.

The second fundamental interaction in the temperament model is between the perceiving and judging processes, and leads to two temperaments among those who prefer intuition over sensing. The Promethean temperament (NT) describes those who desire powers of competence and achievement. Prometheans seek knowledge and proficiency, and can be troubled by ignorance or incompetence. The Apollonian temperament (NF), in contrast, describes those who need to engage in the search for self and self-actualisation. Apollonians can be caught up in the search for meaning and value their individuality and uniqueness.

Religious affiliation and psychological type

Studies over the last two decades indicate the ways in which members of Christian churches differ in their average personality profiles from the population at large. In the UK, the best available study of the general population is that reported by Kendall (1998), which is based on a sample of 748 men and 865 women, and is often used as the baseline for the population. Among both sexes preferences for introversion versus extraversion, or judging versus perceiving, are fairly evenly balanced, whereas around 70–80% of the population tends to prefer sensing to intuition. Among men, 65% prefer thinking over feeling, whereas in women the opposite is true, with 70% preferring feeling over thinking. The greater preference for feeling among women compared with men is a widespread finding across many cultures and is one reason why comparisons of samples is best done for each sex separately.

The most comprehensive comparison of Anglican churchgoers with the UK population norms comes from a study of 2135 women and 1169 men from 140 Church of England congregations by Francis et al. (2011). Among the women, there was a balance of extraverts (51%) and introverts (49%), but a marked preference for sensing (82%) over intuition (18%), feeling (70%) over thinking (30%), and judging (85%) over perceiving (15%). Compared with UK norms, this implied female churchgoers were more likely to be introverts and much more likely to be judging types, but there was no significant difference in the preference for sensing or feeling, which was similarly high among women generally. Among the men, there was a preponderance of introverts (62%) over extraverts (38%), a preference for sensing (78%) over intuition (22%), thinking (58%) over feeling (42%), and judging (86%) over perceiving (14%). Compared with UK norms, this implied that male churchgoers were more likely than men generally to be introverts, sensing types, feeling types, and judging types. These findings substantiated earlier, smaller-scale studies and suggest that psychological predispositions may influence someone's likelihood of joining the Anglican Church.

The most marked disparity between Anglican churchgoers and the general population is over-representation of judging rather than perceiving types. This, coupled with the generally high level of sensing types (mostly reflected in the population at large), implies a high proportion of Epimetheans (SJs). Studies of Anglican clergy have suggested a higher frequency of intuitives compared with that among congregations, especially for those in full-time stipendiary ministry (Francis, Craig, Whinney, Tilley, & Slater, 2007; Village, 2011). Francis and Village (2012) observed that among ordained local ministers (OLMs) type profiles were more similar to congregations; and their study drew on temperament theory to suggest that this particular group of part-time, locally based ministers who were mostly of Epimethean temperament represented the "guardians" of the Church. Building on Oswald and Kroeger's (1988) notion of the "conserving and serving pastor", Francis and Village (2012) suggested that this ministerial niche attracted those who were particularly interested in preserving traditional order and practices, and who served with a strong sense of duty and care.

The Anglican Church may consist generally of people who tend to favour tradition and who resist change, and Anglican Friends association members might simply reflect this sort of psychological profile. However, as people who have a particular interest in maintaining traditional buildings and the worship associated with them, they might represent a specific subset who are more likely to have an Epimethean temperament. Keirsey and Bates (1978) capture the Epimethean propensity to honour heritage in their description of this temperament: "Heritage and heritability loom large in the perspective of the true Epimethean. The transitory, temporary, and expedient seem almost an affront to the corporate, municipal or family heritage" (p. 43). To examine the idea that the Epimethean temperament may predispose people to join heritage organisations, psychological-type profiles of cathedral Friends association members will be compared with those of Anglican churchgoers, using the Francis et al. (2011) dataset as a baseline.

Method

Procedure

In 2011, the Friends associations of six Anglican cathedrals in England were recruited to take part in a broad survey about the motivations and associational behaviours of their members. Individual cathedral Friends were invited to complete and return a postal questionnaire that included a measure of psychological type. Participation was voluntary, and Friends were assured of their anonymity.

Instrument

The questionnaire included the Francis Psychological Type Scales (Francis, 2005). These consist of 40 forced-choice items with 10 related to each of the four psychological-type dimensions. Items representing opposite characteristics within each of the dimensions were presented in pairs and respondents were asked to select the one in the pair that was closest to how they perceived themselves. Choices were summed to give a score for each preference, and type preferences assigned according to which of the pair scored highest, with the few cases of ties assigned to I, N, F, or J. Internal consistency reliabilities (Cronbach, 1951) of scales for each of the dimensions were satisfactory (EI: .76; SN: .67; FT: .65 and JP: .71), and in line with those reported elsewhere (Francis, Robbins, & Wulff, 2008; Village, 2011; Village et al., 2012).

Sample

A total of 5059 questionnaires were distributed, and 1637 (32%) were returned, of which 1356 had sufficient answers to calculate psychological type (775 women and 581 men). In terms of age, only 1% of Friends were under 40; 3% were in their 40s; 7% in their 50s; and 11% aged between 60 and 64. More than three-quarters of the respondents (78%) were 65 years or older (37% were in their 70s, 23% in their 80s, and 3% in their 90s).

Respondents were invited to say how religious they were, using a scale from 0 to 10: 15% were very religious (9 or 10 on the scale); 46% were rather religious (6–8 on the scale); 27% were moderately religious (3–5 on the scale); and 8% were slightly religious (1 or 2 on the scale). Just 4% reported that they were not at all religious (0 on the scale). Consistent with that was the finding that 4% attended neither church nor cathedral services. Weekly or more regular attendance at their cathedral was reported by 22% of respondents, and attendance monthly or fortnightly by a further 11% of Friends. Weekly or more regular attendance at another church was reported by 44% (of whom 61% said that they also attended their cathedral a few times a year). Thus, contrary to Cameron's suggestion (2003), this sample indicates that cathedral Friendship is typically an additional rather than alternative way to belong to the Church of England.

Analysis

Preferences within a dimension were examined using contingency analyses to test for overall preferences within each sex (chi-squared one-sample test) or differences between the sexes (chi-squared two-sample test). Distributions of the 16 types were examined separately for men and women and compared, using conventional type tables (Myers & McCaulley, 1985; Quenk, 1999), with data reported for Anglican churchgoers by Francis et al. (2011), who also compared their findings with UK population norms reported by Kendall (1998). Type tables include comparisons of the four temperaments. The index of attraction (I) is the ratio of the percentage of occurrence of a temperament in the test population with the base population, values less than one indicating an underrepresentation and values over one indicating an overrepresentation. The statistic is tested using the chi-squared statistic calculated from the observed and expected ratios in the test and base sample, with one degree of freedom.

Results

Psychological types of women and men in the sample

The 775 women in the sample (Table 1) showed preferences for introversion (58%) over extraversion (42%), sensing (86%) over intuition (14%), feeling (58%) over thinking (42%), and judging (91%) over perceiving (9%). The 581 men in the sample (Table 2) showed preferences for introversion (72%) over extraversion (28%), sensing (84%) over intuition (16%), thinking (61%) over feeling (39%), and judging (95%) over perceiving (5%). Thus, compared with women, men showed significantly greater preferences for introversion (72% versus 58%, $\chi^2 = 25.4$, $df = 1$, $p < .001$) and thinking (61% versus 42%, $\chi^2 = 46.2$, $df = 1$, $p < .001$), a slightly greater preference for judging (95% versus 91%, $\chi^2 = 6.1$, $df = 1$, $p < .05$), but an equally high preference (84% versus 86%) for sensing.

Among women, the four most frequent types were ISFJ (27%), ISTJ (20%), ESFJ (19%), and ESTJ (15%) which together accounted for 81% of the sample (Table 1). Among men, the four most frequent types were ISTJ (38%), ISFJ (20%), ESTJ (12%), and ESFJ (11%), which together also accounted for 81% of the sample (Table 2). In both sexes, the SJ temperament was more frequent than the other three combined (81% for both sexes).

Table 1. Type distribution for female Anglican cathedral Friends in England, compared with Anglican churchgoers in England.

The Sixteen Complete Types					Dichotomous Preferences			
ISTJ	ISFJ	INFJ	INTJ	E	$n=323$	(41.7%)	$I=0.82$***	
$n=158$	$n=209$	$n=21$	$n=24$	I	$n=452$	(58.3%)	$I=1.18$***	
(20.4%)	(27.0%)	(2.7%)	(3.1%)					
$I=1.65$***	$I=1.09$	$I=0.78$	$I=1.22$	S	$n=668$	(86.2%)	$I=1.06$**	
+++++	+++++	+++	+++	N	$n=107$	(13.8%)	$I=0.74$**	
+++++	+++++							
+++++	+++++			T	$n=325$	(41.9%)	$I=1.39$***	
+++++	+++++			F	$n=450$	(58.1%)	$I=0.83$***	
	+++++							
	++			J	$n=708$	(91.4%)	$I=1.07$***	
				P	$n=67$	(8.6%)	$I=0.59$***	

				Pairs and Temperaments			
ISTP	ISFP	INFP	INTP				
$n=6$	$n=15$	$n=10$	$n=9$	IJ	$n=412$	(53.2%)	$I=1.24$***
(0.8%)	(1.9%)	(1.3%)	(1.2%)	IP	$n=40$	(5.2%)	$I=0.81$
$I=0.97$	$I=0.63$	$I=0.71$	$I=1.77$	EP	$n=27$	(3.5%)	$I=0.43$***
+	++	+	+	EJ	$n=296$	(38.2%)	$I=0.90$*
				ST	$n=282$	(36.4%)	$I=1.51$***
				SF	$n=386$	(49.8%)	$I=0.87$***
				NF	$n=64$	(8.3%)	$I=0.65$***
ESTP	ESFP	ENFP	ENTP	NT	$n=43$	(5.5%)	$I=0.93$
$n=5$	$n=12$	$n=8$	$n=2$				
(0.6%)	(1.5%)	(1.0%)	(0.3%)	SJ	$n=630$	(81.3%)	$I=1.12$***
$I=2.29$	$I=0.36$***	$I=0.36$**	$I=0.39$	SP	$n=38$	(4.9%)	$I=0.58$***
+	++	+		NP	$n=29$	(3.7%)	$I=0.62$*
				NJ	$n=78$	(10.1%)	$I=0.79$
				TJ	$n=303$	(39.1%)	$I=1.41$***
				TP	$n=22$	(2.8%)	$I=1.19$
				FP	$n=45$	(5.8%)	$I=0.48$***
				FJ	$n=405$	(52.3%)	$I=0.90$**
ESTJ	ESFJ	ENFJ	ENTJ				
$n=113$	$n=150$	$n=25$	$n=8$	IN	$n=64$	(8.3%)	$I=0.97$
(14.6%)	(19.4%)	(3.2%)	(1.0%)	EN	$n=43$	(5.5%)	$I=0.54$***
$I=1.36$**	$I=0.77$**	$I=0.70$	$I=0.49$	IS	$n=388$	(50.1%)	$I=1.22$***
+++++	+++++	+++	+	ES	$n=280$	(36.1%)	$I=0.90$**
+++++	+++++						
++++	+++++			ET	$n=128$	(16.5%)	$I=1.20$
	++++			EF	$n=195$	(25.2%)	$I=0.68$***
				IF	$n=255$	(32.9%)	$I=0.99$
				IT	$n=197$	(25.4%)	$I=1.56$***

Jungian Types (E)				Jungian Types (I)				Dominant Types			
	n	%	Index		n	%	Index		n	%	Index
E-TJ	121	15.6	1.22	I-TP	15	1.9	1.33	Dt.T	136	17.5	1.23*
E-FJ	175	22.6	0.76***	I-FP	25	3.2	0.66*	Dt.F	200	25.8	0.75***
ES-P	17	2.2	0.48**	IS-J	367	47.4	1.28***	Dt.S	384	49.5	1.19***
EN-P	10	1.3	0.36***	IN-J	45	5.8	0.97	Dt.N	55	7.1	0.74*

Note: $N=775$ and $+=1\%$ of n.
*$p<.05$
**$p<.01$
***$p<.001$

Table 2. Type distribution for male Anglican cathedral Friends in England, compared with Anglican churchgoers in England.

The Sixteen Complete Types

ISTJ	ISFJ	INFJ	INTJ
n = 220	n = 118	n = 20	n = 41
(37.9%)	(20.3%)	(3.4%)	(7.1%)
I = 1.32***	I = 1.18	I = 1.18	I = 1.11
+++++	+++++	+++	+++++
+++++	+++++		++
+++++	+++++		
+++++	+++++		
+++++			
+++++			
+++++			
+++			

ISTP	ISFP	INFP	INTP
n = 2	n = 8	n = 4	n = 3
(0.3%)	(1.4%)	(0.7%)	(0.5%)
I = 0.21*	I = 0.73	I = 0.37	I = 0.46
	+	+	+

ESTP	ESFP	ENFP	ENTP
n = 4	n = 3	n = 5	n = 1
(0.7%)	(0.5%)	(0.9%)	(0.2%)
I = 0.50	I = 0.25*	I = 0.37*	I = 0.11**
+	+	+	

ESTJ	ESFJ	ENFJ	ENTJ
n = 70	n = 65	n = 6	n = 11
(12.0%)	(11.2%)	(1.0%)	(1.9%)
I = 0.87	I = 1.01	I = 0.38*	I = 0.55
+++++	+++++	+	++
+++++	+++++		
++	+		

Dichotomous Preferences

	n	%	I
E	165	(28.4%)	0.74***
I	416	(71.6%)	1.16***
S	490	(84.3%)	1.09***
N	91	(15.7%)	0.70***
T	352	(60.6%)	1.05
F	229	(39.4%)	0.94
J	551	(94.8%)	1.10***
P	30	(5.2%)	0.37***

Pairs and Temperaments

	n	%	I
IJ	399	(68.7%)	1.24***
IP	17	(2.9%)	0.45**
EP	13	(2.2%)	0.30***
EJ	152	(26.2%)	0.84*
ST	296	(50.9%)	1.12*
SF	194	(33.4%)	1.04
NF	35	(6.0%)	0.61**
NT	56	(9.6%)	0.77
SJ	473	(81.4%)	1.15***
SP	17	(2.9%)	0.42***
NP	13	(2.2%)	0.32***
NJ	78	(13.4%)	0.87
TJ	342	(58.9%)	1.13**
TP	10	(1.7%)	0.30***
FP	20	(3.4%)	0.42***
FJ	209	(36.0%)	1.06
IN	68	(11.7%)	0.96
EN	23	(4.0%)	0.39***
IS	348	(59.9%)	1.21***
ES	142	(24.4%)	0.87
ET	86	(14.8%)	0.73**
EF	79	(13.6%)	0.75*
IF	150	(25.8%)	1.08
IT	266	(45.8%)	1.21***

Jungian Types (E)

	n	%	Index
E-TJ	81	13.9	0.81
E-FJ	71	12.2	0.89
ES-P	7	1.2	0.35**
EN-P	6	1.0	0.26***

Jungian Types (I)

	n	%	Index
I-TP	5	0.9	0.31**
I-FP	12	2.1	0.55
IS-J	338	58.2	1.27***
IN-J	61	10.5	1.14

Dominant Types

	n	%	Index
Dt.T	86	14.8	0.74**
Dt.F	83	14.3	0.81
Dt.S	345	59.4	1.20***
Dt.N	67	11.5	0.88

Note: N = 581 and + = 1% of n.
*p < .05
**p < .01
***p < .001

Comparisons with Anglican churchgoers

There were significant differences in the type profiles of both women and men Friends compared with those reported for Anglican churchgoers by Francis et al. (2011). In terms of dichotomous preferences, female Friends showed significantly greater preferences for introversion, sensing, thinking, and judging compared with female churchgoers (Table 1). This resulted in a significantly higher proportion of ISTJ and ESTJ and a significantly lower proportion of ESFP, ENFP, and ESFJ types compared with female churchgoers. In terms of dominant type, among female Friends there were higher proportions of dominant thinkers (18% versus 14%) and sensers (50% versus 42%), and lower proportions of dominant feelers (26% versus 35%) and intuitives (7% versus 10%), compared with female churchgoers.

Male Friends showed greater preferences for introversion, sensing, and judging (but not feeling) compared with male churchgoers (Table 2). This resulted in a significantly higher proportion of

Table 3. Comparison of cathedral Friends association members with Anglican churchgoers and UK population norms.

		Cathedral Friends	Anglican churchgoers	UK population
Women	N=	775	2135	865
Dimension	*Preference*	%	%	%
Orientation	Introversion	58	49	43
Perceiving	Sensing	86	81	79
Judging	Feeling	58	70	70
Attitude	Judging	91	73	54
Temperament		%	%	%
Epimethean	SJ	81	71	54
Dionysian	SP	5	9	25
Promethean	NT	6	6	5
Apollonian	NF	8	13	15
Men	N=	581	1169	748
Dimension	*Preference*	%	%	%
Orientation	Introversion	72	62	53
Perceiving	Sensing	84	78	73
Judging	Feeling	39	42	35
Attitude	Judging	95	86	55
Temperament		%	%	%
Epimethean	SJ	81	71	44
Dionysian	SP	3	7	29
Promethean	NT	10	13	15
Apollonian	NF	6	9	12

Note: Data for Anglican churchgoers are as reported in Francis, Robbins and Craig (2011); UK norms from Kendall (1998).

ISTJ and a significantly lower proportion of ISTP, ESTP, ENFP, and ENTP types compared with male churchgoers. In terms of dominant type, the main differences were a higher proportion of dominant sensers (59% among Friends versus 49% among male churchgoers) and a lower proportion of dominant thinkers (15% among Friends versus 20% among male churchgoers).

Comparison of Friends in this study with Anglican churchgoers and the UK population generally are summarised in Table 3, which indicates preferences among the four dimensions of the type model and among the four temperaments. For women, Friends were significantly different from either the UK norms or Anglican churchgoers in all four dimensions of psychological type. For men, Friends were different in three of the four dimensions: the exception was in the judging process.

In both sexes, the Epimethean temperament was more frequent and other temperaments less frequent, among Friends than among Anglicans generally. This represented an intensification of the preference for the Epimethean temperament from the UK population, to Anglicans generally and to cathedral Friends in particular.

Discussion

The most frequent profiles of the cathedral Friends in this sample (ISFJ for women and ISTJ for men) are what might be expected from a group that consisted mainly of Christian churchgoers. Studies in the UK (Francis, Duncan, Craig, & Luffman, 2004; Francis et al., 2011; Francis, Robbins, Williams, & Williams, 2007; Village et al., 2012), Canada (Delis-Bulhoes, 1990; Ross, 1993, 1995), and Australia (Robbins & Francis, 2011) suggest that churchgoers from various Christian denominations show higher preferences for introversion and judging than among the populations from which they are drawn. In this respect, Friends may reflect the general tendency of those who belong to Christian churches to be more inward-orientated and to organise their lives with routines and familiar patterns of behaviours. In both dimensions, however, Friends seem to represent people with stronger preferences than average churchgoers. Male Friends, in particular, seem unusually introverted, with 72% preferring introversion, compared with around half of men in the UK population and 62% of male Anglicans generally. The difference among women was slightly less marked, but introversion preference was still higher than either Anglican churchgoers or the general population. Cathedral Friends seem to be people who are content to belong to an organisation, but may not necessarily join in order to interact directly with others. Joining without socialising or attending services may be a more preferred way of belonging to a religion, especially for introverted men.

Friends, like churchgoers generally, are more likely to prefer judging over perceiving, but the distinction from the population at large is even more marked. Over 90% of Friends prefer judging over perceiving in dealing with the outer world, suggesting people who are organised like planning, and are inclined to join organisations for a specific purpose. This seems to be a powerful motivation for becoming a Friend. Similarly, sensing is more strongly preferred among Friends than among churchgoers generally, in both men and women. Sensing seems to be the preferred mode of perceiving in most of the UK population, and the churchgoers (but not necessarily clergy) seem to follow this trend (Francis, Robbins, Duncan, & Whinney, 2010; Village, 2011). However, Friends are especially likely to prefer sensing over intuition, and this makes them even more different from Anglican clergy than most churchgoers.

In both sexes, the overwhelming majority of Friends (81%) were SJ types, representing the Epimethean temperament described by Keirsey and Bates (1978). In studies of church members, this temperament has been referred to as "guardians" by virtue of their propensity to revere the past and hold on to traditional ways of doing things (Francis & Village, 2012). This would seem to fit very well the interests and preoccupations of people in Friends associations, who dedicate themselves to maintaining ancient buildings and national heritage. They would seem to be even more suited psychologically to doing this than most Anglican churchgoers. Among ordained clergy, the Epimethean temperament seems more suited to the roles of OLM (Francis & Village, 2012; Village, 2011). Among lay Anglicans, the Epimethean temperament may find its expression in those areas of church life that value and express the traditional practices and norms of the Church. Historic buildings such as Church of England cathedrals embody the Anglican tradition both in terms of the services that they offer and in the architecture that is redolent of history and liturgical practice. Guarding this heritage may be a preoccupation driven partly by psychological predisposition.

Conclusions

A few key conclusions emerge from this analysis. First, this is further evidence that the psychological predispositions proposed in the psychological type model seem to be useful predictors of religious orientations and behaviours. Temperament theory predicts that SJs would be people most likely to maintain the traditions and heritage of a society, and cathedral Friends associations consist mainly of SJs.

Second, cathedral Friends seem to represent the typical Anglican churchgoer's psychological profile, but even more so. They are even more introverted, even more sensing and even more judging and as such may represent something of "core" Anglicans. The high sensing preference means they are more different from most Anglican clergy than congregation members generally, and clergy might need to be aware of how differently such members perceive the value of change and innovation.

Third, consistent with Cameron's (2003) suggestion, there is some evidence that Friends associations may offer a way of belonging to church for some people who might otherwise find the usual routes less attractive. Friends need not meet with others to belong (Muskett, in press), and more of them seem to be introverts. Men might find this particularly attractive, especially if they struggle with the rather "feminine" profile of much of the Anglican Church, which can be manifest when Anglicans gather for worship or interact socially. Introverted thinking types may find Friends associations the sort of organisation that they would most want to join to express their commitment to upholding religious institutions.

This study was based on a reasonably large sample, but it was a convenience sample and therefore it is difficult to know how far it is fully representative of this sort of organisation. Further work, especially if it could capture a high proportion of Friends of a given cathedral, might help to indicate if these findings can be more generally applied.

References

Archbishops' Council Research and Statistics. (2013a). *Statistics for mission 2011*. Retrieved December 14, 2013, from http://www.churchofengland.org/media/1737985/attendancestats2011.pdf

Archbishops' Council Research and Statistics. (2013b). *Cathedral statistics 2012*. Retrieved December 14, 2013, from http://www.churchofengland.org/media/1820547/2012cathedralstatistics.pdf

Bayne, R. (1994). The Myers-Briggs versus the "Big Five". *The Psychologist*, 7(1), 14–16. http://www.thepsychologist.org.uk/archive/archive_home.cfm/volumeID_7-editionID_291-ArticleID_2568-getfile_getPDF/thepsychologist/psy7no1.pdf

Bayne, R. (1997). *The Myers-Briggs Type Indicator: A critical review and practical guide*. Cheltenham: Stanley Thornes.

Beeson, T. (2004). *The deans*. London: SCM Press.

Cameron, H. (2003). The decline of the Church of England as a local membership organization: Predicting the nature of civil society in 2050. In G. Davie, P. Heelas & L. Woodhead (Eds.), *Predicting religion. Christian, secular and alternative futures* (pp. 109–119). Aldershot: Ashgate.

Cronbach, L. J. (1951). Coefficient alpha and the internal structure of tests. *Psychometrika, 16*(3), 297–334. doi:10.1007/BF02310555

Crump, J., Furnham, A., & Moutafi, J. (2003). The relationship between the revised NEO-Personality Inventory and the Myers-Briggs Type Indicator. *Social Behavior and Personality: An International Journal, 31*(6), 577–584. doi:10.2224/sbp.2003.31.6.577

Davie, G. (1994). *Religion in Britain since 1945*. Oxford: Blackwell.

Davie, G. (2012). Thinking sociologically about religion: Implications for faith communities. *Review of Religious Research, 54*(3), 273–289. doi:10.1007/s13644-012-0077-y

Day, A. (2011). *Believing in belonging: Belief and social identity in the modern world*. Oxford: Oxford University Press.

Delis-Bulhoes, V. (1990). Jungian psychological type and Christian belief in active church members. *Journal of Psychological Type, 20*(1), 25–33. http://www.capt.org/research/psychological-type-journal.htm

Francis, L. J. (2005). *Faith and psychology: Personality, religion and the individual*. London: Darton, Longman & Todd.

Francis, L. J., Craig, C. L., Whinney, M., Tilley, D., & Slater, P. (2007). Psychological typology of Anglican clergy in England: Diversity, strengths, and weaknesses in ministry. *International Journal of Practical Theology, 11*(2), 266–284. doi:10.1515/IJPT.2007.17

Francis, L. J., Duncan, B., Craig, C. L., & Luffman, G. (2004). Type patterns among Anglican congregations in England. *Journal of Adult Theological Education, 1*(1), 65–77. doi:10.1558/jate.1.1.65.36058

Francis, L. J., & Jones, S. H. (2000). The relationship between the Myers-Briggs Type Indicator and the Eysenck personality questionnaire among adult churchgoers. *Pastoral Psychology, 48*(5), 377–386. doi:10.1023/A:1022036504232

Francis, L. J., & Muskett, J. A. (in press). Shaping cathedral studies: a scientific approach. In L. J. Francis (Ed.), *Anglican cathedrals in modern life: the science of cathedral studies*. Palgrave Macmillan.

Francis, L. J., Robbins, M., & Craig, C. (2011). The psychological type profile of Anglican churchgoers in England: Compatible or incompatible with their clergy? *International Journal of Practical Theology, 15*(2), 243–259. doi:10.1515/IJPT.2011.036

Francis, L. J., Robbins, M., Duncan, B., & Whinney, M. (2010). Confirming the psychological type profile of Anglican clergymen in England: A ministry for intuitives. In B. Ruelas & V. Briseño (Eds.), *Psychology of intuition* (pp. 211–219). New York, NY: Nova Science Publishers.

Francis, L. J., Robbins, M., Williams, A., & Williams, R. (2007). All types are called, but some are more likely to respond: The psychological profile of rural Anglican churchgoers in Wales. *Rural Theology, 5*(1), 23–30. doi:10.1179/rut_2007_5_1_003

Francis, L. J., Robbins, M., & Wulff, K. (2008). The relationship between work-related psychological health and psychological type among clergy serving in the Presbyterian Church (USA). *Journal of Empirical Theology, 21*(2), 166–182. doi:10.1163/157092508X349854

Francis, L. J., & Village, A. (2012). The psychological temperament of Anglican clergy in Ordained Local Ministry (OLM): The conserving, serving pastor? *Journal of Empirical Theology, 25*(1), 57–76. doi:10.1163/157092512X635743

Furnham, A. (1996). The big five versus the big four: The relationship between the Myers-Briggs Type Indicator (MBTI) and NEO-PI Five Factor Model of personality. *Personality and Individual Differences, 21*(2), 303–307. doi:10.1016/0191-8869(96)00033-5

Garden, A.-M. (1991). Unresolved issues with the Myers-Briggs Type Indicator. *Journal of Psychological Type, 22*, 3–14. http://www.capt.org/research/psychological-type-journal.htm

Gill, R. (1999). *Churchgoing and Christian ethics*. Cambridge: Cambridge University Press.

Hayes, D., & Slater, A. (2003). From "social club" to "integrated membership scheme": Developing membership schemes strategically. *International Journal of Nonprofit and Voluntary Sector Marketing, 8*(1), 59–75. doi:10.1002/nvsm.201

Hood, R. W. Jr., Hill, P. C., & Spilka, B. (2009). *The psychology of religion: An empirical approach* (4th ed.). New York, NY: Guildford Press.

Inge, J. (2006). Cathedrals, outreach and education. In S. Platten & C. Lewis (Eds.), *Dreaming spires? Cathedrals in a new age*. (pp. 26–38). London: SPCK.

Jung, C. G. (1923). *Psychological types*. London: Routledge.

Keirsey, D. (1998). *Please understand me II: Temperament, character and intelligence*. Del Mar, CA: Prometheus Nemesis.

Keirsey, D. & Bates, M. (1978). *Please understand me* (3rd ed.). Del Mar, CA: Prometheus Nemesis.

Kendall, E. (1998). *Myers-Briggs Type Indicator: Step 1 manual supplement*. Palo Alto, CA: Consulting Psychologists Press.

Lloyd, J. B. (2012). The Myers-Briggs Type Indicator and mainstream psychology: Analysis and evaluation of an unresolved hostility. *Journal of Beliefs & Values*, 33(1), 23–34. doi:10.1080/13617672.2012.650028

MacDonald, D. A., Anderson, P. E., Tsagarakis, C. I., & Holland, C. J. (1995). Correlations between the Myers-Briggs Type Indicator and the NEO Personality Inventory facets. *Psychological Reports*, 76(2), 449–450. doi:10.2466/pr0.1995.76.2.449

McCrae, R. R., & Costa, P. T. (1989). Reinterpreting the Myers-Briggs Type Indicator from the perspective of the Five-Factor Model of personality. *Journal of Personality*, 57(1), 17–40. doi:10.1111/j.1467-6494.1989.tb00759.x

Muskett, J. A. (2011). Deferential or dazzled? Rural cathedral Friends' associations and their royal patronage, past and present. *Rural Theology*, 9(1), 7–25. doi:10.1558/ruth.v9i1.7

Muskett, J. A. (2012). From sixpenny entry to five shilling subscription: Charting cathedral outreach and Friends' associations in the 1920s and 1930s. *Journal of Anglican Studies*, 10(1), 94–118. doi:10.1017/S1740355311000106

Muskett, J. A. (2013). "Friends" of Anglican cathedrals: Norms and values. Befriending, friending or misnomer? *Journal of Beliefs & Values*, 34(2), 189–203. doi:10.1080/13617672.2013.801655

Muskett, J. A. (in press). Reflections on the shop-windows of the Church of England. Anglican cathedrals and vicarious religion. *Journal of Contemporary Religion*.

Muskett, J. A. (in press). Cathedrals making Friends: Building associations. In L. J. Francis (Ed.), *Anglican cathedrals in modern life: the science of cathedral studies*. Palgrave Macmillan.

Myers, I. B. (2006). *MBTI manual: A guide to the development and use of the Myers-Briggs Type Indicator*. Palo Alto, CA: Consulting Psychologists Press.

Myers, I. B., & McCaulley, M. H. (1985). *Manual: A guide to the development and use of the Myers-Briggs Type Indicator*. Palo Alto, CA: Consulting Psychologists Press.

Myers, I. B., & Myers, P. B. (1980). *Gifts differing*. Palo Alto, CA: Consulting Psychologists Press.

Oswald, R. M., & Kroeger, O. (1988). *Personality type and religious leadership*. Washington, DC: Alban Institute.

Pargament, K. I. (Ed.). (2013). *APA handbook of psychology, religion, and spirituality*. Washington, DC: American Psychological Association.

Platten, S., & Lewis, C. (Eds.). (1998). *Flagships of the spirit: Cathedrals in society*. London: Darton, Longman & Todd.

Platten, S., & Lewis, C. (Eds.). (2006). *Dreaming spires? Cathedrals in a new age*. London: SPCK.

Quenk, N. L. (1999). *Essentials of Myers-Briggs Type Indicator assessment*. New York, NY: John Wiley & Sons.

Robbins, M., & Francis, L. J. (2011). All are called, but some psychological types are more likely to respond: Profiling churchgoers in Australia. *Research in the Social Scientific Study of Religion*, 22, 212–229. doi:10.1163/ej.978900420721.i-360.44

Ross, C. F. J. (1993). Type patterns among active members of the Anglican Church: Comparisons with Catholics, evangelicals and clergy. *Journal of Psychological Type*, 26(1), 28–35. http://www.capt.org/research/psychological-type-journal.htm

Ross, C. F. J. (1995). Type patterns among Catholics: Four Anglophone congregations compared with Protestants, Francophone Catholics and priests. *Journal of Psychological Type*, 33(1), 33–41. http://www.capt.org/research/psychological-type-journal.htm

Rowe, P. (2010). *The role of the modern cathedral* (Unpublished PhD Thesis). University of St, Andrews.

Slater, A. (2003). An audit of Friends' schemes at UK heritage sites. *International Journal of Heritage Studies*, 9(4), 357–373. doi:10.1080/1352725032000155081

Slater, A. (2004). Revisiting membership scheme typologies in museums and galleries. *International Journal of Nonprofit and Voluntary Sector Marketing*, 9(3), 238–260. doi:10.1002/nvsm.251

Slater, A. (2005a). Developing a typology of membership schemes in the UK. *International Review on Public and Non Profit Marketing*, 2(1), 23–39. doi:10.1007/BF02893248

Slater, A. (2005b). *National Friends of Cathedrals and Abbeys* (Final Report, 15 November). London: University of Greenwich.

Slater, A., & Armstrong, K. (2010). Involvement, Tate, and me. *Journal of Marketing Management*, 26(7–8), 727–748. doi:10.1080/0267257X.2010.481868

Theos & The Grubb Institute. (2012). *Spiritual capital: The present and future of English cathedrals*. A Research Report commissioned by The Foundation for Church Leadership and The Association of English Cathedrals. London.

Tobacyk, J. J., Livingston, M. M., & Robbins, J. E. (2008). Relationships between Myers-Briggs Type Indicator measure of psychological type and NEO measure of Big Five personality factors in Polish university students: A preliminary cross-cultural comparison. *Psychological Reports, 103*(2), 588–590. doi:10.2466/PR0.103.6.588-590

Tucker, I. F., & Gillespie, B. V. (1993). Correlations among three measures of personality type. *Perceptual and Motor Skills, 77*(2), 650. doi:10.2466/pms.1993.77.2.650

Village, A. (2011). Gifts differing? Psychological type among stipendiary and non-stipendiary Anglican clergy. *Research in the Social Scientific Study of Religion, 22*, 230–250. doi:10.1163/ej.978900420721.i-360.49

Village, A., Baker, S., & Howat, S. (2012). Psychological-type profiles of churchgoers in England. *Mental Health, Religion & Culture, 15*(10), 969–978. doi:10.1080/13674676.2012.686479

Walker, D. (2011). Marks of mission and ways of belonging; shaping the Anglican agenda for occasional churchgoers in the countryside. *Journal of Anglican Studies, 9*(1), 100–116. doi:10.1017/S1740355310000082

Woodhead, L., & Catto, R. (Eds.). (2012). *Religion and change in modern Britain*. Abingdon: Routledge.

Unsettling the guardian: quest religiosity and psychological type among Anglican churchgoers

David S. Walker

Both psychological type and religious orientation have provided tools for understanding the make-up of church congregations and for examining the extent to which different styles of church services may appeal to distinct congregational profiles; however the relationship between the two instruments is relatively little studied to date. Some 390 individuals who attended a Christmas carol service in a Church of England cathedral completed both the Francis Psychological Type Scales and the New Indices of Religious Orientation. Higher Quest scores were found among Intuitive types than Sensing types, replicating an earlier finding by Ross and Francis. Unlike the earlier study, the present survey also identified significantly higher Quest scores for perceiving rather than judging types. A further comparison of the combined SJ type with the remainder of the sample showed the former to have lower Quest scores. The findings are discussed and suggestions made for further research.

Introduction

Psychological type theory and the Francis Psychological Type Scales

Psychological type theory, in the form used in many studies of religious institutions and practices, follows the framework established and operationalised in the Myers–Briggs Type Indicator (MBTI; Myers & McCauley, 1985). A distinctive feature of this instrument and of others that have followed it is that rather than locate individuals at points along a continuum it seeks to conceptualise the four aspects of the human psyche (the perceiving and judging processes, the orientations, and attitudes) by way of polar opposites. For the purpose of the practical study of large samples, especially where the type instrument needs to be administered alongside a variety of other questions or scales, alternative and simpler operationalisations have been proposed, tested, and adopted. An important aspect of psychological type is that, whilst it has been found to be a very useful theory for church-related studies, both the concepts and the operationalisations enable clear comparisons to be made between churchgoers and the general population.

The Francis Psychological Type Scales (FPTS; Francis, 2005), employed in the present cathedral survey, assign to each individual respondent one or other type for each of the four scales: orientation (introvert or extravert), perceiving process (sensing or intuition), judging process (thinking or feeling), and attitudes (judging or perceiving). This particular operationalisation is well established in the literature for the study of churchgoers.

Significant research results using this instrument include those of Francis, Robbins, and Craig (2011), who compared some 3300 Anglican churchgoers with the wider UK population norms. This study found for women more introverts and judging types and for men more introverts, sensing types, feeling types, and judging types among those who attend church. Walker (2012a) compared data for cathedral Sunday morning congregations studied by Francis and Williams (in press) with data for the cathedral carol service congregations and found, inter alia, that the cathedral carol service attracted a larger proportion of thinking types than those present in the wider regular churchgoing population. More recently and most strikingly, Church of England (2014) examined a wide range of possible correlates for Anglican church growth in England, on behalf of the Church Commissioners. The highest single positive correlation was with the minister being an extravert. It would appear from these results that psychological type theory has a major role to play within the field of mission studies.

Alongside the above examples, other studies have looked at the relationship between psychological type and various scales and measures related to religious affiliation, belief, and practice. Francis and Ross (2000) provide a bibliography of some of these, including explorations of links to: attitude towards Christianity, mystical orientation, charismatic experience, styles of believing, dogmatism, preferred ways of interpreting scripture, religious affiliation, and the experience and appreciation of cathedral visitors.

There is no reason why either men or women should be evenly distributed across the 16 psychological types. Walker (2012a) sets out the type tables for those who attend cathedral carol services and compares them with those for male and female UK churchgoers previously identified by Francis et al. (2011). Both sets of figures are heavily weighted towards sensing types and judging types. Among the wider churchgoers, some 78% of men and 81% of women were sensing types, with the cathedral figures a little lower at 70% and 73%, respectively. Some 86% of both male and female churchgoers were judging types with the cathedral figures almost exactly the same at 84% and 85%. Unsurprisingly, this was reflected in a very large proportion of SJ types in both samples, 71% of men and 73% of women among the churchgoers, plus 62% of men and 68% of women at the cathedral carol service. These figures are in all cases significantly above the UK population norms, provided by Kendall (1998) and employed by Francis et al. (2011) who identify that UK church worship appears to attract disproportionately some psychological types and not others.

The SJ combination is often referred to by the descriptor "Guardian". The Guardian type is one that honours customs and traditions, seeking familiarity and stability in a fast changing world. They tend to join groups and be hard-working, loyal, and dutiful, not least in sustaining social institutions such as churches. With such a characterisation, it is not surprising that they are found in relatively large numbers in church congregations.

Religious orientation

The study of religious orientation in church settings derives substantially from the work of Allport (1966, p. 454), who distinguished between two groups of churchgoers. *Extrinsic orientation* described those individuals whose membership and communal activity serve other ends, whilst *intrinsic orientation* identified those for whom religion is "an end in itself", providing the whole of life with meaning, context, and purpose. Allport and Ross (1967) provide detailed characterisations of what might appear to be, as with the FPTS, distinct types. Batson and Ventis (1982, p. 150) made a strong case for the model to be extended by the addition of a third index, *quest orientation*. This will be discussed in more detail in the next section.

Unlike psychological type, the theory of religious orientation is not readily applicable to compare churchgoers with wider populations that include those who do not espouse religious faith. It is focussed on "how" religious people are religious rather than on factors relevant to the general population. Many of the statements found in the various operationalisations of religious orientation would make little sense to an individual to whom religion was of limited or no importance.

As the theory of religious orientation has developed, it has increasingly been seen that the three dimensions of intrinsic, extrinsic, and quest are not descriptions of three distinct and differently motivated groups of individuals, rather they are best operationalised as scales, so that any given person will have a personal score on each of the three. The positive correlations of around .3 to .4 found for example by Walker (2012b) between the three, along with strong positive correlations also found between frequency of churchgoing and both the Intrinsic Scale (.66 $p < .001$) and the Quest Scale (.26 $p < .001$), establish that a person for whom religion is a central aspect of their life is likely to score higher on both of these scales than would a person with more limited engagement. No correlation was found between the Extrinsic Scale and churchgoing frequency.

Quest and the new indices of religious orientation

As the concept of quest orientation is central to the present paper, it is worth quoting the characterisation given by Batson and Ventis in full:

> An individual who approaches religion in this way recognises that he or she does not know, and probably never will know, the final truth about such matters. But still the questions are deemed important and however tentative and subject to change, answers are sought. There may not be a clear belief in a transcendent reality, but there is a transcendent, religious dimension to the individual's life. (Batson & Ventis, 1982, p. 150)

This general characterisation is later refined by Batson and Schoenrade (1991), who distinguish between three components of the quest orientation, defining them as: readiness to face existential questions without reducing their complexity; self-criticism and perception of religious doubt as positive; and openness to change.

Various scales have been produced over the period since Allport proposed his model and the measures have been used in a variety of ways. For the purposes of the present paper, the statements used to construct the Quest Scale found in the *New Indices of Religious Orientation* (NIRO) proposed by Francis (2007), and demonstrated therein to satisfy the requirements for internal consistency have been adopted. The advantages of the NIRO Scales include that they are designed to distinguish between individuals whose religiosity has been shaped by engagement with the institutional church; they also distinguish between the different components of each index. The three components of the NIRO Quest Scale are then each compiled from three individual statements, rated on a 5-point Likert scale: "disagree strongly" (1), "disagree" (2), "not certain" (3), "agree" (4), and "agree strongly" (5). These statements are set out below:

Existentialism

- I was driven to ask religious questions by a growing awareness of the tensions in my world.
- My life experiences have led me to rethink my religious beliefs.
- Religion only became very important for me, when I began to ask questions about the meaning of my life.

Self-criticism

- I value my religious doubts and uncertainties.

- For me, doubting is an important part of what it means to be religious.
- Questions are more important to my religious faith than are answers.

Openness to change
- As I grow and change, I expect my religion to grow and change as well.
- I am constantly questioning my religious beliefs.
- There are many religious issues on which my views are still changing.

A total score is constructed for each respondent by adding up their scores for each of the nine elements. It is clear from their wording that the nine statements used to create the Quest Scale presume a level of religiosity.

The value of studying quest orientation by means of the NIRO Scales has been established in a number of recent papers. Walker (2012b) compared the three scale means for the cathedral carol service congregations with those found among Sunday morning churchgoers by Francis and Williams (in press). The mean of the Intrinsic Scale was significantly lower for the carol services (27.5 as opposed to 32.7, $p < .001$) than the Sunday worship. The same was true for the Extrinsic Scale, with the carol service mean again (25.0) significantly lower than that found on Sundays (26.8, $p < .001$). However, the Quest Scale means show no significant difference between the two samples, being 28.7 and 28.9, respectively. This would suggest that different types of Church of England worship have different levels of appeal to the three orientations. Moreover Walker (2013) identified that, after controlling for age, sex, and the other two religious orientations, higher levels of quest religiosity were associated with more positive opinions regarding both same sex marriage and the appointment of gay men as bishops. Walker (in press) further established a clear negative association between literal beliefs with respect to the Christmas story and Quest.

Quest religiosity and psychological type

The widespread availability of research based on psychological type theory among UK churchgoers, especially by comparison with the much more limited material that makes use of the concept of quest religious orientation, provides in itself grounds for exploring the relationship between the two. If associations are to be found between them, then it might be possible to infer from this associations between quest and the various fields within the study of religion that have proven associations with type. Or, where such direct inferences could not be confidently made, at the very least likely areas for further research may be identified.

Francis and Ross (2000) had put forward a hypothesis for a link between three of the four elements of the psychological type theory and quest orientation. With regard to the perceiving process, it was argued that intuitive types are intrigued by complexity and are likely to endorse the view that doubt only strengthens faith, whereas sensing types are more likely to avoid doubt and questioning. Hence, intuitive types might be expected to record higher quest scores than sensing types. For the judging process, it was hypothesised that thinking types are more likely to be stimulated than feeling types by the questions and challenges of faith and hence might be likely to record higher quest scores than them. For the attitudes, it was suggested that judging types are more likely than perceiving types to respond to a faith that is settled and decided. Hence, perceiving types were predicted to record higher quest scores than judging types. They had not identified theoretical grounds on which to propose a link between quest and the two orientations, extraversion, and introversion.

To test this theory, they had invited a sample of 64 active adult Catholic churchgoers to complete the MBTI together with the six-item measure of Quest orientation proposed by Batson and

Ventis (1982), however, perhaps due in part to the small size of the sample, no significant associations were found.

Working with a larger sample, Ross and Francis (2010) explored the links between psychological type and all three aspects of religious orientation. Using data provided by some 481 weekly churchgoing Christians from the UK who completed the MBTI and the NIRO, they found, as had been earlier proposed, that quest religious orientation scores were indeed higher among intuitive types than sensing types, and that there were no links to introversion and extraversion. However, they were also unable to establish any relationships between quest orientation and the judging process or attitudes. A further paper by Francis (2010) examined the relationship between the NIRO indices and the three major dimensions of personality proposed by the short-form Revised Eysenck Personality Questionnaire (Eysenck, Eysenck, & Barrett, 1985) among a sample of 517 first-year undergraduate students. Whilst the Eysenck model for individual personality differences is very different from the one proposed by psychological type theory, the concept of extraversion is common to both. Francis found that quest religious orientation was associated with low extraversion scores. Although extraversion as measured in this way is not conceptualised exactly in the same way as in psychological type theory, this result would appear to be at some variance with the earlier hypothesis.

Finally, when comparing the cathedral carol service with regular Sunday worshippers, Walker (2012a, 2012b) found differences, respectively, in the prevalence of particular types and the religious orientations. To the extent that associations can be found between quest religiosity and psychological type, this might assist in investigating the relative attraction of church worship to those with different scores across the NIRO Scales.

Research questions

In the light of this body of research, three questions arise:

- Is it possible to establish links between quest orientation and psychological type?
- Can the particular four hypotheses put forward by Francis and Ross (2000) be supported or repudiated?
- Does the prevalence of the SJ type among churchgoing populations have implications for the attraction of church worship to those with a strong quest orientation?

Method

Procedure

Some 1500 adults attended one of the two services of nine lessons and carols at Worcester Cathedral on consecutive evenings in December 2009, most arriving with ample time to complete a survey form distributed by the cathedral staff before the service began. Pencils were provided. The completed questionnaires were collected after the service was over. The survey forms were anonymous and confidential.

Measures

Respondents were asked basic information about gender and age (measured largely in decades with a final category for "80 and over"). Frequency of church attendance was assessed by a choice of six responses: "once a week or more", "nearly every week", "at least once a month", "at least 6 times a year", "at least once a year", and "never". Religious affiliation was tested in two ways. Respondents were invited to describe themselves as "Church of England", "other

Christian denomination", "other world faith", or "none". They were also asked to indicate whether or not they had been baptised or confirmed.

In terms of religious orientation, the 27 questions devised by Francis (2007) for the NIRO made use of a 5-point Likert scale: "agree strongly"; "agree"; "not certain"; "disagree"; and "disagree strongly". In terms of psychological type, the Francis Psychological Type Scales (Francis, 2005) comprised 40 forced-choice questions, with 10 exploring each of the four components of psychological type theory. In accordance with common practice, respondents who failed to complete significant numbers of the Likert scale questions were excluded from the study.

Participants

The sample comprised 58% women and 42% men, a figure very close to that found by Francis and Williams (in press) at cathedral Sunday services. The carol service age profile was, by comparison with the latter, much more evenly spread across the decades: 27% of respondents were under 40, with the figures for the next three age decades being 13%, 21%, and 31%, only 8% were aged 70 or above. The corresponding Sunday worship figures were 16% under 40, then 14%, 18%, and 23%, with 27% aged 70 or above.

A very wide range of church attendance was found among the participants, with 20% attending weekly or more, 12% nearly weekly, 9% at least monthly, 14% at least 6 times per year, and 37% at least annually. A further 9% claimed never to attend church. A large majority of respondents (61%) considered themselves to be Church of England. A further 17% were members of other Christian denominations, whilst 1% belonged to other world faiths, and 20% had no religious affiliation. Some 61% had been both baptised and confirmed and a further 28% were baptised.

Analysis

The very high figures for both affiliation and the two aspects of Christian initiation, especially confirmation, suggest that, notwithstanding the low levels of churchgoing reported, enough of the sample would have had the level of engagement with religion that would make the NIRO Scales likely to be reliable and effective.

Results

The Quest Scale was found to be internally reliable with respect to the current sample, with a Cronbach (1951) alpha value of .80. Furthermore, the alpha values for the four Francis Psychological Types Scales: orientation (.79), perceiving process (.70), judging process (.69), and attitudes (.77) also all exceeded the lower bound of .65 proposed for tests of this sort by DeVellis (2003).

The results for the comparisons between Quest orientation and psychological type are set out in Table 1. The numbers of participants falling into each of the psychological type pairings reflect the widely observed phenomenon (see, for example, Kendall, 1998) that not all types occur equally often. Much higher numbers were found to be sensing types (70%) than intuitive types (30%), although the population norms for women (79%) are even more strongly weighted towards sensing types. An even larger disproportionality was observed between judging types (84%) and perceiving types (16%), well above the UK population norms for judging types of 62% for women and 55% for men. Almost two-thirds of the respondents (65%) were found to be both sensing and judging types. Although this *Guardian* combination is relatively common within the general UK population, this present sample significantly exceeds the norms for both men (44%) and women (54%).

Table 1. Quest orientation scores by psychological type preferences.

	Mean	SD	N	p<
Orientations				
Extraversion	28.6	5.86	198	
Introversion	28.7	5.64	192	NS
Perceiving functions				
Sensing	28.2	5.44	274	
Intuition	29.6	6.32	116	.05
Judging functions				
Thinking	28.6	6.21	204	
Feeling	28.8	5.20	185	NS
Attitudes				
Judging	28.2	5.80	326	
Perceiving	30.9	4.91	64	.001
SJ combination				
Guardians	28.1	5.48	252	
Others	29.7	6.09	138	.01

The lack of any significant difference between the quest scores recorded by the two orientations was in line with both the Francis and Ross (2000) hypothesis and the Ross and Francis (2010) findings, over against the results obtained by Francis (2010) which would have suggested higher quest scores for introverts. The significant difference between the two perceiving processes was in line with the Francis and Ross (2000) hypothesis, albeit at the lowest level of statistical significance commonly accepted in such tests, whereas Ross and Francis (2010) had not established any significant association. The lack of any significant difference between the two judging processes was in line with the results of Ross and Francis (2010), which did not support the Francis and Ross (2000) hypothesis. The difference between the two attitudes was significant at the $p < .001$ level. This was in line with the Francis and Ross (2000) hypothesis, which the Ross and Francis (2010) study had failed to produce evidence to support. The mean quest score for the Guardian (SJ) types was higher than for the remainder of the sample, significant at the $p < .01$ level.

Discussion

Francis and Ross (2000) had proposed that no link would be found between the orientations and quest religiosity scores. Whilst Francis (2010) had found lower Eysenck extraversion scores associated with higher quest scores, it would appear from both the present data and the results of Ross and Francis (2010) that, when measured using the FPTS, there is no association to be found between quest scores and the two psychological orientations.

The link between the two perceiving processes hypothesised by Francis and Ross (2000) had not been found in their later study; the present study supports it, albeit only at the $p < .05$ level of significance. In itself this is not a strong result, but may become of greater significance when discussed in the light of the other findings of the paper.

The hypothesis put forward by Ross and Francis (2010) that thinking types would be more likely than feeling types to be stimulated by the challenges and questions of faith, and hence would return higher quest scores, has now failed to be borne out by both their own later research and the present paper, neither of which has identified any association. Indeed the current study showed a slightly higher mean for feeling types than for thinking types. A closer look at the three component parts of the Quest Scale may give some indication as to why this may be; the *existentialism* part of the index may indeed have a focus on the asking of questions and even "rethinking", but the *self-criticism* statements, with a focus on "value" and "what it means", and a negative statement about "answers", are cast in a more "feeling" register. The final section, *openness to change*, ranges in its languages from "beliefs" to "views" and to what I "expect". Overall it can be argued that there is a balance between words in the statements that might appeal to each of the two judging processes. However, it would be simple to recast the words of the nine statements in ways that remained true to the concept of quest religiosity but which favoured one process over the other. That may in itself provide an argument for keeping the questions in their present form.

Francis and Ross (2000) had hypothesised a positive association between quest religiosity and perceiving types on the grounds that "judgers are more likely than perceivers to respond to a faith that is settled and decided". Notwithstanding the relatively small proportion of perceiving types found in the present sample, the study has supported this hypothesis at the highest significance level of $p < .001$. In terms of the three subsections used to form the Quest Scale, it is clear that the notions of *self-criticism* and of *openness to change* have a strong resonance with the perceiving type's preferences. Moreover, the individual statements that build up the scale make many references to having changing views, valuing uncertainties and to the prioritisation of questions over answers. Quest orientation would therefore appear to have a strong association with the perceiving attitude.

The high proportion of SJ or *Guardian* types found commonly in church congregations was reflected in the present sample, with almost two-thirds falling into that category. It has been found that this group has a significantly lower mean quest score than the remainder of the sample. Moreover, the refining of the comparison from S to SJ has both increased the difference between the two means and strengthened the significance level from $p < .05$ to $p < .01$. This finding is consonant with the overall characterisation of quest orientation by Batson and Ventis (1982) in terms of "tentativity" and "uncertainty" and of such answers as an individual may reach to religious questions being "subject to change". The three subdivisions of quest by Batson and Schoenrade (1991) into *existentialism*, *self-criticism*, and *openness to change* again fit ill with the *Guardian* type. Moreover, the wording of the nine NIRO quest statements, with their constant emphases on change, doubt, questioning, and rethinking, would almost without exception be potentially troubling to a *Guardian* type.

These findings raise the issue as to what sort of welcome quest religiosity is likely to receive in an Anglican church dominated by Guardians. With quest scores increasing with frequency of church attendance, it is clear that this orientation is present at the heart of church congregations. It is plausible that it may be an underlying factor in the various church conflicts (such as over same sex marriage) where the battleground is substantially between those seeking a traditional and more uniform position and those who wish to increase diversity and provisionality.

Conclusions

Clear links have been found between both sensing types and judging types and lower quest scores. The combining of these two aspects into the *Guardian* type has further elaborated the distinction and has suggested that this may be a factor in church conflicts. Hence, the relationship between psychological type and religious orientation is not simply a matter for academic interest but potentially of real significance to churches today. Further research might usefully build on the present findings by seeking to determine whether the strength of quest religiosity and the numerical domination of the SJ pairing vary in different types of churches or at different levels of church leadership. Given that the type distributions of men and women are different, research with a larger sample could usefully seek to establish whether the present findings are true for both sexes.

References

Allport, G. W. (1966). The religious context of prejudice. *Journal for the Scientific Study of Religion, 5*, 447–457.

Allport, G. W., & Ross, J. M. (1967). Personal religious orientation and prejudice. *Journal of Personality and Social Psychology, 5*, 432–443.

Batson, C. D., & Schoenrade, P. A. (1991). Measuring religion as quest: 1) Validity concerns. *Journal for the Scientific Study of Religion, 30*, 416–429.

Batson, C. D., & Ventis, W. L. (1982). *The religious experience: A social psychological perspective*. New York, NY: Oxford University Press.

Church of England. (2014). *From anecdote to evidence: Findings from the Church Growth Research Programme 2011–2013*. London: Church of England.

Cronbach, L. J. (1951). Co-efficient alpha and the internal structure of tests. *Psychometrika, 16*, 297–334.

DeVellis, R. F. (2003). *Scale development: Theory and applications* (2nd ed.). London: Sage.

Eysenck, S. B. G., Eysenck, H. J., & Barrett, P. (1985). A revised version of the Psychoticism Scale. *Personality and Individual Differences, 6*, 21–29. doi:10.1016/0191-8869(85)90026-1

Francis, L. J. (2005). *Faith and psychology: Personality, religion and the individual*. London: Darton, Longman and Todd.

Francis, L. J. (2007). Introducing the New Indices of Religious Orientation (NIRO): Conceptualisation and measurement. *Mental Health, Religion & Culture, 10*, 585–602. doi:10.1080/13674670601035510

Francis, L. J. (2010). Personality and religious orientation: Shifting sands or firm foundations? *Mental Health, Religion & Culture, 13*(7), 793–803. doi:10.1080/13674670802187912

Francis, L. J., Robbins, M., & Craig, C. L. (2011). The psychological type profile of Anglican churchgoers in England: Compatible or incompatible with their clergy? *International Journal of Practical Theology, 15*, 243–259. doi:10.1515/IJPT.2011.036

Francis, L. J., & Ross, C. F. J. (2000). Personality type and quest orientation of religiosity. *Journal of Psychological Type, 55*, 22–25.

Francis, L. J., & Williams, E. (in press). The motivational style of cathedral congregations: An empirical enquiry employing the New Indices of Religious Orientation.

Kendall, E. (1998). *Myers-Briggs Type Indicator: Step 1 manual supplement*. Palo Alto, CA: Consulting Psychologists Press.

Myers, I. B., & McCaulley, M. H. (1985). *Manual: A guide to the development and use of the Myers-Briggs Type Indicator*. Palo Alto, CA: Consulting Psychologists Press.

Ross, C. F. J., & Francis, L. J. (2010). The relationship of intrinsic, extrinsic, and quest religious orientations to Jungian psychological type among churchgoers in England and Wales. *Mental Health, Religion & Culture, 13*(7), 805–819. doi:10.1080/13674670802207462

Walker, D. S. (2012a). Attending the service of nine lessons and carols at a rural cathedral: An empirical study in religious orientation and motivational style. *Rural Theology, 10*(1), 56–69.

Walker, D. S. (2012b). O come all ye thinking types: The wider appeal of the cathedral carol service. *Mental Health, Religion & Culture, 15*(10), 987–995. doi:10.1080/13674676.2012.707436

Walker, D. S. (2013). Religious orientation and attitudes towards gay marriage and homosexual bishops: An empirical enquiry inside an Anglican Cathedral. *Theology & Sexuality, 18*(1), 76–92. doi:10.1179/1355835813Z.0000000005

Walker, D. S. (in press). Religious orientation and styles of believing: insights from the psychology of religion for developing Christmas carol services in cathedrals and large churches. *International Journal of Practical Theology*.

Inside Southwark Cathedral: a study in psychological-type profiling

David W. Lankshear and Leslie J. Francis

A series of recent studies have begun to map the psychological-type profile of Anglican churchgoers in England and Wales. This study sets the profile of 120 men and 161 women attending Sunday services in Southwark Cathedral against the profile of 1169 men and 2135 women attending Anglican parish churches. These data found a significantly higher proportion of intuitive types and thinking types within the cathedral congregation and a significantly lower proportion of participants displaying the SJ temperament. The implications of these findings are discussed for appreciating the distinctive style of cathedral worship and of cathedral ministry.

Introduction

Psychological-type theory is beginning to play an increasingly visible role both in the psychology of religion (Lewis, 2012) and in empirical theology (Village, 2011). One example of this development concerns the field of congregational studies where empirical research employing psychological-type theory has been conducted in North America, the UK, and Australia: in North America by Gerhardt (1983), Rehak (1998), Delis-Bulhoes (1990), Ross (1993, 1995), and Bramer and Ross (2012); in the UK by Craig, Francis, Bailey, and Robbins (2003), Francis, Duncan, Craig, and Luffman (2004), Francis, Robbins, Williams, and Williams (2007), Francis, Robbins, and Craig (2011), Village, Baker, and Howat (2012), Francis and Robbins (2012), and Francis (2013); and in Australia by Robbins and Francis (2011, 2012) and Robbins, Francis, and Powell (2012).

Psychological-type theory

Psychological-type theory has its roots in the pioneering work of Jung (1971) and has been developed and popularised through a series of type indicators, type sorters or type scale. The most frequently employed of these measures in church-related research and congregational studies are the Keirsey Temperament Sorter (Keirsey & Bates, 1978), the Myers–Brigg Type Indicator (Myers & McCaulley, 1985), and the Francis Psychological Type Scales (FPTS; Francis, 2005). At its core, psychological-type theory distinguishes between two orientations, two perceiving functions, two judging functions, and two attitudes towards the outer world. In each of these four areas, psychological-type theory conceptualises difference in terms of two discrete categories (or types) rather than in terms of a continuum stretching between two poles.

In psychological-type theory, the two orientations are concerned with contrasting energy sources and distinguish between introversion (I) and extraversion (E). Introverts are energised by the inner world. When tired they prefer to go inwards to regain energy. Extraverts are energised by the outer world. When tired they prefer to congregate with other people to regain energy. Introverts enjoy their own company and appreciate silence. Extraverts enjoy the company of others and prefer to engage in conversation. A congregation shaped by introverts may seem somewhat strange to extraverts, while a congregation shaped by extraverts may seem somewhat strange to introverts.

In psychological-type theory, the two perceiving functions are concerned with contrasting ways of taking in information and distinguish between sensing (S) and intuition (N). Sensing types are concerned with the details of a situation as perceived by the five senses. Intuitive types are concerned with the meaning and significance of a situation. Sensing types feel comfortable with the familiar and with the conventional. They tend to dislike change. Intuitive types feel comfortable with innovation and with new ideas. They tend to promote change. A congregation shaped by sensing types may seem somewhat strange to intuitive types, while a congregation shaped by intuitive types may seem somewhat strange to sensing types.

In psychological-type theory, the two judging functions are concerned with contrasting ways of evaluating situations and distinguish between thinking (T) and feeling (F). Thinking types are concerned with the objective evaluation of a situation, and with identifying the underlying logic. Feeling types are concerned with the subjective evaluation of a situation, and with identifying the underlying values. Thinking types are more concerned with supporting effective systems. Feeling types are concerned with supporting interpersonal relationships. A congregation shaped by thinking types may seem somewhat strange to feeling types, while a congregation shaped by feeling types may seem somewhat strange to thinking types.

In psychological-type theory, the two attitudes towards the outer world are concerned with which of the two psychological processes is employed in the outer world and distinguish between judging (J) and perceiving (P). Judging types employ their preferred judging function (thinking or feeling) in the outer world. Perceiving types employ their preferred perceiving function (sensing or intuition) in the outer world. Judging types display a planned, orderly and organised profile to the outer world. Perceiving types display a flexible, spontaneous and unplanned profile to the outer world. A congregation shaped by judging types may seem somewhat strange to perceiving types, while a congregation shaped by perceiving types may seem somewhat strange to judging types.

As well as discussing the four contrasting pairs independently (introversion *or* extraversion, sensing *or* intuition, thinking *or* feeling, and judging *or* perceiving), psychological-type theory draws these component parts together in a variety of ways, three of which are particularly important. First, the combination of the components allows each individual's strongest, or *dominant* function to be identified: dominant sensing types are practical people; dominant intuitive types are imaginative people; dominant feeling types are humane people; and dominant thinking types are logical people. Second, alongside their dominant preference individuals are given clearer identity by their second strongest, or *auxiliary* function. The auxiliary is the preferred function for the opposite process complementing the dominant function, leading to eight dominant-auxiliary pairs: dominant sensing with thinking, dominant sensing with feeling, dominant intuition with thinking, dominant intuition with feeling, dominant feeling with sensing, dominant feeling with intuition, dominant thinking with sensing, and dominant thinking with intuition. Third, all 4 preferred components of psychological-type theory cohere to generate 16 complete types, usually identified by their initial letter (e.g., INTJ or ESFP).

Working from the same building blocks of psychological-type theory, temperament theory as developed by Keirsey and Bates (1978) proposes four main temperament types defined by the following combinations: SJ, SP, NF, and NT. In the language shaped by Keirsey and Bates (1978), the Epimethean Temperament characterises the SJ profile, people who long to be dutiful, to be useful to the social units to which they belong, and to preserve and hand on to others what they have inherited. The Dionysian Temperament characterises the SP profile, people who want to be engaged, involved, and doing something new. The Promethean Temperament characterises the NT profile, people who want to understand, explain, shape and predict realties, and who prize their personal competence. The Apollonian Temperament characterises the NF profile, people who quest for authenticity and for self-actualisation, who are idealistic and who have great capacity for empathic listening.

Psychological-type theory in congregational studies

Working within the UK, Francis et al. (2007) analysed data from a sample of 185 churchgoers attending small congregations in rural Wales and compared the profile of male and female churchgoers with population norms for the UK published by Kendall (1998). The main finding from this comparison concerned the undue weighting towards sensing, feeling, and judging in church congregations. Among women ISFJ accounts for 32% of churchgoers, compared with 18% of the general population, and ESFJ accounts for 28% of churchgoers, compared with 19% of the general population. Among men ISFJ accounts for 19% of churchgoers, compared with 7% of the general population, and ESFJ accounts for 27% of churchgoers, compared with 6% of the general population. The over-representation of ISFJ and ESFJ among churchgoers leads to under-representation of other types. Francis et al. (2007) choose the descriptive (but challenging) title, "All types are called, but some are more likely to respond" for their study.

The major shortcoming with the study reported by Francis et al. (2007) concerned the interpretative weight carried by a sample of only 185 churchgoers. A more recent study, reported by Francis et al. (2011), addressed this shortcoming by assembling data from 2135 women and 1169 men surveyed in the context of Anglican church services in England and by (again) comparing the psychological-type profile of these churchgoers with the population norms for the UK published by Kendall (1998). The findings from this larger study are remarkably similar to some of the findings from the smaller study (especially among the women). Among the female churchgoers, there were strong preferences for sensing (81%), for feeling (70%), and for judging (85%), with a balance between introversion (49%) and extraversion (51%). In this study, 25% of the women reported ISFJ, 25% reported ESFJ, and 73% reported the SJ temperament. Among the male churchgoers, there were preferences for introversion (62%), for sensing (78%), for thinking (58%), and for judging (86%). In this study, 17% of the men reported ISFJ, 11% reported ESFJ, and 71% reported the SJ temperament.

The major shortcoming with the two studies reported by Francis et al. (2007, 2011) is that both studies were restricted to Anglicans in England and Wales. Another study, reported by Robbins and Francis (2011), addressed this shortcoming by drawing on data collected by the Australian National Church Life Survey from 936 women and 591 men surveyed in the context of church services across 18 participating denominations and by comparing the psychological-type profile of the churchgoers with the population norms for Australia published by Ball (2008). The findings from this Australian study are remarkably similar to the findings reported by Francis et al. (2011). Among the female churchgoers, there were strong preferences for sensing (81%), for feeling (62%), and for judging (87%), with a balance between introversion (52%) and extraversion (48%). In this study, 23% of the women reported ISFJ and 22% reported ESFJ. Among the male churchgoers, there were preferences for introversion (59%), for sensing

(78%), for thinking (60%), and for judging (88%). In this study, 13% of the men reported ISFJ and 14% reported ESFJ.

Overall, when the profiles of the men and women are added together from the three studies (giving a sample of 5016), the ISFJ profile of churchgoers is confirmed with introversion (54%), sensing (80%), feeling (58%), and judging (86%). Given the predominance of the ISFJ profile within church congregations, the hypothesis was advanced in a subsequent study by Francis and Robbins (2012) that extraverts, intuitive types, thinking types, and perceiving types who attend church are the least likely to feel at home in or satisfied with the churches they attend. They tested this hypothesis among a sample of 1867 churchgoers who completed a measure of psychological type, together with a measure of frequency of attendance, and an index of congregational satisfaction. These data confirmed that congregations were weighted towards preferences for introversion, sensing, feeling, and judging (ISFJ), and the individuals displaying the opposite preferences (extraversion, intuition, thinking, and perceiving) recorded lower levels of congregational satisfaction. On the basis of these findings, Francis and Robbins (2012) took the view that, not only were extraverts, intuitive types, thinking types, and perceiving types less in evidence in church congregations, those who were there were expressing lower levels of congregational satisfaction and thus more likely to join the category of church leavers (Francis & Richter, 2007).

Psychological-type theory in cathedral studies

A separate strand of research has also begun to introduce psychological-type theory within the field of cathedral studies, although this strand has focused primarily on understanding the profile of cathedral visitors (Francis, Annis, Robbins, ap Siôn, & Williams, 2012; Francis, Mansfield, Williams, & Village, 2010; Francis, Williams, Annis, & Robbins, 2008). Walker (2012), however, took this strand in a somewhat different direction in order to examine the psychological-type profile of 164 men and 239 women who attended two carol services on consecutive nights in Worcester Cathedral in December 2009. Walker's study found some significant differences between churchgoers and those who attended the cathedral carol services among both men and women.

For women there were no significant differences in terms of the orientations (51% extraverts in the cathedral and 51% extraverts in the parish churches) or in terms of attitudes (85% judging types in the cathedral and 85% in the parish churches). Significant differences emerged, however, with regard to the two processes. In terms of the perceiving process, the proportion of sensing types fell from 81% in the church congregations to 73% in the cathedral congregation, with a consequent increase in intuitive types from 19% to 27%. In terms of the judging process, the proportion of feeling types fell from 70% in the church congregations to 61% in the cathedral congregation, with a consequent increase in thinking types from 30% to 39%. In terms of dominant types, there were significantly more dominant thinking types (19% compared with 14%) and significantly more dominant intuitive types (14% compared with 10%) in the cathedral congregation compared with the church congregations. In terms of temperament theory, the proportion of SJs fell from 73% in the church congregations to 68% in the cathedral congregation.

For men there were no significant differences in terms of the orientations (42% extraverts in the cathedral and 38% in the parish churches) or in terms of the attitudes (84% judging types in the cathedral and 86% judging types in the parish churches). Significant differences emerged, however, with regard to the two processes. In terms of the perceiving process, the proportion of sensing types fell from 78% in the church congregations to 70% in the cathedral congregation, with a consequent increase in intuitive types from 22% to 30%. In terms of the judging process, the proportion of feeling types fell from 42% in the church congregations to 31% in the cathedral congregation, with a consequent increase in thinking types from 58% to 69%. In terms of dominant types, there were significantly more dominant thinking types (28% compared with 20%) in the cathedral congregation compared with the church congregations. In terms of temperament theory, the proportion of SJs fell from 71% in the church congregations to 62% in the cathedral congregation.

Clearly, Walker's (2012) study suggests that the cathedral carol service attracts a distinctive congregation comprising higher proportions of intuitive types and thinking types than found in regular church congregations. Walker argues that the cathedral carol service relates the Christmas story in a way that goes beyond the senses and hints at "a deeper mystery understood or apprehended in the depths of the human soul" (p. 993), an experience enhanced by a professional quality choir, by a professional organist, and by an evocatively lit Grade 1 listed ancient building. Such qualities may resonate with intuitive types. Walker also argues that the cathedral carol service is not couched in a context of emotional and relational engagement or cast in the "feeling" idiom of many church services. Such qualities may resonate with thinking types.

Research question

The question raised by Walker's (2012) study concerns the extent to which the distinctive appeal of the cathedral to intuitive types and to thinking types is mainly limited to the highly distinctive environment of the cathedral carol service, or whether it extends to the routine Sunday worship as well. It is the aim of this study to explore this issue.

Method

Procedure

On one Sunday during late September 2013, the congregation attending services in Southwark Cathedral were invited to assist the cathedral by compiling a questionnaire. The questionnaire comprised three sections exploring background, attitudes, and psychological profile, including psychological type. Participation was voluntary, and anonymity and confidentiality were assured. A total of 288 questionnaires completed by participants aged 20 or over were submitted at the end of the service, of which 281 had full data on psychological-type profile.

Participants

The 281 participants who had fully completed the psychological-type profile data comprised 120 men and 161 women; 5% were in their 20s, 12% in their 30s, 13% in their 40s, 21% in their 50s, 30% in their 60s, 16% in their 70s, and 3% were aged 80 or over. The majority regarded the cathedral as their main place of worship (69%), attended services weekly (63%), and were on the membership roll of the cathedral (56%). The majority were white (90%) and either in part-time (16%) or full-time (43%) work.

Instrument

Psychological type was assessed by the FPTS (Francis, 2005). This is a 40-item instrument comprising four sets of 10 forced-choice items related to each of the four components of psychological type: orientation (extraversion or introversion), perceiving process (sensing or intuition), judging process (thinking or feeling), and attitude towards the outer world (judging or perceiving). Recent studies have demonstrated that this instrument functions well in church-related contexts. For example, Francis, Craig, and Hall (2008) reported alpha coefficients of .83 for the EI Scale, .76 for the SN Scale, .73 for the TF Scale, and .79 for the JP Scale. Participants were asked for each pair of characteristics to check the "box next to that characteristic which is closer to the real you, even if you feel both characteristics apply to you. Tick the characteristics that reflect the real you, even if other people see you differently".

Data analysis

The research literature concerning the empirical investigation of psychological type has developed a highly distinctive method for analysing, handling, and displaying statistical data in the form of "type tables". This convention has been adopted in the following presentation in order to integrate these new data within the established literature and to provide all the details necessary for secondary analysis and further interpretation within the rich theoretical framework afforded by psychological type. Type tables have been designed to provide information about the 16 discrete psychological types, about the four dichotomous preferences, about the six sets of pairs and temperaments, about the dominant types, and about the introverted and extraverted Jungian types. Commentary on this table will, however, be restricted to those aspects of the data strictly relevant to the research question. In the context of type tables, the statistical significance of the difference between two groups is established by means of the selection ration index (I), an extension of chi-square (McCaulley, 1985).

Results

The eight indices of the FPTS all achieved satisfactory internal consistency reliability in terms of the alpha coefficient (Cronbach, 1951): extraversion and introversion, $\alpha = .80$; sensing and intuition, $\alpha = .71$; thinking and feeling, $\alpha = .70$; judging and perceiving, $\alpha = .77$.

Table 1 presents the type distribution for the 161 women engaged in the cathedral congregation. These data demonstrate preferences for introversion (57%) over extraversion (44%), for sensing (54%) over intuition (46%), for thinking (53%) over feeling (47%), and for judging (85%) over perceiving (15%). The hierarchy of dominant-type preferences is dominant sensing (29%), followed by dominant intuition (29%), dominant feeling (21%), and dominant thinking (21%). In terms of the 16 complete types, the four predominant types are INTJ (16%), ISTJ (14%), ISFJ (14%), and ESTJ (12%).

Table 1 also draws attention to the ways in which women engaged in the cathedral congregation differ from women engaged in parish church congregations. In terms of dichotomous preferences, significant differences emerge in the perceiving process (sensing and intuition) and in the judging process (thinking and feeling), but neither in the orientations (extraversion and introversion) nor in the attitudes (judging and perceiving). While in the church congregation 19% of the women preferred intuition, the proportion rose to 46% in the cathedral congregation. While in the church congregation 30% of the women preferred thinking, the proportion rose to 53% in the cathedral congregation. In terms of dominant-type preferences, among women in the cathedral congregation, compared with church congregations, there are a higher proportion of dominant intuitive types (29% compared with 10%), and of dominant thinking types (21% compared with 14%), and lower proportions of dominant sensing types (29% compared with 42%) and dominant feeling types (21% compared with 35%). In terms of temperament theory, among women in the cathedral congregation there is a lower proportion of SJs (49% compared with 73%).

Table 2 presents the type distribution for the 120 men engaged in the cathedral congregation. These data demonstrate preferences for introversion (60%) over extraversion (40%), for sensing (59%) over intuition (41%), for thinking (58%) over feeling (43%), and for judging (86%) over

Table 1. Type distribution for women in cathedral congregation compared with female churchgoers.

The Sixteen Complete Types

ISTJ	ISFJ	INFJ	INTJ
n = 22	n = 22	n = 11	n = 25
(13.7%)	(13.7%)	(6.8%)	(15.5%)
I = 1.11	I = 0.55**	I = 1.97*	I = 6.13***
+++++	+++++	+++++	+++++
+++++	+++++	++	+++++
++++	++++		+++++
			+

ISTP	ISFP	INFP	INTP
n = 4	n = 1	n = 4	n = 2
(2.5%)	(0.6%)	(2.5%)	(1.2%)
I = 3.12*	I = 0.20	I = 1.36	I = 1.89
+++	+	+++	+

ESTP	ESFP	ENFP	ENTP
n = 0	n = 3	n = 6	n = 4
(0.0%)	(1.9%)	(3.7%)	(2.5%)
I = 0.00	I = 0.43	I = 1.28	I = 3.79**
	++	++++	+++

ESTJ	ESFJ	ENFJ	ENTJ
n = 19	n = 16	n = 13	n = 9
(11.8%)	(9.9%)	(8.1%)	(5.6%)
I = 1.10	I = 0.40***	I = 1.76*	I = 2.65**
+++++	+++++	+++++	+++++
+++++	+++++	+++	+
++			

Dichotomous Preferences

	n =		I =
E	70	(43.5%)	0.86
I	91	(56.5%)	1.14
S	87	(54.0%)	0.67***
N	74	(46.0%)	2.45***
T	85	(52.8%)	1.75***
F	76	(47.2%)	0.68***
J	137	(85.1%)	1.00
P	24	(14.9%)	1.03

Pairs and Temperaments

	n =		I =
IJ	80	(49.7%)	1.15
IP	11	(6.8%)	1.07
EP	13	(8.1%)	0.99
EJ	57	(35.4%)	0.83
ST	45	(28.0%)	1.16
SF	42	(26.1%)	0.46***
NF	34	(21.1%)	1.65**
NT	40	(24.8%)	4.17***
SJ	79	(49.1%)	0.67***
SP	8	(5.0%)	0.59
NP	16	(9.9%)	1.64*
NJ	58	(36.0%)	2.84***
TJ	75	(46.6%)	1.68***
TP	10	(6.2%)	2.60**
FP	14	(8.7%)	0.72
FJ	62	(38.5%)	0.67***
IN	42	(26.1%)	3.07***
EN	32	(19.9%)	1.94***
IS	49	(30.4%)	0.74**
ES	38	(23.6%)	0.59***
ET	32	(19.9%)	1.44*
EF	38	(23.6%)	0.64***
IF	38	(23.6%)	0.71*
IT	53	(32.9%)	2.02***

Jungian Types (E)

	n	%	Index
E-TJ	28	17.4	1.35
E-FJ	29	18.0	0.61**
ES-P	3	1.9	0.41
EN-P	10	6.2	1.74

Jungian Types (I)

	n	%	Index
I-TP	6	3.7	2.56*
I-FP	5	3.1	0.63
IS-J	44	27.3	0.74*
IN-J	36	22.4	3.73***

Dominant Types

	n	%	Index
Dt.T	34	21.1	1.48*
Dt.F	34	21.1	0.61***
Dt.S	47	29.2	0.70**
Dt.N	46	28.6	2.99***

Notes: N = 161; NB: + = 1% of N.
*p < .05.
**p < .01.
***p < .001.

Table 2. Type distribution for men in cathedral congregation compared with male churchgoers.

The Sixteen Complete Types					Dichotomous Preferences			
ISTJ $n = 22$ (18.3%) $I = 0.64*$ +++++ +++++ +++++ +++	ISFJ $n = 13$ (10.8%) $I = 0.63$ +++++ +++++ +	INFJ $n = 8$ (6.7%) $I = 2.29*$ +++++ ++	INTJ $n = 17$ (14.2%) $I = 2.24***$ +++++ +++++ ++++	E I S N T F J P	$n = 48$ $n = 72$ $n = 71$ $n = 49$ $n = 69$ $n = 51$ $n = 103$ $n = 17$	(40.0%) (60.0%) (59.2%) (40.8%) (57.5%) (42.5%) (85.8%) (14.2%)	$I = 1.04$ $I = 0.97$ $I = 0.76***$ $I = 1.83***$ $I = 0.99$ $I = 1.01$ $I = 1.00$ $I = 1.02$
ISTP $n = 1$ (0.8%) $I = 0.51$ +	ISFP $n = 1$ (0.8%) $I = 0.44$ +	INFP $n = 4$ (3.3%) $I = 1.77$ +++	INTP $n = 6$ (5.0%) $I = 4.50***$ +++++	Pairs and Temperaments			
				IJ IP EP EJ ST SF NF NT SJ SP NP NJ	$n = 60$ $n = 12$ $n = 5$ $n = 43$ $n = 41$ $n = 30$ $n = 21$ $n = 28$ $n = 69$ $n = 2$ $n = 15$ $n = 34$	(50.0%) (10.0%) (4.2%) (35.8%) (34.2%) (25.0%) (17.5%) (23.3%) (57.5%) (1.7%) (12.5%) (28.3%)	$I = 0.91$ $I = 1.54$ $I = 0.57$ $I = 1.16$ $I = 0.75*$ $I = 0.78$ $I = 1.78**$ $I = 1.87***$ $I = 0.81**$ $I = 0.24*$ $I = 1.80$ $I = 1.84***$
ESTP $n = 0$ (0.0%) $I = 0.00$	ESFP $n = 0$ (0.0%) $I = 0.00$	ENFP $n = 4$ (3.3%) $I = 1.44$ +++	ENTP $n = 1$ (0.8%) $I = 0.51$ +				
ESTJ $n = 18$ (15.0%) $I = 1.09$ +++++ +++++ +++++	ESFJ $n = 16$ (13.3%) $I = 1.21$ +++++ +++++ +++	ENFJ $n = 5$ (4.2%) $I = 1.52$ ++++	ENTJ $n = 4$ (3.3%) $I = 0.97$ +++	TJ TP FP FJ IN EN IS ES ET EF IF IT	$n = 61$ $n = 8$ $n = 9$ $n = 42$ $n = 35$ $n = 14$ $n = 37$ $n = 34$ $n = 23$ $n = 25$ $n = 26$ $n = 46$	(50.8%) (6.7%) (7.5%) (35.0%) (29.2%) (11.7%) (30.8%) (28.3%) (19.2%) (20.8%) (21.7%) (38.3%)	$I = 0.97$ $I = 1.16$ $I = 0.92$ $I = 1.03$ $I = 2.38***$ $I = 1.16$ $I = 0.62***$ $I = 1.00$ $I = 0.95$ $I = 1.15$ $I = 0.90$ $I = 1.02$

Jungian Types (E)				Jungian Types (I)				Dominant Types			
	n	%	Index		n	%	Index		n	%	Index
E-TJ	22	18.3	1.07	I-TP	7	5.8	2.13	Dt.T	29	24.2	1.21
E-FJ	21	17.5	1.27	I-FP	5	4.2	1.11	Dt.F	26	21.7	1.24
ES-P	0	0.0	0.00*	IS-J	35	29.2	0.63***	Dt.S	35	29.2	0.59***
EN-P	5	4.2	1.06	IN-J	25	20.8	2.26***	Dt.N	30	25.0	1.90***

Notes: $N = 120$; NB: + = 1% of N.
*$p < .05$.
**$p < .01$.
***$p < .001$.

perceiving (14%). The hierarchy of dominant-type preferences are dominant sensing (29%), followed by dominant intuition (25%), dominant thinking (24%), and dominant feeling (22%). In terms of the 16 complete types, the 4 predominant types are ISTJ (18%), ESTJ (15%), INTJ (14%), and ESFJ (13%).

Table 2 also draws attention to the ways in which men engaged in the cathedral congregation differ from men engaged in parish church congregations. In terms of the dichotomous preferences, significant differences emerge in the perceiving process (sensing and intuition), but not in the judging process (thinking and feeling), the orientations (extraversion and introversion) and the attitudes (judging and perceiving). While in the church congregations 22% of the men preferred intuition, the proportion rose to 41% in the cathedral congregation. In terms of dominant-type preferences among men in the cathedral congregation, compared with church congregations, there is a higher proportion of dominant intuitive types (25% compared with 13%) and a lower proportion of dominant sensing types (29% compared with 49%). In terms of temperament theory, among men in the cathedral congregation there is a lower proportion of SJs (58% compared with 71%).

Conclusion

The research question addressed by this study was framed against a body of knowledge concerning the psychological-type profile of men and women attending Anglican church services in England reported by Francis et al. (2011) and in light of the findings of Walker (2012), who reported on the psychological-type profile of men and women attending carol services in an Anglican cathedral in England. Walker found that the cathedral carol service attracted higher proportions of intuitive types and thinking types. What is not clear from Walker's study is whether these differences in psychological-type profile reflect the specific attraction of the carol service or may reflect the attraction of cathedral services more generally.

In order to address this research question, data were provided by 120 men and 161 women aged 20 or over who attended the Sunday services in Southwark Cathedral on one Sunday during late September 2013. Three main conclusions emerge from these data set alongside the data provided by Francis et al. (2011) provided by 1169 men and 2135 women who attended Anglican parish churches.

The first conclusion concerns the perceiving process. Compared with church congregations, the cathedral congregation attracted a higher proportion of intuitive types, not only at the carol service but also at the regular Sunday morning service. This finding may suggest that some people who prefer intuition may deliberately seek out the cathedral in preference to the parish church. Intuitive types may be seeking a particular kind of worship environment for which the architecture, the ceremony, and the music may all contribute an imaginative gateway into transcendence. Intuitive types may also be seeking a particular kind of teaching ministry in which questions may be more attractive than answers and a liberal interpretation of the Christian message may be more attractive than a conservative presentation (Francis & Village, 2008).

The second conclusion concerns the judging process. Compared with church congregations, the cathedral attracted a higher proportion of thinking types. This was the case for both men and women at the regular Sunday morning service. This finding may suggest that some people who prefer thinking may deliberately seek out the cathedral in preference to the parish church. Thinking types may be seeking a particular kind of worship environment where the objective approach of the liturgy carries more weight than the relational activity of the participants. Thinking types may also be seeking a particular kind of teaching ministry in which more weight is given to the analysis of theological issues than to the human story within the gospel narrative (Francis & Village, 2008).

The third conclusion concerns the temperaments. Compared with church congregations, the cathedral attracted a lower proportion of SJs, not only at the carol service but also at the regular Sunday morning service. The SJ temperament is styled by Oswald and Kroeger (1988) as the "guardian". Here are people who are concerned to safeguard the tradition and to resist innovation and change. Because the SJ temperament is so dominant in church congregations (accounting for over 70% of the participants), individuals shaped by other temperament preferences may find it difficult to feel that they really fit in with these congregations. In particular, it is the NF and NT temperaments that seem to make their way from the local parish churches and into the cathedral congregation. In this sense, cathedrals may provide greater opportunities for innovation, experimentation, development, and change than is the case in many parish churches. The fact, however, that over half of the people in cathedral congregations are shaped by SJ temperaments suggest plenty of opportunity for conflict, opposition, and misunderstanding between the NF and NT tendency to welcome innovation and change and the SJ tendency to resist innovation and change.

The main limitation with this study is that the data have been drawn from just one cathedral and it would be misleading to assume that Southwark Cathedral may be representative of all cathedrals. The findings are, nonetheless, intriguing and the study properly deserves replication within other cathedrals in order to test the generalisability of what has been found in this one place.

References

Ball, I. L. (2008). Australian data on the distribution of psychological types. *Bulletin of Psychological Type*, *31*, 53–55.

Bramer, P. D. G., & Ross, C. F. J. (2012). Type patterns among evangelical Protestants in Ontario. *Mental Health, Religion & Culture*, *15*, 997–1007. doi:10.1080/13674676.2012.678577

Craig, C. L., Francis, L. J., Bailey, J., & Robbins, M. (2003). Psychological types in Church in Wales congregations. *The Psychologist in Wales*, *15*, 18–21.

Cronbach, L. J. (1951). Coefficient alpha and the internal structure of tests. *Psychometrika*, *16*, 297–334.

Delis-Bulhoes, V. (1990). Jungian psychological types and Christian belief in active church members. *Journal of Psychological Type*, *20*, 25–33.

Francis, L. J. (2005). *Faith and psychology: Personality, religion and the individual*. London: Darton, Longman and Todd.

Francis, L. J. (2013). The psychological type profile of a church: A case study. *Comprehensive Psychology*, *2*, 6. doi:10.2466/01.09.CP.2.6

Francis, L. J., Annis, J., Robbins, M., ap Sion, T., & Williams, E. (2012). National heritage and spiritual awareness: A study in psychological type theory among visitors to St Davids Cathedral. In F-V. Anthony & H-G. Ziebertz (Eds.), *Religious identity and national heritage: Empirical theological perspectives* (pp. 123–147). Leiden: Brill. doi:10.1163/9789004228788_008

Francis, L. J., Craig, C. L., & Hall, G. (2008). Psychological type and attitude toward Celtic Christianity among committed churchgoers in the United Kingdom: An empirical study. *Journal of Contemporary Religion*, *23*, 181–191.

Francis, L. J., Duncan, B., Craig, C. L., & Luffman, G. (2004). Type patterns among Anglican congregations in England. *Journal of Adult Theological Education*, *1*, 65–77. doi:10.1558/jate.1.1.65.36058

Francis, L. J., Mansfield, S., Williams, E., & Village, A. (2010). Applying psychological type theory to Cathedral visitors: A case study of two cathedrals in England and Wales. *Visitor Studies*, *13*, 175–186. doi:10.1080/10645578.2010.509695

Francis, L. J., & Richter, P. (2007). *Gone for good? Church-leaving and returning in the twenty-first century*. Peterborough: Epworth.

Francis, L. J., & Robbins, M. (2012). Not fitting in and getting out. Psychological type and congregational satisfaction among Anglican churchgoers in England. *Mental Health, Religion & Culture*, *15*, 1023–1035. doi:10.1080/13674676.2012.676260

Francis, L. J., Robbins, M., & Craig, C. L. (2011). The psychological type profile of Anglican churchgoers in England: Compatible or incompatible with their clergy? *International Journal of Practical Theology*, *15*, 243–259. doi:10.1515/IJPT.2011.036

Francis, L. J., Robbins, M., Williams, A., & Williams, R. (2007). All types are called, but some are more likely to respond: The psychological profile of rural Anglican churchgoers in Wales. *Rural Theology*, *5*, 23–30.

Francis, L. J., & Village, A. (2008). *Preaching with all our souls*. London: Continuum.

Francis, L. J., Williams, E., Annis, J., & Robbins, M. (2008). Understanding cathedral visitors: Psychological type and individual differences in experience and appreciation. *Tourism Analysis*, *13*, 71–80. doi:10.3727/108354208784548760

Gerhardt, R. (1983). Liberal religion and personality type. *Research in Psychological Type*, *6*, 47–53.

Jung, C. G. (1971). *Psychological types: The collected works* (Vol. 6). London: Routledge and Kegan Paul.

Keirsey, D., & Bates, M. (1978). *Please understand me*. Del Mar, CA: Prometheus Nemesis.

Kendall, E. (1998). *Myers–Briggs Type Indicator: Step 1 manual supplement*. Palo Alto, CA: Consulting Psychologists Press.

Lewis, C. A. (2012). Psychological type, religion, and culture: Theoretical and empirical perspectives. *Mental Health, Religion & Culture*, *15*, 817–821. doi:10.1080/13674676.2012.721534

McCaulley, M. H. (1985). The selection ratio type table: A research strategy for comparing type distributions. *Journal of Psychological Type*, *10*, 46–56.

Myers, I. B., & McCaulley, M. H. (1985). *Manual: A guide to the development and use of the Myers–Briggs Type Indicator*. Palo Alto, CA: Consulting Psychologists Press.

Oswald, R. M., & Kroeger, O. (1988). *Personality type and religious leadership*. Washington, DC: The Alban Institute.

Rehak, M. C. (1998). Identifying the congregation's corporate personality. *Journal of Psychological Type*, *44*, 39–44.

Robbins, M., & Francis, L. J. (2011). All are called, but some psychological types are more likely to respond: Profiling churchgoers in Australia. *Research in the Social Scientific Study of Religion*, *22*, 213–229. doi:10.1163/ej.9789004207271.i-360.44

Robbins, M., & Francis, L. J. (2012). The psychological type profile of Australian Catholic congregations: Psychological theory and congregational studies. In A. W. Ata (Ed.), *Catholics and Catholicism in contemporary Australia: Challenges and achievements* (pp. 262–281). Melbourne, Victoria: David Lovell Publishing.

Robbins, M., Francis, L. J., & Powell, R. (2012). Congregational bonding social capital and psychological type: An empirical enquiry among Australian churchgoers. *Mental Health, Religion & Culture*, *15*, 1009–1022. doi:10.1080/13674676.2012.676264

Ross, C. F. J. (1993). Type patterns among active members of the Anglican church: Comparisons with Catholics, Evangelicals and clergy. *Journal of Psychological Type*, *26*, 28–35.

Ross, C. F. J. (1995). Type patterns among Catholics: Four Anglophone congregations compared with Protestants, Francophone Catholics and priests. *Journal of Psychological Type*, *33*, 33–41.

Village, A. (2011). Introduction to special section: Psychological type and Christian ministry. *Research in the Social Scientific Study of Religion*, *22*, 157–164. doi:10.1163/ej.9789004207271.i-360.28

Village, A., Baker, S., & Howat, S. (2012). Psychological type profiles of churchgoers in England. *Mental Health, Religion & Culture*, *15*, 969–978. doi:10.1080/13674676.2012.686479

Walker, D. (2012). O Come all ye thinking types: The wider appeal of the cathedral carol service. *Mental Health, Religion & Culture*, *15*, 987–995. doi:10.1080/13674676.2012.707436

Spiritual well-being and psychological type: a study among visitors to a medieval cathedral in Wales

Leslie J. Francis, John W. Fisher and Jennie Annis

This study explores the theoretical and empirical connections between spiritual well-being and psychological type by drawing on Fisher's model of spiritual well-being as assessed by the Spiritual Health And Life-Orientation Measure and Francis' classification of psychological type as generated by the Francis Psychological Type Scales. Data provided by 2339 visitors to St David's Cathedral in rural west Wales demonstrated that, when the four components of psychological type were considered independently, higher levels of spiritual well-being were associated with extraversion rather than introversion, with intuition rather than sensing, with feeling rather than thinking and with perceiving rather than judging. Further examination of these data suggested that the judging process (distinguishing between the feeling function and the thinking function) was of greatest importance in shaping individual differences in spiritual health.

Introduction

Spiritual well-being

Spiritual well-being is an established, but nonetheless contested construct (Hill & Pargament, 2003). Current empirical research has been informed by many different measures of spiritual well-being, each of which operationalises a distinctive perspective on this contested construct. The instruments generally reflect the worldview of their authors (Berry, 2005). These range from a traditional theistic view that considers religion as the over-arching concept, which embraces spirituality as one of its expressions (Idler et al., 2003; Pargament, 1997), through views that posit similarities but also differences between the two constructs (King & Benson, 2006), to contemporary views that see religion as one potential expression of spirituality (Polanski, 2002) or contend that it is possible to have spirituality without religion (van Dierendonck & Mohan, 2006; du Toit, 2006). For example, the Spiritual Assessment Inventory (Hall & Edwards, 1996) and the Spiritual History Scale in Four Dimensions (Hays, Meador, Branch, & George, 2001) mainly comprise questions on transcendental issues and religion. Ellison's Spiritual Well-Being Survey presents 10 items for each of two factors, labelled Existential Well-Being and Religious Well-Being (Ellison, 1983) and the Search Institute Inventory of Youth Spiritual

Development has 156 items related to self, to others, to the environment, to the transcendent and to religion (Center for Spiritual Development, 2007). Daaleman's Spirituality Index of Well-Being contains 12 items solely relating with self (Daaleman & Frey, 2004). According to Fisher (2009), the composition of 25 extant spiritual health and well-being measures reveals their authors' dominant emphases on relating with self (100%) and with God (72%), with lesser concern for relating with other people (56%) and the environment (44%).

One clear conceptualisation of spiritual well-being has been advanced by Fisher (1998, 2011). In this work, spiritual well-being is perceived as the lived expression revealing the underlying state of a person's spiritual health. Spiritual health is posited as a, if not the, fundamental dimension of health which undergirds and integrates the other dimensions of health (namely the physical, mental, emotional, social and vocational). Spiritual well-being is reflected in the quality of relationships that each person has in four domains, namely with the self (the personal domain, assessed in terms of meaning, purpose and values); with other people (the communal domain, assessed in terms of morality, culture and religion); with the environment (the environmental domain, assessed in terms of connectedness beyond care, nurture and stewardship) and with a (personal or impersonal) transcendent other (the transcendental domain, assessed in relation to something or someone beyond the human and natural world).

In his foundation study, Fisher (1998) develops his understanding of these four domains of spiritual well-being in the following ways. The personal domain concerns the ways in which individuals relate to and evaluate their inner selves. It is concerned with meaning, purpose and values in life. In the personal domain, the human spirit creates self-awareness, relating to self-worth and identity. The communal domain concerns the quality and depth of interpersonal relationships, between self and others, relating to morality and culture. In the communal domain, the human spirit generates love, justice, hope and faith in humanity. The environmental domain concerns not only care and nurture for the physical and biological aspects of the world around us, but also a sense of awe and wonder. In the environmental domain, the human spirit nurtures, at least for some, the experience of unity or connectedness with the environment. The transcendental domain concerns the relationship of the self with something or someone beyond the human level, with a transcendent other, whether this be known as ultimate concern, cosmic force, transcendent reality or God. In the transcendent domain, the human spirit nurtures a sense of trust and faith in, and a sense of adoration and worship for, the source of mystery at the heart of the universe.

Fisher's conceptualisation of spiritual well-being has been operationalised through several instruments: the Spiritual Health in Four Domains Index (SH4DI; Fisher, Francis, & Johnson, 2000), the Spiritual Health And Life-Orientation Measure (SHALOM; Fisher, 1999, 2010) and Feeling Good, Living Life (Fisher, 2004). Gomez and Fisher (2003) demonstrated that SHALOM showed good reliability (Cronbach's alpha, composite reliability and variance extracted) and validity (construct, concurrent, discriminant, predictive and factorial independence from personality). Subsequent studies have examined the psychometric properties of SHALOM from a range of perspectives. For example, SHALOM is one of the only two spiritual well-being questionnaires that have reported item response theory (IRT) analysis on them (Hall, Reise, & Haviland, 2007). There was general support for the psychometric properties of this spiritual well-being questionnaire from an IRT perspective (Gomez & Fisher, 2005a). Multi-group confirmatory factor analysis showed that the statistical fit results supported the invariance of the measurement model, and of both the measurement and structural models. The results also showed little gender differences. Together, these findings support gender equivalencies for this spiritual well-being questionnaire (Gomez & Fisher, 2005b).

A series of studies employing Fisher's instruments has begun to build up a coherent body of knowledge about the correlates, antecedents and consequences of individual differences in spiritual well-being. An early study investigated the relationship of spiritual well-being to other measures of subjective well-being among psychology students at the University of Ballarat (Stott, 2002). Another project with similar students investigated how the domains of spiritual well-being predict the current quality of life and general well-being (Hall, 2005).

The relationship between ethical orientation in decision-making and spiritual well-being was examined via a survey of business executives in Australia. Each of the four domains of spiritual well-being in SHALOM was examined in relation to idealism and relativism. Spiritual well-being, especially in the communal domain, was shown to be predictive of idealism among these executives (Fernando & Chowdhury, 2010).

SHALOM was also used to help assess the impact of an Interim Protection Order on victims of domestic violence in South Africa, in English, Afrikaans and Xhosa (Vogt, 2007). A study among adolescents in South Africa reported that a high valuing of religion and spirituality, more frequent church attendance or spiritual activity, and more frequent prayer, all related to higher levels of transcendental spiritual well-being. Spiritual salience and more frequent prayer are also related to higher levels of personal spiritual well-being and to higher levels of global spiritual health (van Rooyen, 2007). This and the following study also used the Sesotho language. Further study with these adolescents showed that seeking spiritual support for coping was highly correlated with transcendental spiritual well-being and moderately so with communal spiritual well-being (Moodley, 2008).

A study with Canadian primary school children found that their personal and communal spiritual well-being, as measured by SHALOM, was strongly linked to their happiness, although their religious practices were not. Spirituality remained a significant predictor of happiness even after removing the variance associated with temperament (Holder, Coleman, & Wallace, 2010). Three independent studies were undertaken to show the factorial validity of the German translation of SHALOM (Rowold, 2011). They also showed that each of the four scales on SHALOM was discriminant to mental, physical and emotional well-being. In addition, SHALOM-G predicted levels of subsequent happiness, and was related positively with psychological well-being and negatively with stress.

The underlying theme of "connectedness", or building relationships, undergirds research in spiritual well-being and resiliency. Studies were reported with 9- to 19-year-old students in Australia using SHALOM and an instrument to gauge the strength of relationships (in terms of connectedness) of each student with family, friends, school and/or church, areas which have been shown to provide support for resiliency (Fisher, 2012). How well students connected, especially with themselves and God, was shown to influence their spiritual well-being and resilience. The students, who showed marked differences between their ideals and lived experience on SHALOM, reported lower levels of support from themselves, parents, school teachers, principals, female friends and God, in building relationships with self, others, environment and/or God. These students also showed higher levels of psychoticism and lower levels of happiness.

As yet, however, little research has focused specifically on the connection between personality and Fisher's model of spiritual well-being. One important pioneering study in this area by Gomez and Fisher (2003) revealed the factorial independence of the spiritual well-being domains on SHALOM from the personality domains operationalised in the short-form of Eysenck's Personality Questionnaire Revised (Eysenck & Eysenck, 1991). Another study using Eysenck's dimensional model of personality employed the SH4DI, a precursor of SHALOM, to investigate personal and social correlates of spiritual well-being among primary school teachers (Fisher, Francis, & Johnson, 2002). These data demonstrated that higher levels of spiritual health were found among older teachers who recorded low scores on the Psychoticism Scale and who practised religious faith through church attendance and personal prayer.

Using the NEO Five-Factor Inventory (FFI; Costa & McCrae, 1992) with SHALOM, among employees in the general Australian workforce, Becker (2002) found that neuroticism correlated negatively with personal and communal spiritual well-being, whereas extraversion correlated positively with these two as well as with environmental spiritual well-being. Openness, agreeableness and conscientiousness correlated positively with the four domains of spiritual well-being on SHALOM.

Streukens (2009) used the Clinical Analysis Questionnaire (CAQ; Krug & Cattell, 1980) together with SHALOM to examine what relationship existed between personality and spiritual well-being among alcoholics in Canada. This study concluded that neuroticism correlated negatively with all four domains of spiritual well-being, whereas extraversion correlated positively with all four. Psychoticism was shown to correlate negatively with only communal and environmental spiritual well-being.

The aim of the present study is to build on the earlier work reported by Becker (2002) using the NEO FFI, by Fisher et al. (2002) and Gomez and Fisher (2003) using the Eysenck Personality Questionnaire Revised, and by Streukens (2009) using the CAQ, and to do so by drawing on the model of personality proposed by psychological type theory. In this way, the present study proposes to link research on Fisher's model of spiritual well-being with a broader and growing body of research exploring the connection between psychological type and spirituality (see review by Francis, 2009).

Psychological type

Like spiritual well-being, psychological type is an established, but nonetheless contested construct. Psychological type theory has its roots in the pioneering work of Jung (1971). Subsequently, Jung's theory has been developed and extended in association with a series of psychometric instruments, including the Keirsey Temperament Sorter (Keirsey & Bates, 1978), the Myers–Briggs Type Indicator (Myers & McCaulley, 1985) and the Francis Psychological Type Scales (FPTS; Francis, 2005). Psychological type theory is contested because it conceives of individual differences in personality in terms of discrete type categories, in contrast with the way in which other personality theories conceive of individual differences in terms of location on continua. It is continua, not typology, that characterise the 16 personality factors proposed by Cattell, Cattell, and Cattell (1993), the big five factors proposed by Costa and McCrae (1985) and the three major dimensions proposed by Eysenck and Eysenck (1991).

It is this attachment to typology that makes psychological type theory so distinctive in the field of personality assessment. The core of psychological type theory distinguishes between two fundamental psychological processes, styled the perceiving process and the judging process. Both processes are experienced in two opposing functions.

The perceiving process was styled by Jung as the irrational process, since it is concerned wholly with the gathering of information and not with the evaluation of that information. The two opposing functions of the perceiving process are known as sensing and as intuition. On the one hand, sensing types (S) focus on the realities of a situation as perceived by the senses. They tend to focus on specific details, rather than on the overall picture. They are concerned with the actual, the real and the practical; they tend to be down to earth and matter of fact. On the other hand, intuitive types (N) focus on the possibilities of a situation, perceiving meanings and relationships. They may feel that perception by the senses is not as valuable as information gained from the unconscious mind as indirect associations and concepts impact on their perception. They focus on the overall picture, rather than on specific facts and data.

The judging process was styled by Jung as the rational process, since it is concerned wholly with the evaluation of information. The two opposing functions of the judging process are known as thinking and as feeling. On the one hand, thinking types (T) make decisions and judgements based on objective, impersonal logic. They value integrity and justice. They are known for their truthfulness and for their desire for fairness. They consider conforming to principles to be of more importance than cultivating harmony. For thinkers, impersonal objectivity is more important than interpersonal relationships. For them, the mind is more important than the heart. On the other hand, feeling types (F) make decisions and judgements based on subjective, personal values. They value compassion and mercy. They are known for their tactfulness and for their desire for peace. They are more concerned to promote harmony, than to adhere to abstract principles. For feelers, interpersonal relationships are more important than impersonal objectivity. For them, the heart is more important than the mind.

In psychological type theory, these two fundamental psychological processes (perceiving and judging) are situated within the context of two opposing orientations and two opposing attitudes. The orientations are concerned with identifying the source and focus of psychological energy, and distinguish between introversion and extraversion. On the one hand, extraverts (E) are orientated towards the outer world; they are energised by the events and people around them. They enjoy communicating and thrive in stimulating and exciting environments. They tend to focus their attention on what is happening outside themselves. They are usually open people, easy to get to know and enjoy having many friends. Introverts (I), on the other hand, are orientated towards their inner world; they are energised by their inner ideas and concepts. They enjoy solitude, silence and contemplation, as they tend to focus their attention on what is happening in their inner life. They may prefer to have a small circle of intimate friends rather than many acquaintances.

The attitudes, better styled as the "attitudes towards the outer world", are concerned with identifying which psychological process (perceiving or judging) is exercised in the outer world. On the one hand, judging types (J) exercise their preferred judging function (either thinking or feeling) in the outer world. They seek to order, rationalise and structure their outer world, as they actively judge external stimuli. They enjoy routine and established patterns. They prefer to follow schedules in order to reach an established goal and may make use of lists, timetables or diaries. They tend to be punctual, organised and tidy. They prefer to make decisions quickly and to stick to their conclusions once made. On the other hand, perceiving types (P) exercise their preferred perceiving function (either sensing or intuition) in the outer world. They do not seek to impose order on the outer world, but are more reflective, perceptive and open, as they passively perceive external stimuli. They have a flexible, open-ended approach to life. They enjoy change and spontaneity. They prefer to leave projects open in order to adapt and improve them. Their behaviour may often seem impulsive and unplanned.

These four constructs provide the building blocks of psychological type theory, distinguishing between two perceiving functions (sensing and intuition), two judging functions (thinking and feeling), two orientations (introversion and extraversion) and two attitudes towards the outer world (judging and perceiving). The first research question to be raised by the present study concerns the connection between these four constructs, considered separately, and spiritual well-being.

According to Jungian theory, each individual needs access to all four functions (sensing, intuition, thinking and feeling) for normal and healthy living. The two perceiving functions (sensing and intuition) are needed to gather information about the inner and outer worlds inhabited by the individual. These are the irrational functions concerned with collecting information, with seeing reality and possibility. The two judging functions (thinking and feeling) are needed to organise and evaluate information. These are the rational functions concerned with making decisions and determining courses of action. Although each individual needs access to all four functions, Jungian theory posits the view that the relative strengths of these four functions vary from one individual to another. The analogy is drawn with handedness. Although equipped with two hands, the majority of individuals tend to prefer one hand, to develop skills with that preferred hand, and to neglect the development of the other hand. Similarly, empirical evidence suggests that individuals will develop preference for one of the perceiving functions (sensing or intuition) and neglect the other, and that they will develop preference for one of the judging functions (thinking or feeling) and neglect the other.

According to Jungian theory, for each individual either the preferred perceiving function (sensing or intuition) or the preferred judging function (thinking or feeling) takes preference over the other, leading to the emergence of one dominant function which shapes the individual's dominant approach to life. Dominant sensing shapes the practical person; dominant intuition shapes the imaginative person; dominant feeling shapes the humane person and dominant thinking shapes the analytic person. The definitions of these four dominant types pose the second research question addressed by the present study. This question concerns the connection between dominant-type preferences and spiritual well-being.

According to Jungian theory, for each individual, the dominant-type preference is complemented and supported by the auxiliary function. The auxiliary function is defined as the preferred function from the other process. The dominant sensing types and dominant intuitive types are supported by auxiliary thinking or by auxiliary feeling; dominant feeling types and dominant thinking types are supported by auxiliary sensing or by auxiliary intuition. It is the auxiliary function that adds depth, tone and perspective to the dominant function. The third research question to be raised by the present study concerns the connection between spiritual well-being and the eightfold typology proposed by the dominant and auxiliary pairs.

The four basic building blocks of psychological type theory (the two perceiving functions, the two judging functions, the two orientations and the two attitudes) are employed to construct the four dominant types and the eight dominant and auxiliary pairs. The full richness of psychological type theory is achieved in the definition of the 16 complete types. The fourth research question to be raised by the present study concerns the connection between spiritual well-being and the 16 complete types.

Psychological type and spiritual well-being

Hypotheses regarding the link between psychological type and spiritual well-being can be guided by two existing bodies of knowledge shaped by previous research exploring the connection between psychological type and spirituality and the connection between psychological type and well-being. Currently less is known about the connection between psychological type and well-being than is known about the connection between psychological type and spirituality.

Two main and relevant strands of research within the psychology of religion have investigated the connection between psychological type and spirituality. The first strand has explored the connection between psychological type and the profile of individuals attracted to the Christian Church, either as members of congregations or as clergy. For example, the psychological type profiles of church congregations and church members have been explored in studies in North America by Gerhardt (1983), Delis-Bulhoes (1990), Ross (1993, 1995), and Rehak (1998), in Australia by Robbins and Francis (2011, 2012), and in the UK by Craig, Francis, Bailey, and Robbins (2003), Francis, Duncan, Craig, and Luffman (2004), Francis, Robbins, Williams, and Williams (2007), and Francis, Robbins, and Craig (2011). The general consensus of these findings is that, compared with the general population norms, a higher proportion of feeling types are attracted to church participation in comparison with thinking types.

The psychological type profiles of clergy have been explored in studies in North America by Cabral (1984), Harbaugh (1984), Holsworth (1984), Bigelow, Fitzgerald, Busk, Girault, and Avis (1988), Francis, Robbins, and Wulff (2011), and Burns, Francis, Village, and Robbins (2013), in Australia by Francis, Powell, and Robbins (2012), and in the UK by Francis, Payne, and Jones

(2001), Francis and Robbins (2002), Craig, Duncan, and Francis (2006), Francis, Craig, Whinney, Tilley, and Slater (2007), Francis, Gubb, and Robbins (2009), Francis, Hancocks, Swift, and Robbins (2009), Burton, Francis, and Robbins (2010), Francis, Littler, and Robbins (2010), Francis, Robbins, Duncan, and Whinney (2010), Village (2011), Francis and Holmes (2011), and Francis and Village (2012). The general consensus of the findings from these studies is that, compared with the general population norms, among male clergy in particular, higher proportions of feeling types are attracted to the clerical profession in comparison with thinking types.

On the basis of this strand of research, if spiritual well-being follows the same trajectory as attraction to church membership or religious vocation, the hypothesis can be advanced that feeling types will record higher levels of spiritual well-being compared with thinking types.

The second strand of relevant research within the psychology of religion has explored the connection between psychological type and spiritual experience, with special reference to mystical experience. Studies employing either the Mystical Orientation Scale (Francis & Louden, 2000a) or the Short Index of Mystical Orientation (Francis & Louden, 2004) alongside measures of psychological type have been reported by Francis and Louden (2000b), Francis (2002), Francis, Village, Robbins, and Ineson (2007), Francis, Robbins, and Cargas (2012), and Francis, Littler, and Robbins (2012). Testing a thesis first developed by Ross (1992) regarding the centrality of the perceiving process (the sensing function and the intuitive function) in shaping individual differences in religious experience, expression and belief, the general consensus of the findings from these studies, is that, intuitive types record higher scores of mystical orientation in comparison with sensing types.

On the basis of this strand of research, if spiritual well-being follows the same trajectory as spiritual or mystical experience, the hypothesis can be advanced that intuitive types will record higher levels of spiritual well-being compared with sensing types.

Two main and relevant strands of research within positive psychology have investigated the connection between psychological type and aspects of well-being. The first strand has explored the connection between psychological type and general happiness. For example, Francis and Jones (2000) reported on the responses of 284 adults who had completed the Myers–Briggs Type Indicator (Myers & McCaulley, 1985) and the Oxford Happiness Inventory (Argyle, Martin, & Crossland, 1989). These data found that extraverts recorded significantly higher happiness scores than introverts. On the other hand, happiness scores were unrelated to preferences for sensing or intuition, for thinking or feeling, or for judging or perceiving.

The second strand of relevant research within positive psychology has explored the connection between psychological type and work-related positive psychological health. For example, a series of five studies by Francis, Wulff, and Robbins (2008), Francis, Robbins, Kaldor, and Castle (2009), Robbins and Francis (2010), Brewster, Francis, and Robbins (2011), and Robbins, Francis, and Powell (2012) administered the FPTS (Francis, 2005) alongside the Satisfaction in Ministry Scale (Francis, Kaldor, Shevlin, & Lewis, 2004) to samples of clergy in Australia, the UK and the USA. All five of these studies have agreed that the distinction between introversion and extraversion functions as a stable predictor of individual differences in work-related psychological health.

On the basis of these two strands of research, if spiritual well-being functions in the same way as psychological well-being, the hypothesis can be advanced that extraverts will record higher levels of spiritual well-being compared with introverts.

Research question

Against this background, the aim of the present study is to explore the association between psychological type (employing the FPTS) and spiritual well-being (employing the Fisher measure of spiritual health) among a broad sample of adults (aged 18-years or above) who were invited to complete both measures during their visit to St David's Cathedral in west Wales. Cathedral visitors provided an appropriate constituency among whom to test the association between psychological type and spiritual health for two reasons. Previous research among visitors to the cathedral reported by Williams, Francis, Robbins, and Annis (2007) has demonstrated that this constituency comprises a good mix of religious pilgrims and secular tourists. Many of these visitors come as holiday-makers and are well disposed to being invited to participate in research on spirituality-related issues.

The review of relevant related research has advanced three specific hypotheses concerning the connection between psychological type and spiritual well-being:

(1) in terms of orientations, it is hypothesised that extraverts will record higher scores of spiritual well-being in comparison with introverts;
(2) in terms of the perceiving process, it is hypothesised that intuitive types will record higher scores of spiritual well-being in comparison with sensing types;
(3) in terms of the judging process, it is hypothesised that feeling types will record higher scores of spiritual well-being in comparison with thinking types.

There is no evidence from relevant related research to link individual differences in spiritual well-being with attitudes towards the outer world. The fourth hypothesis is therefore:

(1) in terms of the attitudes towards the outer world, it is hypothesised that there will be no significant difference between judging types and perceiving types on scores of spiritual well-being.

Method

During July, August and September 2006, one member of the research team invited visitors to St David's Cathedral who were at least 18 years of age to complete a copy of the questionnaire. A total of 2697 visitors accepted the invitation to do so and returned the completed questionnaire. The researcher first welcomed the visitors when they entered the cathedral by the west door and ensured that they received the visitor information leaflet about the cathedral. Then as the visitors were about to leave the building, they were invited to complete a questionnaire reflecting on their visit. Visitors were assured of confidentiality, anonymity and the voluntary nature of their participation. Completed questionnaires were left in the cathedral.

Participants

Of the 2697 questionnaires returned, 2339 were suitable for analysis in the present study. The remaining 358 were excluded because of missing data. The 2339 participants comprised 1026 men and 1313 women; 359 individuals under the age of 20, 214 in their 20s, 263 in their 30s, 497 in their 40s, 529 in their 50s, 352 in their 60s and 125 aged 70 or over. The majority of the visitors had travelled over 20 miles to visit St David's Cathedral (94%), although comparatively few of these had travelled from overseas. The majority of the visitors identified their religious affiliation as Christian (76%), with most of the others claiming no religious affiliation (21%), leaving only 3% of the visitors affiliated with other religions. In terms of religious practice, St David's Cathedral attracted almost equal proportions of weekly churchgoers (23%) and of people who never attended church (24%), with 9% attending at least monthly,

10% at least 6 times a year, 34% attending less than 6 times a year and 1% declining to answer the question.

Measures

Psychological type was assessed by the FPTS (Francis, 2005). This instrument proposes four 10-item scales designed to distinguish preferences between introversion and extraversion, sensing and intuition, feeling and thinking, and judging and perceiving. Recent studies have reported good qualities of internal consistency reliability for these scales. For example, Francis, Craig, and Hall (2008) reported the following alpha coefficients: .83 for the extraversion and introversion scales; .76 for the sensing and intuition scales; .73 for the thinking and feeling scales; and .79 for the judging and perceiving scales. The participants were asked to choose between each of the 40 pairs of characteristics "which is closer to the real you, even if you feel both characteristics apply to you. Tick the characteristic that reflects the real you, even if other people see you differently".

Spiritual well-being was assessed by the SHALOM (Fisher, 1999, 2010). This instrument comprises four five-item scales designed to assess the quality of relationships reflecting a person's spiritual well-being in four domains: the personal domain (relationship with self), the communal domain (relationship with others), the environmental domain (relationship with the natural world) and the transcendental domain (relationship with transcendent matters of ultimate concern or with God). The four domains of SHALOM have also been shown to cohere into a single higher order factor, called spiritual well-being (Gomez & Fisher, 2003). The participants were asked to rate on a five-point scale, from "low" (1) to "high" (5), how much in their "normal day-to-day life" they experience each of the 20 issues itemised in the measure.

Analysis

The scientific literature concerned with psychological type has developed a highly distinctive way of presenting type data in the form of "type tables". This convention has been adopted in the current study in order to integrate these new data within the established literature and to provide all the details necessary for secondary analysis and further interpretation.

Results and discussion

The four scales of the FPTS achieved satisfactory consistency reliabilities in terms of the alpha coefficients (Cronbach, 1951): extraversion and introversion, .75; sensing and intuition, .64; thinking and feeling, .60; judging and perceiving, .70.

Table 1 presents the type profile of the 2339 visitors to St David's Cathedral. These data show that among the visitors, there were preferences for introversion (58%) over extraversion (42%), for sensing (72%) over intuition (28%), for thinking (54%) over feeling (46%) and for judging (82%) over perceiving (18%). Considering these indicators together, 4 of the 16 Jungian complete types accounted for almost two-thirds of the visitors (63%): ISTJ (24%), ISFJ (15%), ESTJ (13%) and ESFJ (11%). In terms of dominant types, dominant sensing accounted for 43% of the visitors, dominant thinking for 21%, dominant feeling for 20% and dominant intuition for 16%.

Table 2 presents the mean scores recorded on the measure of spiritual well-being according to the four component parts of psychological type theory. The data are consistent with the first three hypotheses proposed by the present study: extraverts recorded significantly higher scores of spiritual well-being compared with introverts; intuitive types recorded significantly higher scores of

Table 1. Type distribution for cathedral visitors.

The Sixteen Complete Types					Dichotomous Preferences		
ISTJ	ISFJ	INFJ	INTJ	E	$n =$ 974	(41.6%)
$n = 557$	$n = 350$	$n = 107$	$n = 149$	I	$n =$ 1365	(58.4%)
(23.8%)	(15.0%)	(4.6%)	(6.4%)			
+++++	+++++	+++++	+++++	S	$n =$ 1688	(72.2%)
+++++	+++++		+	N	$n =$ 651	(27.8%)
+++++	+++++					
+++++				T	$n =$ 1267	(54.2%)
++++				F	$n =$ 1072	(45.8%)
				J	$n =$ 1921	(82.1%)
				P	$n =$ 418	(17.9%)
ISTP	ISFP	INFP	INTP		Pairs and Temperaments	
$n = 62$	$n = 53$	$n = 53$	$n = 34$	IJ	$n =$ 1163	(49.7%)
(2.7%)	(2.3%)	(2.3%)	(1.5%)	IP	$n =$ 202	(8.6%)
++	++	++	++	EP	$n =$ 216	(9.2%)
				EJ	$n =$ 758	(32.4%)
				ST	$n =$ 966	(41.3%)
				SF	$n =$ 722	(30.9%)
				NF	$n =$ 350	(15.0%)
ESTP	ESFP	ENFP	ENTP	NT	$n =$ 301	(12.9%)
$n = 40$	$n = 61$	$n = 84$	$n = 31$			
(1.7%)	(2.6%)	(3.6%)	(1.3%)	SJ	$n =$ 1472	(62.9%)
++	+++	++++	+	SP	$n =$ 216	(9.2%)
				NP	$n =$ 202	(8.6%)
				NJ	$n =$ 449	(19.2%)
				TJ	$n =$ 1100	(47.0%)
				TP	$n =$ 167	(7.1%)
				FP	$n =$ 251	(10.7%)
				FJ	$n =$ 821	(35.1%)
ESTJ	ESFJ	ENFJ	ENTJ			
$n = 307$	$n = 258$	$n = 106$	$n = 87$	IN	$n =$ 343	(14.7%)
(13.1%)	(11.0%)	(4.5%)	(3.7%)	EN	$n =$ 308	(13.2%)
+++++	+++++	+++++	++++	IS	$n =$ 1022	(43.7%)
+++++	+++++			ES	$n =$ 666	(28.5%)
+++	+					
				ET	$n =$ 465	(19.9%)
				EF	$n =$ 509	(21.8%)
				IF	$n =$ 563	(24.1%)
				IT	$n =$ 802	(34.3%)

Jungian Types (E)			Jungian Types (I)			Dominant Types		
	n	%		N	%		n	%
E-TJ	394	16.8	I-TP	96	4.1	Dt.T	490	20.9
E-FJ	364	15.6	I-FP	106	4.5	Dt.F	470	20.1
ES-P	101	4.3	IS-J	907	38.8	Dt.S	1008	43.1
EN-P	115	4.9	IN-J	256	10.9	Dt.N	371	15.9

Note: $N = 2339$ (NB: + = 1% of N).

Table 2. Spiritual well-being scores by dichotomous-type preferences.

Comparisons	N	mean	SD	F	$p <$
Extraversion	974	3.42	.66		
Introversion	1365	3.32	.65	3.4	.001
Sensing	1688	3.33	.65		
Intuition	651	3.44	.66	−3.4	.001
Thinking	1267	3.22	.64		
Feeling	1072	3.53	.64	−11.5	.001
Judging	1921	3.35	.65		
Perceiving	418	3.43	.68	−2.4	.05

spiritual well-being compared with sensing types and feeling types recorded significantly higher scores of spiritual well-being compared with thinking types. At the same time, these data question the fourth hypothesis, namely that the attitudes towards the outer world were not related to individual differences in spiritual well-being; perceiving types recorded significantly higher scores of spiritual well-being compared with judging types.

Table 3 takes the analysis one stage further by analysing spiritual well-being scores by dominant-type preference. The highest level of spiritual well-being is reported by dominant feeling types, followed by dominant intuitive types, with lower levels of spiritual well-being reported by dominant thinking types and dominant sensing types.

Table 4 examines the additional insights generated when the auxiliary function is taken into account alongside the dominant function. This analysis makes clear the primary role of the judging process (distinguishing between thinking and feeling) in shaping individual differences in spiritual well-being. The four highest scoring dominant-auxiliary pairs all involve the preference for feeling, either as the dominant function or as the auxiliary function. The four lowest scoring dominant-auxiliary pairs all involve the preference for thinking, either as the dominant function or as the auxiliary function.

Table 5 completes the analysis by examining the association between spiritual well-being and the 16 complete types. These data confirm the centrality of the judging process (distinguishing between thinking and feeling) in shaping individual differences in spiritual well-being. The eight highest scoring psychological types all prefer feeling, while the eight lowest scoring psychological types all prefer thinking. After the judging process has been taken into account, the other components of type theory occupy no consistent location within the rank ordering the mean scores of spiritual well-being. Among the four highest scoring psychological types, there were two sensing types (ISFP and ESFJ) and two intuitive types (INFJ and INFP); and among the four lowest scoring psychological types, there were two sensing types (ESTP and ISTJ) and two intuitive types (INTP and INTJ). Among the four highest scoring psychological types, there were two judging types (INFJ and ESJF) and two perceiving types (ISFP and INFP); and among the four

Table 3. Spiritual well-being scores by dominant-type preferences.

Dominant types	N	mean	SD	F	$p <$
Dominant feeling	470	3.56	.64		
Dominant intuition	371	3.43	.66		
Dominant thinking	490	3.29	.65		
Dominant sensing	1008	3.28	.64	23.1	.001

Table 4. Spiritual well-being scores by dominant and auxiliary type preferences.

Dominant and auxiliary types	N	mean	SD	F	p <
Dominant intuition with feeling	191	3.61	.64		
Dominant feeling with sensing	311	3.58	.63		
Dominant feeling with intuition	159	3.50	.64		
Dominant sensing with feeling	411	3.45	.63		
Dominant thinking with intuition	121	3.35	.66		
Dominant thinking with sensing	369	3.27	.65		
Dominant intuition with thinking	180	3.25	.64		
Dominant sensing with thinking	597	3.16	.63	22.4	.001

lowest scoring psychological types, there were two judging types (INTJ and ISTJ) and two perceiving types (INTP and ESTP). Among the four highest scoring psychological types, there were three introverted types (INFJ, ISFP and INFP) and one extraverted type (ESFJ); and among the four lowest scoring psychological types, there were three introverted types (INTP, INTJ and ISTJ) and one extraverted type (ESTP).

Table 5 draws attention to INFJ as the psychological type that records the highest level of spiritual well-being. Myers (1998, p. 7) describes the INFJ in the following terms:

> Succeed by perseverance, originality and desire to do whatever is needed or wanted. Put their best efforts into their work. Quietly forceful, conscientious, concerned for others. Respected for their firm principles. Likely to be honoured and followed for their clear visions as to how to serve the common good.

Table 5 draws attention to ISTJ as the psychological type that records the lowest level of spiritual well-being. Myers (1998, p. 7) describes the ISTJ in the following terms:

> Serious, quiet, earn success by concentration and thoroughness. Practical, orderly, matter-of-fact, logical realistic and dependable. See to it that everything is well organised. Take responsibility. Make up their own minds about what should be accomplished and work towards it steadily, regardless of protests or distractions.

Table 5. Spiritual well-being scores by 16 complete types.

Type	N	mean	SD	F	p <
INFJ	107	3.67	.59		
ISFP	53	3.60	.68		
ESFJ	258	3.58	.62		
INFP	53	3.57	.64		
ENFP	84	3.54	.70		
ENFJ	106	3.47	.64		
ISFJ	350	3.46	.62		
ESFP	61	3.44	.70		
ENTJ	87	3.39	.66		
ENTP	31	3.34	.72		
ISTP	62	3.29	.67		
ESTJ	307	3.26	.64		
INTP	34	3.26	.65		
ESTP	40	3.24	.56		
INTJ	149	3.23	.62		
ISTJ	557	3.16	.63	10.8	.001

Conclusion

This paper sets out to draw together two well-established research traditions, one concerned with the definition and measurement of spiritual well-being and one concerned with the definition and classification of psychological types, in order to assess whether psychological type theory can help to explain individual differences in spiritual well-being. In order to explore this research question, data were gathered from 2339 visitors to St David's Cathedral in west Wales who completed the FPTS alongside Fisher's measure of spiritual well-being (SHALOM). These data were analysed through four distinctive levels offered by psychological type theory, drawing on: the four preferences (defined by the two orientation, the two perceiving functions, the two judging functions and the two attitudes), each considered separately; the four dominant-type preferences (dominant sensing, dominant intuition, dominant thinking and dominant feeling), considered together; the eight dominant-auxiliary pairs and the 16 complete types. Five main conclusions emerge from these analyses.

First, considered independently, the two orientations have a part to play in shaping spiritual well-being. Extraverts enjoy a higher level of spiritual well-being than introverts. This finding is consistent with the broader research tradition reviewed in the introduction to this paper that found higher levels of psychological well-being among extraverts than among introverts, as defined in terms of the positive affect associated with personal happiness and with work-related satisfaction. In this sense, there seems to be some continuity between spiritual well-being (as defined by Fisher) and a broader understanding of psychological well-being.

Second, considered independently, the two perceiving factors have a part to play in shaping spiritual well-being. Intuitive types enjoy a higher level of spiritual well-being than sensing types. This finding is consistent with the broader research tradition reviewed in the introduction to this paper that found higher levels of spiritual experience among intuitive types than among sensing types, as defined in terms of mystical orientation. In this sense, there seems to be some continuity between spiritual well-being (as defined by Fisher) and a broader understanding of spiritual experience.

Third, considered independently, the two judging functions have a part to play in shaping spiritual well-being. Feeling types enjoy a higher level of spiritual well-being than thinking types. This finding is consistent with the broader research tradition reviewed in the introduction to this paper that found a higher proportion of feeling types than thinking types associated with conventional religious participation, as defined in church membership, church attendance and religious vocations. In this sense, there seems to be some continuity between spiritual well-being (as defined by Fisher) and a broader engagement with an interest in religious and spiritual practices.

Fourth, considered independently, the two attitudes towards the outer world have a (small) part to play in shaping spiritual well-being. Perceiving types enjoy a (slightly) higher level of spiritual well-being than judging types. At present, there is no body of research with which to link and by which to interpret this (small) association.

Fifth, when the components of psychological type theory are considered in combination to generate the four dominant-type preferences, the eight dominant-auxiliary pairs or the 16 complete types, the judging process (distinguishing between the feeling function and the thinking function) emerges as the strongest, and clearest factor in predicting individual differences in spiritual well-being (as defined by Fisher). This finding is consistent with the theoretical connection between the way in which Fisher originally construed spiritual well-being theory and the way in which Jung originally construed psychological type theory. For Fisher, at the heart of good spiritual well-being resides a concern for a valuing of relationships. On Fisher's account, good spiritual well-being is reflected in good relationships with self (the personal domain), good relationships with others (the communal domain), good relationships with the environment (the environmental domain) and good relationships with the transcendent (the transcendental domain). Good relationships of this nature are a consequence of a rational process of evaluation and prioritisation. For Jung, at the heart of the feeling function is a rational process of evaluation and prioritisation shaped by personal values and by concern for interpersonal relationships. The finding, then, that *the key* connection between spiritual well-being (as defined by Fisher) and psychological type (as defined by Jung) resides in the feeling function provides support for the internal coherence of these two separate and distant theories, and support for the construct validity of the two measures through which these theories have been operationalised, namely the FPTS (Francis, 2005) and the Fisher measure of spiritual well-being (SHALOM; Fisher, 1999, 2010).

A clear limitation with the present study concerns the distinctive nature of the population from which the sample was drawn, namely visitors to a cathedral in rural west Wales. While this aspect of the study facilitated the generation of a large data set (2339 men and women across a wide range of ages), it nonetheless remains difficult to claim that cathedral visitors are representative of the wider general population. For this reason, the study now needs replication among other groups.

References

Argyle, M., Martin, M., & Crossland, J. (1989). Happiness as a function of personality and social encounters. In J. P. Forgas & J. M. Innes (Eds.), *Recent advances in social psychology: An international perspective* (pp. 189–203). Amsterdam: Elsevier Science Publishers.

Becker, P. L. (2002). *Spirituality in Australian organizations employee attitudes and impact on wellbeing* (D. Psychol. dissertation). Swinburne University of Technology, Victoria.

Berry, D. (2005). Methodological pitfalls in the study of religiosity and spirituality. *Western Journal of Nursing Research, 27*(5), 628–647. doi:10.1177/0193945905275519

Bigelow, E. D., Fitzgerald, R., Busk, P., Girault, E., & Avis, J. (1988). Psychological characteristics of Catholic sisters: Relationships between the MBTI and other measures. *Journal of Psychological Type, 14*, 32–36.

Brewster, C. E., Francis, L. J., & Robbins, M. (2011). Maintaining a public ministry in rural England: Work-related psychological health and psychological type among Anglican clergy serving in multi-church benefices. In H.-G. Ziebertz & L. J. Francis (Eds.), *The public significance of religion* (pp. 241–265). Leiden: Brill. doi:10.1163/ej.9789004207066.i-495.90

Burns, J., Francis, L. J., Village, A., & Robbins, M. (2013). Psychological type profile of Roman Catholic priests: An empirical enquiry in the USA. *Pastoral Psychology, 62*, 239–246. doi:10.1007/s11089-012-0483-7

Burton, L., Francis, L. J., & Robbins, M. (2010). Psychological type profile of Methodist circuit minister in Britain: Similarities with and differences from Anglican clergy. *Journal of Empirical Theology, 23*, 64–81. doi:10.1163/157092510X503020

Cabral, G. (1984). Psychological types in a Catholic convent: Applications to community living and congregational data. *Journal of Psychological Type, 8*, 16–22.

Cattell, R. B., Cattell, A. K. S., & Cattell, H. E. P. (1993). *Sixteen Personality Factor Questionnaire: Fifth edition (16PF5)*. Windsor: NFER-Nelson.

Center for Spiritual Development. (2007). *Spirituality measures*. Retrieved August 29, 2008, from http://www.spiritualdevelopmentcenter.org/CMS/FrontEnd/pop

Costa, P. T., & McCrae, R. R. (1985). *The NEO Personality Inventory*. Odessa, FL: Psychological Assessment Resources.

Costa, P. T., & McCrae, R. R. (1992). *Revised NEO Personality Inventory (NEO PI-R) and NEO Five Factor Inventory (NEO-FFI): Professional manual*. Odessa, FL: Psychological Assessment Resources.

Craig, C. L., Duncan, B., & Francis, L. J. (2006). Psychological type preferences of Roman Catholic priests in the United Kingdom. *Journal of Beliefs and Values, 27*, 157–164. doi:10.1080/13617670600849812

Craig, C. L., Francis, L. J., Bailey, J., & Robbins, M. (2003). Psychological types in Church in Wales congregations. *The Psychologist in Wales, 15*, 18–21.

Cronbach, L. J. (1951). Coefficient alpha and the internal structure of tests. *Psychometrika, 16*, 297–334. doi:10.1007/BF02310555

Daaleman, T. P., & Frey, B. B. (2004). The spirituality index of well-being: A new instrument for health-related quality of life research. *The Annals of Family Medicine*, *2*(5), 499–503. doi:10.1370/afm.89

Delis-Bulhoes, V. (1990). Jungian psychological types and Christian belief in active church members. *Journal of Psychological Type*, *20*, 25–33.

van Dierendonck, D., & Mohan, K. (2006). Some thoughts on spirituality and eudaimonic wellbeing. *Mental Health, Religion & Culture*, *9*, 227–238. doi:10.1080/13694670600615383

Ellison, C. (1983). Spiritual well-being: Conceptualization and measurement. *Journal of Psychology and Theology*, *11*, 330–340.

Eysenck, H. J., & Eysenck, S. B. G. (1991). *Manual of the Eysenck Personality Scales*. London: Hodder and Stoughton.

Fernando, M., & Chowdhury, R. M. (2010). The relationship between spiritual well-being and ethical orientations in decision making: An empirical study with business executives in Australia. *Journal of Business Ethics*, *95*, 211–225. doi:10.1007/s10551-009-0355-y

Fisher, J. W. (1998). *Spiritual health: Its nature, and place in the school curriculum* (Unpublished PhD dissertation). The University of Melbourne, Melbourne. Retrieved from http://eprints.unimelb.edu.au/achieve/00002994/

Fisher, J. W. (1999, October 15). Developing a Spiritual Health And Life-Orientation Measure for secondary school students. In J. Ryan, V. Wittwer, & P. Baird (Eds.), *Research with a regional/rural focus: Proceedings of the University of Ballarat inaugural annual research conference* (pp. 57–63). Ballarat: University of Ballarat, Research and Graduate Studies Office.

Fisher, J. W. (2004). Feeling good, living life: A spiritual health measure for young children. *Journal of Beliefs and Values*, *25*, 307–315. doi:10.1080/1361767042000306121

Fisher, J. W. (2009). *Reaching the heart: Assessing and nurturing spiritual well-being via education* (EdD dissertation). University of Ballarat, Victoria. Retrieved from http://archimedes.ballarat.edu.au:8080/vital/access/HandleResolver/1959.17/13481

Fisher, J. W. (2010). Development and application of a spiritual well-being questionnaire called SHALOM. *Religions*, *1*, 105–121. doi:10.3390/rel1010105

Fisher, J. W. (2011). The four domains model: Connecting spirituality, health and well-being. *Religions*, *2*, 17–28. doi:10.3390/rel2010017

Fisher, J. W. (2012). Connectedness: At the heart of resiliency and spiritual well-being. In C. A. Stark & D. C. Bonner (Eds.), *Handbook on spirituality: Belief systems, societal impact and roles in coping* (pp. 265–277). New York, NY: Nova Science Publishers Inc.

Fisher, J. W., Francis, L. J., & Johnson, P. (2000). Assessing spiritual health via four domains of spiritual wellbeing: The SH4DI. *Pastoral Psychology*, *49*, 133–145. doi:10.1023/A:1004609227002

Fisher, J. W., Francis, L. J., & Johnson, P. (2002). The personal and social correlates of spiritual well-being among primary school teachers. *Pastoral Psychology*, *51*, 3–11. doi:10.1023/A:1019738223072

Francis, L. J. (2002). Psychological type and mystical orientation: Anticipating individual differences within congregational life. *Pastoral Sciences*, *21*, 77–99.

Francis, L. J. (2005). *Faith and psychology: Personality, religion and the individual*. London: Darton, Longman and Todd.

Francis, L. J. (2009). Psychological type theory and religious and spiritual experience. In M. De Souza, L. J. Francis, J. O'Higgins-Norman, & D. G. Scott (Eds.), *International handbook of education for spirituality, care and wellbeing* (pp. 125–146). Dordrecht: Springer. doi:10.1007/978-1-4020-9018-9_8

Francis, L. J., Craig, C. L., & Hall, G. (2008). Psychological type and attitude toward Celtic Christianity among committed churchgoers in the United Kingdom: An empirical study. *Journal of Contemporary Religion*, *23*, 181–191. doi:10.1080/13537900802024543

Francis, L. J., Craig, C. L., Whinney, M., Tilley, D., & Slater, P. (2007). Psychological profiling of Anglican clergy in England: Employing Jungian typology to interpret diversity, strengths, and potential weaknesses in ministry. *International Journal of Practical Theology*, *11*, 266–284. doi:10.1515/IJPT.2007.17

Francis, L. J., Duncan, B., Craig, C. L., & Luffman, G. (2004). Type patterns among Anglican congregations in England. *Journal of Adult Theological Education*, *1*, 65–77. doi:10.1558/jate.1.1.65.36058

Francis, L. J., Gubb, S., & Robbins, M. (2009). Psychological type profile of Lead Elders within the Newfrontiers network of churches in the United Kingdom. *Journal of Belief and Values*, *30*, 61–69. doi:10.1080/13617670902784568

Francis, L. J., Hancocks, G., Swift, C., & Robbins, M. (2009). Distinctive call, distinctive profile: The psychological type profile of Church of England full-time hospital chaplains. *Practical Theology*, *2*, 269–284. doi:10.1558/prth.v2i2.269

Francis, L. J., & Holmes, P. (2011). Ordained local Ministers: The same Anglican orders, but of different psychological temperaments? *Rural Theology, 9*, 151–160.

Francis, L. J., & Jones, S. H. (2000). Psychological type and happiness: A study among adult churchgoers. *Journal of Psychological Type, 54*, 36–41.

Francis, L. J., Kaldor, P., Shevlin, M., & Lewis, C. A. (2004). Assessing emotional exhaustion among the Australian clergy: Internal reliability and construct validity of the Scale of Emotional Exhaustion in Ministry (SEEM). *Review of Religious Research, 45*, 269–277. doi:10.2307/3512264

Francis, L. J., Littler, K., & Robbins, M. (2010). Psychological type and Offa's Dyke: Exploring differences in the psychological type profile of Anglican clergy serving in England and Wales. *Contemporary Wales, 23*, 240–251.

Francis, L. J., Littler, K., & Robbins, M. (2012). Mystical orientation and the perceiving process: A study among Anglican clergymen. *Mental Health, Religion & Culture, 15*, 945–953. doi:10.1080/13674676.2012.676257

Francis, L. J., & Louden, S. H. (2000a). The Francis-Louden Mystical Orientation Scale (MOS): A study among Roman Catholic priests. *Research in the Social Scientific Study of Religion, 11*, 99–116.

Francis, L. J., & Louden, S. H. (2000b). Mystical orientation and psychological type: A study among student and adult churchgoers. *Transpersonal Psychology Review, 4*(1), 36–42.

Francis, L. J., & Louden, S. H. (2004). A Short Index of Mystical Orientation (SIMO): A study among Roman Catholic priests. *Pastoral Psychology, 53*, 49–51. doi:10.1023/B:PASP.0000039325.40451.65

Francis, L. J., Payne, V. J., & Jones, S. H. (2001). Psychological types of male Anglican clergy in Wales. *Journal of Psychological Type, 56*, 19–23.

Francis, L. J., Powell, R., & Robbins, M. (2012). Profiling Catholic priests in Australia: An empirical study applying psychological type theory. In A. W. Ata (Ed.), *Catholics and Catholicism in contemporary Australia: Challenges and achievements* (pp. 282–298). Melbourne: David Lovell Publishing.

Francis, L. J., & Robbins, M. (2002). Psychological types of male evangelical church leaders. *Journal of Belief and Values, 23*, 217–220. doi:10.1080/1361767022000010860

Francis, L. J., Robbins, M., & Cargas, S. (2012). The perceiving process and mystical orientation: An empirical study in psychological type theory among participants at the Parliament of the World's Religions. *Studies in Spirituality, 22*, 341–352.

Francis, L. J., Robbins, M., & Craig, C. L. (2011). The psychological type profile of Anglican churchgoers in England: Compatible or incompatible with their clergy? *International Journal of Practical Theology, 15*, 243–259. doi:10.1515/IJPT.2011.036

Francis, L. J., Robbins, M., Duncan, B., & Whinney, M. (2010). Confirming the psychological type profile of Anglican clergymen in England: A ministry for intuitives. In B. Ruelas & V. Brisero (Eds.), *Psychology of intuition* (pp. 211–219). New York, NY: Nova Science.

Francis, L. J., Robbins, M., Kaldor, K., & Castle, K. (2009). Psychological type and work-related psychological health among clergy in Australia, England and New Zealand. *Journal of Psychology and Christianity, 28*, 200–212.

Francis, L. J., Robbins, M., Williams, A., & Williams, R. (2007). All types are called, but some are more likely to respond: The psychological profile of rural Anglican churchgoers in Wales. *Rural Theology, 5*, 23–30.

Francis, L. J., Robbins, M., & Wulff, K. (2011). Psychological type profile of male and female clergy serving in The Presbyterian Church (USA): Implications for strengths and weaknesses in ministry. *Research in the Social Scientific Study of Religion, 22*, 192–211. doi:10.1163/ej.9789004207271.i-360.38

Francis, L. J., & Village, A. (2012). The psychological temperament of Anglican clergy in ordained local ministry (OLM): The conserving, serving pastor? *Journal of Empirical Theology, 25*, 57–76. doi:10.1163/157092512X635743

Francis, L. J., Village, A., Robbins, M., & Ineson, K. (2007). Mystical orientation and psychological type: An empirical study among guests staying at a Benedictine Abbey. *Studies in Spirituality, 17*, 207–223. doi:10.2143/SIS.17.0.2024649

Francis, L. J., Wulff, K., & Robbins, M. (2008). The relationship between work-related psychological health and psychological type among clergy serving in The Presbyterian Church (USA). *Journal of Empirical Theology, 21*, 166–182. doi:10.1163/157092508X349854

Gerhardt, R. (1983). Liberal religion and personality type. *Research in Psychological Type, 6*, 47–53.

Gomez, R., & Fisher, J. W. (2003). Domains of spiritual well-being and development and validation of the Spiritual Well-Being Questionnaire. *Personality and Individual Differences, 35*, 1975–1991. doi:10.1016/S0191-8869(03)00045-X

Gomez, R., & Fisher, J. W. (2005a). Item response theory analysis of the spiritual well-being questionnaire. *Personality and Individual Differences, 38*, 1107–1121. doi:10.1016/j.paid.2004.07.009

Gomez, R., & Fisher, J. W. (2005b). The Spiritual Well-Being Questionnaire: Testing for model applicability, measurement and structural equivalencies and latent mean differences across gender. *Personality and Individual Differences, 39*, 1383–1393. doi:10.1016/j.paid.2005.03.023

Hall, H. J. (2005). *How the domains of spiritual well being predict current quality of life and general well being* (Postgraduate Diploma of Psychology Research Report). Victoria: University of Ballarat.

Hall, T. W., & Edwards, K. J. (1996). The initial development and factor analysis of the Spiritual Assessment Inventory. *Journal of Psychology and Theology, 24*, 233–246.

Hall, T. W., Reise, S. P., & Haviland, M. G. (2007). An item response theory analysis of the Spiritual Assessment Inventory. *International Journal for the Psychology of Religion, 17*, 157–178. doi:10.1080/10508610701244197

Harbaugh, G. L. (1984). The person in ministry: Psychological type and the seminary. *Journal of Psychological Type, 8*, 23–32.

Hays, J. C., Meador, K. G., Branch, P. S., & George, L. K. (2001). The Spiritual History Scale in Four Dimensions (SHS-4): Validity and reliability. *The Gerontologist, 41*, 239–249. doi:10.1093/geront/41.2.239

Hill, P. C., & Pargament, K. I. (2003). Advances in the conceptualization and measurement of religion and spirituality. *American Psychologist, 58*(1), 64–74. doi:10.1037/0003-066X.58.1.64

Holder, M. D., Coleman, B., & Wallace, J. M. (2010). Spirituality, religiousness, and happiness in children aged 8–12 years. *Journal of Happiness Studies, 11*, 131–150. doi:10.1007/s10902-008-9126-1

Holsworth, T. E. (1984). Type preferences among Roman Catholic seminarians. *Journal of Psychological Type, 8*, 33–35.

Idler, E. L., Musick, M. A., Ellison, C. G., George, L. K., Krause, N., Ory, M. G., ... Williams, D. R. (2003). Measuring multiple dimensions of religion and spirituality for health research. *Research on Aging, 25*, 327–365. doi:10.1177/0164027503025004001

Jung, C. G. (1971). *Psychological types: The collected works, volume 6*. London: Routledge and Kegan Paul.

Keirsey, D., & Bates, M. (1978). *Please understand me*. Del Mar, CA: Prometheus Nemesis.

King, P. E., & Benson, P. L. (2006). Spiritual development and adolescent well-being and thriving. In E. C. Roehlkepartain, P. E. King, L. M. Wagener, & P. L. Benson (Eds.), *The handbook of spiritual development in childhood and adolescence* (pp. 384–398). Thousand Oaks, CA: Sage Publications. doi:10.4135/9781412976657.n27

Krug, S., & Cattell, R. (1980). *Clinical Analysis Questionnaire Manual*. Champaign, IL: Institute for Personality & Ability Testing.

Moodley, T. (2008). *The relationship between coping and spiritual well-being during adolescence* (PhD dissertation). University of the Free State, Bloemfontein, South Africa.

Myers, I. B. (1998). *Introduction to type: A guide to understanding your results on the Myers–Briggs Type Indicator (Fifth edition, European English version)*. Oxford: Oxford Psychologists Press.

Myers, I. B., & McCaulley, M. H. (1985). *Manual: A guide to the development and use of the Myers–Briggs Type Indicator*. Palo Alto, CA: Consulting Psychologists Press.

Pargament, K. I. (1997). *The psychology of religion and coping: Theory, research and practice*. London: Guilford Press.

Polanski, P. J. (2002). Exploring spiritual beliefs in relation to Adlerian theory. *Counselling and Values, 46*, 127–136. doi:10.1002/j.2161-007X.2002.tb00283.x

Rehak, M. C. (1998). Identifying the congregation's corporate personality. *Journal of Psychological Type, 44*, 39–44.

Robbins, M., & Francis, L. J. (2010). Work-related psychological health among Church of England clergywomen: Individual differences and psychological type. *Review of Religious Research, 52*, 57–71.

Robbins, M., & Francis, L. J. (2011). All are called, but some psychological types are more likely to respond: Profiling churchgoers in Australia. *Research in the Social Scientific Study of Religion, 22*, 213–229. doi:10.1163/ej.9789004207271.i-360.44

Robbins, M., & Francis, L. J. (2012). The psychological type profile of Australian Catholic congregations: Psychological theory and congregational studies. In A. W. Ata (Ed.), *Catholics and Catholicism in contemporary Australia: Challenges and achievements* (pp. 262–281). Melbourne: David Lovell Publishing.

Robbins, M., Francis, L. J., & Powell, R. (2012). Work-related psychological health among clergywomen in Australia. *Mental Health, Religion & Culture, 15*, 933–944. doi:10.1080/13674676.2012.698044

van Rooyen, B. M. (2007). *Spiritual well-being in a group of South African adolescents* (PhD dissertation). University of the Free State, Bloemfontein, South Africa.

Ross, C. F. J. (1992). The intuitive function and religious orientation. *Journal of Analytical Psychology, 37,* 83–103.

Ross, C. F. J. (1993). Type patterns among active members of the Anglican church: Comparisons with Catholics, Evangelicals and clergy. *Journal of Psychological Type, 26,* 28–35.

Ross, C. F. J. (1995). Type patterns among Catholics: Four Anglophone congregations compared with Protestants, Francophone Catholics and priests. *Journal of Psychological Type, 33,* 33–41.

Rowold, J. (2011). Effects of spiritual well-being on subsequent happiness, psychological well-being, and stress. *Journal of Religion & Health, 50,* 950–963. doi:10.1007/s10943-009-9316-0

Stott, A. (2002). *The relationship of spiritual well-being to other measures of subjective well-being* (Postgrad. Dip. Psych. dissertation). Department of Psychology, University of Ballarat, Victoria.

Streukens, J. P. (2009). *Alcoholism: Spirituality and personality dynamics* (PhD dissertation). University of Calgary, Alberta, Canada.

du Toit, C. W. (2006). Secular spirituality versus secular dualism: Towards postsecular holism as a model for a natural theology. *Theological Studies, 62,* 1251–1268.

Village, A. (2011). Gifts differing? Psychological type among stipendiary and non-stipendiary clergy. *Research in the Social Scientific Study of Religion, 22,* 230–250. doi:10.1163/ej.9789004207271.i-360.49

Vogt, T. (2007). *The impact of an Interim Protection Order (Domestic Violence Act 116 of 1998) on the victims of domestic violence* (D. Pyschol. dissertation). University of Stellenbosch, South Africa.

Williams, E., Francis, L. J., Robbins, M., & Annis, J. (2007). Visitor experiences of St Davids Cathedral: The two worlds of pilgrims and secular tourists. *Rural Theology, 5,* 111–123.

The perceiving process and mystical orientation: a study in psychological type theory among 16- to 18-year-old students

Christopher F.J. Ross and Leslie J. Francis

This study builds on earlier work to test Ross' thesis that the perceiving process is core to individual differences in religious experience. Data provided by 149 adolescents (16–18 years of age) who completed the Francis Psychological Type Scales alongside the Mystical Orientation Scale supported Ross' thesis. Intuitive types recorded a significantly higher score than sensing types on the index of mystical orientation, while no significant differences were recorded in terms of the judging process (thinking and feeling), the orientations (extraversion and introversion), or the attitudes (judging and perceiving).

Introduction

Psychological type theory has become more visible within the empirical psychology of religion, as a growing body of evidence has established the power of type theory to predict individual differences in religious expression, experience, and belief (for recent reviews, see Francis, 2009; Ross, 2011). Particular contributions to this growing body of knowledge have been made by recent special issues of *Research in the Social Scientific Study of Religion* (Village, 2011) and *Mental Health, Religion & Culture* (Lewis, 2012). Psychological type theory distinguishes between two core psychological processes, the perceiving process and the judging process. Each of these processes is expressed through two contrasting functions. The perceiving process is expressed through the sensing function and the intuitive function. The judging process is expressed through the thinking function and the feeling function. Psychological type theory also distinguishes between two orientations or directions of energy, introversion and extraversion, and between two attitudes towards the external world, judging and perceiving.

Jung (1971) considered the perceiving process as the irrational process, concerned with the ways in which people gather information. Sensing types focus on the realities of a situation as perceived by the senses. They are concerned with the actual, the real, and the practical. They tend to be down to earth and matter of fact. Intuitive types focus on the possibilities of a situation, perceiving meanings and relationships. The judging process, on the other hand, Jung considered as the rational process, based on the Latin root *ratio* meaning ordering. This ordering process is concerned with the ways in which people judge or evaluate information. Thinking types focus on the abstract, logical, and systematic aspects of a situation, thereby privileging consistency. They evaluate through the mind. Feeling types focus on the interpersonal values and the relational aspects of a situation, thereby privileging consideration and sensitivity to the human consequences. They evaluate through the heart.

The two orientations are concerned with the sources of psychological energy. Introverts are energised by the inner world of ideas and can be drained by too much engagement with the outer world of people and events. Extraverts are more energised by the outer world and by interaction with people and events. They can be drained or immobilised by too much solitude and isolation. The two attitudes are concerned with identifying which of the two processes (judging or perceiving) are engaged in the external world. Perceiving types engage their preferred perceiving function (sensing or intuition) in the outer world and consequently present an open, flexible, and spontaneous approach to the outer world. Judging types engage their preferred judging function (thinking or feeling) in the outer world and consequently present an organised, planned, and disciplined approach to the outer world.

Psychological type theory and religiosity

Assessing the connection between psychological type theory and individual differences in religious expression, experience, and belief, Ross (1992) argued that the perceiving process (sensing and intuition) is of central importance. In his initial empirical examinations of this thesis, Ross began to chart the distinctive profiles of religiosity among sensing types and among intuitive types. For example, Ross, Weiss, and Jackson (1996) found intuitives contrasted to sensers in terms of greater comfort with regard to complexity of religious belief, while sensers tended to be more definite in regard to what counted as religious to them. Sensers evidenced firmer boundaries between what was secular and what was sacred. Intuitives showed a more welcoming attitude towards religious change, viewing new insights as essential for a healthy religious life and viewing narrow-minded religion as a significant problem. Sensing types, by contrast, saw religious change as a problem, and change in personal faith as an indication of weakness. Ross and Jackson (1993) concluded in their study of Catholics that the pattern of responses to individual items suggested that religion functioned in different ways for sensing and for intuitive types. According to this study, religion tended to function as a guide to right living for sensers, and as a source of insight for intuitives. Studies of college students by Burris and Ross (1996) confirmed the relevance of the perceiving preference of sensing or intuition for orientation to religion, even among less religiously committed groups.

In a subsequent paper, Francis and Ross (1997, p. 95) set out to examine differences between sensing types and intuitive types with regard to preferences in Christian spirituality, and to test the following two specific hypotheses:

> As consistent with a preference for more traditional patterns of worship and more conservative forms of belief, it is hypothesised that sensers will display a greater preference for traditional expressions of Christian spirituality (like church attendance and personal prayer) in comparison with intuitives, while intuitives will display a greater openness to the experiential aspects of spirituality (like witnessing a fine sunset or being inspired by a star filled sky) in comparison with sensers.

Ross' general theory that the perceiving process (sensing or intuition) plays a central role in predicting preferred ways of being religious or expressing religiosity, together with the findings presented by Francis and Ross (1997) that intuitive types show a higher appreciation than sensing types of experiential spirituality, leads to the clear hypothesis that intuitive types will record higher scores than sensing types on indices of mystical orientation.

Exploring mystical orientation

From the early work of James, the psychology of religion has shown both a theoretical and an empirical interest in mysticism (1982). Two theoretical discussions of mysticism in particular have led to the development of well-calibrated measures. The theoretical framework proposed by Stace (1960) formed the basis for the Hood Mysticism Scale (Hood, 1975). The theoretical framework proposed by Happold (1963) formed the basis for the Francis–Louden Mystical Orientation Scale (MOS; Francis & Louden, 2000a). The present study is set within the framework proposed by Happold (1963) as operationalised by the Francis–Louden MOS, an instrument that has been used in a range of studies, including work reported by Bourke, Francis, and Robbins (2004), Francis, Village, Robbins, and Ineson (2007), Edwards and Lowis (2008a, 2008b), Francis, Littler, and Robbins (2012), and Francis, Robbins, and Cargas (2012). A shorter instrument derived from the MOS, the Short Index of Mystical Orientation (SIMO), was proposed by Francis and Louden (2004) and has been used by Francis and Thomas (1996), Francis and Louden (2000b), and Francis (2002).

Happold's (1963) definition of mysticism embraces seven key characteristics, the first four of which were taken directly from James (1982): ineffability, noesis, transiency, passivity, consciousness of the oneness of everything, sense of timelessness, and true ego (or self). The Francis–Louden MOS proposes three indicators of each of these seven characteristics in order to construct a 21-item measure. In their foundation paper, Francis and Louden (2000a) reported an alpha coefficient of internal consistency reliability of .94 for this instrument (Cronbach, 1951).

Ineffability is a negative description emphasising the private or incommunicable quality of mystical experience. According to James (1982, p. 380), those who have this kind of experience report that "it defies expression, that no adequate report of its content can be given in words". The MOS accesses ineffability with items like "experiencing something I could not put into words".

Noesis emphasises how mystical experiences carry states of insight into levels of truth inaccessible to the discursive intellect. According to James (1982, pp. 380–381), those who have this kind of experiences regard them "to be also states of knowledge ... They are illuminations, revelations, full of significance and importance, all inarticulate though they remain". The MOS accesses noesis with items like "knowing I was surrounded by a presence".

Transiency emphasises how mystical experience is brief, inconstant, passing, and intermittent. According to James (1982, p. 381), mystical states do not endure for long though they may recur "and from one recurrence to another it is susceptible of continuous development in what is felt as an inner richness and importance". The MOS accesses transiency with items like "the passing moments of divine revelation".

Passivity emphasises both the experience of being controlled by a superior power, and the undeserved, gratuitous nature of the mystical experience. According to James (1982, p. 381), mystical states are "not passive interruptions, an invasion of the subject's inner life with no residual recollection of significance, and this distinguishes them from phenomenon like prophetic speech, automatic writing, and mediumistic trance". The MOS accesses passivity with items like "being grasped by a power beyond my control".

Consciousness of the oneness of everything emphasises how mystical experience conveys the sense in which existence is perceived as a unity. According to Happold (1963, p. 47), although it may be expressed in different ways by Hindu, Buddhist, Sufi, and Christian contemplatives, the resolution of the dilemma of duality through this sense of the oneness of everything "is at the heart of the most highly developed mystical consciousness". The MOS accesses consciousness of the oneness of everything with items like "sensing the unity of all things".

Sense of timelessness emphasises how mystical experiences appear to have a timeless quality and to occupy an entirely different dimension from that of any known sense of time and to be wholly unrelated to anything that can be measured by what is known as clock time. According to Happold (1963, p. 48), "the mystic feels himself to be in a dimension where time is not, where 'all is always now'". The MOS accesses sense of timelessness with items like "being conscious only of timelessness and eternity".

True ego (or self) emphasises how mystical experience speaks to the deep, the true inner-self, and how such experience addresses the soul or the inner spirit. According to Happold (1963, p. 48), mystical experience gives rise to "the conviction that the familiar phenomenal *ego* is not the real *I*". The MOS accesses this notion of the true ego with items like "feeling my everyday self absorbed in the depths of being".

Psychological type and mystical orientation

So far, five studies have examined the association between scores recorded on the MOS or the SIMO and individual differences recorded on the Jungian perceiving process. Two of these studies employed the SIMO. Francis and Louden (2000b) administered the SIMO together with the Keirsey Temperament Sorter (Keirsey, 1998) to a sample of 100 student and adult churchgoers. These data supported Ross' hypothesis with significantly higher scores of mystical orientation reported among intuitive types ($M = 30.6$, $SD = 7.5$) than among sensing types ($M = 25.6$, $SD = 8.7$). Francis (2002) administered the SIMO together with the Myers–Briggs Type Indicator (Myers & McCaulley, 1985) to a sample of 543 participants attending workshops concerned with personality and spirituality. These data did not support Ross' hypothesis with no significant differences reported between intuitive types ($M = 30.2$, $SD = 7.6$) and sensing types ($M = 29.0$, $SD = 7.7$).

The other three studies employed the MOS. Francis et al. (2007) administered the MOS together with the Francis Psychological Type Scales (FPTS; Francis, 2005) to a sample of 318 guests who had stayed at a Benedictine Abbey. These data supported Ross' hypothesis with significantly higher scores of mystical orientation reported among intuitive types ($M = 77.9$, $SD = 17.4$) than among sensing types ($M = 71.4$, $SD = 18.3$). Francis, Robbins, et al. (2012) administered the MOS together with the FPTS (Francis, 2005) to a sample of 580 participants from a range of religious and spiritual traditions attending the Parliament of the World's Religions in Barcelona, 2004. Again these data supported Ross' hypothesis with significantly higher scores of mystical orientation reported among intuitive types ($M = 78.7$, $SD = 18.5$) than among sensing types ($M = 71.3$, $SD = 15.8$). Francis, Littler, et al. (2012) administered the MOS together with the FPTS (Francis, 2005) to a sample of 232 Anglican clergymen serving in the Church in Wales. Again these data supported Ross' hypothesis with significantly higher scores of mystical orientation among intuitive types ($M = 65.1$, $SD = 15.8$) than among sensing types ($M = 59.8$, $SD = 15.1$).

Research question

The aim of the present study is to build on this research tradition by adding a sixth study to the series in order to discover whether there may be further support for the aberrant finding reported by Francis (2002) or further support for the growing consensus in favour of Ross' thesis as evidenced by Francis and Louden (2000b), Francis et al. (2007), Francis, Robbins, et al. (2012), and Francis, Littler, et al. (2012).

Method

Procedure

Within the school system of England and Wales, year 12 and year 13 students (16–18 years of age) are given the opportunity to study a range of subjects that may prepare them for access to higher education programmes within the university sector. Religious studies is one of the options. Groups of students taking this option within year 12 or year 13 were invited to participate in a research exercise. Participation was voluntary, with assured anonymity and confidentiality. Completed data were provided by 149 participants.

Measures

Mystical orientation was assessed by the Francis–Louden MOS (Francis & Louden, 2000a). This is a 21-item measure containing three items to access each of the seven key characteristics of mysticism identified by Happold (1963): ineffability, noesis, transiency, passivity, consciousness of the oneness of everything, sense of timelessness, and true ego. Respondents were asked to assess "how important each experience is to your own faith", using a five-point scale anchored by 1 = "low importance", 3 = "medium importance", and 5 = "high importance".

Psychological type was assessed by the FPTS (Francis, 2005). This 40-item instrument comprises four sets of 10 forced-choice items related to each of the four components of psychological type: orientation (extraversion or introversion), perceiving process (sensing or intuition), judging process (thinking or feeling), and attitude towards the outer world (judging or perceiving). A number of studies have demonstrated this instrument to function well in church-related contexts. For example, Francis, Craig, and Hall (2008) reported alpha coefficients of .83 for the EI Scale, .76 for the SN Scale, .73 for the TF Scale, and .79 for the JP Scale.

Sample

The participants ($N = 149$) comprised 77% male and 23% female; 32% aged 16, 50% aged 17, and 18% aged 18; 37% self-identified as having no religion, 49% as Christian, 6% as Hindu, 6% as Muslim, 2% as Sikh; 24% never attended a place of worship, 44% did so weekly, 5% once a month, 5% at least six times a year, and 21% occasionally.

Data analysis

The data were analysed by the SPSS package, using the correlation, reliability, and *t*-test routines. The scientific literature concerned with psychological type has developed a highly distinctive way of presenting type-related data. The conventional format of "type tables" has been employed in the present paper to allow the findings of this study to be located easily alongside other relevant studies in the literature.

Results

The first step in the data analysis concerned an examination of the internal consistency reliability of the FPTS. Adequate alpha coefficients (Cronbach, 1951) were reported for all four scales: EI, .73; SN, .65; TF, .61 and JP, .78.

The type distribution of the sample of 149 adolescents is presented in Table 1 in the conventional format. In this study, the participants displayed preferences for extraversion (60%) over introversion (40%), for intuition (58%) over sensing (42%), for thinking (58%) over feeling (42%), and for judging (73%) over perceiving (27%). The most frequently occurring types were ESTJ (13%) and ENTJ (12%).

The second step in the data analysis comprised an evaluation of the measure of mystical orientation. Table 2 presents the 21 items of the Francis–Louden MOS, together with the item rest-of-test correlations and the proportions of the respondents who rated the importance of the

Table 1. Type distribution for religious studies students.

The Sixteen Complete Types					Dichotomous Preferences		
ISTJ	ISFJ	INFJ	INTJ	E	$n=$ 89	(59.7%)
$n=15$	$n=10$	$n=16$	$n=11$	I	$n=$ 60	(40.3%)
(10.1%)	(6.7%)	(10.7%)	(7.4%)			
+++++	+++++	+++++	+++++	S	$n=$ 63	(42.3%)
+++++	++	+++++	++	N	$n=$ 86	(57.7%)
		+				
				T	$n=$ 87	(58.4%)
				F	$n=$ 62	(41.6%)
				J	$n=109$	(73.2%)
				P	$n=$ 40	(26.8%)
ISTP	ISFP	INFP	INTP	Pairs and Temperaments		
$n=1$	$n=0$	$n=3$	$n=4$	IJ	$n=$ 52	(34.9%)
(0.7%)	(0.0%)	(2.0%)	(2.7%)	IP	$n=$ 8	(5.4%)
+		++	+++	EP	$n=$ 32	(21.5%)
				EJ	$n=$ 57	(38.3%)
				ST	$n=$ 40	(26.8%)
				SF	$n=$ 23	(15.4%)
				NF	$n=$ 39	(26.2%)
ESTP	ESFP	ENFP	ENTP	NT	$n=$ 47	(31.5%)
$n=5$	$n=3$	$n=10$	$n=14$			
(3.4%)	(2.0%)	(6.7%)	(9.4%)	SJ	$n=$ 54	(36.2%)
+++	++	+++++	+++++	SP	$n=$ 9	(6.0%)
		++	++++	NP	$n=$ 31	(20.8%)
				NJ	$n=$ 55	(36.9%)
				TJ	$n=$ 63	(42.3%)
				TP	$n=$ 24	(16.1%)
				FP	$n=$ 16	(10.7%)
				FJ	$n=$ 46	(30.9%)
ESTJ	ESFJ	ENFJ	ENTJ			
$n=19$	$n=10$	$n=10$	$n=18$	IN	$n=$ 34	(22.8%)
(12.8%)	(6.7%)	(6.7%)	(12.1%)	EN	$n=$ 52	(34.9%)
+++++	+++++	+++++	+++++	IS	$n=$ 26	(17.4%)
+++++	++	++	+++++	ES	$n=$ 37	(24.8%)
+++			++			
				ET	$n=$ 56	(37.6%)
				EF	$n=$ 33	(22.1%)
				IF	$n=$ 29	(19.5%)
				IT	$n=$ 31	(20.8%)

Jungian Types (E)			Jungian Types (I)			Dominant Types		
	n	%		n	%		n	%
E-TJ	37	24.8	I-TP	5	3.4	Dt.T	42	28.2
E-FJ	20	13.4	I-FP	3	2.0	Dt.F	23	15.4
ES-P	8	5.4	IS-J	25	16.8	Dt.S	33	22.1
EN-P	24	16.1	IN-J	27	18.1	Dt.N	51	34.2

Note: $N=149$ (NB: $+=1$% of N).

Table 2. Scale of mystical orientation: correlation coefficients for each item with the rest-of-test and item endorsement.

	r with rest of test	% important
Ineffability		
Experience something I could not put into words	.38	53
Feeling moved by a power beyond description	.59	26
Being aware of more than I could ever describe	.64	36
Noesis		
Sensing God in the beauty of nature	.64	21
Knowing I was surrounded by a presence	.69	20
Hearing God speak to me	.58	7
Transiency		
Brief glimpses into the heart of things	.61	23
Transient visions of the transcendental	.72	8
Passing moments of divine revelation	.71	13
Passivity		
Being overwhelmed by a sense of wonder	.65	35
Being in a state of mystery outside my body	.73	14
Being grasped by a power beyond my control	.69	11
Oneness		
Feeling at one with the universe	.69	16
Feeling at one with all living things	.73	12
Sensing the unity in all things	.67	21
Timelessness		
Losing a sense of time, place and person	.55	24
Being conscious only of timelessness and eternity	.68	13
The merging of past, present, and future	.64	17
True ego		
Being absorbed within the divine	.79	8
Losing my everyday self in a greater being	.75	9
Feeling my everyday-self absorbed in the depths of being	.72	13

experience for their own faith as 4 or as 5 on the 5-point scale. The scale achieved the satisfactory alpha coefficient of .92. All the 21 items contributed positively to the homogeneity of the scale, with the item rest-of-test correlations ranging between .39 and .71.

The third step in the data analysis explored the connection between psychological type and scores recorded on the MOS in terms of the four dichotomous type preferences. The data presented in Table 3 supported Ross' hypothesis with significantly higher scores of mystical orientation reported among intuitive types ($M = 49.7$, $SD = 18.6$) than among sensing types ($M = 42.7$, $SD = 15.3$). These data also demonstrate that there is no significant difference in the scores of mystical orientation recorded by introverts and extraverts (the two orientations), by thinking types and feeling types (the two judging functions), or by perceiving types and judging types (the two attitudes).

Discussion and conclusion

The present study has built on previous research by means of careful and deliberate replication, in order to test the empirical grounds for Ross' thesis that individual differences in mystical orientation are related to the perceiving process (sensing and intuition). Now in four

Table 3. Mean mystical orientation scores by dichotomous preference.

	N	Mean	SD	t	P<
extraversion	89	44.8	15.8		
introversion	60	49.6	19.8	1.6	NS
sensing	63	42.7	15.3		
intuition	86	49.7	18.6	2.5	.05
thinking	87	44.8	16.4		
feeling	62	49.5	18.9	1.6	NS
judging	109	48.0	18.4		
perceiving	40	43.2	14.9	1.5	NS

studies the measures have been held constant (the Francis–Louden MOS and the FPTS) and the samples have been varied to include 318 guests who had stayed at a Benedictine Abbey (representing Christians from a range of denominations), 580 participants attending the 2004 Parliament of the World's Religions (representing a wide range of spiritual and religious traditions), 232 Anglican clergymen (representing religious professionals within one tradition), and 149 religious studies students (representing a mix of adolescents actively engaged with public worship attendance and adolescents not so engaged). Data from all four studies confirmed Ross' thesis by demonstrating significantly higher mystical orientation scores among intuitive types than among sensing types.

As well as providing further evidence in support of the general thesis that significantly higher mystical orientation scores are recorded by intuitive types than by sensing types, the present study adds to knowledge by demonstrating for the first time that this association holds true relatively early in the human life cycle. While previous research had been conducted among groups of adults, the present study was conducted among adolescents between the age of 16 and 18 years. The questions arise "What is it about intuition that makes for more openness to mystical experience" and "Why do more intuitive perceivers report more experiences that share characteristics with customary definitions of mysticism"?

The findings are indeed consonant with classical formulations of type theory. Whereas sensation or sensing types (Ross, 2012) preserve specific sensations (extraverted sensing) and registration of details (introverted sensing) in consciousness, intuitives immediately cognise patterns of meaning between or within discrete sensory experiences, and resonate to and store these patterns. As a result, the boundaries between different entities are blurred making it more likely that intuitives will cognise "wholes" rather than "parts". Mysticism is usually understood to encompass a sense of oneness.

Future studies might investigate the possible reasons and dynamics that may account for the lower occurrence of mystical experiences among those with sensing preferences. An important question that deserves investigation is whether those with sensing preferences may in fact have mystical experiences but do not remember or report them because they are appraised in a different manner, because their habitual way of perceiving is more defined, boundaried, and focused, and therefore more discrepant with mystical experience. From the perspective of cultural psychology (Shweder, 1991) mysticism occurs in a particular socio-historical context, and use of the term mysticism in its current meaning can be traced to when science and technology became dominant in the eighteenth and nineteenth centuries. The sensation function plays an essential role in scientific method and in the application of its findings through technology. Furthermore, an empirical philosophy undergirds both science and technology. As a result, it can be argued that a sensing preference becomes privileged in the problem-solving culture of scientific modernity. If sensing then has become the "normal" form of perceiving because of its central role in problem-solving, then it should come as no surprise that intuition and mysticism may be associated as both are marginalised and rarer in technologised societies.

Two further conclusions emerge from these studies that are of wider significance within the empirical psychology of religion. The first conclusion concerns the conceptualisation and measurement of the construct of mystical orientation. These four studies, together with other studies that have used the same instrument (Bourke et al., 2004; Edwards & Lowis, 2008a, 2008b; Francis & Louden, 2000a), have demonstrated the usefulness of the MOS both in the sense of high internal consistency reliability and in the sense of generating stable findings over different studies. This instrument can be commended for further use. The second conclusion concerns the contribution made to the empirical psychology of religion by psychological type theory. These four studies, together with the wider developing literature reviewed by Francis (2009) and by Ross (2011), have demonstrated that psychological type theory is capable of generating useful, insightful, and empirically testable theories relevant to illuminating individual differences in religious experience, religious expression, and religious belief.

This study has also demonstrated the contribution that can be made to the psychology of religion through patient replication and extension of previous work. Further studies testing the present findings among different samples should be welcomed.

References

Bourke, R., Francis, L. J., & Robbins, M. (2004). Mystical orientation among church musicians. *Transpersonal Psychology Review*, 2, 14–19.

Burris, C., & Ross, C. F. J. (1996). *Jungian type and religious orientation: Extrinsic, intrinsic, quest or immanence*. Unpublished paper presented to American Psychological Association Convention, Toronto.

Cronbach, L. J. (1951). Coefficient alpha and the internal structure of tests. *Psychometrika*, 16, 297–334. doi:10.1007/BF02310555

Edwards, A. C., & Lowis, M. J. (2008a). Construction and validation of a scale to assess attitudes to mysticism: The need for a new scale for research in the psychology of religion. *Spirituality and Health International*, 9, 16–31. doi:10.1002/shi.330

Edwards, A. C., & Lowis, M. J. (2008b). Attitudes to mysticism: Relationship with personality in Western and Eastern mystical traditions. *Spirituality and Health International*, 9, 145–160. doi:org/10.1002/shi.342

Francis, L. J. (2002). Psychological type and mystical orientation: Anticipating individual differences within congregational life. *Pastoral Sciences*, 21, 77–99.

Francis, L. J. (2005). *Faith and psychology: Personality, religion and the individual*. London: Darton, Longman and Todd.

Francis, L. J. (2009). Psychological type theory and religious and spiritual experiences. In M. De Souza, L. J. Francis, J. O'Higgins-Norman, & D. G. Scott (Eds.), *International handbook of education for spirituality, care and wellbeing* (pp. 125–146). Dordrecht: Springer. doi:10.1007/978-1-4020-9018-9_8

Francis, L. J., Craig, C. L., & Hall, G. (2008). Psychological type and attitude toward Celtic Christianity among committed churchgoers in the United Kingdom: An empirical study. *Journal of Contemporary Religion*, 23, 181–191. doi:10.1080/13537900802024543

Francis, L. J., Littler, K., & Robbins. (2012). Mystical orientation and the perceiving process: A study among Anglican clergymen. *Mental Health, Religion & Culture*, 15, 945–953. doi:10.1080/13674676.2012.676257

Francis, L. J., & Louden, S. H. (2000a). The Francis–Louden Mystical Orientation Scale (MOS): A study among Roman Catholic priests. *Research in the Social Scientific Study of Religion*, 11, 99–116.

Francis, L. J., & Louden, S. H. (2000b). Mystical orientation and psychological type: A study among student and adult churchgoers. *Transpersonal Psychology Review*, 4(1), 36–42.

Francis, L. J., & Louden, S. H. (2004). A Short Index of Mystical Orientation (SIMO): A study among Roman Catholic priests. *Pastoral Psychology*, 53, 49–51. doi:10.1023/B:PASP.0000039325.40451.65

Francis, L. J., Robbins, M., & Cargas, S. (2012). The perceiving process and mystical orientation: An empirical study in psychological type theory among participants at the Parliament of the World's Religions. *Studies in Spirituality, 22*, 341–352.

Francis, L. J., & Ross, C. F. J. (1997). The perceiving function and Christian spirituality: Distinguishing between sensing and intuition. *Pastoral Sciences, 16*, 93–103.

Francis, L. J., & Thomas, T. H. (1996). Mystical orientation and personality among Anglican clergy. *Pastoral Psychology, 45*, 99–105. doi:10.1007/BF02260016

Francis, L. J., Village, A., Robbins, M., & Ineson, K. (2007). Mystical orientation and psychological type: An empirical study among guests staying at a Benedictine Abbey. *Studies in Spirituality, 17*, 207–223. doi:10.2143/SIS.17.0.2024649

Happold, F. C. (1963). *Mysticism: A study and an anthology*. Harmondsworth: Penguin.

Hood, R. W. (1975). The construction and preliminary validation of a measure of reported mystical experience. *Journal for the Scientific Study of Religion, 14*, 29–41. doi:10.2307/1384454

James, W. (1982). *The varieties of religious experience*. Harmondsworth: Penguin.

Jung, C. G. (1971). *Psychological types: The collected works* (Vol. 6). London: Routledge and Kegan Paul.

Keirsey, D. (1998). *Please understand me: 2*. Del Mar, CA: Prometheus Nemesis.

Lewis, C. A. (2012). Psychological type, religion, and culture: Theoretical and empirical perspectives. *Mental Health, Religion & Culture, 15*, 817–821. doi:10.1080/13674676.2012.721534

Myers, I. B., & McCaulley, M. H. (1985). *Manual: A guide to the development and use of the Myers–Briggs Type Indicator*. Palo Alto, CA: Consulting Psychologists Press.

Ross, C. F. J. (1992). The intuitive function and religious orientation. *Journal of Analytical Psychology, 37*, 83–103. doi:10.1080/13674676.2012.721534

Ross, C. F. J. (2011). Jungian typology and religion: A perspective from North America. *Research in the Social Scientific Study of Religion, 22*, 165–191. doi:10.1163/ej.9789004207271.i-360.30

Ross, C. F. J. (2012). Religion and the sensation function. *Mental Health, Religion & Culture, 15*, 823–835. doi:10.1080/13674676.2012.678576

Ross, C. F. J., & Jackson, L. M. (1993). *Orientation to religion and Jungian type preference among Canadian Catholics*. Unpublished paper presented to American Psychological Association Convention, Toronto.

Ross, C. F. J., Weiss, D., & Jackson, L. M. (1996). The relation of Jungian psychological type to religious attitudes and practices. *International Journal for the Psychology of Religion, 6*, 263–279. doi:10.1207/s15327582ijpr0604_3

Shweder, R. (1991). *Thinking through cultures*. Cambridge, MA: Harvard University Press.

Stace, W. T. (1960). *Mysticism and philosophy*. Philadelphia, PA: Lippincott.

Village, A. (2011). Introduction to special section: Psychological type and Christian ministry. *Research in the Social Scientific Study of Religion, 22*, 157–164. doi:10.1163/ej.9789004207271.i-360.28

The personality of the Fourth Evangelist

Derek Edwin Noel King[†]

The technique of personality-critical analysis (PCA) has been applied to the Fourth Gospel, identifying its major author as INFJ. The author is shown to have the personality type for developing both the high Christology of the preface and the meditations which characterise this Gospel. The bitter arguments with the Jews would have been particularly debilitating for him, but his faith would have helped him to win through this period so that he could then promote a time of renewal for the community. Many of the striking, and yet puzzling, features of this Gospel can be explained through a knowledge of the author's personality, together with an understanding of his view of the validity of that part of Jesus' teaching which came through the Paraclete. The study also explains the widely differing reactions (ranging from inspiration to confusion) exhibited by different readers. Finally, it shows that the Elder (the author of the Johannine letters) could have written the final chapter of the Gospel as a Redactor.

Introduction

"The origin of this Gospel is veiled in obscurity", so wrote Barrett (1962, p. 844). Nevertheless, for 18 centuries, the author of this volume was described as *John the Apostle*. However, in the nineteenth century critics moved towards a view that it was dependent on the three Synoptic Gospels and hence it could have no intrinsic historical value. In an opposite swing in the middle of the twentieth century, Dodd (1953, p. 423) stated that the Fourth Gospel was not unlike the others; that is, it had been composed through three stages: memories of Jesus, influence from church experience and, finally, the writing down by a skilled preacher. Smalley states: "In John, we have an unexpectedly traditional evangelist, and an unusually perceptive interpreter" (1998, p. 283). However, Robinson (1962, p. 95) warns us that "this work is a serious witness not to the Jesus of history but the Christ of faith".

The text does give clues about the source of its basic tradition. On two occasions the author seems to identify the "one who testifies to the tradition" (19: 26–27; 21: 24) with "the disciple whom Jesus loved" (19: 35; 21: 20). Recent suggestions on the person of this witness range from "the witness (and author) is John the Son of Zebedee" (Ratzinger, 2007, pp. 218–238), through "the Beloved Disciple is the eyewitness who provides the account and wrote it" (Bauckham, 2006, pp. 412–437), to "the Beloved Disciple is not fictional and is the originating (but not

---

[†]The Revd Dr Derek King died shortly after this study was completed.

the final) source" (Moloney, 2012, p. 420). Although most agree about the unity of the bulk of this volume, doubts have been raised over one section: the Epilogue (Chapter 21), because Chapter 20 already has a clear ending. Thus, Chapter 21 might be a later insertion by a redactor with a particular aim.

In a magisterial review of 23 recent commentaries, Moloney (2012, p. 322) sighs: "It is no doubt time for fewer commentaries on the Gospel of John". However, there should still be room for novel techniques which throw further light on this extraordinary Evangelist.

Brown (1999, pp. 373ff) proposed a helpful history of the Johannine community which can be summarised as follows: it began with an initial group of Jewish Christians who had a picture of Jesus as a Davidic Messiah, followed by a second group of Anti-Temple Jews and Samaritan converts with a picture of a Mosaic Messiah. This Mosaic picture catalysed the development of the high Christology (for which the Gospel is noted) which precipitated a theological battle with the Jews who finally expelled the Christians from their synagogues. After this period of hostility, the community stressed an extreme realised eschatology which overcame all that they had lost. The Beloved Disciple received his title through making this transition and helping others through it. The Evangelist (a person of great literary skill) wrote his gospel and the community probably moved from Palestine to the Diaspora (Ephesus?). They saw themselves as quite separate from the world, the Jews and other Christians who failed to believe their high Christology. However, the Gospel's one-sided emphasis on the divinity of Jesus opened the way for some members to develop exaggerated views which led to schism. The first two Johannine Epistles indicate this split and we see the writer complementing the Gospel by emphasising the humanity of Jesus. Yet there was still no leadership structure which was sufficiently authoritative to discipline the secessionists. A Redactor probably added the final chapter of the Gospel, putting Peter on the same level as the Beloved Disciple, as the community started to look out towards other Christians. The third Epistle shows signs of this change of outlook. This model shows the Fourth Evangelist as a community member with great literary potential taking up his pen to write down the community's theological reflections through the window of their experiences – rejection and renewal.

In an alternative approach, Bauckham (2007, p. 15), following a suggestion by Hengel (1989), proposed that both the internal evidence and the most reliable external evidence, when properly understood, attribute the Gospel (and the Johannine letters) to a John who had been a personal disciple of Jesus, though not one of the Twelve. He described himself as the Beloved Disciple who was present sitting next to Jesus (possibly as the host) at the Last Supper and standing at the foot of the cross where Jesus gave his Mother into his care. He brought together his own experience of Jesus with that of others and wrote the Gospel, drawing on the Jewish traditions which he knew so well. Known later as "John the Elder" he could have been confused with John the Apostle.

Background to PCA

Jung (1971) first identified and described the notion of psychological type. Jung's system for determining psychological type was honed by Myers and McCauley (1985) through the Myers–Briggs Type Indicator (MBTI). These concepts have been used in the fields of teaching (Lawrence, 1979), career advice (Hammer, 2007), management consultancy (Hirsh & Kummerow, 1998), preaching (Francis & Village, 2008) and spirituality (Duncan, 1993) with each exponent encouraging individuals to "go with the grain" of their particular type.

Duncan (1993, pp. 63–69) employed the concept of psychological type in an analytical mode to discover the most distinctive personality characteristics of each of the authors of the four Gospels. He demonstrated that each Gospel had a particular "colouring" which mirrored one of the four central personality functions: Sensing, Intuition, Feeling and Thinking (in Mark, John, Luke, and Matthew, respectively).

Recently, King has shown (2010, p. 2012) that a full personality description can be derived from several authors of New Testament letters through a technique which he termed personality-critical analysis (PCA) in order to align it with the other critical techniques listed by Hayes and Holladay (1982). Recognised type descriptions can then be used to understand the author who is being studied. For example, King has shown that Paul's strengths and needs were both crucial to his success in evangelism, and that he was followed by a successor (the author of Colossians and Ephesians) who was highly suitable for presenting Pauline teaching in a more attractive style after Paul's death (2012, p. 8). The New Testament letters are particularly suited to PCA techniques because most are written in an intense style which readily betrays psychological type characteristics.

Research aim

This paper aims to demonstrate that a PCA of a New Testament Gospel can determine the psychological type of the author, even though the pointers may be less obvious than those in the letters (because the authors are primarily telling a story). A secondary aim is the illustration of the strong influence which an author's psychological type can have on his writing. Burrage writes: "John's gospel is an excellent example of the use of a deliberate style – carefully worked out through prayer, meditation and teaching" (1994, p. 140).

Method
Personality-critical analysis

A recognised way to determine an individual's psychological type profile is to administer the MBTI, a self-report questionnaire designed to identify individual preferences, distinguishing between two orientations (introversion and extraversion), two perceiving functions (sensing and intuition), two judging functions (thinking and feeling) and two attitudes towards the outer world (judging and perceiving) (Myers & McCauley, 1985). However, since we cannot ask the ancient writers to take the MBTI, we must rely on their favourite words and styles of writing to indicate their basic preferences and so their personality traits. The following preferences provide access to the eight components of Jungian psychological type theory:

- *Introvert*: Reflection, quiet, depth, prefers writing.
- *Extravert*: Action, busy, noise, prefers speaking, socialising.
- *Sensing*: Simplicity, conciseness, storytelling, facts, detail, practicality, the present moment, experience, repetition, and words connected with the senses.
- *Intuitive*: Images, metaphors, ideas, patterns, hunches, the future, the big picture.
- *Feeling*: Values, harmony, persuasion, relationships, sympathy.
- *Thinking*: Logic, objectivity, fairness, justice.
- *Perceiving*: Flexibility, discovery, adaptability, variety.
- *Judging*: Planning, closure, deadlines, control, structure.

Thus, in PCA, one seeks the greater of two characteristics in each personality choice: introversion versus extraversion; sensing versus intuition; feeling versus thinking; and judging versus perceiving. A great advantage of this technique is the fact that, through seeking the greater of two alternative characteristics in each personality preference, one is unlikely to become confused by any extraneous additions from redactors or scribes.

Results

Intuition versus sensing

First, Duncan (1993, pp. 63–69) found indications of a strong preference for intuition in the Fourth Gospel, claiming that "John's Gospel is a supreme example of God's gift to us of intuitive perception." The prologue is an excellent example of intuitive writing (combined with introversion). Many conceptual words are used throughout this text: glory, truth, knowledge, re-birth, belief, word, life, light, love, etc. The long, complex discourses point towards intuition, images abound, and many are highlighted in the dramatic *Egō Eimi* (I Am) phrases. The Evangelist is always highlighting the significance of the Gospel.

Brown (1999, pp. 333–337), in his analysis of the gospel, describes several creative (N) styles:

- Misunderstandings: Images which Jesus' questioners will misunderstand (2: 19–21; 3: 3–4; 4:10–11; 6: 26–27; 8: 33–35; 11: 11–13).
- Double-Meaning: In a dialogue, a questioner will pick up one meaning while Jesus intends another, for example, "lifted up" (3:14; 8: 28; 12:34).
- Irony: When opponents make derogatory statements which are true in a sense which they cannot realise (3: 2; 4: 12; 6:42; 7:35; 9: 40–41; 11: 50).
- Knowing: (2: 24–25; 4: 19; 5: 6; 6: 64b; 18: 34).

By contrast, the Evangelist has little interest in facts or details (a Sensing characteristic). He only describes a few events in Jesus' life and we can see that most have been chosen as a starting point for a reflection. This confirms Bruce Duncan's identification of intuition as predominant.

Introversion versus extraversion

The Fourth Gospel does not open in Bethlehem or even Galilee, but in *eternity* – making the prologue a deep theological reflection (an introvert's preference). The Gospel continues as a collection of reflections, of which some are written as Jesus' theological reflections, to teach individuals (3: 1–10), while in other passages the Evangelist takes several events and reflects theologically on each at length (10: 1–18). Another indication of his preference for introversion is his stress on the one-to-one contacts between Jesus and a questioner, rather than his regular contacts with crowds detailed in the synoptic Gospels. The Evangelist also presents Jesus as having a solemnity of speech in order to set his message as heavenly. There are 25 examples of statements preceded by a double "amen" to alert us (3: 3, etc.). The blind man (9: 1–17) and the Samaritan woman (4: 7–30) can be seen as personifying different faith reactions. He describes the Paraclete as making Jesus available (15: 26), and an ideal picture of worship (4: 23–24) closes this list.

Jesus' dramatic action in the Temple might be seen as a solitary occasion of extraversion when quiet persuasion would have had no effect, but it was clearly a prophetic act (2: 13–16). Thus the Evangelist's preference for introversion is clear.

Feeling versus thinking

The Evangelist declares "love" (a feeling characteristic) to be a characteristic of God from the outset as he describes it as the source of salvation (3: 16). The sole commandment in this gospel is "Love one another" (13: 34; 15: 17). He stresses love throughout the gospel (5: 42; 8: 42; 13:1; 14: 15, 21, 23, 24, 31; 15: 9, 10, 12, 13, 19; 17: 26; 21: 15–17). He appears to be comforting his community over their loss of Jewish festivals by showing Jesus doing things which are more dramatic (5: 1–47; 6:1–71; 7:1–10: 21; 10: 22–42). In Jesus' prayer in the garden, he prays for unity (harmony is a prime aim for NFs).

Conversely, the Evangelist does not stress righteousness (a thinking characteristic) as Matthew and Paul do. Thus the Evangelist exhibits a clear preference for feeling.

Judging versus perceiving

The Evangelist highlights those individuals who come to believe in Jesus: John the Baptist (1: 29), the disciples (16: 30), Nathaniel (1: 45), the Samaritan woman (4: 39) and Martha (11: 27). The world is divided between light and darkness (3:19–21). The Evangelist draws a clear line around his community – the Johannine Jesus does not pray for the world (17:9); the Good Shepherd knows *his own* sheep (10, 14b; 10: 16). The Evangelist pictures Jesus as preferring judging (3: 18–21; 3:36; 5: 30), that is, drawing a line around the community. The Paraclete is described as continuing this role (16: 8).

Thus, without any sign of openness, we find that the Evangelist had a preference for judging. Overall, in each of the four preference categories, he exhibits an overwhelming indication for one function, thus giving a description of a strong INFJ; that is, one exhibiting introverted intuition with extraverted feeling.

Discussion

The Evangelist's preferences are found to be so strong that his personality has shone out, despite the diluting effect of the story which he is telling.

Goldsmith and Wharton (1993, p. 43) say that "INFJs dominant preference and driving force is their intuition, which generates a flow of insights, meanings, patterns and ideas". This description beautifully fits the Evangelist: his Gospel is full of these features. Quenk says: "Their spiritual, sometimes mystical, bent have been frequently noted" (2002, p. 90). We may well imagine the Christology of the prologue as having evolved from the Mosaic picture of Jesus brought by the second group of converts, as suggested by Brown (1999, p. 374). But, once we discover that the Evangelist was a gifted INFJ, we should see him as the central mover in this innovative process. With his deep spirituality, the Evangelist was the ideal person to create the vision of the pre-existent Jesus and present it in a succinct (and even liturgical) form in the Prologue. Dodd (1963, p. 285) saw the words "The word became flesh" (1: 14a) as an ideal title to the whole volume, while Stanton (2002, p. 107) described the Prologue as "the most sustained and profound exposition of the significance of Jesus found in the New Testament". Keirsey and Bates (1978, p. 171) state "They (INFJs) may be attracted to writing as a profession, and often use language which contains an unusual degree of imagery". It would have been natural for the Evangelist to pick up his pen to capture the community's tradition together with his own visions and meditations.

Myers states that "At their best, INFJs have faith in their insights which often takes on a sense of sureness, of *knowing*" (1993, p. 13). This would have strengthened his arguments during the period of controversy with the Jews. The Evangelist frequently describes Jesus in just that way, as when talking to Nathaniel, Nicodemus and the Samaritan woman. These events also show Jesus "understanding the feelings and motivations of others before the others do so themselves". Here, we are watching the Evangelist either projecting his own characteristics onto his picture of Jesus, or vividly recognising his own personal characteristics in the accounts of Jesus which he was retelling. Furthermore, the Evangelist's "sureness" and strength of personality make it most unlikely that he would have described himself in a whimsical style as the *Beloved Disciple*, as suggested by Bauckham (2007, p. 15). Surely he was distancing himself (as author) from the Beloved Disciple by giving him a characteristic description and indicating two important times of close contact with Jesus (once again, he is drawing a line between different people).

Myers (1993, p. 13) also writes: "They prefer to lead persuasively", so the Evangelist would have found the period of intense disagreement with their former Jewish friends extremely upsetting. Goldsmith and Wharton (1993, p. 44) explain that "They are devastated by too much criticism and unpleasant working relationships lead them to lose confidence", while Quenk (2002, p. 18) describes how "Under stress they may come across as picky, fault-finding, narrow minded, and unimaginative". This period in his inferior (sensing) mode would have probably left him, according to Quenk (2002, p. 202), "to rely on his religious beliefs to help cope". However, Quenk goes on to explain that "There are also occasions when a lengthy time in the grip of inferior can stimulate new awareness and positive growth". So, in a period of renewal, the Evangelist might well have preached to his community: "This is what Jesus is saying to you today" by putting Jesus right in the middle of their recent controversies (Chapters 8 and 9). Similarly, he was inspired to take the divine name "I Am" from their Greek scriptures (Isaiah 41: 4; 43: 13; 46: 4; 48: 12; Deuteronomy 32: 39) and put it into Jesus' direct words on three occasions to make powerful statements about Jesus' divinity (8: 24; 8: 28; 8: 58). He also used this crucial phrase, together with a set of seven dramatic predicates, in order to highlight Jesus in his relation with this world and its inhabitants (6: 35; 8: 12; 10: 7; 10: 11; 11: 25; 14: 6; 15: 1). He could do this without any qualms because he believed that this powerful post-resurrection teaching through the Paraclete, which had supported them through the bitter controversies, had been validated by Jesus' promise (14: 26). For the Evangelist, the Jesus who had spoken to the community through the Paraclete was the same Jesus who had previously walked on earth. The sudden leaps from Jesus' spoken words to a narrator's comment are probably also explained by John's understanding of the Paracletal teaching (3: 11–16). Today, some of these profound statements rank among the most-quoted verses of this Gospel. However, the bitter references to "the Jews" (when he was referring to the religious authorities) show that he remained permanently scarred by the synagogue battles of the past. His negative attitude towards "the World" is also explained by Quenk (2002, p. 193): "They have a readiness to distrust the outer world and to assume that things or people will fail them." It is surprising that one whose strong judging characteristic governs his distrust of other groups does not set his community rules or commandments as Paul had (John only set one). This may also be explained by his attitude towards the Paraclete: if he had handed control of his own life over to the Paraclete, he would have expected his followers to do likewise.

This attitude, together with the Evangelist's preference for persuasion, would have led him to encourage the community to listen to the Paraclete rather than to follow a hierarchical leadership. This would have resulted in a greater diversity of views during a later period of the community, and some views could have been heretical. He also clearly "took his eyes off the ball". As Quenk (2002, p. 317) explains: "They may see the goal so clearly that they fail to look at other things that might conflict with the goal." Clearly, he ignored the growing dissent within the community while, at the same time, the Elder (the writer of the Johannine letters), although recognising this problem, also failed to speak out because, as King (2010, p. 86) explained, he was "afraid to rock the boat". It was only after the actual secession that the Elder spoke out through his three letters, struggling to keep the remnant together. His resounding message was a "return to fundamentals", the original testament of the Beloved Disciple and his friends (1 John 1: 1–2). "We may note that the agendas of the Beloved Disciple and the Elder were similar, but with a gap of something like 70 years between the crucifixion and the writing of the letters it is unlikely that they could have been the same person. However, one might suggest that the Elder could have written the last chapter of the Gospel (as a Redactor). For example, he uses repetition very effectively (21: 15–17) and the risen Jesus calls his disciples "little children" (21:5) in the same manner as the Elder writes "little children/children" (1 John 2:1; 1 John 2, 18) to his community members.

Thus many of the strange, but wonderful, characteristics of the Fourth Gospel can be explained in the light of the Evangelist's psychological type. This confirms Smalley's (1998, p. 30) assessment that "John's sophisticated style and language are his own, just as the other evangelists use their individual, and possibly more traditional, diction". This study shows the Evangelist as a prophet of his times who was deeply involved in the faith and the life of the community from his arrival, through the development of exciting new theology, bitter arguments with the Jews and then a period of renewal with an outpouring of Paracletal teaching. This wider role points to the need for some revision of Raymond Brown's proposed history of the community (see below). Although this study makes no attempt to identify the author, it is obvious that so great a writer must have had his skills honed by schooling in Jewish and general philosophical writings.

Reception

Bauckham (2008, p. 139) states "the origins and reflective maturation of this testimony is idiosyncratic"; yet it clearly represents the faith of his community prior to the secession. I suggest that Bauckham is certain of the credentials of the Evangelist, but baffled by his style. PCA can give us a better understanding of the Evangelist's supremely creative style and of our own individual reception of the message in the text. We are each drawn towards writers with a similar personality to our own (we seek a literary resonance), while we may be repelled by an opposite type. Therefore, the Fourth Evangelist's strong meditative style draws intuitive types, but confuses sensing types when they try to take it literally. So, Vanier (2004) describes the reading process as "being drawn into the mystery of Jesus through the Gospel of John", but some sensing types will wish to force the "I Am" phrases into the timeframe of Jesus' earthly ministry. Feeling types will warm to the Fourth Evangelist's values, but thinking types may look towards Matthew for more teaching. Judging types may endorse the statement "No one comes to the Father except through me" (14: 6b), yet perceiving types may prefer to turn towards Luke's openness. So, in the same way that we can experience either a resonance or a clash of human personalities, we also may experience a similar resonance or clash with a text. However, a clash can sometimes be very helpful when we need to be confronted by a particular truth. As Brown has recommended: "We should read our Bibles to discover where we have not been listening" (1984, p. 158).

A revised history for the Johannine community

We can postulate a scenario with two leading characters in the initial community: first, a disciple of Jesus (the Beloved Disciple), who had been very close to Jesus at times and later brought his testimony to the community; then secondly, a creative and prophetic type who was inspired to conceive the high Christology, argue with the Jews and bring himself and the community through a period of revival by his powerful preaching. This second person committed the testimony of the Beloved Disciple and his friends, plus much of his own meditation and preaching, into the Gospel, thus becoming the Fourth Evangelist. As time went on, he failed to foresee a fragmentation within the community. The Elder (a later leader) also failed to speak out against the divisions, but finally fought to retain a remnant by writing three letters to bring them back to the original tradition. In his third letter, one may see in Diotrephes a sign of a new leadership which does not rely solely on the Paraclete (1 John 3: 9). The Elder might well have added a final post-resurrection chapter to the Gospel.

Conclusions

The primary conclusion is that the major author of the Fourth Gospel stands out as a Jungian INFJ. This result shows that he would have been ideal for conceiving (through inspiration) the powerful preface and the meditations which characterise this Gospel. His depiction of Jesus as the Christ of faith is a theological and artistic *tour de force*. He has clearly used dramatic post-resurrection teaching which he has received through the Paraclete to revive and encourage his community and he has recorded this in Jesus' direct speech (because he believed it to be equally valid). Thus, this Gospel draws many readers closer into the fellowship of Jesus but perplexes some others. It is best understood as a carefully crafted amalgam of the testimony of the Beloved Disciple, together with the author's inspired meditations and preaching, all validated by the spiritual life of the Johannine community and affirmed by the Church ever since. The Evangelist clearly draws a line between himself (as author) and the Beloved Disciple who testifies to the Jesus tradition. The findings also reinforce the differences found between the Evangelist (an INFJ) and the Elder (an ESFJ) (King, 2010). However, the Elder may well have composed the final chapter of the Gospel, as a Redactor.

Acknowledgements

The Scripture quotations contained herein are from The New Revised Standard Version of the Bible, Anglicised Edition, copyright 1989, 1995 by the Division of Religious Education of the National Council of the Churches of Christ in the United States of America, and are used by permission. All rights reserved.

References

Barrett, C. K. (1962). John. In M. Black & H. H. Rowley (Eds.), *Peake's commentary on the Bible* (pp. 844–869). London: Nelson.
Bauckham, R. (2006). *Jesus and the eyewitnesses*. Grand Rapids, MI: Eerdmans.
Bauckham, R. (2007). *The testimony of the beloved disciple*. Grand Rapids, MI: Baker Academic.
Bauckham, R. (2008). The fourth Gospel as testimony of the beloved disciple. In R. Bauckham & C. Mosser (Eds.), *The Gospel of John and Christian theology* (pp. 120–142). Grand Rapids, MI: Eerdmans.
Brown, R. E. (1984). *The churches the Apostles left behind*. New York, NY: Paulist Press.
Brown, R. E. (1999). *An introduction to the New Testament*. New York, NY: Doubleday.
Burrage, R. A. (1994). *Four Gospels: One Jesus*. London: SPCK.
Dodd, C. H. (1953). *The interpretation of the fourth Gospel*. Cambridge: Cambridge University Press.
Dodd, C. H. (1963). *Historical tradition in the fourth Gospel*. Cambridge: Cambridge University Press.
Duncan, B. (1993). *Pray your way*. London: Darton, Longman and Todd.
Francis, L. J., & Village, A. (2008). *Preaching with all our souls*. London: Continuum.
Goldsmith, M., & Wharton, M. (1993). *Knowing me; knowing you*. London: SPCK.
Hammer, A. L. (2007). *Introduction to type and careers*. Oxford: Oxford Psychologists Press.
Hayes, J. H., & Holladay, C. R. (1982). *Biblical exegesis*. Atlanta, GA: John Knox Press.
Hengel, M. (1989). *The Johannine question* (J. Bowden Trans.). London: SCM.
Hirsh, S. K., & Kummerow, J. M. (1998). *Introduction to type in organisations*. Mountain View, CA: CPP.
Jung, C. G. (1971). *Psychological types: The collected works* (Vol. 6). London: Routledge and Kegan Paul.
Keirsey, D., & Bates, M. (1978). *Please understand me*. Del Mar, CA: Prometheus Book.
King, D. E. N. (2010). The author of John's letters – the Evangelist, or another? *Journal of Beliefs and Values, 31*, 81–87. doi:10.1080/13617671003666795
King, D. E. N. (2012). The four Pauls and their letters: A study in personality-critical analysis. *Mental Health, Religion & Culture, 15*, 863–871. doi:10.1080/13674676.2012.677591

Lawrence, G. (1979). *People types and tiger stripes*. Gainesville, FL: Centre for Applications of Psychological Type.
Moloney, F. J. (2012). Recent Johannine studies: Part two: Monographs. *The Expository Times*, *123*, 417–428. doi:10.1177/0014524612442266
Myers, I. B. (1993). *Introduction to type*. Oxford: Oxford Psychologists Press.
Myers, I. B., & McCauley, M. H. (1985). *Manual: A guide to the development and use of the Myers–Briggs Type Indicator*. Palo Alto, CA: Consulting Psychologists Press.
Quenk, N. L. (2002). *Was that really me?* Boston, MA: Davies-Black.
Ratzinger, J. A. (2007). Jesus, the Apostles, and the early Church: General audiences 15 March 2006–14 February 2007. San Francisco, CA: Ignatius Press.
Robinson, J. A. T. (1962). The new look on the fourth Gospel. In J. A. T. Robinson (Ed.), *Twelve New Testament studies* (pp. 94–106). London: SCM Press.
Smalley, S. (1998). *John – Evangelist and interpreter*. Carlisle: Paternoster Press.
Stanton, G. (2002). *The Gospels and Jesus*. Oxford: Oxford University Press.
Vanier, J. (2004). *Drawn into the mystery of Jesus through the Gospel of John*. London: Darton, Longman and Todd.

Do different psychological types look for different things in sermons? A research note

Leslie J. Francis, Christopher Stone and Mandy Robbins

A sample of 76 Evangelical Anglican churchgoers completed the Francis Psychological Type Scales and rated the importance that they attribute to a sermon speaking to their imagination. The data demonstrated that sermons speaking to the imagination were rated more highly by intuitive types, feeling types, and perceiving types than by sensing types, thinking types, and judging types. Different psychological types look for different things in sermons.

Introduction

Reader perspective has come to play an increasingly important part in contemporary hermeneutical theory regarding the reading and interpretation of scripture. Sociological categories have become established in defining and shaping distinctive reader perspectives as illustrated by liberation readings, feminist readings, and black readings. Psychological categories are also growing in prominence as documented by works like Rollins and Kille (2007), Francis and Village (2008), and Ellens (2012).

In their study of preaching, Francis and Village (2008) link contemporary hermeneutical theory with psychological-type theory, as advanced initially by Jung (1971) and as subsequently developed and extended by a range of psychological-type indicators, especially the Myers–Briggs Type Indicator (Myers & McCaulley, 1985), the Keirsey Temperament Sorter (Keirsey & Bates, 1978), and the Francis Psychological Type Scales (Francis, 2005). They argue that different psychological types read and proclaim scripture in distinctive ways that reflect their type preferences both in terms of the perceiving functions (sensing and intuition) and in terms of the judging functions (thinking and feeling).

Currently empirical support for this theory has been derived primarily from research conducted among preachers using both quantitative methods (Francis, Robbins, & Village, 2009; Village, 2010) and qualitative methods (Francis, 2010, 2012a, 2012b, 2013; Francis & Jones, 2011; Francis & Smith, 2012). The aim of the present study is to test the connection between the different psychological-type profiles of churchgoers and their perception of listening to the same sermon. In particular, type theory suggests that intuitive types and feeling types are more likely than sensing types and thinking types to report that sermons speak to their imagination.

Method

A sample of 76 churchgoers (38 men and 38 women, of whom 17% were under 40, 51% in their forties or fifties, and 31% 60 or over) who had attended the same sermon in an Evangelical Anglican Church in England completed the Francis Psychological Type Scales (Francis, 2005), a 40-item forced choice instrument that distinguishes between introversion and extraversion, sensing and intuition, thinking and feeling, and judging and perceiving. They also rated the question, "How important for you is it that a sermon speaks to your imagination?" on a five-point scale: "agree strongly", "agree", "not certain", "disagree", and "disagree strongly".

Results

The congregation reported preferences for extraversion (56%) over introversion (44%), for sensing (70%) over intuition (30%), for feeling (56%) over thinking (44%), and for judging (94%) over perceiving (7%). Correlations between the continuous psychological-type scores (with introversion, sensing, thinking, and judging as the high scoring poles) and the item concerning imagination demonstrated negative correlations with sensing ($r = -.36$, $p < .01$), thinking ($r = -.29$, $p < .01$), and judging ($r = -.25$, $p < .05$) and independence with introversion ($r = -.02$, n.s.).

Conclusion

Two main conclusions emerge from these data, one primary and one secondary. The primary conclusion is that intuitive types, feeling types, and perceiving types are more likely than sensing types, thinking types, and judging types to look for sermons to speak to their imagination. Different psychological types may look for different things in sermons and consequently also hear different things in sermons. The secondary conclusion is that the Evangelical Anglican congregation reflects the general type preferences of Anglican churchgoers as reported by Francis, Robbins, and Craig (2011) in terms of preferring sensing, feeling, and judging. On the other hand, this congregation prefers extraversion compared with the general Anglican profile of introversion. This is consistent with the view that Evangelical Anglican congregations may give greater emphasis to social engagement and social interaction among its members.

The limitation with the present study is that it was restricted to one congregation and reported on only one aspect of sermon evaluation. The findings, however, suggest that the study deserves replication and extension.

References

Ellens, H. J. (Ed.). (2012). *Psychological hermeneutics for biblical themes and texts: A festschrift in honour of Wayne G. Rollins*. London: Bloomsbury.

Francis, L. J. (2005). *Faith and psychology: Personality, religion and the individual*. London: Darton, Longman and Todd.

Francis, L. J. (2010). Five loaves and two fishes: An empirical study in psychological type and biblical hermeneutics among Anglican preachers. *HTS Theological Studies*, *66*(1), Art. #811, 1–5. doi:10.4102/hts.v66i1.811

Francis, L. J. (2012a). What happened to the fig tree? An empirical study in psychological type and biblical hermeneutics. *Mental Health, Religion & Culture*, *15*, 873–891. doi:10.1080/13674676.2012.676252

Francis, L. J. (2012b). Interpreting and responding to the Johannine feeding narrative: An empirical study in the SIFT hermeneutical method among Anglican ministry training candidates. *HTS Theological Studies*, *60*(1), Art. #1205, 1–9. doi:10.4102/hts.v68i1.1205

Francis, L. J. (2013). Ordinary readers and reader perspectives on sacred texts: Drawing on empirical theology and Jungian psychology. In J. Astley & L. J. Francis (Eds.), *Exploring ordinary theology: Everyday Christian believing and the Church* (pp. 87–96). Farnham: Ashgate.

Francis, L. J., & Jones, S. H. (2011). Reading and proclaiming the resurrection: An empirical study in psychological type theory among trainee and experienced preachers employing Mark 16 and Matthew 28. *Journal of Empirical Theology*, *24*, 1–18. doi:10.1163/157092511X571141

Francis, L. J., Robbins, M., & Craig, C. L. (2011). The psychological type profile of Anglican churchgoers in England: Compatible or incompatible with their clergy? *International Journal of Practical Theology*, *15*, 243–259. doi:10.1515/IJPT.2011.036

Francis, L. J., Robbins, M., & Village, A. (2009). Psychological type and the pulpit: An empirical enquiry concerning preachers and the SIFT method of biblical hermeneutics. *HTS Theological Studies*, *65*(1), article #161, 7 p. doi:10.4102/hts.v65i1.161

Francis, L. J., & Smith, G. (2012). Separating sheep from goats: Using psychological type theory in a preaching workshop on Matthew 25: 31–46. *Journal of Adult Theological Education*, *9*, 175–191.

Francis, L. J., & Village, A. (2008). *Preaching with all our souls*. London: Continuum.

Jung, C. G. (1971). *Psychological types: The collected works* (vol. 6). London: Routledge and Kegan Paul.

Keirsey, D., & Bates, M. (1978). *Please understand me*. Del Mar, CA: Prometheus Nemesis.

Myers, I. B., & McCaulley, M. H. (1985). *Manual: A guide to the development and use of the Myers-Briggs Type Indicator*. Palo Alto, CA: Consulting Psychologists Press.

Rollins, W. G., & Kille, D. (Eds.). (2007). *Psychological insight into the Bible: Texts and readings*. Grand Rapids, MI: William B. Eerdmans.

Village, A. (2010). Psychological type and biblical interpretation among Anglican clergy in the UK. *Journal of Empirical Theology*, *23*, 179–200. doi:10.1163/157092510X527349

Index

Note: Page numbers in **bold** refer to tables

Allport, G. W. 126
American Religious Identification Survey (2008) 92
Amsterdam Biographical Questionnaire 37, 38
Andersen, J. A. 15
Anglican clergy 18–19, 20, 23–4, 28, 38; serving in Wales (case study) 2, 5–12, **10**
Annis, J. 2, 145
Apollonian temperament (NF) 114, 136
Atlas of Type Tables 38
attitudes, toward outer world 6–7, 27–8, 32–3, 106–7, 113–14, 135–139, 178
Avis, J. 150

Bailey, J. 106, 134, 150
Baker, M. J. 2, 92–4, 103
Baker, S. 134
Ball, I. L. 53, 136
Barrett, C. K. 173
Barrick, M. R. 15
Bates, M. 112, 114, 115, 120, 136, 177
Batson, C. D. 126–9, 132
Bauckham, R. 174, 178, 179
Becker, P. L. 147, 148
Beloved Disciple 173–4, 178, 179, 180
Best, J. 37
Bible, the 76, 77
biblical scholarship, psychological type functions and (case study) 75–87; dependent variables 80; discipline/method **83**, 83–4, 90–1; limitations and future work 86–7; predictor variables 80; psychological type 81; research questions and analyses 81; sample 79–80; sex and religiosity 80–1; subject area, method and psychological functions 85; survey 79; text-handling 79, 81–3, **82**, **83**, 84, **84**, 85–6
Bigelow, E. D. 150
Bono, J. E. 14
Boomsma, D. I. 37
Bourke, R. 165
brain-storming links 77
Bramer, P. D. G. 134
Brewster, C. E. 48, 67, 151

Brown, R. E. 174, 176, 177, 179
Burns, J. 150
Burris, C. 164
Burton, L. 151
Busk, P. 150

Cabral, G. 150
Caldwell-Harris, C. L. 103
Cameron, H. 116, 121
CAQ *see* Clinical Analysis Questionnaire (CAQ)
Cargas, S. 165
Castle, K. 151
cathedral Friends associations, England (case study) 111–13, 120–1; analysis 116; comparisons with Anglican churchgoers **119**, 119–20; distribution **117**, **118**; psychological type 113–14, 114–15, 116; sample 116
cathedral studies, psychological type theory in 137–8
Chao, A. 37
Chen, R. 37
churchgoers, and church-leavers (case study) 94–5, 102–3; data analysis 95; distribution 95, **96–101**, 102; measurement 95
church-leavers *see* churchgoers, and church-leavers (case study)
clergy: leadership 17; training, psychological type theory and 28–9; *see also* Anglican clergy; Protestant denominations, clergymen and clergywomen in (case study); Reformed Church in America (RCA), clergywomen and clergymen in (case study)
Clinical Analysis Questionnaire (CAQ) 148
Colbert, A. E. 15
congregational studies 106–7; psychological type theory in 136–7
consciousness, of oneness of everything 165
Costa, P. T. Jr. 14
Craig, C. L. 7–8, 11, 48, 95, 106–7, 126, 134, 139, 150–1, 153, 167
Craighill, P. 37
Crea, G. 2, 63

INDEX

criticism, of cultural studies 91; historical 75; ideological 76, 84, 85; reader-centred 76, 84; *see also self-criticism*
Cronbach, L. J. 130
curates, and training incumbents (case study): attitude 32–3; clergy training 28; judging process 31–2; perceiving process 30–1; psychological type theory 26–8
Curtin, M. 36
Curtin, R. 37

decision-making: process 66; value-based 86
Delis-Bulhoes, V. 106, 134, 150
Depersonalisation Scale 66
DeVellis, R. F. 39, 53, 130
Dimock, M. 37
Dionysian (SP) temperament 114, 136
Dodd, C. H. 173
Duncan, B. 106, 134, 150–1, 176

Edwards, A. C. 165
Edwards, P. 36
Ellens, H. J. 182
Emotional Exhaustion Scale 66
Epimethean (SJ) temperament 114, 115, 120, 121, 136
evangelists, traditional 173; *see also* Fourth Evangelist
existentialism 127, 132
extraversion 1, 5–6, 16, 27, 93; *vs.* introversion 176
extraverts 33, 38, 106
extrinsic orientation 126
Extrinsic Scale 127, 128
extroversion + intuition (EN) psychological type 23
Eysenck, S. B. G. 1, 37, 48, 129, 147

Farkas, C. M. 15
feelers 77, 93, 149
feeling types 27, 78–9, 93–4, 113, 135; *vs.* thinking types 6, 33, 38, 66–7, 176–7
Fisher, J. W. 2, 145–8, 157
Fitzgerald, R. 150
Fourth Evangelist 174, 176–9
Fourth Gospel 173–4, 176–80
FPTS *see* Francis Psychological Type Scales (FPTS)
Francis Burnout Inventory (FBI) 64; scale properties 68, **68**
Francis, L. J. 2, 7–9, 11, 16–18, 28, 33, 47–8, 56, 63, 67, 93–5, 103, 105–7, 114–15, 119, 126–9, 131–9, 142, 145, 150–1, 153, 163–7, 182–3
Francis–Louden Mystical Orientation Scale 165
Francis Psychological Type Scales (FPTS) 2; in questionnaires 37, 39; use on biblical scholars 81; use on cathedral visitors 151, 153; use on Christians in fellowship or study groups 105, 107; use on churchgoers 93, 95, 125–6, 134, 182–3; use on church-leavers 93, 95; use on clergy 8, 16, 47, 53, 57, 65; use on curates and training incumbents 26; use on students 166–7
Freudian theory 1

Gerhardt, M. 14
Gerhardt, R. 106, 134, 150
Girault, E. 150
Goldsmith, M. 177, 178
Gomez, R. 146–8
gospel *see* Fourth Gospel
Gubb, S. 47, 151

Hall, G. 8, 95, 139, 153, 167
Hancocks, G. 151
Happold, F. C. 165–7
Harbaugh, G. L. 150
Hayes, J. H. 175
Hengel, M. 174
Holbrook, A. 37
Holladay, C. R. 175
Holmes, P 151
Holsworth, T. E. 150
Hood Mysticism Scale 165
Howat, S. 134
Hsu, G. 37

ICS *see* Index of Consumer Sentiment (ICS)
Ilies, R. 14
Index of Consumer Sentiment (ICS) 37
ineffability 165
Ineson, K. 107, 151, 165
International Church Life Survey (2001) 48
intrinsic orientation 126
Intrinsic Scale 127, 128
introversion 5, 27, 93; *vs.* extraversion 176
introversion, sensing, feeling, and judging (ISFJ) 93, 137
introversion + sensing (IS) psychological type 23
introverts 33, 38, 106
intuition 38, 93; *vs.* sensing 176
intuitive types 30–1, 38, 77–9, 81–6, **82**, 108–9, 135, 137–9, 151–7, 163–4
ISFJ *see* introversion, sensing, feeling, and judging (ISFJ)
item response theory (IRT) 146

Jackson, L. M. 164
James, W. 165
Johannine community 174, 179–80
Johannine letters 174, 178
John the Apostle 173, 174
Jones, S. H. 28, 150, 151
Journal of Psychological Type 38
Judge, T. A. 14

INDEX

judging 93–4, 148–50; functions 27, 29, 33–4, 38, 76–7, 85, 105–8; *vs.* perceiving 95, 102–3, 114–15, 135, 177, 163–4; process 31–2, 66, 80–1, **83**, 85, 113–14, 155; types 28, 32, 105–8, 128
Jung, C. G. 16, 26, 47, 56, 65–6, 76, 92, 105, 113–14, 134, 163, 174, 182; psychological type theory 1, 37, 49, 149, 150, 175; Jungian types 9, **10**

Kainz, R. I. 38
Kaldor, K. 151
Keeter, S. 37
Keirsey, D. 112, 114, 115, 120, 136, 177
Keirsey Temperament Sorter 47, 80, 105, 134, 166, 182
Kendall, E. 7, 9, 106, 114, 116, 126, 136
Kennedy, C. 37
Kille, D. 182
King, Derek Edwin Noel 173, 175, 178
Kroeger, O. 28, 33, 115, 143
Krosnick, J. A. 36, 37

Lankshear, D. W., 2, 134
Larkin, Thomas 56
leadership: clerical 17; effectiveness 14, 15
leadership, and personality (case study) 14, 15, 23–4; descriptive statistics **18**, 18–19, **19**; leadership measurement 16–17, 22–3; leadership ratings **21**, 23; leadership strengths, bivariate associations with 19–20, **20**; multivariate analysis 22; multivariate *vs.* bivariate analyses 20–2, **21**; psychological type measurement 16–17; psychological type ratings **21**, 23; sample method 16
Lewis, C. A. 1, 2, 5
Lie (L) Scale 1, 37
Likert scale 17, 127, 130
linear regression models **21**
Littler, K. 7–9, 151, 165
Louden, S. H. 151, 165, 166
Lowis, M. J. 165
Luffman, G. 106, 134, 150

Macdaid, G. P. 38
Marquette, J. 36
MBTI *see* Myers–Briggs Type Indicator (MBTI)
McCauley, M. H. 38, 174
McCrae, R. R. 14
Mental Health, Religion & Culture 1, 3, 163
Moloney, F. J. 174
Mount, M. K. 15
Muskett, J. A., 2, 111
Myers–Briggs Type Indicator (MBTI) 16, 29, 38, 47, 80, 93, 125, 134, 175
Myers, I. B. 38, 42, 56, 174, 178
mystical orientation 169–70; data analysis 167; distribution for religious studies **167**; exploring 165–6; measurement 167; psychological type and 166; scale 151, **169**; scores by dichotomous preference **170**
mysticism 165, 167, 170–1

National Church Life Survey (NCLS), Australia 17, 47–8, 105, **108**, 109; analysis 108; congregational studies 106–7; measurement 107–8; research question 107
NEO Five-Factor Inventory (FFI) 147, 148
neuroticism 1, 16, 18
Neuroticism (N) Scale 37
New Indices of Religious Orientation (NIRO) 127; NIRO Quest Scale 127
noesis 165
Norton, Jon 56

Oh, I. S. 15
openness to change 128, 132
orientation: *extrinsic* 126; Francis–Louden Mystical Orientation Scale 165; *intrinsic* 126; religious orientation 126–8; Short Index of Mystical Orientation (SIMO) 165, 166; Spiritual Health And Life-Orientation Measure (SHALOM) 146, 147–8, 153; *see also* mystical orientation; *New Indices of Religious Orientation* (NIRO)
Oswald, R. M. 28, 33, 115, 143

Paganini-Hill, A. 37
passivity 165
Payne, V. J. 2, 5, 7–9, 11, 28, 33, 47, 150
PCA *see* personality-critical analysis (PCA)
perceiving 93, 166; functions 27, 38, 65, 135; process 30–1, 65; *vs.* judging 27–8, 85, 135, 177; types 34
personality: Cattell's 16-factor Model of Personality 1; Costa and McCrae's Five-factor Model of Personality 1; Eysenck dimensional model for individual 1, 48, 129, 147; five-factor model of 14; psychological type model of 37, 76, 112; traits 14, 20
personality-critical analysis (PCA) 173–6, 179
Personality Questionnaire Revised 147, 148
Personality type and religious leadership (Oswald and Kroeger) 28
Pfent, A. 37
Powell, R. 2, 46, 105, 134, 150, 151
Presser, S. 37
Promethean temperament (NT) 114, 136
Protestant denominations, clergymen and clergywomen in (case study) 46–9; data analysis 49; distribution **50–2**, 53; measurement 49
psychological functions: biblical text-handling and 85–6; discipline/method and **83**, 83–4; handling texts and 84, **84**
psychological health, work-related 63–5, 66–7
psychological type: and biblical scholarship 75–87; conceptualisation and measurement of 65–6; and

INDEX

mystical orientation 166; quest religiosity and 128–9; work-related 66–7; *see also specific psychological types*
psychological type theory 5, 26, 37–8, 47, 92, 105–6, 134–5, 163; application to biblical scholarship 78; in cathedral studies 137–8; and clergy training 28–9; in congregational studies 106–7, 136–7; Jungian 1, 16, 37, 49, 149, 150, 175; and religiosity 164; and religious research 93,125–6, 134, 163; and studies of clergy 65

Quenk, N. L. 178
questionnaires, responders to (case study) 36–8; analysis 38; distribution for early responders **40**, 42; distribution for late responders **41**, 42; ESFJ 42–3; INTJ 42; measurement 38
quest religiosity, and psychological type 128–33, **131**; analysis 130; measurement 129–30
Quest Scale 127, 128, 130, 132

Randall, K. J. 2, 36
Reformed Church in America (RCA), clergywomen and clergymen in (case study) 56–7, 61–2; data analysis 57–8; distribution 58, **59**, **60**, 61, **61**; measurement 57
Rehak, M. C. 106, 134, 150
Reid, J. 66
religion: affiliation, and psychological type 114–15; orientation 126–8
religiosity, psychological type theory and 164
Research in the Social Scientific Study of Religion 1, 163
Revised Eysenck Personality Questionnaire (EPQR-S) 37, 129
Robbins, M. 2, 7, 11, 28, 46–8, 56, 67, 93–4, 103, 105–7, 126, 134, 137, 150–1, 165–6, 182–3
Robinson, J. A. T. 173
Rollins, W. G. 182
Ross, C. F. J. 2, 106, 126, 128–9, 131–2, 134, 150–1, 163–4, 169, 171
Ross, R. K. 37
Royle, M. H. 2, 56
Rutledge, C. 48

Saraglou, V. 94, 103
Satisfaction in Ministry Scale 151
SBL *see* Society of Biblical Literature (SBL)
Schoenrade, P. A. 127, 132
Scripture 78, 85, 126, 178, 182
self-criticism 127–8, 132
sense of timelessness 165–6, 167
sensers 6, 65, 77, 164
sensing types 38, 93, 105, 113, 135; engagement 85; *vs.* intuition types 33, 77–8, 105, 135, 164, 176
SHALOM *see* Spiritual Health And Life-Orientation Measure (SHALOM)

Short Index of Mystical Orientation (SIMO) 165, 166
Silverthorne, C. 14
SIMO *see* Short Index of Mystical Orientation (SIMO)
Singer, E. 37
SJ temperament 47
Slater, P. 48, 151
Smalley, S. 179
Smith, G. 2, 26
Society of Biblical Literature (SBL) 75
Southwark Cathedral services (case study): cathedral studies 137–8; congregational studies 136–7; data analysis 139; gender distribution in cathedral congregation **140**, **141**; psychological type theory 134–6
Spiritual Assessment Inventory 145
Spiritual Health And Life-Orientation Measure (SHALOM) 146, 147–8, 153
Spiritual History Scale in Four Dimensions 145
spiritual well-being 145–8, 151–3, 157–8; analysis 153; distribution for cathedral visitors 153, **154**; by dominant-type preferences 155, **155**; measurement 153; psychological type 148–51; scores by dichotomous-type preferences 153, **155**; scores by dominant and auxiliary type preferences 155, **156**
Stace, W. T. 165
Stone, C. 2, 182
Streukens, J. P. 148
Swift, C. 151
Syme, P. D. 37

temperaments: Apollonian (NF) 114, 136; Dionysian (SP) 114, 136; Epimethean (SJ) 114, 115, 120, 121, 136; Keirsey Temperament Sorter 47, 80, 105, 134, 166, 182; Promethean (NT) 114, 136; SJ temperament 47; theory 114, 121
text-handling style: instrument development 79; and psychological functions 84, **84**; scales 81–3, **82**, **83**
thinkers 77
thinking types 6, 33–4, 77–8, 113, 135, 105–6; engagement 85; *vs.* feeling types 6, 27, 33–4, 38, 66–7, 163–4, 176–7
Thomas, T. H. 165
Tilley, D. 28, 33, 48, 151
transiency 165
true ego 166

Vanier, J. 179
Ventis, W. L. 126–9, 132
Village, A. 2, 16, 75–6, 78, 85, 107, 115, 134, 150–1, 165, 182–3
Vink, J. M. 37
Visser, P. S. 36
Voas, D. 2, 14, 16

INDEX

Walker, D. S. 2, 125–8, 137, 138
Wang, G. 15
Watt, L. 2, 14, 16
Wei, L. 37
Weiss, D. 164
Wetlaufer, S. 15
Wharton, M. 177, 178
Whinney, M. 7, 8, 11, 48, 151
Wilde, G. J. S. 37
Williams, A. 106, 134, 150
Williams, E. 126, 128
Williams, R. 106, 134, 150

work-related psychological health (case study) 66–8, 71; conceptualisation and measurement 63–5; data analysis 68; emotional exhaustion and satisfaction 69, **70**; FBI, scale properties 68, **68**; measurement 68; SEEM and SIMS 69, **70**
work-related psychological type (case study) 66–7; data analysis 68; emotional exhaustion and satisfaction 69, **70**; FBI, scale properties 68, **68**; measurement 68; SEEM and SIMS 69, **70**
Wulff, K. 56, 150, 151

Yik, M. S. M. 14